WINNER OF THE

PEN HESSELL-TILTMAN PRIZE

SHORTLISTED FOR THE

JAMES TAIT BLACK MEMORIAL PRIZE

A BEST BOOK OF THE YEAR

FINANCIAL TIMES · NEW STATESMAN

HISTORY TODAY · THE SPECTATOR

"Like a Renaissance wonder cabinet,
full of surprises and opening up into a lost world."
—STEPHEN GREENBLATT, author of *The Swerve*

"[A] superb biography . . . [Wilson-Lee] affords an intriguing glimpse
into the Renaissance mind and its rage for order, as well as a beguiling
preview of the modern library and, very possibly, what lies beyond."
—*THE WALL STREET JOURNAL*

"Astonishing for both its geographic and intellectual breadth . . . A
potent reminder that a great library originates as a bold adventure."
—*BOOKLIST* (starred review)

MORE PRAISE FOR

THE CATALOGUE OF SHIPWRECKED BOOKS

"The stuff of a Hollywood blockbuster."

—NPR

"Absorbing, adventure-packed . . . Hernando's life, then, was one packed with wonders."

—*The Washington Post*

"A captivating adventure . . . For lovers of history, Wilson-Lee offers a thrill on almost every page. . . . *The Catalogue of Shipwrecked Books* is an intellectual biography, but its beating heart is the tangled love of a son for his father. . . . Magnificent."

—*The New York Times Book Review*

"Read this transporting book. Take it to the beach, to the countryside, wherever—and thank you, Edward Wilson-Lee, for writing it, and with such a sense of vital grace."

—Simon Schama

"Edward Wilson-Lee's fascinating and beautifully written account of how Hernando conceived and assembled his library is set within a highly original biography of the compiler. It's a work of imagination restrained by respect for evidence, of brilliance suitably alloyed by erudition, and of scholarship enlivened by sensitivity and acuity."

—Felipe Fernández-Armesto, *The Literary Review*

"Superbly researched and remarkably well-written . . . Colon was obviously a man ahead of his time; his story is expansive, and in Wilson-Lee's hands, absolutely compelling."

—*Fine Books & Collections*

"Thoroughly absorbing . . . Wilson-Lee's pioneering study makes Hernando's life every bit as compelling as his father's. But that is not all: as we accompany Hernando on his various European journeys of compulsive acquisition, we are not only led through a richly evoked early modern world, but also prompted to reflect on our own data-saturated age."

—*The Times Literary Supplement*

"Hernando Columbus deserves to be as famous as his father, Christopher. . . . Wilson-Lee's greatest strength is the subtlety with which Hernando's public life as a courtier and his private life as a collector are interwoven. Unless you like libraries a lot then the most important thing about Hernando is not the most interesting. But in these elegantly handled parallels, Wilson-Lee leads us almost by stealth to an understanding of his subject's greatest achievement."

—*The Spectator*

"A wonderful book, not least in the literal sense of an epic unfolding in a nonstop procession of marvels, ordeals, and apparitions. . . . The true measure of Wilson-Lee's accomplishment, delivered in a simile-studded prose that is seldom less than elegant and often quite beautiful, is to make Hernando's epic, measured in library shelves, not nautical miles, every bit as thrilling as his father's story."

—*Financial Times*

"Wilson-Lee's book—the first modern biography of Hernando written in English—is far more than just a straight account of a life, albeit a rich one. . . . Moving . . . Wilson-Lee does a fine job of capturing the intellectual excitement of a moment in European history."

—*New Statesman*

"Reading about Christopher Columbus's illegitimate son and his bibliomania is not everyone's idea of a beach read, but that's exactly what I want to dive into this summer. . . . I love the parallel between these two searches for the known world and can't wait to set sail!"

—Dominic Smith, author of *The Electric Hotel*

"Lively and evocative . . . A fresh postimperialist perspective on the age of European exploration, the emergence of modern printing, modern libraries, and the concept of a global world."

—*AudioFile*

"An elegantly written, absorbing portrait of a visionary man and his age."

—*Kirkus Reviews* (starred review)

"This is a truly remarkable book, a work of immense scholarship, and of history that reads like fiction, with a protagonist from the early sixteenth century who would not be out of place in our modern world as he grappled with the growing and almost insoluble problem of what to do with more and more data, how to organize it, how to catalogue it, how to manage it."

—*Hispanic Research Journal*

"[Edward Wilson-Lee] has created a cabinet of wonders with this book. . . . Wilson-Lee's fascinating account brings back to wholeness 'the largest private library of the day' while revealing the son of a renowned man as, among other things, a master librarian."

—*Publishers Weekly* (starred review)

"At once an adventure tale and a history of ideas that continue to resonate. . . . Wilson-Lee's insightful and entertaining work refreshes the memory of Colón's sweeping vision."

—*BookPage* (starred review)

ALSO BY EDWARD WILSON-LEE
Shakespeare in Swahililand

The
CATALOGUE
of
SHIPWRECKED
BOOKS

*Christopher Columbus,
His Son, and the Quest
to Build the World's
Greatest Library*

EDWARD WILSON-LEE

SCRIBNER
New York   London   Toronto   Sydney   New Delhi

for Kelcey

Scribner
An Imprint of Simon & Schuster, Inc.
1230 Avenue of the Americas
New York, NY 10020

First Scribner paperback edition March 2020

SCRIBNER and design are registered trademarks of The Gale Group, Inc.,
used under license by Simon & Schuster, Inc., the publisher of this work.

For information about special discounts for bulk purchases, please contact Simon & Schuster
Special Sales at 1-866-506-1949 or business@simonandschuster.com.

The Simon & Schuster Speakers Bureau can bring authors to your live event.
For more information or to book an event contact the Simon & Schuster Speakers Bureau
at 1-866-248-3049 or visit our website at www.simonspeakers.com.

Manufactured in the United States of America

1   3   5   7   9   10   8   6   4   2

Library of Congress Cataloging-in-Publication data is available.

ISBN 978-1-9821-1139-7
ISBN 978-1-9821-1140-3 (pbk)
ISBN 978-1-9821-1141-0 (ebook)

Achilles' shield is therefore the epiphany of Form, of the way in which art manages to construct harmonious representations that establish an order, a hierarchy. . . . Homer was able to construct (imagine) a closed form because he . . . knew the world he talked about, he knew its laws, causes and effects, and this is why he was able to *give it a form*. There is, however, another mode of artistic representation, i.e., when we do not know the boundaries of what we wish to portray, when we do not know how many things we are talking about and presume their number to be, if not infinite, then at least astronomically large. . . . The infinity of aesthetics is a sensation that follows from the finite and perfect completeness of the thing we admire, while the other form of representation we are talking about suggests infinity almost *physically*, because in fact *it does not end*, nor does it conclude in form. We shall call this representative mode the *list*, or *catalogue*.

UMBERTO ECO, *The Infinity of Lists*

Como todos los hombres de la Biblioteca, he viajado en mi juventud; he peregrinado en busca de un libro, acaso del catálogo de catálogos; ahora que mis ojos casi no pueden descifrar lo que escribo, me preparo a morir a unas pocas leguas del hexágono en que nací.

JORGE LUIS BORGES, "El Biblioteca de Babel"

The use of letters was invented for the sake of remembering things, which are bound by letters lest they slip away into oblivion.

ISIDORE OF SEVILLE, *Etymologies* I.iii

So if the invention of the Shippe was thought so noble, which carryeth riches, and commodities from place to place, and consociateth the most remote regions in participation of their fruits: how much more are letters to be magnified, which as Shippes, passe through the vast Seas of time, and make ages so distant, to participate of the wisdome, illuminations, and inventions the one of the other?

FRANCIS BACON, *Advancement of Learning*

CONTENTS

CONTENTS

PART III
AN ATLAS OF THE WORD

PART IV
SETTING THINGS IN ORDER

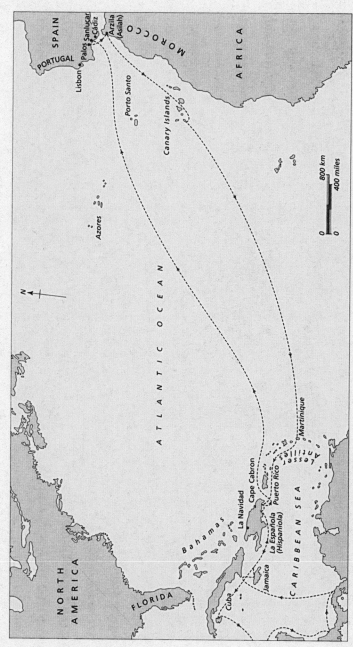

The route of Columbus's Fourth Voyage, 1502–4, on which he was accompanied by Hernando.

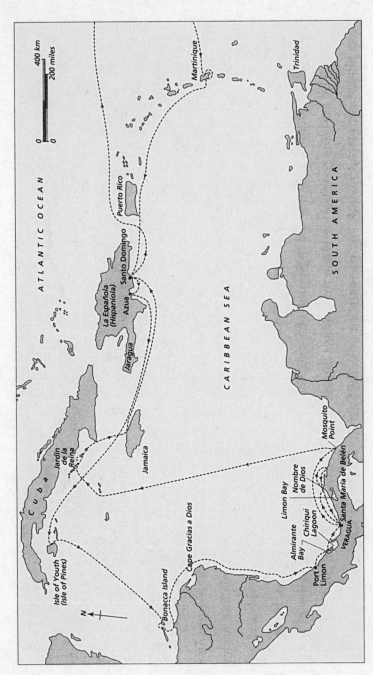

Detail of Hernando and Columbus's route around the Caribbean and Central America in 1502–4.

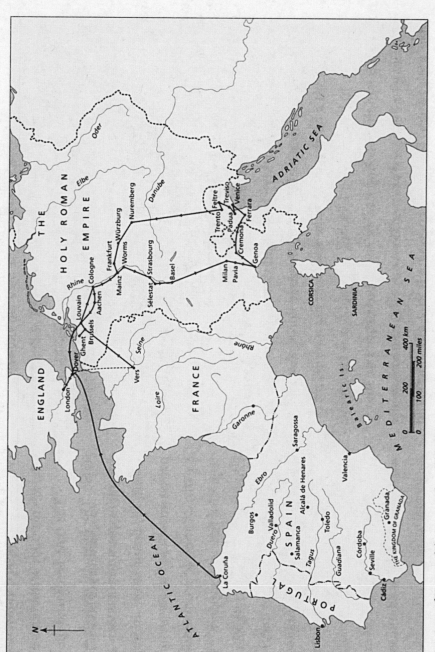

The route of Hernando's journey through Europe in 1520–22; the dashed portions are conjectured.

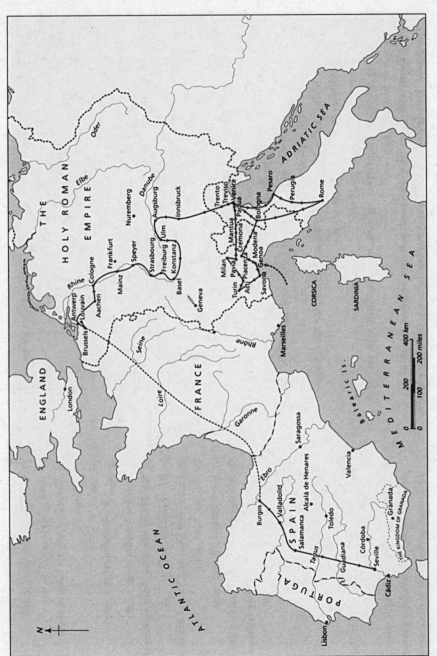

The route of Hernando's journey through Europe in 1529–31; the dashed portions are conjectured.

PROLOGUE
Seville, 12 July 1539

O n the morning of his death, Hernando Colón called for a bowl of dirt to be brought to him in bed. He told his servants that he was too weak to raise his arms and instructed them to rub the soil on his face. While many of them had been with him for a decade or more and were intensely loyal, they refused on this occasion to obey his orders, thinking he must finally have taken leave of his senses. Hernando mustered the strength he needed and reached into the bowl by himself, smearing his face with the silt of the Guadalquivir, the river that meandered through Seville and held his house in the crook of its arm. As he painted himself with mud, Hernando spoke some words in Latin that began to make sense of this performance for those who had gathered at his side: *Remember that you are dust,* he said, *and unto dust you will return.* On the opposite bank of the river, Hernando's father—Christopher Columbus, Admiral of the Ocean Sea—had recently been raised from the same soil, from a grave in which he had lain for thirty years. If Hernando's word is to be believed (and for many things in Columbus's life we have only Hernando's word), the men who opened his tomb may have been surprised to find, along with the explorer's bones, a pile of chains. These chains were a link to a moment in Hernando's past, when at twelve years old his mostly absent father appeared bound in them, returning as a prisoner from the paradise he looked upon as his discovery and his gift to Spain.[1]

The meaning of the great explorer's grave-goods, of these chains that he wished to be placed with him in his tomb, was something Hernando only divulged late in life, when he came to write his father's story. But the dust with which he painted himself on the morning of his death would have made sense to all around him: it was a symbol of abject humility, humility he knew he could afford to vaunt because there was no doubt he had achieved something extraordinary. Hernando, the man who was welcoming his impending decay with open arms, had built an engine capable of withstanding forever the onslaught of time. He died shortly after this performance, at eight o'clock in the morning.

An hour later the next act in Hernando's strange death pageant began. Those closest to him had gathered at his house for the reading of his will, reaching his Italianate villa by the river by passing through the Puerta de Goles (Hercules Gate) and the garden of unknown plants. Hernando had an extraordinary memory, an obsession with lists, and a delicate conscience, so his will tabulated in minute detail the people to whom he felt he owed something, right down to a mule driver whom he had shortchanged nearly two decades previously. But after the tables of his conscience had been cleared, his testament moved on to its great crescendo, a declaration all but incomprehensible to his time. The main heir to his fortune was not a person at all, but rather his marvelous creation, his library. As this was the first time in living memory that someone in Europe had left their worldly wealth to a group of books, the act itself must have been somewhat confusing; but it was even harder to make sense of given the form of the library in question. Most of Hernando's books were not like the precious manuscripts treasured by the great libraries of the day— venerated tomes of theology, philosophy, and law, books that were often sumptuously bound to reflect the great value placed upon them. Instead, much of Hernando's collection consisted of books by authors of no fame or reputation, flimsy pamphlets, ballads printed on a single page and designed for pasting on tavern walls, and other such things that would have seemed just so much trash to many of his contemporaries. To some eyes, the great explorer's son had left a legacy of rubbish. Yet to Hernando these things were priceless because they brought him closer to the goal of a library that would collect everything, becoming *universal* in a sense never before imagined. It was not even clear where this strange and multifarious collection began and ended: in addition to all these written works, there were chests and chests of printed images—the largest collection ever gathered—and more printed music than had ever been brought together before. As some accounts would have it, even the garden outside had begun to collect the plant life of the world and arrange it in its beds. There was, however, no word yet for such a botanical garden.[2]

Visitors to the library would have been greeted by the strangest of sights. The scale of the collection must surely have been impressive, by far the largest private library of the day, blurring the vision as the number of individual items expanded beyond what could be taken in at a glance. Contributing to this disorientation, they might have noticed next that the walls of the library had disappeared. In their place were row upon row of books standing upright on their spines, stacked in this new vertical way in specially designed wooden cases. To the modern viewer these kinds of bookshelves are so familiar as to escape notice, but visitors to the library were encountering these as the first of their kind. This was just one of many elements in Hernando's fabulous library design that defied explanation, beginning with the inscription at the entrance proudly declaring the edifice was founded on shit. Inside the library, the baffling marvels multiplied: the bookless cages in which readers were supposed to sit, the chests full of volumes that should be turned over two or three times a year but were not for reading, the bookshop of useless titles. Then there was the army of paid readers, and the fiendishly complex system of security and surveillance. Most mysterious of all, perhaps, was the master blueprint for the library, which lay in pieces: more than ten thousand scraps of paper, to be precise, each bearing a different hieroglyphic symbol. Each of the myriad ways these pieces could be put together suggested a different path through the library.[3]

It was possible to puzzle out some elements of the design by simple logic: the creation of the bookshelves, for instance, had been a matter of necessity. While previous collections, with hundreds of volumes or at most a few thousand, might be stacked on tables or in chests and could be found at will by a librarian of good memory, a library on the scale of Hernando's would have overwhelmed even the most capacious of human minds and quickly overflowed from most rooms. The new bookshelves took little space from any room and displaced the weight of the books onto the walls behind them. They formed orderly ranks, so that their call numbers could be read from left to right, in a sequence like a line of text; storing the books vertically also meant each could easily be removed, unlike the horizontal stacks, where removing the bottom book would make those above topple. But here the logic of the library explorer may have broken down. What did the line of text, made up of the titles of the books in sequence, actually say? How were wanderers in the library to navigate their way through this world of books? As anyone who has ambled through a library will know, order is everything. The ways in which books can be organized multiplies rapidly as the collection grows, and each shows the universe in a slightly different light. Order the books alphabetically by author and the wanderer will find all of the Pérezes and the Patels together, whether or not their books share anything else. Ordering by size will save space by fitting books of the same height into snug shelves, but this puts pocket novels in the same place as prayer books.

The wanderer in the library is lost without the order that catalogues and shelving systems create; Hernando referred to such unmapped collections as "dead." But even with a map the wanderer is stuck with the order given to them by the librarian, unable to go through the collection in any other way, especially in a book hoard flooded as Hernando's was with the kind of cheap print previously excluded from these civilized spaces. Breaking old paradigms, whether by discovering a new continent or by allowing a new universe of information into the decorous space of the library, was useless or even dangerous unless there was a new paradigm to take its place, a new vision of what these expanded worlds meant. Without this, those who had once felt at home in the world would simply be stranded in a pathless sea of information. As a solution, Hernando's library aimed not simply to be universal but to provide a set of propositions about how that universe fit together. Some of these propositions could be found in the books kept at the center of the library—color-coded in leather that was black, red, or white, or embossed—which contained his catalogues (including the enchanting and mysteriously named *Catalogue of Shipwrecked Books*), while others can only be pieced together from the ten thousand pieces of the final map to the collection, with their hieroglyphic signs.

But not everything in the library fitted on the shelves or could be put in the catalogues. Hernando's will left strict instructions that as soon as both of his executors were together, they were to open in each other's presence a chest containing his personal papers. An inventory of these survives, though now worm-eaten and delicate as a form left in ash. Among other things, it lists

> designs for a house
> ballads for singing
> recipes for medicine
> a catalogue of plants and gardens
> the case of Doña Isabel de Gamboa
> the art of making nautical maps
> a book of the travels of the emperor
> plans for the conquest of Persia and Arabia
> a system of charity for the poor
> a verse life of Columbus
> a poetical treatise
> certain geographical writings on Spain
> a dictionary
> a dialogue between Goodwill, Power, and Justice
> a ledger of Columbus's writings
> certain papers on the de Arana family

Most of the hundred-odd entries in the inventory are illegible, but the parts that can be deciphered begin to give some sense of the myriad adventures of Hernando's extraordinary mind. Some of these works by Hernando survive—the immense dictionary he compiled by hand, the geographical encyclopedia he began on a personal tour around the whole of Spain—but many are lost entirely. The list, moreover, is not complete and omits many of the things in which he played a part, including the maps he helped create, some of which changed the shape of the known world. Some of his works were likely not listed because they were no longer in his possession at the time of his death.[4]

Among those writings mysteriously missing from this list is perhaps the most famous document of all: the biography of Columbus that was printed, in Italian translation, under Hernando's name in Venice three decades after his death. To this *Life and Deeds of the Admiral* we owe much of what we know about the great explorer, including the details of his early life and many of his voyages, especially the Fourth Voyage, the part of Columbus's life we know most richly and intimately because Hernando was there as an eyewitness. Though Hernando was not quite eighteen when his father died, he had an intense knowledge of him that no one else could possibly have—not only as his son, but as someone who had lived with him, in a confined space and facing death, for more than a year in a strange land. That the *Life* was not mentioned among Hernando's papers, and the curious circumstances surrounding its appearance in Italy long after his death, has led to endless controversies. The original Spanish version of this work has never been found, so we are entirely reliant on the Italian translation. Various theories emerged, many proposing a forgery undertaken in Hernando's name, a conspiracy to falsify the life of one of history's greatest figures.

But the missing pieces of this puzzle were waiting to be found in the labyrinthine remnants of Hernando's library. Somewhat over four thousand titles today form the Biblioteca Colombina, housed in a wing of Seville Cathedral, all silence and spotless marble like a mausoleum. These are only a fraction of the books that made up this once-immense library, but this fraction—along with the map of the original collections that survives in the catalogues—is more than enough to reconstruct the life of an extraordinary man in resplendent detail, detail almost unthinkable for most people who lived in his time. This is because Hernando's books contain within their covers not just an exquisitely detailed picture of the Renaissance world, but also a map of his life. In every book he bought, Hernando recorded the date and place of its acquisition and how much it cost, often also noting where and when he read it, if he met with the author, or from whom he received the book if it was a gift. He also responded in many cases to what the books said, though as will become apparent, he had his own singular way of doing so. These many fragments, when pieced together, give an account of one of the most fascinating lives in a period filled with entrancing characters; of a man who not only saw more of the world and what it had to offer than almost any of his contemporaries, but also one whose insights into this changing world were astonishingly prescient.[5]

To reconstruct Hernando's life from his books is to find him present at many of the most significant events of the age of Renaissance, Reformation, and exploration. But Hernando's view of these events is rather like one of the deceptive anamorphic paintings of which the age was so fond, in which a picture viewed from another angle reveals something entirely different. This is in part because Hernando's mind moved ceaselessly from *event* to *system*, from a single thing to a general framework into which it could be fitted. This will quickly become clear in the story of his life, for while most biographies start with a list of documents about their subject that need to be set in order, many of the documents through which we know about Hernando are themselves *lists*: catalogues, encyclopedias, inventories, logbooks, which he compiled obsessively and compulsively. We should not be deceived by the staid and impersonal appearance of these lists, documents that at first seem all fact and no interpretation. To the trained eye, each contains a story: how the list maker imagines the place for which he has packed the items, his way of seeing the world that lies behind a particular kind of ordering, the secrets being hidden by omissions from the list.

If Hernando attempted to bring order to his rapidly expanding world by reducing it to catalogue entries and finding ways of organizing these lists that seemed logical, he was far from immune to distorting influences, distortions that can be traced to the core of his being. Much of his life can be explained by his desire to become worthy of, perhaps even equal to, the father he worshipped, though this was a father whom he in a sense created, as he slowly and deliberately shaped our collective memory of Columbus into the man known today. In death and in life, many of Hernando's actions were in conversation with the father he last saw in his youth, but whose voice he continued to hear and record long after. Their relationship, both before and after the explorer's death, was inevitably affected by the fact that Hernando was not the product of a legitimate union—he was, in the delicate Spanish phrase, a *natural son*. Although Columbus never paid this distinction much mind, the circumstances of his birth meant Hernando could win legitimacy only by showing himself to be his father's son in spirit. Hernando's travels in the realm of knowledge and the new routes he pioneered through it were in a real sense akin to what his father had achieved.

For all that he died nearly five centuries ago, Hernando's discovery of his world bears striking, sometimes uncanny, resemblance to the one we are collectively discovering every day. Perhaps no one has been as helpless in the face of information as those who have lived through the beginning of the twenty-first century: the digital revolution has increased the amount of available information exponentially, and as a result we are wholly reliant on the search algorithms developed to navigate it, tools whose modes of ordering and ranking and categorizing are quickly remaking our lives. The invention of print was another such revolution, and the tools developed in response to it profoundly shaped the world of yesterday, during the age of print. The way of seeing things created by the print library has become so natural to us as to be all but invisible; we forget that its form is far from inevitable, that it was the product of specific decisions with immense consequences, consequences that our current age, sleep-walking into new ways of organizing knowledge by search algorithms, seems likely to face on an even larger and more pervasive scale. Hernando was, in a sense, one of the first and greatest visionaries of the age of print. If his life has escaped the notice of previous generations, it was perhaps because the power of tools that order our reservoirs of information was not as obvious. To reconstruct his life is not only to recover a vision of the Renaissance age in unparalleled depth, but also to reflect upon the passions and intrigues that lie beneath our own attempts to bring order to the world.

PART I

The

SORCERER'S
APPRENTICE

I

The Return from Ocean

Hernando Colón's earliest recorded memory is characteristically precise. It was an hour before sunrise on Wednesday, the twenty-fifth of September 1493. He was standing next to his older half brother, Diego, looking out at the harbor of Cadiz. Dancing on the water in front of him was a constellation of lamps, on and above the decks of seventeen ships about to weigh anchor, preparing to return to the islands in the west where their father had first made landfall less than a year before. Christopher Columbus was now the "Admiral of the Ocean Sea" and was of sufficient fame that chroniclers took down each detail of the scene in front of the five-year-old Hernando. The fleet was formed of a number of lighter craft from Cantabria in the north of Spain, vessels made with wooden joinery so as not to be weighed down with iron nails, as well as the slower but more durable caravels. On board the ships were thirteen hundred souls, including artisans of every sort and laborers to reap the miraculous and uninterrupted harvests of which Columbus had told, but also well-bred caballeros who went for adventure rather than work.[1]

A favorable wind had begun to freshen, and as the dawn grew behind the city, the dots of lamplight would slowly have been connected by the cabins and masts and riggings to which they were fixed. The scene and the mood were triumphant: tapestries hung from the sides of the ships and pennants fluttered from the braided cables, while the sterns were draped in the royal ensigns of the *Reyes Católicos* (Catholic Monarchs), Ferdinand of Aragon and Isabella of Castile,

13

the great sovereigns whose marriage had united a fragmented Spain. The piercing fanfare of hautboys, bagpipes, trumpets, and clarions was so loud, according to one observer, that the Sirens and the spirits of the water were astonished, and the seabed resounded with the cannonades. At the harbor mouth a Venetian convoy, returning from a trade mission to Britain, augmented the noise with their own gunpowder salutes, preparing to follow Columbus part of the way in the hope of learning something of his course.

It is unclear whether, in later life, Hernando could reach back beyond this earliest recorded memory to the rather different circumstances in which, earlier that year, his father had returned from his first voyage across the Atlantic. Columbus had arrived back in Europe with only one of the three vessels with which he had left Spain on 3 August 1492: his flagship, *Santa Maria*, had run aground off Hispaniola on Christmas Eve, and on the return voyage he had lost sight of the *Pinta* during a storm near the Azores. Thirty-nine of Columbus's original crew of ninety or so had been left on the other side of the ocean, in the newly founded settlement of La Navidad in Hispaniola, a town built from the shipwrecked lumber of the *Santa Maria* with the assistance of the local king or cacique, Guacanagarí, and named in honor of the Christmas Day on which it was founded. Columbus's skeleton crew for the return voyage had been reduced to just three men when the rest were taken prisoner by unfriendly islanders in the Azores, though he did eventually secure their release. And when the great explorer finally did reach Europe in the only ship remaining to him, the *Niña*, he was running under bare poles after another heavy storm had split the sails. To make matters worse, he had arrived back not in Spain but in Portugal, dragging his ship past the Rock of Sintra to take shelter under the Castle of Almada in Lisbon estuary, where he was treated with suspicion before eventually receiving a summons to make his report to King João. Though later

(*opposite*) A contemporary drawing (1509) of the harbor of Cadiz, site of Hernando's earliest recorded memory.

reports would focus on the crowds who covered the harbor in their skiffs, swarming to see the island natives whom Columbus had brought home as part of his plunder, Columbus's royal audience was for all intents and purposes an imprisonment, and his release was in part prompted by João's doubts regarding the discoverer's claims. Hernando's written records of these early events would record the hardship but leave out much of the confusion of this first return, of the forlorn man and his outlandish claims.[2]

Hernando's early life was unusual—perhaps unprecedented—because from the youngest age his personal recollections of his father would have contended with widely circulated written accounts of Columbus's exploits. Hernando may have been present at Córdoba in March when a letter was read aloud at the cathedral announcing his father's discoveries, and he kept as central relics in his library several editions of the letter, printed first at Barcelona, through which the discoveries were announced to the world. Hernando's later collecting was to place at the heart of his universal library precisely this kind of cheap print whose first rustlings could be heard in these reports on Columbus's voyage. The letter that was to be the common reading matter of Europe was written by Columbus when he landed in Portugal, and the crowds of Jews embarking from Lisbon harbor for Fez in North Africa would have served as a reminder that his ocean crossing would be forced to compete for public attention. The tumultuous course of recent events had reached a peak of intensity in the early months of 1492, when with the taking of Granada Ferdinand and Isabella finally completed the *Reconquista*, the capture of the Spanish peninsula from the Muslims who had ruled it (almost whole or in parts) for seven hundred years, a crusade that was cast as the righteous restoration of Christian rule. In an attempt to transform the small symbolic victory at Granada into a turning point in the ancient clash between the Abrahamic faiths, the *Reyes Católicos* celebrated their military triumph by presenting the Jews in their dominions with an ultimatum: forced conversion or exile. This was only an escalation of a long-standing Spanish history of persecuting those of the Jewish faith, but it proved a decisive one. Despite the fact that the Jewish community had been established in Iberia even longer than the Muslims and had been central to the flourishing of culture and society in Arabic Spain, many of them could not stomach the price of keeping their homes, which included agreeing that their sacred Talmud was merely a forgery designed to stop the onward march of the Christian faith. Those who chose to stay also faced the prospect of having their property confiscated by the likes of Tomás de Torquemada, the leader of the Inquisition, set up in 1478, who would use this fortune to finance a golden age of Spanish art and exploration. A great multitude prepared to leave, and in their number went many of the greatest intellectuals of fifteenth-century Spain. Forced, as one chronicler records, to sell their houses for a donkey and their vineyards for a little bread, they made the most of the disaster by casting it as a new Exodus, in which the Lord of Hosts would lead them in triumph to the Promised Land. Observing this pathetic scene did not restrain the same chronicler from accusing them of secretly taking much of the kingdom's gold with them. The rabbis attempted to alleviate any feeling of desperation by having the women and children sing to the sounds of timbrels as they walked away from their homes. Though the Jews were given temporary asylum in Portugal, their safe haven there lasted only as long as Columbus's first voyage, and when their paths crossed in Lisbon, the Jews were on the move again, boarding ships bound for North Africa.[3]

Even in his travel-worn state Columbus was quick to find a way for his own expedition to play a part in this grand historic narrative. His voyage west had, after all, been given royal sanction from the camp at Santa Fe outside the walls of Granada, at which Ferdinand and Isabella were celebrating the recent capitulation of the city's last Muslim king, Boabdil, and from which they would also later issue the edict expelling the Jews. The letter Columbus sent ahead to Barcelona from Portugal sang of the marvelous fertility of the islands he had found, in perpetual bloom, and the naked innocence of the native people, who were willing to part with the abundant gold of that region for a few trifles from the visitors they regarded as descended from heaven. If the Jews had a new Exodus, Columbus offered Christians a new Eden. The letter announced that even if the natives knew nothing of Castile or of Christ, they showed themselves miraculously ready to serve both. As a token of their part in an expanded Spanish empire, Columbus had renamed these islands as he took possession of them, so that they now reflected the hierarchy of Spanish power, from Christ the Savior on down through the Monarchs and royal children:

> San Salvador
> Santa Maria de la Concepción
> Fernandina
> Isabela
> Juana
> Hispaniola

In its final paragraph the letter makes clear what has been implicit in the preceding pages, namely that these islands Columbus had encountered should be added to the list of famous victories achieved by the Catholic Monarchs, one that—like the conquest of the Moorish kingdoms and the expulsion of the Jews—would expand both the dominion of the Church and fill the coffers of Spain. This letter, soon printed again in Latin at Rome and Basel, and accompanied by a picture showing a single man guiding a ship toward an endless and fertile archipelago, was one of the central relics of Hernando's childhood, at once cheap and priceless, flimsy and timeless, manufactured and intimate, widely distributed and intensely personal.[4]

Overwriting the native place names with Spanish ones was only one of the word tricks by which this New World was transformed, tricks that included set speeches through which Columbus and others legally "took possession" of the islands, even though these speeches meant nothing to the indigenous peoples listening to them. The former names began to lose their authority and were often soon lost altogether, as Spanish power came to seem natural in a place with so

An image from *De insulis nuper in mari Indico repertis* (Basel, 1494),
showing Columbus manning a ship among the newly renamed islands.

many Spanish names. For all the momentous consequences of their actions, Columbus and his crew often seemed little conscious of the power of this act of naming. As Hernando was later to record, the last-named island, Hispaniola, was so called because they caught there the same fish available in Spain (gray mullet, bass, salmon, shad, dory, skate, corvinas, sardines, crayfish). The power of Columbus's names to change the world was often at odds with the casual way in which he chose them: to commemorate a particular event or an impression of the landscape, or, as here, because it brought back a memory of somewhere he had been before. One of the most powerful experiences for Columbus the explorer, and for the European audience of his feats, was the feeling of having found the familiar in an unexpected place, and around these familiar things the European imagination of the New World began to form.

Yet the letter that reached print and would later be found on the shelves of his son's library was not the first Columbus had written, and Hernando was later to record an original, lost letter penned during the storm off the Azores a few weeks before the return to Europe. Despairing of ever reaching Spain to make his report in person, Columbus in this letter lamented that he would leave his two sons without help in a strange land, far from his ancestors (who, as Spain would soon learn to forget, were Genoese). He had dipped a copy of this first letter in wax, sealing it inside a barrel and turning it overboard with a notice to the discoverer that they could exchange the contents for a reward of a thousand ducats at the Spanish court. It is the first of the documents key to Hernando's life that probably sits at the bottom of the sea.

The letter Columbus wrote from Lisbon not only inaugurated his fame but also saved him from the fate of those who come second. Arriving back in the Spanish port of Palos on 15 March, he learned that in fact the *Pinta* had not sunk in the storm off the Azores, and that its captain, Martín Alonso Pinzón, had himself gone ahead to Barcelona to break the news of the discovery and conquest to Ferdinand and Isabella. Crucially, Columbus's luck held out a few days longer, and Pinzón died before he could gain an audience with the Monarchs. The explorer arrived in Barcelona in mid-April, bringing with him eyewitness reports and gifts from the lands (in the words of one contemporary report) "where the sun sets in the month of March": pineapples, cotton, parrots, cinnamon, canoes, peppers four times as hot as those eaten in Spain, a group of natives, and (most important) a small amount of gold. The intended effect of this list— the argument it makes without seeming to—is simple: In a land of such varied and unrelated wonders, who can doubt that anything could be true? In this, Columbus's gifts were like the great medieval collection of Jean, duc de Berry, which among its three thousand items contained a unicorn's horn, St. Joseph's engagement ring, an embalmed elephant, an egg found inside another egg, and other such marvels. The force of this argument, of these incomprehensible novelties, seems to have been enough to gain widespread acceptance for Columbus's claims that gold was marvelously abundant in those regions, even if he had only a meager sample at present. He knelt before Ferdinand and Isabella, who quickly raised him to his feet and recognized him as the Admiral of the Ocean Sea, going on to reconfirm the rewards that had been promised at Santa Fe in January 1492, which conferred upon him in the event of a successful voyage extraordinary rights over lands he claimed in the Monarchs' names.[5]

In a remarkable display of Columbus's new status, he then rode on horseback through Barcelona in triumph, flanking Ferdinand with his heir, the Infante Juan. If, as is likely, Columbus rode on Ferdinand's left side, he would have seen the still-tender scar running from the king's ear down to his shoulder, the result of an attempted assassination a few months earlier. The wide variety of groups suspected of being behind this attack—the French, the Catalans, the Navarrese, the Castilians—was a reminder of the fragile state of Ferdinand and Isabella's Spanish union, which faced opposition from within the Iberian Peninsula and outside it. Isabella had wrested her kingdom not only from the Moors but before that from her half brother, Enrique IV, and those loyal to his line, then forming with Ferdinand an unlikely but effective partnership to rule over their fractured and restive king-doms; but the threat of a return to civil war was always present. That the blame for the assassination attempt was eventually pinned on a madman, one Juan de Cañamares, who claimed the devil had incited him to kill the king, served, like Columbus's victorious return, con-veniently to distract attention from local difficulties and to recast peninsular affairs as a battle between divine forces of Good and Evil.

For now Hernando was probably sheltered by his youth from the fact that not everyone shared this triumphal account of his father's return. There were contemporary mutterings that his stop in Portugal was part of Columbus's plan to cut a deal with that great exploring nation for even more privileges over the islands he had visited. Peter Martyr d'Anghiera, an Italian man of letters who had come to Spain to fight the Moors and had stayed to join the illustrious court of Ferdinand and Isabella, wrote from Barcelona in May and only mentions in passing "a certain Christopher Columbus, from Liguria," who had recently returned from the western Antipodes and had discovered marvelous things, before quickly moving on to discussing more pressing matters of European politics. It is understandable, perhaps, that Peter Martyr should recall Columbus was a fellow Italian, but Columbus's origins, and those of his children, muddied somewhat the waters of this Spanish feat. Similarly, the chronicler Bernáldez, who would later come to know Columbus intimately, first speaks of the explorer as a man from the territory of Milan, *a seller of printed books* who traded in Andalusia and especially in the city of Seville, a man of great ingenuity yet not well educated, who knew the art of cosmography and mapmaking well. Hernando was later to defend his father vigorously against this charge of being involved in a *mechanical*, menial occupation such as selling books. The heroic account of the New World discoveries had to compete, from the earliest days, against the eroding effects of rumor, which attributed to the discoverer an origin that seemed unsuitable.[6]

In Hernando's library the books from his father's pen were listed under the entry "Cristophori Colón," a firmly Spanish name rather than the Latinate *Columbus* by which the rest of Europe would claim him, or his Italian birth name, *Colombo*. As well as modifying his name, Columbus seems to have drawn a veil over his early life, leaving modern biographers to unearth his modest origins in a family of weavers, from whose traditional craft and native region of Genoa he departed in his late teens, and the evidence is clear now that Columbus did get his start in mercantile ventures, notably working in the fledgling sugar trade for the Centurione family of his native Genoa. It is also wholly possible that books were part of his stock-in-trade, a trade for which his son seemed to inherit an instinctive familiarity. But even after centuries of digging, evidence of his activities is fragmentary before his arrival in Lisbon in the late 1470s, when he was around thirty years old. His early years were a blank except when, occasionally and in later life, he needed them not to be.[7]

With Columbus's arrival in Lisbon we begin to know something of his life, and documents from this period start to find their way into the library. Among these may have been the papers and maps Columbus inherited—in Hernando's telling of it—from the father of his Portuguese wife, a match that not only gave him an heir in Hernando's brother, Diego, but also a connection to a Portuguese maritime dynasty: the father of Dona Filipa Moniz Perestrelo had been among those who had claimed and settled the Madeira archipelago in the mid-fifteenth century. Also in the library, copied into one of the books Columbus left his son, was a letter from the Italian geographer Paolo dal Pozzo Toscanelli that may have shaped Columbus's thinking at this stage. The letter from Toscanelli to a Portuguese priest outlined his "narrow Atlantic" hypothesis, which estimated that the distance from Lisbon to Cathay was approximately a third of the globe—130 degrees, 26 *espacios*, or 6,500 miles. Though the later claim that the as-yet-undistinguished Columbus was directly in contact with Toscanelli is likely untrue, he was clearly influenced by the geographer's theories, as well as the Italian's mouthwatering description of "Zaiton" (modern Quanzhou), a great port in which a hundred ships' worth of pepper was delivered every year, and only one of the numberless cities over which the Grand Khan ruled. For his description of Cathay, and the regions of "Antillia" and "Cipangu," which Columbus believed would make convenient stopping points on the way, Toscanelli was largely indebted to the thirteenth-century travelers Marco Polo, William of Rubruck, and Giovanni da Pian del Carpine, right down to the use of the Mongol word *Cathay* (Khitai) for China—a name that had not been current in China itself for several hundred years.[8]

One of the great achievements of the Columbuses—begun by Christopher but brought to perfection by Hernando—was turning the series of events that followed into a narrative of personal destiny. Where historians today might focus on the grand historical forces that pushed European expansion into the Atlantic, and the coincidences that gave the voyage of 1492 its specific form, the Columbus legend saw it as a moment in which history focused its stare on the explorer and guided his hand at every turn. This was especially true when recounting the series of failed bids for patronage that came before Columbus's eventual success. Hernando was to acknowledge that the Portuguese were wary of further investment in Atlantic exploration, which had so far proved costly and unprofitable (in Guinea, the Azores, Madeira, and Cape Verde), but in Hernando's telling the Portuguese refusal to support Columbus, when he first turned to them for funding, was one of those moments in which God hardened the heart of one to whom He had not allotted victory. Similarly, Hernando acknowledged openly that Columbus had dispatched his brother Bartholomew to seek English backing for the voyage, even recording in his library a map that was presented to Henry VII and the verses that were written on it; but he saw further evidence of God's manifest hand in that Bartholomew arrived too late with Henry's offer of support, leaving Spain to reap the rewards. And while it was later to be claimed that many prominent Spaniards supported Columbus's project long before his triumph, Hernando was to reserve the vindication to his father alone, depicting him as a solitary voice against the stubbornness of the learned and the powerful. The image of Columbus as a visionary who was mocked and derided but lived to have the last laugh was one molded in large part by his son.[9]

The verses on the map presented to Henry VII, which Hernando retrieved from the library and copied into his biography, give an abbreviated version of the tripartite argument the Columbus brothers presented to skeptics of his westward passage to Cathay and India:

> You who wish to know the limits of the earth
> can read them in this picture:
> What was known to Strabo, Ptolemy, Pliny, and
>   Isidore
> though they did not always agree;
> Yet also here are the lands unknown of old
> but now found by Spanish ships and in every man's
>   thoughts.
> (*by Bartholomew Columbus, in London on 13*
>   *February 1488*)

Hernando was later to codify this argument into three parts, namely *the nature of things, the sayings of ancient and modern writers,* and *reports from sailors.* This threefold case brought together the common-sense reasoning that it was possible to circle a round world with thoughts from classical and medieval writers on the likely circumference of the globe, and rumors of promising sightings during voyages in the eastern Atlantic. Columbus's detailed examination of ancient geographers, mostly through medieval compendiums such as the *Picture of the World* by Pierre d'Ailly and the *History* of Eneas Silvius Piccolomini, are strikingly attested to by the dense notes he left in the margins of his copies, which were to be inherited by Hernando and to make his library a site of pilgrimage for those seeking to understand the explorer. Hernando was to portray his father as amassing a vast body of authorities on the circumference of the earth, and to ignore entirely the willfulness that made Columbus prefer the smallest of the estimates of circumference, following the Arabic cosmographer Alfragan (al-Faragani)—the one that would make his voyage most likely to succeed. To those opposing Columbus, Hernando allows only a series of points designed to seem immensely contemptible in retrospect. Among these were assertions that the Ocean was interminably broad or impossible to navigate, and that those sailing back from the west would be going "uphill"; also that the great Church father St. Augustine was on record as doubting the existence of undiscovered Antipodean lands, an opinion that satisfied them and that it might be heretical to question.[10]

The versions of the Columbus story that descended from Hernando—as most do—would pass over the growing body of support for Columbus at the Spanish court and focus instead on a dramatic climax in which the explorer forced the hand of an unwilling world. Neither of the learned gatherings to whom Columbus presented his arguments (in 1487 and 1491) reached a conclusion favorable to Columbus's design, and Ferdinand and Isabella understandably remained reluctant, given the cost of the war against the Moors and the terms Columbus was demanding, to invest in a venture whose promise rested on the word of an unproven if undoubtedly charismatic stranger. Hernando would portray his father, scorning to beg his destiny from the blind, as abandoning the Spanish court to look for other means of advancing his plans. Only the eleventh-hour intercession of the queen's confessor, Fray Juan Pérez, gained Columbus a favorable hearing, and the offer of the secretary of the exchequer, Luis de Santangel, to front the costs himself seems to have persuaded the Monarchs to come to terms with Columbus. Later accounts of these events were to heighten the dramatic tension, with stories of Columbus being called back even as he rode away from the city, and the queen offering to pawn her own jewels to pay for the expedition.

This narrative of events in 1491 and early 1492 was later honed to epic perfection by those seeking to paint a picture of Spanish destiny and by the vision of Columbus promoted by the explorer himself and by his faction. The legend obscures many of the mundane and practical contexts that might detract from this messianic version of events. Among these were the Monarchs' need for new sources of gold now that the Moors of Spain would no longer be paying tribute drawn on the North African trade routes, the pressure for European expansion (especially from mercantile nations including the Venetians and Genoese) to look west as the Ottoman Turks began to absorb the eastern Mediterranean regions that had once supplied many of their goods, and the comparability of Columbus's voyage to many fifteenth-century expeditions that had enlarged the European orbit south down the coast of Africa and west to islands in the Atlantic.

Another effect of the narrowing of the Columbus narrative to focus on the single Man of Destiny was to obscure his family life, obliterating the personal circumstances of his actions and instead making those around him conform to the patterns of his mythmaking. Columbus's abrupt departure from Portugal after the failure of his bid for King João's support was attributed to his unwavering focus on his destiny, but may also have been driven by the death of Dona Filipa, who had given him Hernando's elder brother but whose premature passing abruptly cut Columbus's ties to Portugal. It was her relatives who determined where he went in Spain by providing links when he arrived there, especially in Palos, which was to be the launching point for his first expedition. The legend also glosses over the change in Columbus's name at this point, from the Italian *Colombo* to the Spanish *Colón*, by which he was known for the rest of his life, though Hernando was later to argue that all of these names were symbolically appropriate to Columbus: "*Colombo*," "the dove," who like Noah's messenger reaches out into the flood and brings back evidence of land as a covenant between God and His nation; and *Colón*, which in Greek made Columbus a "member" of Christ, an arm doing his bidding, and foretold he would make of the natives *coloni*, "members of the Church"—though with no small irony this is also the root for *to colonize*. And the picture of the lonely visionary, pursuing his destiny in the face of blind opposition from the Spanish court, is somewhat complicated by his being, during his years of lobbying in Córdoba, in a liaison with the young orphan Beatriz Enríquez de Arana. Beatriz's parents had been of lowly station—from the same class of weavers from which Columbus himself derived—but Columbus likely came to know her through the circle of doctors in Córdoba who surrounded her uncle and guardian, Rodrigo Enríquez de Arana. Though Hernando, who was born of this affair, was not disloyal to his Arana relatives, noting the significant role many of them later played in Columbus's voyages, he did not pause in the narrative of his father's life so much as to write his mother's name, and his own birth on 15 August 1488 is passed over in silence, preserving the smooth course of the explorer's story. Columbus did not mention, in the first draft of the letter he cast overboard in the storm, that both Diego and Hernando during the voyage were under the care and protection of Beatriz in Córdoba, and his triumphant return largely meant for Beatriz that these children were taken from her. Though she was still living in 1506 when Columbus died, the explorer hardly ever mentioned her again in his letters. The anguished way in which her name was spoken in his final testament reflects a pattern in the life of Columbus and his sons, who showed themselves at once to be of tender conscience and yet also coldly willing to cast aside those near them in pursuit of the destiny they believed to be theirs, a trait that saw Beatriz even being largely written out of her own son's life.[11]

It is easy to see, however, how the events of the First Voyage drove an already determined man to such extraordinary levels of narcissism. Columbus had sailed west into the Ocean Sea, the body of water thought to surround the landmass of the earth, far beyond where any other person on record had gone, and according to his own account (and there is no other), he had resisted the nearly mutinous opposition of his crew almost single-handedly. He did this through a combination of threat and encouraging interpretations of the signs, which Hernando was later to record in detail:

a mast adrift, strange behavior of the compass needle, a prodigious flame falling from the sky, a heron, greenish weed, a flock of birds flying west, a pelican, small birds, a *junco de rabo*, a whale, gulls, songbirds, crabs, a freshness in the air, reef fish, ducks, a light in the distance

A less determined person would have seen this as a jumble of flotsam rather than signs of approaching land. Columbus also practiced downright deception, intentionally giving his sailors a significantly lower figure than his true estimation of the distance traveled, to limit the blank fear they felt at being farther and farther from the world they knew. In what he saw as a reward for his resilience, he found land precisely where he had predicted it to be, at 750 leagues west of the Canary Islands, exactly the distance to east Asia estimated by his calculation of the number of degrees and using al-Faragani's figure of 56⅔ miles to the degree. (No one was aware then that al-Faragani was using an Arabic mile significantly longer than the European one, so that his figure was not in the least confirmed by the voyage.) In the view of Columbus and most others, he was the first man to have sailed west to reach the other side of the known world, reaching the island of Cipangu (Japan), for which the local name was Cuba. For the first time in history someone had broken the bounds of Ocean, and had closed the circle of the globe within the compass of human knowledge. What was more, he had on arriving there met a people who—despite (or because of) his inability to speak to them—he was able to make conform to European notions of prelapsarian innocence, a people who did not know the shame of nakedness or the use of iron or the worth of gold, and who (by extension) must live in or near some version of Eden, as confirmed by the perpetual and uncultivated fertility of those lands. Given the deeply ingrained beliefs of the time the only possible conclusion was that Columbus had triggered an event not just of geographical and political expansion, but one in the providential history of the world: a beginning of the return of man to paradise and the end of secular history.

Yet if Columbus's First Voyage could in some ways be neatly shoe-horned into a narrative of Christian providence, it was harder to square with the existing worldview in other ways. If the voyage confirmed the claims of Ptolemy and Marco Polo, it also proved them unquestionably wrong in other respects, exploding the notion of a world neatly bounded by the uncrossable Ocean Sea, and made it hard to argue that St. Augustine was right to doubt. The observations on these voyages and those that followed were increasingly incompatible with the writings of Pliny, Aristotle, Plato, and others. If they had been wrong about this—the very shape of the world—what else might the ancient authorities have been wrong about? Nor did the native people conform entirely to expectations: for all their Edenic nature they seemed not to understand any of the ancient languages spoken by the converted Jewish interpreters Columbus had taken with him. What knowledges might these people have outside the ambit of classical thought? More troublingly, although Columbus spoke with great enthusiasm about the natural piety of the people he had met and their readiness to be evangelized and converted to Christianity, they clearly had no existing notion of the Gospel. What could be the plan of a God who had kept humans in the dark for a millennium and a half over the secrets that would promise them salvation and eternal life?

These questions, unavoidably provoked by Columbus's discoveries, would take European thinkers decades to articulate and hundreds of years to answer to their own satisfaction. In the meantime, Columbus and his patrons focused on more immediate and pressing practical matters, successfully petitioning the recently installed Spanish pope, Alexander VI (Rodrigo Borja, the second Borgia pope), for bulls that conferred upon Spain the same legal rights (and spiritual duties) over their "discovered" territories as those given to Portugal over its new colonies in west Africa and the Atlantic islands. Furthermore, the Catholic Monarchs seem to have employed a painstakingly secret process to copy the exceptionally detailed logs of Columbus's First Voyage, spreading the pages among a large number of scribes so no one of them could leak the information to other interested parties (particularly the Portuguese). This process took so long Columbus received back his copy of the log only three weeks before his departure for the Second Voyage on 25 September 1493, in a packet that also contained a letter from Isabella conceding that everything he had predicted regarding the location of the Indies had been proved true and urging him on to complete his map of these western lands so that any remaining territorial disputes with the Portuguese could be settled once and for all.[12]

When Hernando stood on the dock in Cadiz in his first-recorded memory, then, he was looking at a man who had made the world anew, a man setting off in triumph to secure the victorious conquests that seemed to be within his grasp. His father was going to rejoin his mother's cousin, Diego de Arana, who had been left as one of those in charge of the first city in the Spanish New World—La Navidad—and they would in turn be joined by his uncle Bartholomew Columbus, who had heard the news of his brother's triumphant return while in Paris, on the way back from England to deliver the rival offer from Henry VII. Hernando himself was, through his father's ambitious maneuvering at this the dawn of his influence, set to join his brother Diego as part of the household of the heir apparent to the throne, the Infante Juan, placing Hernando right at the center of the kingdom God had chosen to transform the globe.

II

In the Chamber of Clean Blood

Whatever roles the child Hernando had played by the time his father left for his Second Voyage—son to his mother, younger sibling, *natural child* to a father who was rarely present—none of them would have prepared him for his arrival at the court of the *Reyes Católicos* early in 1494. Though he and Diego were officially joining the household of the Infante Juan, there was nothing homely about this institution. The heir to the throne, at sixteen, still followed the itinerant court of his parents around their kingdoms, but he nevertheless had a personal following of several hundred people, each of whom had a distinct office relating to one of the prince's needs. This household was constantly on the move and mostly did not live in palaces owned by the crown but were billeted in the mansions of the local nobility, always shifting, reshuffling to make the household hierarchy fit each new royal residence. Hernando probably first joined this outfit in the austere Castilian town of Valladolid, a center of royal power whose bare and imposing character must have seemed even less hospitable during the biting winter months after Hernando's arrival. The weather may not have been the only thing adding a chill to the reception. The hauteur of northern Castilians, derived in part from boasts about their early victories over the Muslim invaders, often led them to treat Andalusians like Hernando with suspicion, given their longer history of mingling with the Islamic residents of the peninsula.

Hernando's first home in Valladolid was perhaps the Palacio de

Pimentel, a short walk from the Palacio de los Vivero, where Ferdinand and Isabella had been married in 1469 and where the itinerant Castilian government was just beginning to put down its first roots. These solid, square structures, unadorned on the outside and set around plain colonnaded courtyards, were a world apart from the willful asymmetry of Hernando's hometown of Córdoba, with its warren of streets slinking between the houses toward the cathedral, where a forest of horseshoe arches provided a constant reminder of its long history as a mosque. If the houses of Valladolid were rather spare, though, Hernando would have found some relief looking out of the windows of the Palacio de Pimentel to where, across the street, the art of the Flamenco-Spanish high Gothic was reaching its apex. For the newly completed façade of the Colegio de San Gregorio and the adjoining Iglesia de San Pablo, the master masons Simón de Colonia and Gil Silóe had created riotous sculptural marvels, whittling the local stone until it became encrusted with images—wild men, pomegranate trees, stars, figures of chivalry—and foliage so delicate in appearance it seems to be carved from eggshell, in defiance of the rough winds of the north Castilian plain. Around the corner from this, in the façade of the Colegio de Santa Cruz by Juan Vázquez, Hernando would have seen the garbled first beginnings of neoclassicism in Spanish architecture. The court would soon pass on from Valladolid, but the art of these master masons would become a constant in the years to come. Hernando would spend the remainder of his childhood years moving between the centers of royal power in northern Spain, a landscape he would later chart in minute detail. Among the most familiar places would have been the redbrick Mudéjar palace on the corner of Medina del Campo's great market square; russet Salamanca, given its distinctive hue by the rusting iron in the sandstone from León; and Burgos, by the gentle river Arlanzon, with its immense and terraced cathedral, strikingly topped by hollow spires of delicate Gothic tracery—the work of the German artist Juan de Colonia—like crowns of paper lace cut from the living stone. In each of these places the household would reconfigure itself like a puzzle box, and Hernando would have to find order in an ever-shifting world.[1]

The huge retinue Hernando joined was presided over by a lord steward (*mayordomo*), who in turn delegated duties for the household finances to a lord chancellor (*contador mayor de castilla*) for major transactions, and a privy chancellor (*contador mayor de la despensa e raciones*), who dealt with the day-to-day expenses and arrangements. Beneath them a lord chamberlain (*camarero mayor*) took charge of the Infante's immediate personal needs, in which task he was assisted by the Ten Choice Companions (five old and five young). In addition, there were other officers including secretaries, chamberlains, master of the horse, master of the hounds, master of the hunt, and lord privy seal who were not under the lord steward. At the very bottom of the hierarchy were the pages—the rank to which Hernando and Diego were assigned—who were members of the household but who did not enjoy the dignity of having a personal role about the prince's body.

To make matters even more confusing, many of the duties belonging to these posts were actually performed by other people: the tasks assigned to the chancellor were usually handed on to his secretary, and while the Ten Choice Companions counted among their official duties waiting upon the prince while he dressed and ate, these tasks were in practice undertaken by a number of trenchermen and attendants. Hernando would eventually have understood that while the official duties of these posts were rather lowly—looking after the Infante's clothes, his meals, his accounts, and even his toilette— the posts were greatly sought after and held by the most powerful nobles in the kingdoms of Ferdinand and Isabella. To be near the body of the heir apparent was not merely a ceremonial honor: it held the promise of influencing the future king of a united Spain in matters of policy and patronage. These grandees could not be expected to perform the actual physical acts of serving food and folding laundry, so those labors were delegated elsewhere. The power of the political symbolism nevertheless remained: the Infante was of such importance that even his menial chores were performed by great aristocrats, and when one day he assumed the throne, they would be bound to him as those who had been his household companions, men who had grown up at the same table. Even lowly pages were the sons of the most eminent noblemen of the kingdom. If for Hernando losing his mother and finding himself at the bottom of a hierarchy of strangers must have been painful and confusing, it nevertheless represented Columbus's reception among the principal men of the realm. It also meant that Beatriz Enríquez's child was publicly and royally recognized as a son of the Admiral of the Ocean Sea.

The social advantages of joining the prince's household were probably of little comfort to the five-year-old boy who entered this forbidding and unfriendly place. As is clear from the writing of Gonzalo Fernández de Oviedo (a fellow page whose later *Book of the Royal Chamber of Prince Juan* provides us with an intimate and detailed picture of the household), great importance was placed upon the lineage of those who belonged to Juan's entourage. In his account Oviedo insists repeatedly that everyone near the prince was of "clean blood" (*limpia sangre*), by which he means there was no hint of Moorish or Jewish ancestry to be found in their genealogies. Even as Ferdinand and Isabella moved into the Alhambra, whose Moorish aesthetic of calligraphy and lemon trees and vaulted baths made one contemporary visitor call it a little peerless paradise, the belief that the infidelity of one's ancestors remained in the blood was gaining ground. Turning from enemies without to enemies within, the belief became widespread that conversion to Christianity was not enough to cleanse those of Moorish or Jewish descent of the stain of their forefathers. Oviedo asserts with unmixed pride that no one who waited at the Infante's table, in his pantry or his cellar, nor anyone from the doorman of the palace inward who exercised *any* office, was not of pure gentlemanly stock or at the very least an "Old Christian," someone who could trace his lineage back through many generations of high standing. Hernando could not even establish his descent from his own parents with any legally valid evidence, let alone rest upon the venerable ancestry of a father who seems deliberately to have kept his origins vague. Hieronymus Munzer, a German who traveled in Spain in these years and left a detailed account of what he saw, records the widespread paranoia that all of the principal offices of the realm were held by Marranos—Jews whose conversion to Christianity was, he says, a devious pretense—who oppressed Spain's Christians and taught children to curse them in private. It is hard to imagine Hernando not being included among those "two or three" outcasts at the court whom Oviedo mentions as appointed (as Columbus's sons were) by the queen before the prince came of age, and who he says were treated as strangers and kept apart from the circle and the person of the prince. The same high genealogical standards were not required, it seems, of the Infante's piebald dog, Bruto, which was an unusual mixture of whippet and mastiff, and which regularly delighted the prince by fetching specific garments and courtiers according to his master's need.[2]

Hernando was not the only stranger introduced to the prince's court by Columbus. Although many of the Taino people that Columbus had brought back with him from Hispaniola had, after evangelization and instruction, accompanied him on the return to the island to act as translators during further exploration, a few had been left behind to add luster to the royal court. The oddity of this situation, in which the Spanish court dress must only imperfectly have covered the red, black, and white tattoos customary to the Taino, would have been increased by their having taken the names of their Spanish godparents, so that shadowing the court were an Indio Ferdinand of Aragon and an Indio Juan of Castile. The Indio Juan remained in the household of the Infante Juan after Columbus left to return to the Taino homeland in Hispaniola, and though we know sadly little of his life during the two years this "Juan" survived the unfamiliar climate, the subsequent reports from Hispaniola take on a different tone when we imagine them heard by this unfortunate exile.

If Hernando and the Indio Juan were excluded from the inner circle of Juan's court, there may have been little to regret. While Oviedo's nostalgic account of life in the household paints it as a center of virtue in a Golden Age, the humanist Peter Martyr, who was one of the Infante's tutors, leaves an altogether less flattering picture of the prince as an unprepossessing youth who had no wit and little intellectual curiosity, and who gave his time over almost entirely to hunting. The intensely studious, bookish, and solitary character that Hernando was to have in later life may have developed during years in which snobbery and boorishness excluded him from the main activities of the household; though he was an excellent horseman, it seems he looked upon the aristocratic pastimes of hawking and hunting with disdain. The only surviving portrait of Hernando, made late in his life, also suggests his appearance may not have helped him to fit in. His lower lip juts out, perhaps the result of an underbite, his ears are too prominent, his nose is strangely formed at the bridge, and his face seems to slant to one side. It is not clear at what age a child would notice his looks are unpleasing to others, though it could only be too soon. For one reason or another, Hernando likely had time during these years quietly to observe the workings of this complex household and to absorb some of the cultural riches that went ignored by the dullard prince.[3]

Though it may have seemed a tiresome chore to many, one of the special duties of the pages was distinctly suited to Hernando's unique predilections: the keeping of the great books of the household, which ordered the myriad possessions of the prince into a series of lists. There were four of these great books, namely:

> Manual or Diary
> Book of Everything or The Book of Jewels
> Great Book
> Book of the Inventory

Juan's personal tastes were every bit as voluptuous as one would expect from one of the great princes of Europe, as suggested by the shopping list Oviedo copied down from 13 March 1496, in which the chamberlain was asked to acquire

satin brocade of cloth of gold for a *ropa bastarda*
crimson silk for doublets
purple silk for doublets
black silk for doublets
crimson velvet for a canopy
black Genoese velvet for my private room
cochineal-dyed cloth for gifts to my grooms [*moços
    despuela*]
green woolen cloth for hunters' hoods and tabards
Dutch linen for my private room
cloths to cover my tables and sideboards
crimson and tawny velvet to decorate my stable

If the pages were to compete with the dog Bruto for the Infante's affection, they would have to be at least as good as the dog in finding these garments once they had been acquired and stored away. The *Manual*, which was completed by the page who held the keys to the Infante's chamber, kept track of everything that came in and went out of the household, while *The Book of Jewels* was a list of the gold and silver vessels, tapestries, jewels, canopies, curtains, furs, and chapel plate belonging to the prince's household. Moreover, it described each of these things using their various weights, dimensions, and the stories depicted on the treasures. In a household that would have had scores of tapestries and hundreds of items of treasure, an accurate record could only be kept by using the distinctive qualities of each piece, which made a thorough knowledge of generic scenes used by artisans essential. A page asked to find for the Infante's bedroom a tapestry of nymphs bathing might think this a welcome task, but if he could not see the bow of Diana or the horns of Actaeon that made the scene a warning against the dangers of lust, then he was no better than a dog.

The *Great Book* sought to avoid such confusions by using another

(*opposite*) A print of Giovanni Battista Palumba's, *Diana Bathing with Her Attendants*, c.1500; Hernando's inventory number 2150.

inventory method, adopting the tools used by bankers and employing their accounting techniques not only to compile the household accounts but also to reconcile everything that was in the *Manual* and *The Book of Jewels*, as well as providing an alphabetical list of entries and a guide to the location of each object described. As with the increasingly complex and manifold financial transactions being undertaken by the great mercantile houses of Europe, comfort could be gained in reducing each entry to a docket number or giving it a place on an alphabetic list. The final book, the *Book of the Inventory*, also used an alphabetical list to register the voluminous incoming and outgoing correspondence of the Infante, and to provide a guide to the ledgers so that old letters could be revisited. From his earliest days, some of the most prized books in Hernando's world were ones that tamed a wilderness of miscellaneity through the magic of lists, making a curtain and a cup part of the same order by reducing them to name, number, cost, and location.

Life at court not only introduced Hernando to a bewildering variety of people and things but also to a world of complex and often contradictory ideas. He would have attended lectures by the great scholars recruited to train the aristocracy at court, probably from an early age, like the little boy who, much younger than the rest, kneels at the feet of the great humanist Antonio de Nebrija in a contemporary manuscript illumination of Juan's court. It may have helped that two opposing camps of ideas were embodied in the two tutors who were in charge of the education of the Infante and (more important, given his lack of interest) of the pages of the court. The first of these was the Dominican friar Diego de Deza, a theologian educated at Spain's greatest seat of learning, the University of Salamanca, who had risen through the church hierarchy as bishop of Zamora and then of Salamanca itself, even if his duties at court gave him little time for church business. Deza seems to have been among Columbus's earliest and most reliable supporters, and Hernando would quickly have learned to count him among the faction at the court who spoke well of his father and his projects. Yet Deza's backing may have been slightly confusing to the young Hernando: the friar was, after all, a staunch Thomist, meaning that he dedicated his scholarly life to championing the work of Thomas Aquinas and his use of Aristotelian logic to understand and explain the mysteries of the Christian faith. An extraordinary addition to Deza's teachings may have come in the person of Beatriz Galindo, a rare female scholar, whose prodigious talents had made her a celebrated Aristotelian at Salamanca, and who was also brought to court to teach, though likely only the princesses and their households. Deza and Galindo taught their charges to read nature firstly as the Book of God, in which the divine was revealed through the order installed at creation. As this scholastic kind of learning was focused on the cloister, the university, and the library, it would have had less obvious connection to the world of ships and islands inhabited by Hernando's father.[4]

The other tutor, however, represented a wholly different attitude to learning: this was Peter Martyr, the letter-writing man of arms who was to become one of the first and most important historians of the New World. Peter Martyr was very much a humanist in the mold created during the Italian Renaissance of the previous hundred years: someone who valued beautiful speech and writing and had little time for the knotty problems of the Thomists, someone who believed in the worth of the active life rather than the contemplative one, and who moved easily between roles as author, tutor, diplomat, soldier, and citizen of the Republic of Letters that connected men of the same grain across Europe. His teaching, as suggested by one eyewitness account, consisted of having his pupils recite the poetry of Horace and Juvenal, absorbing by repetition the rhythms and the values of classical Rome. Peter Martyr counted among his chief correspondents the genius of the Roman intellectual scene, Giulio Pomponio Leto, a pioneering humanist whose devotion to the learning of pre-Christian Rome led him to affect classical dress and set up an academy among the ruins of the Quirinal Hill, from which he led his disciples on tours of the half-buried Roman monuments and even under them to the catacombs that had lain hidden for a thousand years. So great was

Leto's success in fostering this culture that his academy was disbanded in 1468 by Pope Paul II amid accusations that would have made its guiding spirit, Socrates, proud: republican conspiracy, sexual immorality, anticlericalism, and even pagan irreligion. As one of Leto's disciples, Peter Martyr provided Juan's household with a direct link to the most daring currents of Italian humanism, from a Rome that would later play a central part in Hernando's own life. Indeed, Hernando would have seen this neoclassicism springing up all around him, as at Burgos, where inside the miraculous Gothic cathedral the Roman-trained French artist Felipe Bigarny was carving classical buildings into the transept, and across the street where the printer Fadrique de Basilea was switching from Gothic fonts in his books to Roman ones, freshly imported from Italy where humanists copied their letterforms from the inscriptions on ancient ruins. Peter Martyr in turn directed many of his most important letters on the New World discoveries to Leto, creating a strange symbiosis between the new learning and how the expanding world was written about and conceived. In the persons of his two tutors Hernando would have confronted the stark questions that were driving intellectual debates: whether learning should be directed toward a place in heaven or a triumph on earth, toward the eternal or the present, the metaphysical or the physical, and whether its materials should be Christian only or should take in the thought of other, pagan worlds.[5]

Some maternal comfort in this overwhelmingly male world might have been provided by the Infante's nursemaid Juana de Torres y Ávila, who as well as being one of the few female members of the household was another staunch supporter of the Columbus faction. She was over the years to be the recipient of a number of Columbus's letters to the court, and many of those not directly addressed to her were nonetheless carried back to Spain by her brother, Antonio de Torres, who was to serve as a trusted go-between during Columbus's long absences from the court. The first of his letters from the New World reached court as early as April 1494, only a few months after Hernando had arrived there—though the court had already moved on from Valladolid to Medina del Campo. Having crossed the ocean with seventeen ships this time, and having quickly established reliable shipping routes between the Iberian Peninsula and the Caribbean archipelago, the Admiral could now maintain a reasonably frequent correspondence with the court. While this meant Columbus could continue to provide encouraging reports to the Catholic Monarchs on their new territories and could in turn ask for supplies that could not be sourced on that side of the ocean, the new communication links were fraught with danger for the Admiral. Unlike on the First Voyage, when, despite the efforts of his rival Pinzón, Columbus had been able to disappear, reappear, and provide the only report of what had happened in between, the returning fleet of twelve ships in April 1494 brought a number of letters and eyewitnesses to the New World. As would quickly become clear, it was no longer possible for Columbus to control the narrative of events beyond the sea.[6]

Indeed, not even the court itself could wholly contain and control public understanding of the New World anymore. Among the first letters sent back from the Second Voyage was one from Dr. Chanca, the chief physician of the new settlement, addressed to the city of Seville and evidently intended for wide public circulation. In the great trade fair at Medina del Campo, Hernando would find a growing book fair among the long-standing markets for silver, paintings, and Castilian wool returning to Spain in the form of Flemish tapestries, as well as the currency exchange which drew crowds of merchants from across Europe and connected this dusty outpost with the great banking centers of Lyons, Antwerp, and Venice. In the immense market square, alongside books from Salamanca, Barcelona, and Seville, Hernando found works from the centers of European print—Venice, Basel, Antwerp—perhaps including foreign editions of his father's letter of 1493 reporting his discoveries. But by now Columbus's accounts were not the only ones on the market, and it may have been in these bookstalls that Hernando first sensed the cacophony of printed voices competing to hold the public's attention. While Dr. Chanca's letter repeats Columbus's official reports about the perpetual springtime of the islands, he is not quite as deft as the Admiral in moving swiftly from the vegetal riches of the New World to the mineral ones that will surely follow, as (for instance) when Columbus instructs Antonio de Torres to report the abundant evidence of spices that can be found by simply standing on the shores of these islands, without any effort to penetrate inland, which surely was proof of the unlimited riches within—and the same, he reasons, *must* be true of the gold on the new islands he has found:

> Dominica
> Mariagalante
> Guadeloupe
> Santa Cruz
> Monserrate
> Santa Maria la Redonda
> Santa Maria la Antigua
> San Martin

After recognizing in the first-named island the auspiciousness of their making landfall on a Sunday (*domingo*) and paying tribute to his flagship, the *Mariagalante*, Columbus named these islands after the chief pilgrimage sites in Spain. Dr. Chanca's letter, however, marks a departure from the party line—noting for instance the exotic fruit that some of those on the fleet, perhaps trusting to the Edenic reports they had heard, attempted to taste, only to be rewarded for nothing more than a lick by grotesquely swollen faces and a raving madness.

The first cloud may have been cast for Hernando upon his father's golden world by the succession of reports that slowly revealed the macabre fate of La Navidad, Columbus's original fortress-settlement in the New World. Though Columbus attempted to gloss over this in his communication of January 1494, even the child Hernando might have noticed something amiss in that his father's letters were addressed not from La Navidad but from the new settlement of La Isabela. Readers of Hernando's later account of events might have had a premonition of this disaster, given how often he insists upon the care with which his father recorded the place where he had left thirty-nine men from varied backgrounds, including an Englishman, an Irishman from Galway, and a relation of Hernando's on his mother's side. But when the fleet of the Second Voyage finally made their way back to Hispaniola, they hardly had need of Columbus's directions. On a riverbank near the first landmark of Monte Cristo they found two corpses, one with a noose around his neck and another with his feet tied, though some may have deceived themselves that these bodies, too decomposed for identification, were not those of men who had been left behind in La Navidad. Hernando meticulously recorded further details of this scene: one of the men was young and the other old; the noose was made of esparto grass and the strangled man's arms were extended, his hands tied to a piece of wood like a cross. The hope that these were not Spaniards became harder to sustain when, the next day and farther up the river, they came across two more bodies, one thickly bearded—in a land of natives without facial hair. When they finally anchored off La Navidad, reluctant to come closer to shore for fear of grounding as the *Santa Maria* had, a canoe bearing envoys from Guacanagarí approached, its men wearing masks that they then handed to Columbus. They initially reported all was well but were finally pressed to admit that a few of the settlers of La Navidad had died of disease and fighting. Guacanagarí himself, they said, could not come to greet Columbus because he was lying in his hut, gravely wounded after having battled with two other caciques—Caonabó and Marieni—who had attacked La Navidad.[7]

Hernando's account of these events, which draws upon Columbus's lost expedition diaries but must also have been colored by his own memories, shows all the signs of trauma as it recounts the disintegration of Columbus's idyll. Hernando describes the further bodies that were found, with an estimate of how long they had been dead, and the story that unfolded piece by piece of how a party of settlers had broken with the rest and embarked on a course of rape and pillage, leading the cacique Caonabó to march on them and put the stockade to

the flame. Yet there were discrepancies in the stories told by Guacanagarí and his men, and the belief the Taino were simply and naively
honest became harder to sustain. After narrating this bloodcurdling
episode, Hernando turns strangely to his father's pleasure when Guacanagarí gave him a gold belt, crown, and grains worth four gold
marks, in exchange for items valued at only three reales (equivalent to
less than one two-thousandth of the value). It is unclear whether
Columbus was truly so cold-blooded in his mercantile calculations at
this moment or if he was desperately grasping for positive news in the
face of a massacre for which the real guilt was unlikely ever to be
determined. Similarly, Hernando's recording of this exchange in his
biography of his father, shortly after what must have been a brutal
childhood memory, has the feel of those misdirections often prompted
by trauma.

Hernando's presence at court made him an eyewitness to the competing interpretations of these events. Dr. Chanca's account of the La
Navidad affair played into a dawning belief in the deceitful bloodiness
of these new Spanish subjects, something that would have been rein-
forced by reports of a further disaster for Spanish Atlantic expansion
that also arrived in April 1494. In an attempt to complete the conquest
of the Canary Islands by taking the final holdout of Tenerife, the conquistador Alonso de Lugo had refused to accept the surrender of the
pastoralist Guanches who lived there and attacked instead, only to be
roundly beaten back to the sea with the loss of eight hundred Christian lives. The heartwarming triumph of the natives of Tenerife was
sadly short-lived: de Lugo returned the following year with a larger
force and captured them en masse, a pattern of hardening attitudes
toward Atlantic peoples that was only to worsen in the coming years.
The German traveler Hieronymus Munzer was soon to see these
"beasts trapped in human form" for sale in Valencia and to note without irony the "sweetening effect" of religion on these slaves, many of
whom were put to work harvesting sugarcane. To counter this mount-
ing bigotry, Columbus had a tightrope to walk: even as he attempted
to conjure out of nothing a belief in the New World as a gold-paved

Eden, he had to admit the settlement was faltering at the outset. In the same breath with which Antonio de Torres was to report that vines and wheat sprang marvelously and untended out of the New World ground, he was obliged to request the Monarchs send supplies from Spain, namely:

> wine, hardtack, wheat, salt pork, other salted meat, cattle, sheep, lambs, male and female calves, donkeys, raisins, sugar, almonds, honey, rice, and medicine

And all this if possible before the summer arrived. The reason Columbus gave for this want in his land of milk and honey was the poor quality of what had been stocked for the Second Voyage: the wine had been lost through poorly made barrels, the horses supplied by the farrier in Seville were all broken-backed nags, and the fine strapping men he expected to find when they disembarked in Hispaniola turned out to be layabouts who expected simply to feast on manna, gather the gold that was lying about, and return to Europe rich men. They could not survive on the local cassava bread and required the food they were used to in Spain, and they constantly fell ill in that climate. To prove this de Torres carried with him a list of the healthy and a list of the sick. Just as Columbus was quick to blame the fate of La Navidad on the viciousness of some of the men he left there, so the failure of the New World settlements over the coming years was increasingly to be laid (by Columbus himself, and later Hernando) at the feet of men whom the Admiral disdained for not being willing to suffer like him to turn his vision into a reality. But even Columbus's adherence to the picture of naked innocence among the New World natives was beginning to crumble: not only does he detail the defensive measures he has taken against local aggression, he also in his struggle to make his discoveries profitable proposes a trade be set up in which Spanish cattle be exchanged for New World slaves. Though the Monarchs firmly resisted this suggestion, Columbus continued to push for it in hopes of saving his vision of the New World, being tempted for the sake of expediency into an execrable history of kidnap and enslavement.[8]

The letters from Columbus over the succeeding years followed these familiar patterns. Hernando would have learned in his seventh year, during the early months when the court was at Madrid, of his father's expedition against the aggressor Caonabó in the province of Cibao, where the rivers ran with grains of gold but they faced constant attacks from Caonabó's warriors. At the same time Hernando would have heard tell of his father's expedition in search of terra firma, the continental landmass of Cathay, when instead he got no farther than the coasts of Cuba and Jamaica, becoming marooned amid a labyrinth of hundreds of islets he named the Jardines de la Reina, "The Queen's Gardens." There they witnessed flamingos, pilot fish that hitched rides on the dorsal fins of other swimmers, turtles as big as shields in numbers that blanketed the sea, a cloud of butterflies so large it cast the ship in darkness, and a breeze so sweet the soldiers felt themselves surrounded by roses and the finest perfumes in the world. The Admiral boasted they would have returned to Castile via the East on that very journey, if not for the fact that their supplies were exhausted, as was the Admiral, having not (he claimed) changed clothes or slept in a bed for eight months. On returning to Hispaniola Columbus found his brother Bartholomew, who had finally caught up with him after more than six years, and succumbed to a fever that for five months deprived him of his sight, his memory, and his senses.[9]

Columbus's letters and the objects he sent back to Spain with them are witnesses to a mind struggling to put this flood of new things into order, when every day produced some unheard-of wonder, a struggle that is the prehistory to his son's lifelong quest to organize the world. Insofar as Columbus did attempt to impose a system on what he was seeing, he usually fell back on the worldview of medieval cosmography, in which the oddity of men and their customs showed how far from the center of the world any given place was, whereas the perfumes of Araby and the abundance of gold were clues that one was approaching the earthly Jerusalem or the boundaries of the lost Eden.

Columbus's New World was to him strangely both of these things, both center and periphery, both far from the known and approaching man's point of origin. More often than not his reports of the New World simply never progressed beyond incoherent lists. We should not, however, assume that because the lists lacked order and seemed chaotic, this was a dispassionate and scientific record of what he was seeing: in the tradition of the medieval *enumeratio*, the rambling list was often a way of describing God, whose divine incomprehensibility could not be expressed except by the use of dissimilar images. One such list, for instance, described Christ as the

source, way, right, rock, lion, light bearer, lamb—door, hope, virtue, word, wisdom, prophet—victim, scion, shepherd, mountain, nets, dove—flame, giant, eagle, spouse, patience, worm . . .

Perhaps in imitation of this Columbus most often fell back on protestations of inexpressibility—that the marvelous beauty of the New World was something that could not be put into words but simply had to be seen, to be experienced in rapt admiration. This move at once produced a mystical impression of these new territories and postponed giving them a meaning, leaving Columbus the sole authority, having been the only one to see what could not be properly described.[10]

Some observations did manage to breach this defensive wall of conventional interpretation and blank wonder. The bafflement Columbus felt, for instance, at the natives of Cibao province "locking" the doors of their huts by placing single canes across the entry, slender barriers that none of them would dream of breaching, witnesses the effect of a custom that could not be fitted into these schemes. These cane locks could not be explained by either of the simple narratives used to understand the New World, of Edenic innocence on the one hand or barbaric bestiality on the other; instead, they confronted the viewer with a version of *privacy* unique to that culture. In time it would be precisely these oddities of custom that would lead European thinkers to wonder if their own customs—of dress, of behavior, of morality—were not the natural and necessary practices of a *civilized* people but were equally arbitrary and nonsensical when viewed from outside of that culture. But these awakenings would for a long time remain dormant. In the meantime Columbus and his sponsors at court saw no irony in sending "cannibals" back to Spain to cure them of their sinful appetite for human flesh by converting them to Christianity, membership of which cult they would regularly celebrate by eating the body of the Son of God during Mass. No one appeared to flinch at subjecting the stone *cemies* or idols of the Taino to derision and mockery, as mere pieces of wood and stone that the natives thought could speak and to which they made offerings, while renaming Taino places after statues of the Virgin and saints that had equally proved their blessedness by miraculous acts.

This growing body of knowledge about the western Atlantic gave rise during Columbus's Second Voyage to the first systematic attempts to write about this New World, a process in which Hernando played a key part. In response to Columbus's letters of 1494 Hernando's tutor Peter Martyr declared his intention to write a history of the voyages of exploration and the lands they had encountered, a task that was to occupy him intermittently for the rest of his life. And a mail packet that arrived late in 1495, as the court toured Catalonia, contained the first attempt to write an ethnographic account of a New World people, in the form of Fray Ramón Pané's extensive study of the habits and customs of the Taino, a text that survives only because Hernando copied it wholesale into his writings about his father, and to which we owe most of our knowledge about a culture that was quickly eradicated by massacre, conversion, and disease. Pané's survey begins with a description of the Taino sky deity and his five-named mother, and their belief that mankind emerged from two caves, Cacibayagua and Amayauba, guarded by a man named Marocael ("without eyelashes") who was turned to stone for failing to guard the caves. The description then relates a story of how the first female humans disappeared to an Island of Women, leaving behind children whose cries turned into the croaking of frogs; the men who remained, like the Christians who first arrived from the sea, were a people without women, ones who took what they lacked. Pané records the two caves, from which the sun and moon emerge, contained two stone *cemi* idols named Boinayol ("son of the serpent-formed storm god") and Maroya ("cloudless"), as well as the Taino belief that dead men roam the earth without navels, endlessly seeking to embrace the female *Coaybay* ("absent ones"). His account of native culture ends with a description of their ritual chants (which he likens to those performed by Muslims), their shamanic witch doctors, and the way their idols were made, from trees that move from their rooted spot and reveal to the shaman the form they wish to take during a psychotropic *cohoba* trip. Perhaps Hernando would have felt some sympathy with the frogs central to Taino culture, who were once children left by their mothers and whose croaking is the sound of them calling out to the parent they have lost.

Many of the stories that Hernando transcribed from Pané are jumbled and difficult to understand, and Pané modestly admits the limitations of his account, noting he did not have enough paper to write on and was forced to attempt to memorize everything in order, and that furthermore the linguistic and cultural barrier prevented him from understanding many things fully. But this humility should not distract from the system quietly imposed by Pané on what he heard, which proceeds from an account of the Taino gods, through their story of the creation of man, to their understanding of the shape of the cosmos and of the afterlife, and finally the social institutions that are an expression of their way of seeing the world, from their rituals and sacred objects to the way in which they believe bodies can be healed by their form of medicine. This European way of describing "exotic" peoples, moving from religious beliefs to social practices, was not an invention of Pané's, and since Pané it has become so naturalized that we are in danger of missing the argument that it contains. Hernando may well have recognized that the description of the Taino follows the form set down by classical works including Pliny's *Natural History* and transmitted through the Middle Ages by Isidore of Seville's *Etymologies*: both Pliny and Isidore attempt to describe the entirety of the world as it is known to them, and one might be tempted to see their encyclopedias as merely randomly ordered lists. Closer inspection, however, reveals a clear organizational principle based on Aristotelian philosophy, moving (as one description has put it) from "the original to the derived, and from the natural to the artificial." As in Pané's description of the Taino, this creates order by starting with the things from which the world is seen to come (the gods, Creation), before moving on to the things created (man) and in turn the things created by these creations (religious ceremonies, medical practices, etc.). This seems a reasonable enough way of proceeding, but in practice it allows the Christian reader to dismiss the entirety of another culture on the basis of an incorrect belief in God: if the *premises* on which the culture is based are false (i.e., their notion of God), all practices, beliefs, and customs derived from those premises must also be false. Tellingly, Pané's document ends with an account of his part in the first New World conversion to Christianity, of the attempts by a violent opponent of the Christians (the cacique Guarionex) to destroy the Christian icons, and the public burning of Guarionex's men by Bartholomew Columbus.[11]

The pattern of Hernando's life at court, and of learning about the New World through his father's letters, was interrupted by the sudden return of Columbus in 1496, after an absence of three years, almost half the life of his younger son. Joyful as the reunion must have been for Hernando, the Admiral was not returning in triumph this time, and no fanfare greeted him on his arrival at Cadiz in June nor when he was received by the *Reyes* at the Casa del Cordón in Burgos. The proliferation of different accounts of the New World at court had given substance to increasingly widespread and urgent complaints regarding the conduct of the Admiral as governor of the new territories, and that of his brother Bartholomew during Columbus's extended absences for further exploration. The charges focused not on the tyrannical exploitation of the native population but rather on the high-handed treatment of the Spanish settlers who had come to Hispaniola, with the anti-Columbian party deriding the New World as a place of harshness and violence only made worse by Columbus's leadership, and the Admiral responding that the troubles were largely produced by the viciousness of the Spanish settlers and their needless provocation of the native population. Though the judicial commission didn't find against Columbus, the Admiral seemed to have sensed that his long absence from court was allowing those who opposed him to fill the silence this created.[12]

Columbus was reunited with his children at Burgos during a particularly tumultuous period, one in which a less talented showman might have failed to make his case heard over the cacophony of things competing for the Monarchs' attention. Ferdinand and Isabella were restructuring their court to strengthen the position of their heirs, transferring the Infante Juan to a household of his own, strategically located at Almazán on the border between Ferdinand's province of Aragon and Isabella's of Castile. They had also arranged a double marriage that would link their house solidly to the ascendant House of Habsburg, betrothing their children to the heirs of Maxmilian I, ruler of the Holy Roman Empire. Shortly before Columbus arrived at court an armada of 130 ships, bearing an estimated twenty-five to thirty-five thousand passengers, had departed from the Basque country to take the princess Juana to Flanders, where she would marry Duke Philip of Burgundy, and to bring back on the return trip Maximilian's eldest daughter Margaret. For the princess's private retinue of three thousand, they stocked two hundred cows, a thousand chickens, two thousand eggs, four thousand barrels of wine, and nearly a quarter of a million salted fish. The fleet's size was not only an expression of the great importance of the event, it was also a necessary defense against aggression from the French, with whom Spain was at war as both countries sought to secure and extend their control over the Italian peninsula. The nuptial celebrations party had turned to horror, however, when as many as ten thousand of the Spanish party died of cold and illness during the harsh Flanders winter of 1495–96.[13]

If Hernando sensed his father's showmanship was wearing thin when, presenting another assortment of wonders from the New

World, he could offer only a small amount of gold "as earnest of what was to come," the Admiral nonetheless found a way to use his peculiar talents to bring himself to the fore. Both Columbus and Hernando were later to recall in writing how in March 1497, during the fleet's return from Flanders bearing Juan's intended bride, Princess Margaret, Columbus had convinced the worry-stricken Monarchs not to move with the rest of the court to the inland town of Soria, but instead to stay behind in Burgos to be nearer to Laredo, the port at which he predicted the fleet would dock, even forecasting the exact day they would arrive and the route they would take. This unusual mode of turning a *portolan*—the sailor's description of the routes and distances between ports—into a form of prophecy served Columbus well, and both he and Hernando were over the coming years to exploit the almost mystical authority it conferred on them. As Hernando would later learn, the Italian polymath Angelo Poliziano even had a word for this practice, calling it a *mixed* science, falling halfway between the "inspired" knowledge that came from divine revelation and the practical kind that comes from human invention.[14]

The wedding of Princess Margaret to the Infante Juan was celebrated in Burgos on Palm Sunday, 19 March 1497, after which the Monarchs moved quickly to secure further alliances, with Isabella leaving shortly after to celebrate the marriage of their eldest daughter, Isabel, to King Manuel of Portugal. The nuptial joy was to be short-lived. Juan fell ill while Isabella was away and died soon after in the arms of his father, who tried to comfort his son by telling him God had reserved greater realms for him in the hereafter than those he would now never inherit on earth. It was said that Juan's dog, Bruto, lay down at the head of his master's coffin in Salamanca Cathedral and refused to move for any other reason than to make water outside the church. The dog was still to be found where he last saw his master long after the body was moved to Ávila for burial, though by then a pillow and food had been provided for him at his new post. It is also said Ferdinand joined Isabella for the marriage of their elder daughter but did not tell his wife of the death of their son until the festivities were over. Their daughter, the newly crowned queen consort of Portugal, was also to die, ten months later, only to be replaced as queen by her younger sister Maria, who married the same Portuguese king after two years had elapsed.

During Columbus's two-year residence back in Spain Hernando would have watched his father battle to push his plans forward through the fog of these family and dynastic events, which were themselves being played out in a European context of war against France in Italy, the Turks in the Mediterranean, and the North African Arabs along the Barbary Coast. Columbus followed the court in its cumbersome progress around Aragon, and then from Burgos to Valladolid, Medina del Campo, Salamanca, and Alcalá de Henares. Slowly but surely the Admiral secured a further restatement of the Monarchs' promises to him in the *Capitulaciones de Santa Fe* of 1492, procured desperately needed resupply for the settlers at Hispaniola, saw his sons, Diego and Hernando, transferred from the household of the dead prince to that of the queen herself, and gained permission to return to the New World on a third voyage. Yet Columbus was continually and understandably nervous about the ability of his fortunes to weather the onslaughts against him during his long absences, much less after his death, and in addition to the reiterated promises of Ferdinand and Isabella he took advantage of his presence in Spain to draw up an entail on his estate. This document not only further cemented the Admiral's status by involving him in a legal procedure reserved for members of the nobility, it also vaulted Hernando into the highest elites of Spanish society. On the one hand it held out the promise of substantial revenue in the event of Columbus's death—1 to 2 million maravedís in annual rent, putting Hernando on a footing surpassed only by a few heirs in the land—and on the other hand, perhaps more important for a ten-year-old boy, it named both Diego and Hernando in a single breath as *mis hijos legítimos*, "my legitimate sons."[15]

Exactly what Diego and Hernando would be legitimate heirs to, however, was much less certain than Columbus's entail tried to suggest. His lavish bequests were made on the basis of projected income that existed only in Columbus's imagination and would depend on the crown's continued adherence to the agreements of 1492. While these agreements were notarized and Columbus could appeal in case of any doubt to the importance of the sovereigns' word within the chivalric code, in reality the *Capitulaciones* posed an unacceptable threat to the Spanish monarchy, conferring on Columbus and his heirs in perpetuity virtual autonomy over a kingdom beyond the sea and an income that would rival that of the crown itself.

The tenuousness of Columbus's vision of the future became apparent during the Third Voyage, on which he departed at the end of May 1498. Unwilling simply to return to the islands of which he was governor and oversee their resupply, he had split his fleet in two at the Canary Islands, sending three ships on to Hispaniola and taking three himself south toward the equator before heading west in search of the elusive mainland. This expedition lasted three months and conferred on Columbus the distinction of being the first European to see the American continental landmass, a part of modern-day Venezuela that he called Paria, even if it is not wholly clear he recognized it as such at the time and though later cartography was famously to accord that honor to Amerigo Vespucci. But Columbus's delay in arriving at Hispaniola was nothing short of disastrous: when he did land at the end of August 1498 in the town of Santo Domingo, founded by his brother Bartholomew on the west bank of the deep-drawing river Ozama and named after their father, he once again found the island in open revolt. This rebellion, like that of 1495, was directed first against Columbus's brothers and stoked by poor conditions on the island, but increasingly and uncontrollably turned against the Admiral himself after his return.

Columbus's sons were not in the least shielded from this complete collapse of their father's power, his reputation, and his prospects:

instead, they were directly in the firing line as settlers from Hispaniola began to bypass the New World administration and present their complaints directly to the Monarchs. Hernando recalled many years later, with the vividness reserved for experiences of shame, the mob of fifty or so returned settlers who had installed themselves (with a barrel of wine) outside the gate of the Alhambra, where the court was in residence. The mob took to shouting loud complaints about how the Admiral had ruined them by withholding their wages and brayed their petition to Ferdinand every time he attempted to leave the palace, shouting, "Pay us! Pay us!" However, the most virulent of their attacks were reserved for Diego and the eleven-year-old Hernando, who in a rare instance quotes the direct speech hurled at them by the mob:

Look at the Sons of the Admiral of Mosquitoes, of him who discovered the Land of Vanity and the Land of Deceit, to be the sepulchre and the misery of the Gentlemen of Castile!

Hernando remembers how after this he and his brother avoided the mob, presumably now leaving the palace only through the back doors.[16]

The length of time the Monarchs withstood this onslaught of complaints speaks of their fidelity to Columbus and the strength of his supporters at court, but eventually even they could not resist the dispatch of a second inquest into affairs in the New World territories, this time led by Francisco de Bobadilla. A mere three months after Bobadilla landed in Santo Domingo on 23 August 1500, Hernando was to have the long-awaited reunion with his father. But the Columbus of Hernando's twelfth year was not the gift-laden conjurer of his eighth. Instead, Columbus returned to Spain half-stricken with blindness, to report that he and his brothers had been led, in the town named after their father, through crowds shouting insults and blowing horns at the fallen Admiral, past street corners covered with ballads lampooning the discoverer of the New World, and subjected to a show trial in which the judge, Bobadilla, incited the witnesses to pour their scorn upon Columbus. He landed at Cadiz on 20 November 1500, stripped of his governorship and his dignity, and bound in chains hand and foot.[17]

III

The Book of Prophecies

Following Columbus's appearance in chains, the weather-beaten, aging explorer shared with his son Hernando a secret project, one that promised to reveal the world in an entirely new light. This work was designed to lift Columbus's discoveries above the petty cost-benefit calculations on which many of the courtly debates were centered, framing them instead as events in a grand religious narrative of history, in which they would set the stage for the triumph of the Christian faith and the coming of the End of Time. The manuscript in which he compiled his evidence now survives as eighty-four leaves of badly damaged paper, sporadically filled with writing in a number of different hands. Each sheet of paper, originally made in Italy, is watermarked with a splayed hand below a six-pointed star. The work was initially given the rather bland, descriptive title of the "Book or collection of *auctoritates* [authoritative writings], sayings, opinions, and prophecies concerning the need to recover the Holy City and Mount Zion, and the finding and conversion of the islands of the Indies and of all peoples and nations." Hernando was to rename it *The Book of Prophecies*, and the role he played in its creation is the first evidence of his growing genius for ordering.[1]

The chains were soon removed from the Admiral of the Ocean Sea—indeed, they would have been taken off sooner had Columbus not refused the offer from the captain escorting him back, preferring to satisfy his fine sense of the theatrical by landing in Spain in the guise of a slave. The shackles neatly captured, for Columbus, the disparity between what he had achieved and how he had been rewarded: in the words of a prophecy he grew fond of quoting, he was the man who had *broken the chains of Ocean* that bounded the ancient world, yet the chains of a captive were the only thing he had been given in return. This was the reason (Hernando recalled toward the end of his life) Columbus had them set aside as a relic, to be placed in his tomb as a token of the world's ingratitude. After ordering his release, Ferdinand and Isabella asked him to come to them at Granada, and over the coming months Columbus resumed his Sisyphean task of reestablishing the legitimacy of his claims to power and wealth from the New World. The Monarchs were quick to condemn Bobadilla's treatment of their Admiral, and to appoint a new commission under Nicolás de Ovando to scrutinize Bobadilla's own conduct, which must have afforded Columbus considerable satisfaction.[2]

Columbus was no longer content, however, to attend to these practical and administrative tasks, and during this period of residence in Spain he seems to have devoted increasing amounts of attention to *The Book of Prophecies*. This was not a sudden development in Columbus's thinking: after all, he had sought since the earliest accounts of the New World to evoke the Edenic feel of the Caribbean, using its fertile climate and the nakedness of its inhabitants to suggest the enterprise was a step toward a blessed Golden Age (and, by extension, toward gold). But Columbus's letters of October 1498 and February 1500 marked a significant shift in his thinking. In the first of these he reported his detour, at the beginning of the Third Voyage, around a three-headed island (he christened it Trinidad) toward another landmass, which he initially named "Isla Santa" but later learned was terra firma—a continent—that the inhabitants of this region called Paria. Columbus's three-month detour around Paria included some of the most harrowing events to date, even for a man whose life had been a catalogue of near-death experiences. First among these was a period shortly after they reached the equator sailing south, during which they were becalmed for eight days in a heat so intense the ships' holds turned to ovens and the decking planks began to groan and split. Drawing on his father's logbooks, Hernando later ventured the opinion that had it not been for the relative cool of night and the occasional shower of rain, the ships would have been burned with everyone inside them. When the wind finally rose and they reached Trinidad, their relief was cut short as they passed in horror through a sea channel between Trinidad and Paria, one that flowed as fast as a furious river, and in which waves from either end crashed in the middle, causing the water to rise like a cliff along the whole length of the strait. They called this strait at the southern end of Trinidad the Boca de la Sierpe, the Serpent's Mouth. Their fear increased when they realized they were now trapped in a gulf between Trinidad and the mainland: they could not sail back south against the current of the Boca de la Sierpe, and it became clear their only route back toward Hispaniola lay through a similar channel to the north, to which they gave the twin name Boca del Drago, Dragon's Mouth. As if the moment were not fraught enough with danger, the crew had to do without the guidance of their leader: Columbus hadn't been sleeping again and his eyes were so bloodshot with continual wakefulness that he was losing his sight. For a man obsessed with observing and recording every detail, and convinced he had a God-given sight that revealed things to him before others, this blindness must have been torture. Under these circumstances they took the only option open to them and ran the Boca del Drago. They survived but were spat out at such a pace that they only regained control after being carried on the current for sixty-five leagues.[3]

Though Columbus may have had to rely on the eyes of others on the visit to Paria, he began to believe he had been given a vision of something more. Struggling to fit the extraordinary experiences of Paria into a model he could understand, he reasoned that the ship's movement had not been determined by simple natural phenomena, but by an irregularity in the shape of the earth. He now saw that the earth was not perfectly spherical: it was shaped like a woman's breast, globular in form but rising to a peak like a nipple, a peak he reasoned was located at the easternmost point of this landmass, just below the equator, and on top of which was to be found the Celestial Paradise. As evidence for this he adduced a number of arguments: the as-yet-unexplained behavior of the compass needle in the middle of the ocean, which confoundingly ceased to point exactly to the north every time he passed a certain point one hundred leagues west of the Azores; the speed at which they had exited the Boca del Drago, suggesting they were going downhill; and the doldrums where they had baked for eight days, there to ensure (he speculated) that no one could approach the Celestial Paradise without God's permission. Further to this he pointed to how the people of Paria failed to conform to late-medieval understandings of racial geography, in which the hottest places on earth were supposed to hold the darkest-skinned people, who had been singed by the climate. He not only found people in Paria braver, more astute, and more talented than most he had encountered, but they were also lighter skinned—because, he argued, they lived where the earth began to rise to a point, "like the stem of a pear."[4]

Columbus had been prevented from developing his theories further at that point by illness and by the immediate urgency of dealing with the open rebellion when he arrived at Santo Domingo. In December 1499, however, he once again found himself stranded aboard a small caravel when, touring Hispaniola during a lull in the rebellion, he was attacked by a band of Tainos and forced to put out to sea without supplies or an adequate crew. On the day after Christmas, weltering in the ocean and staring into an abysm of despair, Columbus experienced the first of a series of visions during which God chastised him for his doubt and told him He would stand by him. On his return to Santo Domingo in February—after forty-odd days afloat—Columbus wrote again to the court, recounting this vision and urging Ferdinand and Isabella to take the discovery of the Indies as a divine signal that they should embark on a last, fatal push to bring about the triumph of the Christian Church, one that must begin with the conquest of Jerusalem.[5]

In a sense Columbus was harping on an old theme: he had long been waging a campaign for the Monarchs to think of his western discoveries as part of a wider crusade that would be followed by the subjection of the Indies and the Holy Land. As part of this he stood in fierce opposition to the mainstream reading of the Treaty of Tordesillas, the 1494 power-sharing agreement with Portugal, which had been brokered by the pope and which divided the world into Portuguese and Spanish zones of activity in an attempt to keep the two nations from going to war over their new discoveries. The treaty granted Spain the right to occupy everything to the west of the Tordesillas meridian—an imaginary line 370 leagues west of the Cape Verde Islands—and Portugal everything to the east of this line. This secured for Portugal its possessions in the Atlantic (the Azores and Madeira), as well as exclusive rights to deal with the west-African territories (Ife, Benin, and the Kingdom of Kongo), and gave Spain a free hand in the New World. In one of the greatest oversights in history, however, the treaty failed, in setting down where the zones of influence began, to make any mention of where they would end. The Portuguese could be forgiven for thinking their zone took in one hemisphere of the globe, ending halfway around the world going east—though it wasn't remotely clear at the time where exactly "halfway" would be. Columbus, on the other hand, was almost alone in maintaining that the Portuguese zone only covered the area from the Tordesillas Line as far east as they had sailed by the treaty date of 1494—the Cape of Good Hope—making the Spanish portion stretch west right from the mid-Atlantic all the way around the world and back to the Cape. Crucially for Columbus, this kept the symbolic centers of late-medieval thought—Cathay, India, Persia, Ethiopia, and (most important) Jerusalem—firmly within the part projected for Spanish expansion.[6]

Columbus's letter of February 1500, however, began to make a theological argument that the discovery of the New World was in itself evidence of God's apportioning Jerusalem to Spain, and a prompt to begin preparations to take back the Holy Land. On his return to Spain in November of the same year, and now free of the judgments of

Bobadilla against him, Columbus had time to pursue these thoughts and was now in a position to begin to put them into some kind of systematic order, a task that may have first brought Hernando's unusual and extraordinary talents into the open. Columbus also recruited the help of a Carthusian monk, Gaspar Gorricio, and periodically stayed at Gorricio's charterhouse, the Cartuja de las Cuevas, across the Guadalquivir from the part of Seville where Hernando would eventually build his library. This place would become increasingly central to Columbus's world and to Hernando's, offering then as now a sanctuary removed from the bustling town, with cool and solid brick buildings lit by the sun from the cloister, expanding effortlessly through the spindly Mudéjar pillars of the colonnade. Here, beneath the refectory mural of St. Christopher carrying the infant Christ across the water, Columbus seemed to find a perfect setting for his increasingly monastic temperament, and it was here he would store his most precious papers when he went once more over the ocean.[7]

Though Columbus had always had a mind for a good quotation and was likely in contact with Gorricio and collecting authorities supporting his thinking in some fashion before his return from the Third Voyage, his activities now were on a wholly different scale. Among the passages copied into the eighty-four leaves of *The Book of Prophecies* as it survives today are excerpts from

> Angelus de Clavasio, Guillielmus Durandus, St. Augustine, Isidore of Seville, Nicholas of Lyra, Daniel, King Alphonso the Wise, Joachim of Fiore, the Psalms, Rabbi Samuel of Fez, Zephaniah, Jeremiah, Alfonso Fernández de Madrigal (El Tostado), Pierre d'Ailly, Albumazar, Ezekiel, Seneca, the Gospels, St. John Chrysostom, Joachim of Calabria, the Book of Kings

These passages from the Bible, the early Church Fathers, medieval mystics and scholastics, as well as more recent figures, are stitched together by a series of short original passages, including a letter from

Columbus to the *Reyes Católicos* (for whom it was evidently designed), a prayer by Gorricio, and verses in Castilian in the hand of Hernando.

Yet as a glance at the list above will quickly suggest, the passages from authorities are not arranged in order of importance, alphabetical order, date, geographical or religious origin, or any other obvious quality. The order also is not determined by how it was compiled, as it seems the book may have passed back and forth between Gorricio and Columbus, with Hernando making his additions in blank spaces left by the other two. After an introduction they are, however, arranged within three sections—*de Praeterito* (On the past), *de Praesenti et Futuro* (On the present and to come), and *de Futuro. In novissimis* (On the future and the end of time)—though even within this framework the thicket of quotations makes little sense. Properly understood, the passages form an argument, a revelation of the nature of things through an inspired act of ordering, as Hernando says in his first set of verses for the book:

> Haré semeiante a este mi siervo
> al sabio varón, sagaz e prudente,
> que funda e hordena por modo exelente

> I will make my servant like him,
> the knowledgeable man, wise and astute,
> who founds and orders in excellent fashion.

Creation, as Hernando's epigram suggests, requires not only strong foundations but the act of arrangement thereafter. The wise man, the Elect, is he who knows how to put things in their proper sequence.[8]

To make sense of *The Book of Prophecies* it is important to start with its first principles. To begin with, the book follows St. Augustine in asserting that God's preordained plan for mankind is not simply a *general* plan, determining the shape of the great events of Christian history from the Fall of Man to the Last Judgment, but instead often affects what happens on a more minute level, right down to the lives of individual people. Importantly, these people need not be great kings or learned sages, as God's power can by itself make great the lowly. As a lovely passage from Gorricio's prayer has it, the God of *The Book of Prophecies* is a

> God who instructs the heart of man without effort or words, and who makes wise the tongues of stammerers, and who is near us in times of need.

Augustine is again brought in to prove that those chosen for God's special favor are *more likely* to be lowly than powerful: they are distinguished "through unusual grace and intelligence rather than nobility of birth," making a strength of the ways in which Columbus and his son were looked down upon by their enemies at court. This special providence does not just take the form of inspiring eloquent speech but can also help the chosen individual in any field of knowledge— including (again following Augustine) a suggestion that God can even instruct His chosen messengers in such technical matters as astronomy. In a dig aimed at those who rejected Columbus's pre-1492 arguments about the extent of the globe's circumference, the book suggests the Admiral's success was in itself evidence that God was on his side, and those opposed to him were, like the Pharisees, willfully rejecting God's call in favor of clever arguments and intellectual pride:

> If indeed they knew so much that they could measure the world, why couldn't they find its Lord more easily?

This is not to say *The Book of Prophecies* portrays Columbus as a kind of holy fool who knows nothing and simply channels God's grace. The prefatory letter to the Monarchs goes to great lengths to point out the Admiral's nautical experience, a passion that trains the sailor to find out the secrets of the world, which Columbus has done through reading widely in cosmography, history, literature, and philosophy. Rather, the argument is that even with all this knowledge and experience man can do nothing without *lunbre*, "light," which Columbus receives in the form of flashes of inspiration. That he has been right about so many things, the argument goes, proves these flashes are not madness but come from God, and that the Admiral has been chosen for a special role in history.[9]

The second major principle of *The Book of Prophecies* was that the words of the Bible should not always be taken literally. This is not to say, as some modern apologists for the Scriptures might, that the Bible is a compendium of traditions and that we should focus (selectively) on its ethical teachings rather than getting stuck on its claims as a record of history. Indeed, it was central to Columbus's claims that many of the more fantastic stories of the Bible, from the Garden of Eden to the Flood, be records of literal truth. It was rather that the book used the common belief that some pronouncements in the Bible, especially the cryptic sayings of the prophets and the Books of Wisdom, could be seen as darkly worded prophecies—even if these predictions were often not revealed as such until after the events in question had come to pass. The example chosen by Columbus and his helpers to illustrate this comes from the Book of Daniel, where the prophet says

I shall be a father to him and he will be a son to me.

While in Old Testament history this was taken as referring to King Solomon, the book points out he is later revealed to be speaking more directly about Christ, "qui est filius Dei *per naturam*," in whom the prophecy is more perfectly fulfilled because he is God's *natural son*. Hernando, the *natural son* of the Admiral, must have thrilled at this choice of example, which served as a reminder that he was just as much his father's son as Jesus, born to Joseph's wife, Mary, was the son of God.[10]

The argument about how to interpret the Bible was central to *The Book of Prophecies* because the great majority of the Scriptures deal not generally with the fate of the world, nor with the role of Christians and Christianity in God's plan, but rather with the special relationship between God and His people of Israel—the Jews. The Christian take on this, once again founded on Augustine but developed into one of the centerpieces of medieval Christian thought, was that the Jews had because of their various crimes in history forfeited their place as God's Chosen People. As a result, when the prophecies of the Old Testament spoke of the future of "Israel," this was to be taken not as speaking of a *physical* Israel (i.e., the Jewish people), but of a *spiritual* Israel, which was none other than the Christian Church itself. Among other evidence for this the book produces a copy of a fourteenth-century letter, popular in Columbus's day (though almost certainly a forgery), from Rabbi Samuel of Fez in North Africa, demonstrating from the Old Testament that the favor of the Lord had passed from the Jews to the Christians, and pointing to the spread of Christianity as evidence of this. Here, then, you had it from the horse's mouth.[11]

The third and final pillar of the book's logic concerns the specific position of Columbus and his contemporaries within the chronological framework of Christian history. In other words, to know *where you figure* in God's plan for mankind, you need to know how long history itself will last and how much time has elapsed since Creation. This had been a central question in Christian thought since the time of the Apostles, when the initial belief that Christ's Second Coming would happen during their lifetime was disappointed and had to be successively replaced by theories positing a longer gap between First and Second Comings, albeit usually ones that kept the Second Coming fairly imminent. *The Book of Prophecies* uses Augustine's prediction that the world would last seven thousand years—one millennium for each day of Creation—along with the calculation of the medieval King Alfonso the Wise that the world was created 5,343 years before the birth of Christ, to predict, as Columbus was writing in 1501, that there were 155 years left until the End of History. This may seem like something of an anticlimax, given that Columbus and his contemporaries could live comfortably in the knowledge they would never see that day, but the number of things that had to happen before the End meant dramatic events would need to start unfolding much sooner.[12]

With these foundations laid down, *The Book of Prophecies* begins to assemble selections from biblical, classical, and medieval authorities to locate Columbus's New World discoveries within God's plan for the world. The argument was that, like Christ's incarnation, the voyages of discovery were predicted long before they happened, though often in ways that didn't make sense until after the fact. And, as with the Christian use of the Jewish Scriptures, these predictions didn't have to be made by Christian prophets, even though they concerned key events in Christian history. One of the most striking passages in *The Book of Prophecies*—and the one that inspired Columbus to be buried with chains—comes not from a religious text but from a piece of theater, the *Medea* by the Roman writer Seneca, in which a chorus toward the end of the play speaks the following lines:

> During the last years of the world,
> the time will come in which Oceanus
> will loosen the chains, and a huge landmass
> will appear; Tiphys will discover new worlds,
> and Thule will no longer be the most remote land.

The playwright Seneca was not a religious authority or even a Christian, but who could deny that these lines seemed to predict Columbus's discoveries, and isn't the ability to prophesy in itself a mark of God's favor?[13]

The discovery of the New World was not, however, simply an isolated event that had been predicted and had come to pass. It was rather the first step toward a central condition in God's plan for the End of Time, namely, the universal evangelization and conversion of the world. Many Christian thinkers believed this had already been fulfilled when, after the destruction of the Temple in Jerusalem by the Roman emperors Titus and Vespasian, the word of God was spread by apostles throughout the world. Others, however, including the medieval theologian El Tostado and biblical scholar Nicholas of Lyra, believed there would be a *second* spreading of the Gospel closer to the End of Time, and this view was obviously supported by the discovery of the New World, which showed without a doubt that the Christian message *hadn't* been spread to every corner of the globe.

Crucially for Columbus, the Bible could be read as predicting not just a second wave spreading the Gospel around the world, but one that took the precise form of his discoveries. For this he was able to take advantage of a quirk of translation that stretched back over a thousand years. A vast number of passages, largely in the Book of Isaiah but also elsewhere, speak poetically about the universal spread of God's name as reaching even אי, a Hebrew term with several meanings. While the general sense is "places where one can take shelter," and the metaphorical sense in Isaiah is likely closer to "coastlands" or "the farthest-outlying places," St. Jerome in translating the Bible into Latin had chosen to render אי as *insula*, "island." This meant the Bible as used by Columbus and his contemporaries was riddled with passages insisting that one sign of the universal conversion that would bring on the End Times was the spread of the word of God to certain unidentified *islands*—an event Columbus had unquestionably brought about. So important were these references to "islands" that Gorricio had set about compiling a concordance listing all relevant mentions of the word in the Bible.[14]

The circumstances of Columbus's life and discovery could be linked to prophecies in the Bible in much greater detail than this. *The Book of Prophecies* noted the verses from Isaiah to the effect that

> my just one is near; my savior has gone out. My arms will judge the peoples; the islands will await me and will welcome my force.

Of these verses fulfillment could be found, for those determined to do so, in the (supposed) welcome given by the Taino to the Christians and their message. Isaiah also said of this "just one" that he would be lowly like Columbus: "So will his appearance be inglorious among

men and his form among the sons of man." A passage from Zepha-
niah confirmed the people the Christians would meet in this Last
Evangelization would be innocent, just as Columbus felt many of the
New World tribes to be: "They will not do evil nor speak lies nor will
a deceitful tongue be found in their mouths, for they will be fed and
will lie nearby and will not have cause to fear."[15]

For Columbus and his faction, placing his discoveries within the
framework of the universal triumph of the Christian faith had the
advantage not only of suggesting the Admiral's actions had divine
blessing, but also of providing some reassurance about the smooth
passage of events to come. A passage from the book of Ezekiel, for
instance, suggested that the immense communication problems they
were experiencing in the New World, which greatly slowed the spread
of the Gospel while the explorers struggled both to teach European
languages and to understand local ones, would be temporary. Crucially for Columbus, given the doubts at court about whether these
new provinces would ever prove profitable, these passages also predicted the discovery of these islands would produce great wealth:

> For the islands await me, the ships of the sea first, so that I may bring
> your sons from afar, their silver and gold with them, in the name of
> the Lord, your God, the Holy One of Israel, because he has glori-
> fied you.

Columbus came increasingly to associate the places he had discovered
with the fabled biblical lands of Tarshish, Ophir, and Kittim, lands
that had sent legendary treasures to King Solomon. Like the gold-
flecked streams of Cibao province in Hispaniola, the richness of
Ophir was said to be so great that sailors needed only to gather the
soil, thrown up by the claws of the lions that dug holes on the shore,
and fire it in a furnace to produce vast quantities of gold. Similarly,
Tarshish (or Tarsus) was important in biblical geography as the homeland of one of the Magi, Caspar, traditionally reputed to have brought
gold to the infant Jesus.

Yet Columbus could not afford to rest on his laurels and wait for this apocalyptic history to take its course, as universal evangelization and conversion was only one of two triggers that would bring on the Second Coming. The other was the conquest of Jerusalem, the city whose symbolic force had set Columbus on the path of collecting the passages for *The Book of Prophecies*, and which he announces as the main thrust of his argument in the prefatory letter to Ferdinand and Isabella. While the defeat of the Moors in the *Reconquista* and the expulsion of the Jews shortly thereafter were already widely seen in Spain as part of God's plan, Columbus was able to cite specific prophecies, attributed to the medieval mystic Joachim of Calabria, to the effect that someone from Spain would recover the wealth of Zion. There were also passages Columbus saw as linking him personally to this destiny, such as the following from Psalm 115:

> You have separated my chains; I shall celebrate a sacrifice of praise to you, and I will invoke the name of the Lord. I will recite my solemn vows to God in the full sight of all his people in the halls of the house of the Lord, in the midst of you, Jerusalem.

This must have appealed strongly to Columbus's heady mix of vanity and paranoia, linking as it did the Chains of Ocean that he saw himself as having broken and the chains in which he had been brought back a prisoner from Santo Domingo in 1500.[16]

It is easy with hindsight to write off *The Book of Prophecies* as an expression of Columbus's narcissistic insanity. We have the advantage of knowing the world did not come to an end in 1656, and that though the discovery of the Americas was the beginning of an extraordinary expansion of the Christian faith, it was hardly either universal or particularly welcome to all subjected to it. Yet the fact that human culture even today regularly falls back upon apocalyptic predictions—in religious fundamentalism, ecological/medical/technological disaster narratives, and stories about clashes of culture—may make us want to pause before passing judgment, not least because many others (including learned clerics such as Gaspar Gorricio) found Columbus's vision of his place in history compelling. Though the dire state of the New World settlements may have meant Columbus had a practical need for just such a narrative, it nevertheless remained the case that the central texts of late-medieval culture provided ample and persuasive evidence that he was onto something. Columbus showed himself able, when medieval certainties about the world had been severely challenged and many might feel themselves adrift in a sea of facts bereft of order, to reassemble the pieces of his culture's belief into a narrative capable of accommodating the new discoveries. In a world exploding with a seeming chaos of new information, the man who provided a sense of order had a significant claim to power, much like the proverbial one-eyed king of the blind.

What, then, was the part of Hernando in all this? At one time many scholars believed that the lion's share of *The Book of Prophecies* was written in the hand of Columbus's younger son, though recently more levelheaded studies have pointed out the unlikelihood of the twelve-year-old Hernando—however astonishing his later career—being able to draw on such a broad range of reading. An examination of the manuscript also reveals that a majority of the passages are in a script that looks nothing like Hernando's increasingly distinctive handwriting; these are probably by a professional scribe employed by Columbus. Yet some sections are unquestionably written by Hernando, and about others we cannot be certain. The most likely sequence of events was that during the last months of 1500 and the first months of 1501, Columbus began to compile extracts he had already come across in his reading, certainly in the presence of Hernando (who was living with him at the time), if we can be sure of nothing more. We do know, from a letter of Columbus's included in the book, that in September 1501 he passed what he had done so far to Gaspar Gorricio, and it seems likely that while Gorricio compiled lists of relevant quotations, the manuscript was then handed to a professional scribe to do the actual work of writing out the texts in question. Gorricio returned it six months later, on 23 March 1502, saying not everything had been copied out but that the book as it was would serve its intended purpose. In its final pages the book is a series of cryptic lists, possibly referring to further passages that could be copied into the manuscript when time permitted.

At some point after this Hernando made his own entries in *The Book of Prophecies*. Like the Castilian verses quoted above, many of his entries are passages of Spanish verse that celebrate the "wide and easy path" that will be opened to the Man of Virtue, helping to underpin the idea that Columbus's successful voyages of exploration were the result of God's special providence. It is perhaps worth pointing out that certain passages, such as the verses from Seneca's *Medea*, would have been unlikely to feature either in the practical reading of Columbus or the theological reading of a monk such as Gorricio, but would certainly have formed part of the humanist curriculum taught by Peter Martyr to Hernando in the household of the Infante Juan. Several copies were later recorded in Hernando's library, which he may already have owned by this stage, including a lost manuscript translation of the plays into Spanish. It is not hard to imagine the young Hernando, daydreaming in the classroom, reading his heroic and absent father into his lessons wherever he could. Certainly the addition from *Medea* was made at a later stage, and in a hand that belongs to neither Columbus nor Gorricio but might belong to Hernando, though we cannot be certain of its authorship.[17]

We can also only guess at Hernando's private feelings about the wild-eyed claims of a father whom he idolized but must, on the brink of manhood, have recognized as increasingly eccentric and misunderstood by those in power. His surviving entries in the book are largely of a general, moralizing nature and steer clear of the occult identification of the Admiral and his acts with biblical events, characters, and prophecies. Yet the experience must have had a profound effect on Hernando, and it is tempting to read the course of his own later life as written also in *The Book of Prophecies*. One of his most extensive entries, and indeed the last in the manuscript as a whole, is another poem about the paths that open to the Virtuous Man; but it is also a code, an acrostic verse whose first words taken together form a sentence, *Memorare Novissima Tua et In Eternam Non Peccabis*— "Remember your death and you will never sin." The addition of an apocalyptic context to the life of a pubescent boy with a megalomanic father can hardly have failed to affect him irreversibly.[18]

As we shall see, in later life Hernando did much to reduce the role of millenarian theories in the public narrative of his father's life, turning Columbus from a provoker of the End Times to the first figure in a new world. But Hernando's attempt to distance himself and his father from these ideas may not tell the whole truth of his role in *The Book of Prophecies*. Large sections are missing from the book, one of which provided the comment "Whoever removed these pages acted badly, for this was the best prophecy in this book." This note was almost certainly written during Hernando's lifetime or shortly thereafter, suggesting perhaps that the pages were removed by Hernando himself or by those close to him. What is more, both of the larger sections missing from the manuscript, including the one lamented above, are flanked by passages in Hernando's handwriting, increasing the likelihood that they contained writings by him. The missing prophecies will likely never be recovered, but we will have cause to return to the question of their contents.[19]

Whatever part Hernando played in creating *The Book of Prophecies*, and however he felt about the father who held it up to himself as a mirror, it is clear Hernando was increasingly close to Columbus during this period. The most dramatic evidence of this came when it was decided that the thirteen-year-old Hernando would accompany his father on his impending Fourth Voyage to the New World. There is no sign Columbus ever considered taking his adult elder son and heir, Diego, with him. There were good practical reasons for this, both to leave someone to argue the Admiral's case at court and to preserve the dynasty in case of disaster. But Hernando would (both then and in later life) have good reason to feel he had a legacy of knowledge and experience from his father that was worth more than a mere monetary inheritance.

Gorricio returned the uncompleted *Book of Prophecies* less than two months before Hernando and his father set sail for the New World, likely prompted by Columbus's desire to take the manuscript with him on the voyage, a theory confirmed by the Admiral's quotation of several passages from the book in letters written during this voyage. A number of entries strongly suggest passages were continuing to be added to the manuscript even as Hernando and his father traveled around the New World. It is mesmerizing to think that not only were the revelations of *The Book of Prophecies* being honed even as father and son explored new reaches of the western Atlantic, but, even more astonishingly, that the book's predictions about Tarshish, Ophir, and Kittim and their place in providential history meant they were in effect carrying with them a guidebook to unknown lands. The prophetic manuscript functioned like a map in reverse, providing them with landmarks that needed to be arranged on the landscape they were about to witness.[20]

IV

Rites of Passage

The fleet that left from Cadiz on 9 May 1502 consisted of four ships, each of which would become a character in the months ahead. References to them can sometimes be hard to sort, given that those on the voyage called them by different names, some proper to the ships themselves, some related to their point of origin, and some related to their crew. These four square-rigged caravels were the *Capitana*, referred to as such because it was the flagship, which carried Columbus and Hernando—its proper name, if it ever had one, is lost to history; the *Vizcaína*, from Biscay; the *Santo* or *Gallega*, from Galicia; and the *Bermuda* or *Santiago de Palos*, from Andalusia. Only three of the four ships could carry a full complement of supplies, as the *Bermuda* (captained by Bartholomew Columbus) drew so low in the water that waves washed onto the deck under full sail. A shipping manifest survives, giving a list of what was stocked for the crew of 140-odd men:

> 2000 arrobas of wine (c. 5,000 gallons)
> 800 quintals of hardtack (ship's biscuit, c. 36 tons)
> 200 pork bellies
> 8 pipes of oil
> 8 tuns of vinegar
> 24 cows' worth salt beef
> 960 fillets of salted mullet

720 other salted fish

2,000 wheels of cheese

12 *cahizes* of chickpeas (c. 750 lbs.)

8 *cahizes* of beans (c. 500 lbs.)

mustard

rocket

garlic

onions

4 fishing nets, plus lines and hooks

20 quintals of tallow (c. 2,000 lbs.)

10 quintals of pitch (c. 1,000 lbs.)

10,000 nails

20,000 carded goods (blankets, caulking oakum,
    hemp)

To these, listed roughly in descending order of volume, can be added a few things we deduce from later references: maps, nautical instruments, paper for logs and letters, and *The Book of Prophecies*. These swiftly dwindling supplies would be the only familiar things to populate Hernando's world over the coming months and years, and they were slowly replaced with new and unheard-of things accumulated along the way. The superbly detailed account of this journey he later wrote was no longer simply reliant on the documents and reports he could gather: this was a record of personal experience, which, as the exquisite observations and interpretations show, laid new foundations of thought in the thirteen-year-old boy and would later shape the order he would bring to the world around him.[1]

If Hernando expected to leave the familiar behind after weighing anchor at Cadiz, he must have been disappointed. The fleet stopped first at Santa Catalina, then crossed in front of the Pillars of Hercules (also known as the Strait of Gibraltar) to North Africa, where they coasted along until they reached the town of Arcila, in modern Morocco. Hernando may have imagined himself on the verge of a chivalric encounter when approaching this place, as Columbus had intended to provide aid to the Portuguese besieged there, relieving them from the onslaught of the Barbary Moors. Sadly for Hernando, by the time they reached Arcila the siege had been lifted, and the whitewashed town rising up a hillside from behind its cove and sea-wall may have seemed little different to the many settlements the Muslims had built along the facing coast of Spain. Hernando did briefly disembark to visit the town's wounded captain, only to find himself surrounded by Portuguese relatives of Columbus's first wife, Filipa Moniz. From Arcila the fleet crossed to the Canary Islands, passing Lanzarote and Fuerteventura, then docking at Maspalomas, on Gran Canaria, for the customary final resupply of wood and water before pushing out into the open ocean. Finally, on the night of 24 May 1502, they set sail on the west-southwesterly course that by now Columbus had mastered.[2]

Experienced sailors of the fleet would have been pleased with the crossing, which at twenty-two days was the fastest westward passage Columbus had yet achieved. In just a few years the Admiral had, through his usual mixture of nautical skill and extraordinary luck, established sea routes between Europe and the Caribbean that were hard to better, and which would remain in use until the coming of steam. But the experience of three weeks without sight of land must have been astonishing for the novice Hernando. He would later write affectingly of the First Voyage's experience of the featureless water, and though he may have been drawing on his father's notes, the description must also have brought back his own first crossing of 1502:

> Because all the men on the fleet were new to this type of voyage and danger and saw themselves so far from any help, they did not hold back from murmuring; and seeing nothing but water and sky, they fixed on every sign that appeared to them, being men who were farther from land than any had been till that time.

The moment of panic when considering the distance from land, unrelieved by any sight to break the flatness of the ocean, and the descent into paranoia, suspicion, and conspiracy as the bored, scared, and enervated mind scrabbles for something to interpret: these reactions are unavoidable among those at sea and cannot have been entirely quelled by the route's being now well established and some of the crew experienced in Atlantic crossing. Columbus had *also* interpreted signs on his First Voyage—albeit in ways designed to confirm his pronouncements that they were nearing land—but Hernando would later recast his father as the exception to this rule, figuring his calm confidence in the threefold logic of his crossing (reason, authority, report) as what set him apart and allowed him to trust in his navigational measurements and projections rather than being pulled about by the promise of every flock of birds or knot of seaweed. Perhaps during his crossing Hernando first sensed the need for such a buttress against the paranoid imaginings of the mind at sea.[3]

The experienced sailors on Columbus's voyages had little reason to share his confidence in his navigational measurements: in the absence of reliable methods for measuring longitude, the Admiral was almost entirely dependent on dead reckoning, using a compass, measurements of time, and estimates of speed to chart the ship's course. Though in retrospect Columbus was impressively accurate, the problems with this method meant there was no way to be completely sure how far west they were at any time: variable wind strength and ocean currents made estimates of speed untrustworthy, and the hourglasses were not only often faulty but also relied on fallible human hands to turn them over at the right times. To make matters worse, even the compasses failed to work consistently during Atlantic crossings. Whereas Columbus and other European sailors would have been used to the compass needle pointing slightly to the east of the North Star, Polaris, the Admiral had noticed with alarm on the First Voyage that, after crossing a line approximately one hundred leagues west of the Azores, the needle suddenly jumped a whole point, now falling to the *west* of Polaris. This phenomenon, incomprehensible without understanding magnetic variation and the difference between magnetic north and true north, deeply challenged contemporary understandings of how the world worked. While some evidence points toward knowledge of this magnetic variation before Columbus, scholars generally agree he was the first to record the phenomenon directly and to posit a cause, namely that the compass needle pointed not to the North Pole but to some other invisible point close to it. This explanation, the first to propose the concept of a magnetic north, is not, however, found in Columbus's writings, but in Hernando's biography of his father. As we have seen, Columbus believed at least as late as the Third Voyage that the variation of the compasses was caused by the bulging of a pear-shaped earth, and his theories hardly became less eccentric from that point on. As shall become clear, there may be good reasons to think this theory was first arrived at by Hernando—not Columbus—and only attributed to his father, one of the many revisions to Columbus's ideas that later developments necessitated. Either way, the world as Hernando knew it tilted sideways as he crossed the Atlantic.[4]

Like the drawn-out process of leaving Europe, arriving on the western edge of the Atlantic may not have felt like the threshold crossing it was supposed to. Ocean faring was not an exact science, and once land was sighted, the pilots had the complex task of orienting themselves before they could proceed to a known port. When the fleet spotted land on 15 June, they eventually recognized the island as one Columbus had sighted on the Second Voyage in 1493 but had not stopped at or named. They took the opportunity to name it now—"La Matinino" or Martinica (modern-day Martinique)—and Hernando was witness to the strange transformation of the unknown to the familiar by the act of naming. From there they were able to follow the same dribble of islands that Columbus had on the Second Voyage, curving north and west like the side of a basin—Dominica, Guadeloupe, the Carib islands, Puerto Rico—up to Hispaniola.[5]

The tension must have been considerable when the Admiral's four ships anchored off Santo Domingo on 29 June. On the one hand, Columbus was for the first time showing the chief town in the New World he had discovered to one of his sons, a place moreover named after the young boy's grandfather. On the other hand, Hernando would probably have been aware the Monarchs, while encouraging Columbus to cross the ocean once more, had forbidden him to land on Hispaniola, fearing his presence there would reignite unrest among settlers for whom opposition to the Columbus brothers was still a rallying cry. Columbus had nevertheless decided the problems with the *Bermuda*, still not able to run under full sail without drawing dangerously low in the water, absolved him of this injunction and made it necessary for him to land at Santo Domingo to exchange the ship for a fitter one. While it is true that a fleet is held back by its weakest craft, and the *Bermuda* would certainly have struggled on the circumnavigation Columbus was planning if he found the passage to China, one suspects he could not resist the dramatic climax of seeking entry to Santo Domingo, either as triumphant founder or to be spurned by his own creation. In the end, the new governor, Nicolás de Ovando—whom Hernando would have known from his days at the court of the Infante Juan, where Ovando was one of the Ten Choice Companions—refused to oblige Columbus in any way and was even deaf to his pleas to be allowed into the harbor to shelter from the vast storm that was collecting over the Caribbean Sea. Even Job, Columbus would later write, would have pitied his state when the land for which he had sweated blood had closed its doors to him. Yet the local news was far more dire than even this: the Admiral would learn they had just missed another fleet of twenty-eight ships departing on the return crossing, including a ship that carried Francisco de Bobadilla (who had unseated Columbus as governor), the leader of the 1498 rebellion, Francisco Roldán, and a great many other settlers who had participated in the revolt against Columbus and his brothers. While the removal of Bobadilla by Ovando may have seemed a triumph, it may also have given way to a greater catastrophe by allowing Columbus's enemies to return in great numbers to the court and tell their side of the story in his absence, spurred on no doubt by the president of the Council of the Indies, Juan Rodríguez de Fonseca, who was an implacable foe to Columbus. Ovando further ignored Columbus's urgings to call this fleet back before the storm hit, though he might reasonably have suspected the motives behind the Admiral's advice. The *hurricane*—from the Taino word for "storm"—reached Hispaniola on Wednesday, 30 June.[6]

Hernando's description of that night records how, in the immense darkness, their fleet was forced to separate, with each ship taking the measures its captain thought best, and each convinced the others had gone down in the storm. While the *Capitana* lay in close to shore to shelter in the lee of the island, the *Bermuda* ran out into the open sea to ride out the storm there. The captain of the *Santo*, returning from begging the obdurate Ovando to change his mind, was forced to cut loose the ship's boat to prevent the swell from sending it like a battering ram into the hull. The crew of the *Capitana* gathered in the driving wind and rain to curse the Admiral, whom they blamed for their being turned away from Santo Domingo when even complete strangers would have been given merciful shelter. At this moment Hernando presumes to record, in a move unusual not only for his biography but for the very practice of life writing at the time, his father's unspoken experience of these events, saying that *in his insides* Columbus felt the misery of his crewmates and indeed felt it worse than them, as the ingratitude and insult were thrown at him in a place he had given to Spain as an addition to its honor and splendor, and moreover at such a fatal time. In the panic and confusion of the storm Hernando had begun, perhaps without thinking, to speak on his father's behalf.[7]

Columbus's fleet finally began to reassemble four days later, on Sunday, at the port of Azúa farther down the coast of Hispaniola, but a series of reports would transform relief into a rather different feeling. It suggested the nautical mastery of Columbus's crew that all four of his ships had survived the storm without significant damage, even the *Bermuda*, the crippled ship that Bartholomew Columbus had brought safely through the hurricane to the great admiration of the other sailors. This began to seem like something more than skill, however, when it was discovered that the fleet heading east had been almost entirely destroyed, with the loss of nearly all of the twenty-eight ships, including the flagship, carrying Bobadilla and Roldán and two hundred thousand gold ducats on its way to Spain. Columbus may have turned with satisfaction to a passage in *The Book of Prophecies*, which predicted that God would "force a commander to cease his insolent conduct" (Daniel 11). Columbus's luck was almost too perfect: rumors began to circulate that he had caused the storm by sorcery to wreak revenge on his enemies, and they seemed to receive confirmation when reports emerged that the only ship to reach Castile, and the least seaworthy craft at that, was the one carrying four thousand gold ducats belonging to Columbus. Even Hernando, who usually resisted unworldly explanations for worldly events, saw the hand of God in preventing his father's enemies from exchanging their false witness for a hero's welcome at court.[8]

The fleet spent two weeks after the hurricane anchored in the port of Azúa, days given over to repairing damage to the ships and restoring the morale of the men, allowing them time to rest and to fish. But Hernando's mind showed itself restless to interpret the new world in which he had found himself, and he records from this time two sights, one a source of pleasure and the other of astonishment. The first moment—of wonder—came when the *Vizcaína*'s boat began, unprompted, to jerk erratically across the water, moving first in one direction and then another as fast as a *saetta* (crossbow bolt). The ship's crew must have thought themselves for a moment still in the sorcery of the storm. When the craft finally fell still, the mystery was revealed: an animal, "big as half a bed," had become snagged on the bottom of the boat and had dragged it around the bay as long as it was able. Hernando calls this creature a *schiavina* because it looked like a cape, and indeed its modern name (manta ray) comes from its looking like a mantle being drawn through the water. Hernando's second observation was of another kind of "fish" not known in Europe, which the Taino called a *manatee*, the gentle sea cow that has now been

(*opposite*) A 1621 print showing Native Americans riding on a manatee, an animal that confounded Europeans and led Hernando to important early speculations.

driven by industry from the Bay of Azúa but can still be found in the coasts and estuaries of the island. A story recorded by Peter Martyr even tells of a manatee tamed by a Taino cacique, whom it would let ride on its back; but the manatee distrusted Christians, recognizing them by their clothes, having once been mistreated by them. This maritime creature, Hernando noted, in many ways did not fit the definition of a fish: it was the size and shape of a calf and grazed like one in the shallows; moreover, it tasted like a calf—even better, because fattier—and resembled a cow more than a fish when cut open. Hernando was here following the classification system of Aristotelian zoology, which grouped animals on the basis of what they ate and how they reproduced. These physiological, anatomical, and behavioral features lent weight, Hernando concluded, to those contemporary natural philosophers who believed that every land animal had its counterpart in the sea: the surface of the ocean, then, acted like an immense zoological mirror, with everything above water having its equivalent beneath.[9]

This theory was wrong, but the episodes of the manatee and the ray give a glimpse into the development of Hernando's mind. While Columbus identified manatees as the "sirens" of legend, noting with disappointment that they didn't resemble human women, his apprentice Hernando is far more inductive, alert to the significance of what he saw before him. The mystery of the moving boat was a cautionary tale against relying on surface appearances, as it required awareness of the hidden depths for its explanation, and the pleasure this provoked is that of having a veil of ignorance torn away. The lesson seems to have been taken to heart as he observed the manatee: Hernando has not attributed to it fishlike qualities simply because it lives in the water, but has followed up the initial impression (that it looks like a calf) by studying its internal qualities (anatomy, taste) and its behavior (grazing). While the grazing provided a false lead (there are plenty of grazing fish), the tissue and organ structure of the manatee allowed Hernando to reach the entirely correct conclusion that it was a mammal, even if there wasn't yet a word for that. His speculation on the presence of this cow in the sea was wrong—the mystery of cetaceans' and Sirenians' return to the water would wait another 450 years for a solution—but it was not unreasonable: the manatee was evidence of some strange symmetry between land and sea, and as symmetry is one of nature's most powerful organizing forces Hernando understandably thought this pattern might extend further. Hernando's father-and-son fishing trip was, then, reflexively absorbed into his obsession with order, in the manatee's suggestion that land and sea animals could be put in two parallel and symmetrical lists.[10]

The fleet departed from Port Azúa on 14 July, sheltering from another storm at Port Brazil farther west along the south coast of Hispaniola, before striking out for Jamaica, where they encountered a string of sandy islets. To these they gave the name Pozze—"puddles"— because though the islets had no freshwater springs the crew still managed to get water on them by digging in the sand. Heading farther west, they encountered another island (Guanaja), where the *Bermuda* captured a gigantic canoe, made of a single trunk but nonetheless eight feet wide and as long as a galley. It carried twenty-five men from the island, as well as women, children, and baggage, all sheltering under a palm-leaf awning; though they did not know it at the time, the people they had encountered were the tribe that came to be known as the Mayans. To Columbus's delight, the canoe contained a gazette of the products of the region, causing him to thank God that so much had been revealed to him at once. The canoe held

> cotton blankets
> sleeveless shirts
> loincloths
> shawls—all in different colors and designs
> long wooden swords with flint edges
> hatchets and

hawksbells—made of copper, with crucibles for
    melting
roots
grains
chica (maize wine)
mandorle (cocoa beans)

Again, in describing this encounter it seems Hernando cannot help attempting to impose some order on what he is seeing, something he achieves by sorting the sights into the common and the unique. So the palm-leaf awning of the canoe is very like the *felzi* or awning of a gondola in Venice, the shawls worn by the women are similar to the veils worn by Moorish women in Granada, and the maize wine is like the beer drunk in England. (Some of these "shawls" may have been made of bark cloth and inscribed with Mayan characters, a form of book, but too alien for Hernando to recognize as such.) On the other hand, for many things in the canoe he can find no equivalent, such as the *ponchos* and swords, and in these instances he simply resorts to description.[11]

But the most interesting discovery seems to fit neither category. While the *mandorle* or cocoa beans were not remarkable in themselves, Hernando notes his surprise that when one of the men from the canoe dropped a bean, he forgot his fear of the Europeans at once and (in a phrase recalling the legend of Perseus), scrabbled around the deck after it *as if he had lost an eye*. In an astonishing moment of insight, Hernando observes that the beans must serve as currency for these people: After all, what else is a currency if not an object to which we assign a value greater than its intrinsic worth, in order that it can serve as a medium of exchange? Though the great value placed upon these beans by the people of Guanaja helps Hernando to think in the abstract about monetary systems, he also sees in it a more general

(*opposite*) A page from the Mayan *Dresden Codex* showing an eclipse, the celestial event that would play a key role in Columbus's Fourth Voyage.

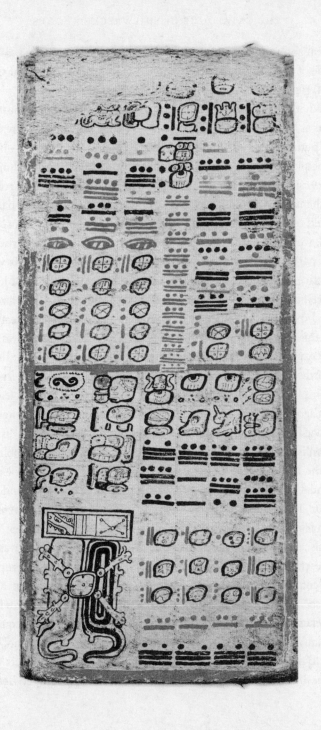

lesson about human nature, in which we forget the merely symbolic value of currency and come to value it more than our physical safety. This, Hernando remarks laconically, is called greed.[12]

What is in many ways *more* fascinating than Hernando's observations as he travels through these islands—manatees in Azúa, freshwater puddles in the Pozze, chocolate money in Guanaja—is the principle of organization that is hidden from even Hernando himself: every island, every landing point, is defined for him and his readers by the unique lesson it has to teach the explorers. The idea that one would record what is distinct about a place seems so obvious, so natural, we might easily miss that doing so belongs within a particular, and particularly European, tradition of thought. In part this was a practice made necessary by the lack of accurate measures of longitude: if a landmass could not be assigned specific spatial coordinates, it could only be identified by its unique human or landscape features. But this had unintended consequences: if each island must present a new experience to the observer, the map becomes little more than a record of the order in which the world is revealed to that observer.

This habit had taken up residence in the European mind at least as long ago as Homer's *Odyssey*, in which Odysseus's ten-year homeward voyage from Troy takes him to a succession of islands, and a distinct lesson is learned on each: the dangers of self-indulgence and oblivion on the Island of the Lotus Eaters, the dangers of greed on Circe's island, the threat posed by carnal enjoyment on Calypso's island, and so on. The tendency can also be seen in medieval maps, where the remote regions of the world were filled in with dog-headed men, cannibals, and wonders, never the same thing twice as the drive was less to describe a place and more to *define* it, to give it a unique property that could then be listed and ordered. The habit would remain, as we will see, deeply embedded in European thought, with narratives from Rabelais's *Quart livre* to Swift's *Gulliver's Travels* featuring a sequence of islands, each of which poses a distinct challenge. This was not limited to the stories Europe told about the world. Several projects were begun in the 1520s (one with links to Hernando) to compile *isolarii*, geographical encyclopedias of every island in the world—even down, as Hernando would later remark, to the Pozze sandbars off Jamaica— noting the distinct features of each. The desire to order the world by splitting it into distinct landmasses that could then be put in particular sequences was so strong that imaginary islands were often *created*, in explorers' narratives and in the most famous *Isolario* (by Bordone), to play host to particular experiences. The physical world, threatening to the European mind in its incomprehensible complexity, becomes more manageable when it is an archipelago of different experiences that can be put in order.[13]

The importance of this underlying order becomes apparent in the pains Hernando took to correct a later map that had reproduced the Guanaja islands *twice*—treating Columbus's visit of 1502 and a subsequent sighting of the islands as evidence of two separate landmasses. The problem this created was not simply that it deprived Columbus of the honor due him as the sole discoverer of the Guanajas (he was, after all, "discoverer" of hundreds of islands), nor even the usefulness of a map as a navigational chart, as until the development of accurate observations of longitude these maps were of limited use in that respect. Rather, the danger of duplicate islands was that they threw into doubt the entire system of organization, creating the prospect of a map filled with infinite shadow islands, each one produced by a different person's experience of them.[14]

Despite the great wealth contained in the canoe from Guanaja, Columbus was determined not to be distracted from continuing in his search for a passage through to the East. They parted from these traders, nevertheless "detaining" one of them, an old man named Yumbe, who acted as translator in the coming months and who seems to have become a firm favorite with the crew. Their ultimate destination was the region north of Paria, which Columbus had visited on the Third Voyage, where he felt sure the passage to the East would be found. Finding this region, however, was easier said than done, and after reaching the mainland they were forced simply to turn south and coast along "like a man groping in the dark," stopping only to note the local particularities: Caxinas Point, named after the paradise plum trees that grew plentifully there, where the locals wore armor of woven cotton capable of deflecting a sword stroke; the Costa de las Orejas, where the dark-skinned people ate raw fish and flesh, wore no clothes, painted themselves with "Moorish" designs as well as lions and turreted castles, and stretched holes in their earlobes (*orejas*) large enough to fit a hen's egg; Cape Gracias a Dios, which they were thankful to reach after progressing just seventy leagues in sixty days, where the land curved south and the winds turned favorable; the Rio de los Desastres, where the canes were as thick as a man's thigh and where a ship's boat was pulled under by a current.

At Cariay, "verdant as a field of basil," and its adjacent island of Quiribiri, the fleet first began to encounter the *guanín* pendants that Columbus had previously seen around Paria: golden disks polished to such a sheen the sailors took to referring to them as "mirrors." In an attempt to win the favor of this people, Columbus ordered presents be distributed among them, only to find them resistant to such obligation; the fleet found all of the gifts on the beach the next morning, tied into a bundle. The following day the natives of Cariay presented them with two young girls of eight and fourteen, naked but covered in *guanín* pendants. While Columbus's memory of the meeting with these girls was vile in the extreme—despite their youth, he would later write, the most practiced whores could not have been more experienced at enticement—this is likely to have been more a projection of the lustful desires of the adult sailors; Hernando, with the bashful nobility of adolescent sexuality, recalled only their braveness among strangers. Columbus clothed them and sent them back to their tribe. Bartholomew captured two natives to act as guides as they progressed down the coast, in response to which the natives sent two wild pigs (peccaries) as ransom, but Columbus insisted on paying for the pigs with gifts. To add to the considerable confusion, one of the peccaries got loose on deck and careened around, only to be attacked by a local catlike creature that one of the sailors had wounded and brought aboard. Hernando concluded from the encounter between the wild pig and the cat that the cats must be used as hunting animals much like greyhounds in Spain, though it becomes clear from his description the "cat" was actually a spider monkey.[15]

During the painfully slow passage along this coast Hernando was drawn even closer to his father by the fever that struck them both down. Columbus later wrote that the suffering of his son, only thirteen at the time, racked his soul, which sank to see Hernando so fatigued. This despair was transformed to boundless feelings of parental pride, however, as the Admiral watched the boy from his sickbed on deck: despite his illness the young Hernando worked so hard that it gave spirit to the other men, and tended to the comfort of his father all the while. It was as if, Columbus said of his son, he had been a sailor for eighty years. This was the kind of intuitive nautical genius Columbus only ever attributed to himself, a testimony of shared character that was cherished as the centerpiece of Hernando's self-image for all his life.[16]

From Cariay onward the avalanche of local customs and curiosities is simplified into records of the steadily increasing numbers of gold guanín mirrors the fleet was able to acquire for little in return, a sure sign for Columbus that they were nearing the gold-rich region for which he had been searching since 1492 and which might also be the beginnings of the realm of Cathay. At Cerabora among the narrow channels a gold mirror weighing ten ducats (paid—three hawksbells); at Alburema, a mirror weighing fourteen ducats and an eagle pendant of twenty-two, whose owners were taken captive after they refused to trade; at Guayga, the herb-spitting, horn-blowing inhabitants were eventually persuaded to trade for sixteen mirrors weighing in at a total of 150 ducats; and at Cateba they took twenty mirrors for a few hawksbells apiece. Also at Cateba they found the first evidence of masonry, in the form of a massive wall made of stone and lime mortar, and farther on they encountered the estuary of Veragua, where five villages of the prettiest houses imaginable were surrounded by cultivated fields.

Then, just when it seemed they must be nearing their Promised Land, the trail went cold. Beyond Veragua the weather turned against them, forcing them eventually to put into a little inlet they named Retrete, where the opening pleasantries with local residents soon turned to hostility. Columbus was able to keep them away from the ships with cannon blasts, bringing to pass the scene foretold in *The Book of Prophecies* in which

> the inhabitants of the islands are stupefied before you, and all their kings are shocked by the thunder (Ezekiel 28).

Despite the natives having an appearance attractive to Hernando, the shore was littered with giant lizardlike crocodiles that smelled "as though all the musk in the world had been gathered" and which would eat any man they found sleeping. With the signs clearly becoming less favorable Columbus reluctantly decided they should return to the region of Veragua, where the trail was last warm, but this volte-face came too late. The climate had turned against them, and they were stranded aboard their ships amid thunder and lightning so intense the sailors closed their eyes, feeling the ships sinking beneath them and the sky collapsing upon them. In the sleeplessness caused by constant rain, Hernando noted that they began to hear phantom distress signals from the other ships, and the endless parade of fears rose once again into their minds: fire from lightning, wind and waves that might capsize the ship, reefs and rocks along unfamiliar coastline. On 13 December the horror increased when a waterspout arose and passed between two of the ships, in a column as thick as a drum and churning like a whirlwind. During the storm they were separated from the *Vizcaína*, and though they managed to find her a few days later, they had in the meantime been surrounded by sharks, an encounter that allowed Hernando to describe the appearance of a bite from one of these creatures and to record that they found, in the sharks' bellies, a whole turtle and the head of another shark. This might seem impossible, Hernando observed, were it not for the fact that the shark's mouth reaches from the tip of its olive-shaped head almost down to its stomach. They caught and ate a number of the sharks, which provided a welcome relief from their usual worm-riddled porridge made of ship's biscuit. The humidity had made it so thick with insects, Hernando writes, that he saw many of the crew wait until after nightfall to eat so they didn't have to face the sight of their food; they had long since given up trying to pick the worms out, as this simply meant throwing away one's dinner.[17]

On the Feast of the Epiphany, 6 January, the fleet finally regained the position they had held two months earlier, among the estuary mouths in Veragua. The name of Belén (Bethlehem) was chosen for the river called Yebra in the local tongue, in honor of the day on which the Magi found Jesus. While the river mouth provided some protection from the storms that continued to trouble the open ocean, it was not without its own dangers. The ships were barely able to enter the shallow inlet, which was no more than four fathoms deep, and although safe from the waves once inside, they soon realized they faced a threat from another direction. Shortly after they arrived in Belén, a flash flood swept down from the mountains a little way inland, snapped loose one of the *Capitana*'s anchors, and sent the ship crashing into the *Gallega*, breaking its bonaventure mizzen (the rearmost mast) and repeatedly smashing them against each other as they swirled in the river.

Driven by the strange mixture of conviction and desperation that characterized many of his actions, Columbus decided a settlement should be founded in Belén and held by a small contingent while the remaining crew should return to Spain for supplies. The inhabitants of an adjacent river mouth had quickly produced gold to trade, claiming they had collected it in the nearby mountains, suffering hunger and missing their wives as they gathered it. Cordial relations had been established with the local chieftain, Quibian, who had also spoken of gold in the mountains, and this had been further confirmed by an expedition inland led by Bartholomew. On their scouting mission they had discovered gold among the roots of the trees, just as the *The Book of Prophecies* predicted would be found in the land of Ophir, where the lions dug it up with their claws and left it to be collected.

This, it seemed, must be the golden region for which Columbus had been searching. But as the houses for eighty men slowly rose in Belén, beyond a gulley "about a lombard's shot" from the river mouth, a strangeness infects the tone of Hernando's notes. The local fisher tribes, he writes, have an uncanny habit of standing with their backs to one another while speaking and are constantly chewing a leaf—*cocaína*—which makes their teeth putrid and rotten. Their main catch comes from the swarms of ocean fish that make their way up the river at various times of the year, but they also catch leaping sardines, sometimes by fixing a palm-leaf partition in the middle of a canoe to block the fish as they are forced to jump over the boat.

The plans for the settlement of Belén included, in addition to the houses, a store and arsenal and the ship *Gallega*, which was to be left for Bartholomew's use as commander of the fort. But the *Gallega* was no longer seaworthy and would not provide an escape route for those left behind in case of need. Besides the loss of its mast in the river flood, it was so riddled with shipworms it was like a delicate lattice or honeycomb. Indeed, it soon became clear that none of the ships could leave the inlet. The mouth had silted up further, leaving only two fathoms' clearance, and while in calm weather they might have considered dragging the unloaded ships over the sandbar, pulling the fragile hulls out in the rough seas was sure to shatter them. Their only hope, then, was to pray for rain to swell the river mouth to allow them passage.

The mood darkened even more when they discovered the apparently friendly Quibian had been maneuvering against them. He had lied, for a start, about the presence of gold in his own region and had instead sent Bartholomew to the gold fields in the lands of a neighboring enemy king, hoping this would draw the travelers to settle there. When they chose to found Belén in Quibian's territory anyway, the incensed king decided to attack and eradicate the Christians' foothold in his land. On learning this, Bartholomew led a band of armed men to Quibian's hut, taking him prisoner and entrusting him to one

Juan Sanchez to take back to the ships. But when Quibian complained about the chafing of his bonds Sanchez loosened them out of pity, allowing Quibian to leap from the boat when Sanchez was momentarily lost in thought. The fugitive swam ashore while the other captives made a cacophony that provided him with some cover. There was no chance of recapturing him in the dense undergrowth. Returning to the ship with the remaining hostages, Sanchez cut off his own beard in fulfillment of the oath he swore to secure his captive.[18]

When the rains did come, Columbus decided to leave immediately for Spain to resupply, unloading the three seaworthy ships and crossing the sandbar using the ship's boats. Before setting sail the skipper of the *Capitana*, Diego Tristan, returned ashore in the sole remaining ship's boat for final supplies and water. The boat did not return, and the crew faced the unpalatable choice of waiting indefinitely for news or turning their backs on Belén. During the days that followed, as Columbus and Hernando anchored in high winds off a dangerous coast with a skeleton crew and no ship's boat, they had little way of knowing what was happening onshore. When Spanish corpses began washing out to sea covered in wounds and perched on by carrion crows, it seemed their darkest fears had been realized. To make matters worse, half the Spaniards' remaining hostages escaped in a daring bid during the night, and those who didn't make it hung themselves belowdecks. Beyond the macabre nature of the scene, this also meant Columbus no longer held anything that might make Quibian deal for a truce.

At this moment Columbus was struck with one of his periodic bouts of blindness, and a high fever. He later remembered himself as being alone aboard the *Capitana*, and he may well have felt alone, though it seems certain Hernando, who is silent about his own role in most things but bears witness to it all, was there with him. At the height of his fever Columbus climbed into the crow's nest, wailing in fear and anguish and calling for help from Spain, though no one from the four winds (Columbus lamented) whispered a response. Having exhausted himself, he collapsed. During this fevered sleep he experienced a vision and later recorded the piteous words spoken to him:

> O foolish man, so slow to trust in your own and the only God! Have I done more for anyone, even my servants Moses and David? I watched you from birth, and when the time was right, I made your name resound marvelously across the earth. I gave you the Indies, a rich portion of the earth, for your own; you parted them as you saw fit, as I gave you power to do. To the sides of the Ocean Sea, fixed with strong chains, I gave you the key. I exalted your name in many lands and brought you honor among Christian people. What greater honor did I do to Israel, when I led them out of Egypt? Or David, whom from a shepherd I raised to be King of the Jews? Return to Him and confess your error; that His pity is boundless. Nor have I held back great things from you in your old age: great inheritance is in your power. Abraham had lived a hundred years when he became a father to Isaac, and nor was Sarah young in age. Yet you cry out for aid into the unknown. Tell me: Who has inflicted woes on you time and time again—God, or the world? The wealth and power God bestows cannot be taken by any, nor shall anyone say he has not been rewarded for his service: even if it appears another way, know that I am letting you fall to bring greater glory in victory. The time is full of ripeness: all that I have promised you will be yours, with more; I have given what was made for you, as I do to all.

The voice in Columbus's vision, which echoes in great perfection the God who speaks to Job out of the whirlwind, now blends the castigation unleashed upon Job with the promises given to Abraham as the maker of a great nation. In his delirium and in front of his young son, Columbus had formed a God for himself out of quotations from *The Book of Prophecies*. Almost more astonishing than the words of Columbus's vision was the fact that he wrote them down after the storm and sent them in a letter to Ferdinand and Isabella. With a breathtaking lack of caution, Columbus speaks of the New World here as God's gift to him personally, to do with what he pleases, and makes Spain the recipient of Columbus's favor directly and God's only indirectly. The storm had closed the gap for Columbus between his inner vision and the world he saw outside, and the predictions of *The Book of Prophecies* were now being confirmed by direct revelation, by a voice speaking to him from out of the maelstrom.[19]

After nine days reports from the land began finally to arrive. Diego Tristan in the *Bermuda*'s boat had reached shore to find Quibian already attacking Belén, having waited only for the moment of Columbus's departure to strike. The forest was thick just thirty yards from the edges of the settlement, allowing Quibian's spearmen to lunge forward unseen. Arriving at the river mouth, Tristan had turned away from the settlers who tried to clamber aboard, choosing instead to save the ship's boat and report back to Columbus if he could. As it turned out, he would not be able to do even this: he died shortly after from a spear driven through his eye socket. In Belén the fighting intensified, with the attackers pressing in close and making it impossible for the Christians to use muskets. When a report did finally reach the Admiral—after one Pedro de Ledesma swam ashore on a scouting mission—it was clear their only option was a full-scale retreat, abandoning Belén and the worm-eaten *Gallega*. The surviving settlers (including Bartholomew Columbus) were ferried aboard under artillery cover provided by the *Capitana*, and they weighed anchor, having profited nothing from Belén but blood, misery, and failure. The *Vizcaína* sank soon after, and now they were reduced from three honeycomb caravels to two, the *Bermuda* and the *Capitana*. To keep these afloat they worked three pumps, night and day, flushing out the water in the hull only just as fast as it came in.

The nearest help, in Hispaniola, was almost a thousand miles away.

V

A Knowledge of Night

As the *Capitana* and the *Bermuda* sailed away from Belén, Hernando saw his father's fortunes at their lowest ebb. Although Columbus would later insist the lands he had visited here were among those eastern kingdoms described in his treasured books, by Marco Polo and by Eneas Silvius Piccolomini in his *Historia rerum*, he admitted they had not found the horses described by Piccolomini, with breastplates and mouthpieces of gold. The report Columbus was to write on this expedition was raw with the knowledge that he had asked for trust too many times: he protested that he would not boast of the riches of Veragua because of his former humiliation, though he could not resist adding as an aside that they saw more signs of gold in two days there than in four years on Hispaniola. This must surely, he reasoned, be the region of *Aurea Chersonesus* (Pliny's name for a "Golden Land" in southeast Asia) that had brought so much wealth to Solomon, and the only reason Columbus had not found the fountainhead of wealth was because he had been confined to the coasts, which were populated only by modest fishermen. There is a sharp historical irony in the fact that as Columbus floundered about to find a positive spin for this disastrous expedition, he was, in some ways, actually right. As Hernando later pointed out, the region of Veragua was indeed the best crossing point for the Pacific and the regions of the East: in Columbus's determination that the "crossing" mentioned by many inhabitants of the region should be a strait through which

100

ships could sail, he had failed to understand that this crossing could instead be a narrow isthmus. The area around Retrete where the trail had gone cold would, four hundred years later, provide the eastern entrance for the Panama Canal.[1]

The damage to Columbus's reputation as a nautical-historical visionary soon began to threaten not just his legacy but also the physical safety of his crews. The sailors on board the swiftly disintegrating ships had a limited number of moves left to them, and the pilots agreed unanimously that they should strike out north for Hispaniola. Columbus, however, was convinced they needed to go farther east before turning north, as once they struck out from land the currents would make it impossible to correct course. They turned north on 1 May 1503, against Columbus's better judgment, and though they sailed as close to the easterly wind as they could, his fears proved true: after passing a series of low islands covered with turtles that they called Las Tortugas (the Cayman Islands), they found their bearings among the labyrinthine islets south of Cuba that Columbus had named the Jardines de la Reina. Hernando would have read from his father the sure knowledge that the game was up: the easterly winds and westerly currents would prevent them from ever making Hispaniola, even if they had not been reliant on ships now more hole than hull. When a night storm drove the *Bermuda* into the *Capitana*, breaking her stern and the other ship's stem, their decision was all but made, and their stomachs sank when at daybreak they discovered a single cable was all that was holding the *Capitana* to its sheet anchor and away from the *Bermuda* and the rocks. Columbus began looking for a place to ground the boats, heading south across the narrow strait to northern Jamaica, where after rejecting the waterless and uninhabited Puerto Bueno, they settled as unchoosing beggars on the harbor of Santa Gloria.

The ships, run aground side by side, were little better than platforms on the open water, with not much room to pace before turning, submerged up to their decks at high tide and propped up at the flanks to keep them from keeling over when the tide went out. These shipwreck fortresses, with their cannons and the clear water between them and unfamiliar country, were still preferable to attempting to survive on land, with depleted supplies and no allies among the local tribes. The bay in which they were planted is sheltered by a reef from the open sea, entered on the western side into waters shallow enough that the white sand makes roads of aquamarine between banks covered by weed. The bay is cut in half by a sandy promontory that fans out into it, now covered by thick mangrove and the occasional shack where fishermen barbecue their catch at midday; a few steps from the beach the land drops off into a deeper lagoon, now a milkier blue. The *Capitana* and the *Bermuda* seem to have settled on the western side of this spit. After a shallow coastal plain, the land in front of where they were rises steeply, into hills serrated like those Hernando knew in Spain but forested with the tangled green that is everywhere in Jamaica. The effect is like an amphitheater, with the grounded ships on the flat stage of the water, looked down upon by the curve of hills to the south, where an unknown number of unseen eyes could watch their every move. Hernando and his father were to live together on this stage, in a cabin built on the poop deck of the *Capitana*—an area of roughly nine square meters—for a year, a month, and four days.[2]

Hernando later wrote how, in response to their desperate situation, Columbus had only a series of lesser evils from which to choose. The Admiral was anxious to prohibit the crew from creating enemies on shore and issued strict prohibitions against pillaging or raping the locals; and with their supplies dangerously low, he took to distributing by lottery what they gained from local trade every day, so those without enough to eat could at least feed themselves on the hope that the next day might be theirs. But these measures would barely sustain them, and their persistence had to depend on a realistic hope of rescue. It was agreed not simply to wait for a passing ship: Jamaica had as yet no European inhabitants, and vessels had no particular reason to pass that way. They also agreed there was no way to build a craft capable of the crossing from the materials they had. They decided then to send twelve Christians in two canoes from the most easterly point of Jamaica across to Hispaniola, with each canoe rowed by ten Jamaican Tainos. This in itself was a desperate measure, as the canoes were not built for the open sea, their sides barely a palm's breadth above water when freighted down. Columbus hoped, nevertheless, that on reaching Hispaniola one of the canoes, "captained" by Bartholomeo Fieschi, would return to Jamaica to reassure those left there of the successful crossing, while the other, under Diego Méndez (who had been with Columbus since the First Voyage), would proceed to Santo Domingo to sound the alarm and prepare a rescue mission. They also carried with them a letter to the Monarchs reporting on what they had found so far, as well as one to Gaspar Gorricio. Bartholomew accompanied the canoes to the launching point at the eastern tip of Jamaica and watched them until they disappeared. Hispaniola was thirty leagues away (more than a hundred miles), with a single waterless rock to break the crossing eight leagues from the end.[3]

And then they waited. Hernando's writings about the minutes, hours, days, and weeks of these first months are fairly sparse; while we might have expected him to have passed the time with conversations through which he would come to know his father better, his testimony records only the peculiar quality of the silence. Years later, lamenting that he had no fuller information on the mysterious earlier parts of his father's life, Hernando reflected that Columbus died before Hernando had the courage to overcome his filial piety and ask his father about these things; reflecting further, he admits he had never even thought to ask these questions in his youth. This has a ring of truth: sharing memories is for those who have the necessary leisure for musing over the past. Those under a suspended death sentence, like the men on board the *Capitana* and the *Bermuda* were, must instead have spent their time in the intense and enervating attunement to each expanding plank, each eroding wave, each hardening and brittle cord. One of Hernando's most vivid memories of this period was of the stormhead that every afternoon would build up over the eastern side of Cuba, threatening with its thunder and lightning an imminent deluge, just like Boina (the dark-serpent rain god of the Taino), only to dissipate as the moon rose. The many pulses must have been nearly unbearable in the silence.[4]

Faced with this yawning lacuna in the life of the explorer, many of those who later wrote epic accounts of Columbus's life invented episodes to fill the void. In one of these, the *Columbus* by the eighteenth-century Jesuit poet Ubertino Carrara, Hernando is swept overboard during a mutiny and trapped in a tree at the bottom of the ocean, where a water nymph, Nerine, saves him. Carrara's dense, baroque neo-Latin verse then tells of how the boy is led by the nymph through the Palace of Aletia, where all the types of truth are reflected in a thousand crystals and mirrors, and where he is taught the principles of Natural Philosophy relating to

> the origins of rivers
> the different states of water
> the nature of wind and fire
> the nature of volcanoes
> the forming of minerals and gems
> etc., etc.

When returning him to shore, the submarine goddesses are on the point of presenting Hernando with a telescope when they are told the invention is reserved for Galileo Galilei. Carrara's underwater allegory rather pleasingly constructs a heroic beginning for Hernando's life of dividing and collecting the many kinds of truth like a refracting crystal, even if there is no basis for any of it in fact. Hernando himself would later experience the great temptation to construct backstories worthy of the monumental figures they describe.[5]

The only true part of Carrara's story is the mutiny. As was perhaps inevitable, after the party dispatched to Hispaniola had not been heard from in four, five, six months, rumors began to swirl. Hernando recalled mutterings among the men that Columbus didn't even want to return to Spain, where he was in disgrace, or to Hispaniola, from which he had been banished, and that he had sent Méndez and Fieschi not to secure their rescue but rather to restore his damaged reputation with the Monarchs. Alternatively, some argued the canoes had sunk on the way to Hispaniola and the bed-bound, gout-ridden Columbus was no longer in a position to lead them in a second bid to cross the strait; instead, they imagined themselves winning the favor of the Admiral's enemies at court if they overthrew him presently. As was perhaps also inevitable, opposition to Columbus coalesced around the head man of the *Bermuda*, Francisco Porras, whose brother Diego was the comptroller of the fleet, assigned by Ferdinand and Isabella to ensure they received their share of the valuable things found on the expedition. Porras brought matters to a head on 2 January 1504, when he presented himself in the Admiral's cabin on the *Capitana* as leader of forty-eight mutineers. Hernando quotes Porras's words in his account of the scene, something he reserves only for the most painful moments of his past:

Sir, what does it mean that you do not wish to return to Castile, but would rather stay here after everything has been lost?

To this the Admiral could only reply that he did not know a way of returning to Castile other than the one they had already tried, and that if Porras disagreed, he should call a meeting of the senior officers to discuss how to proceed. Porras refused to be put off, however, and instead signaled to his followers to begin the mutiny. Brandishing their arms against a nonexistent opposition, they hastened to secure the castles and the roundtops on the mainmasts. In response, Columbus left his bed with some difficulty and hobbled around the deck, attempting to reassert control over the men, who paid him no attention. He was eventually coaxed back to bed by his few remaining friends, who pleaded with the mutineers to take what they wished but to leave the old Admiral unharmed. Finally the mutineers departed in canoes they had taken from the Taino, heading east in a triumphal mood to attempt another crossing from the eastern cape of Jamaica to

Hispaniola. Most of the crew who had until that point remained loyal now joined the mutineers, for fear of being left behind by the healthiest part of the company. Hernando later grimly mused that had it not been for infirmity, he doubted whether twenty men would have stayed behind on the *Capitana*.[6]

Once the vitalizing action was past, Hernando had time to observe his father's response to this desperate situation. Trade with the local tribes had already dwindled as the region became saturated with the goods they had to offer; there were only so many hawksbells, copper points, and glass beads that any curious Taino could want. But worse than this indifference was the growing suspicion of the Admiral's weakness, which received confirmation when the greater part of his men abandoned him, proclaiming their disdain along the way to any Jamaican who would listen. The few inhabitants of the *Capitana* considered going ashore to take food by force, but how long could they hope to hold out against the gathering opposition?

In this condition the Admiral turned again to his old sorcery, this time in the form of a pamphlet in his cabin that had magical properties. Summoning the principal men of the island to a feast, he declared to them that his God was a wrathful god who rewarded the good and punished the bad, and who would visit pestilence and famine upon them in revenge for their failure to trade fairly with the Christians. In token of this, Columbus prophesied, the moon would that very evening be consumed by wrath. Hernando remembered the Taino leaders scoffing at this as they retired, but even Columbus and his crew must have tensed with the fear that the almanac might have been wrong in its prediction of a lunar eclipse for that evening. The volume in question was almost certainly the *Ephemerides*, or *Perpetual Almanac*, of "Abraham Zacuto" (Abraham bar Samuel bar Abraham Zacut), a great Jewish synthesizer of Hebrew, Arabic, and Latin astronomical traditions. Zacuto had been Spanish until the expulsion of the Jews in 1492, when he was among those whose exodus had crossed paths with Columbus in Lisbon at the end of the First Voyage. During a brief residence in the safe haven of Portugal, Zacuto had published his great work of astronomy, before being moved on to North Africa and eventually Jerusalem. Zacuto's *Almanac*—which survives as item 3139 of Hernando's library—provided 11,325 consecutive daily positions of the moon and led Columbus to believe there would be a lunar eclipse on 29 February of that year, 1504, that would last for a total of three hours and thirty-two minutes. The crew may also have worried they no longer really knew what the date was, almost two years after leaving Spain and having weathered all manner of catastrophes, and the formula Hernando wrote into the volume of Zacuto, for calculating which weekday fell at the beginning of each month, may have been a way of double-checking this was indeed the Thursday on which Zacuto predicted the eclipse would fall. Their nerves could hardly have been settled by the uncanny feeling always produced by 29 February, a leap day that does not seem to fit properly into time. But there was a bigger problem even than this. Zacuto's tables were designed to predict the time of eclipses at Salamanca, and while it is now an easy matter to convert these for different time zones, that calculation requires a knowledge of the longitudinal position of the observer—something neither Columbus nor anyone of his day had. Columbus's performance, then, was a nerve-racking gamble: if they were farther west than he thought, the eclipse scheduled to reach its apex at midnight in Spain might not be visible from Jamaica, ruining the intended dramatic effect.[7]

One wonders if Columbus showed any signs of self-doubt in the moments before the moon rose that evening, perfectly succumbing to the earth's penumbra just as dusk fell and engulfing the island in darkness. Hernando recalls the great howl that went up over the islands, and the gathering of Tainos begging the Admiral to intercede with his God on their behalf. Columbus agreed to speak to God for them, and let the charade continue until the midpoint of the eclipse, emerging then to announce that he had entered a covenant on their behalf whereby God would protect them if they supplied the Christians with victuals as needed. If Columbus's ruse was a parody of his usual claims to divine inspiration, turning his nautical know-how into a kind of parlor trick, it was nevertheless put to great use in geographical terms: whereas predicting the exact time of the eclipse was impossible without a measure of longitude, the reverse calculation was quite easy and would allow Columbus to use the time difference between the end of the eclipse in Spain and in Jamaica to demonstrate the precise longitude of his present location. On a page of *The Book of Prophecies*, the following entry nestles his cartographic science among the pages of apocalyptic prophecy:

> Thursday, February 29, 1504, being in the Indies on the Island of Janahica, in the port called Santa Gloria, which is almost in the center of the island on the north part, there was an eclipse of the moon. Because it began before the sun set, I was only able to note the time when the moon had returned to full brightness. This was clearly noted: two hours and a half after nightfall, or exactly five hourglasses.
>
> The difference from the island of Janahica in the Indies to the island of Cadiz in Spain is seven hours and fifteen minutes, so that the sun sets in Cadiz seven hours and fifteen minutes before it does in Janahica. See the *Almanac*.

Using his observations of the eclipse in conjunction with Zacuto's calculation in the *Almanac*, then, had allowed Columbus to make the most accurate measurement of the longitude of the Caribbean to date, and by extension to establish more certainly the breadth of the Atlantic. Perhaps he comforted himself for his cheap conjuring by remembering the beautiful words of Psalm 18 recorded in *The Book of Prophecies*:

> The heavens tell the glory of God, and the firmament proclaims the works of his hand. Day speaks the word to day, and night reveals knowledge to night.

Columbus's night-knowledge had, at least for the time being, saved him and his son from the righteous anger of the disillusioned Taino.[8]

It is not clear at what point Hernando and the others on the *Capitana* became aware that Porras and his fellow mutineers had failed in their attempt to cross to Hispaniola after their departure in January 1504. As it happened, they had managed to get no more than four leagues from Jamaica before turning back, and Hernando suggests that when the seas became rough, they threw their Taino oarsmen overboard to lighten the load. They made two more failed attempts before heading back toward the shipwreck-fortresses in Santa Gloria Bay, where they reappeared in April. It seems there must have been contact between the mutineers and those still with Columbus during this time, as Hernando accused Porras of spreading rumors that an upended canoe was seen floating along the coast, leaving the paranoid survivors to assume the alarm had never been raised in Hispaniola. Whatever the reason, mutiny began to brew again even among the handful of crewmen who had remained on the *Capitana*.

Then, just when Hernando must have been braced for the final coup de grâce that would put the wounded god he called a father out of his suffering, a caravel appeared on the horizon. As the ship came closer and so evaporated the inevitable fear of the marooned, that the passing ship will fail to see them, those around Columbus must have marveled once more at the strange trick of destiny that always seemed to pull the Admiral back from the brink. But Columbus's luck was never simple. When the ship stood by the *Capitana*, it emerged, like some grotesque joke, that it had not come on them by chance, yet also had no intention of taking them back to Hispaniola. Instead the captain brought Governor Ovando's apologies that he did not, at that time, have any ships available suited to the task of rescuing them. The visiting ship presented Columbus with a side of salted pork and a single barrel of wine and left before anyone on the *Capitana* could write any message to send on.

The residents of the *Capitana* may have felt some comfort in the knowledge that their cry for help carried by Diego Méndez had indeed reached Hispaniola, and that they were not lost without a trace. But the letter the ship had brought back from Méndez gave little comfort. When the Jamaican canoes reached Hispaniola—their crews nearly dying of thirst and panic, being saved from both only by a rising moon that picked out the stopping point between Jamaica and Hispaniola in silhouette—Méndez had made his way overland with a raging quartan fever to find Ovando in the western province of Yaragua. None of the Tainos from Jamaica were well enough to bring back news of the successful crossing, and even the seeming miracle of their survival turned dark when Ovando, feigning pleasure at the news of the Admiral's safety, nevertheless showed no urgency in responding to his call for help.

Whatever stay of execution had been granted to the residents of the *Capitana* by the arrival of the caravel was short-lived. While the on-board mutiny seemed to dissipate for the time being, Columbus's attempt to outmaneuver Porras by sending him some of the salted pork, as a peace offering and a reminder that after the impending rescue they would be tried as mutineers, was unsuccessful. Porras cannily refused to allow Columbus or his emissaries to address the shore company directly and rejected a general pardon for the mutineers, countering with a suggestion they be given a sectioned-off half of a rescue ship if one came—something that would allow Porras to keep his followers close for the moment when they landed in Hispaniola and the accusations began. When Columbus's emissaries balked, Porras, in Hernando's later recollection, countered by asking his followers whether the caravel had really been there at all. Would a *real* ship have simply come and gone, leaving Christians stranded in a strange land, without even taking away the Admiral himself and his beloved son? Perhaps the ship was simply a phantasm, conjured by the sorcerer Columbus, who had been known to do such things. It was clear neither side could afford to allow the other to reach Hispaniola and control the narrative of what had happened during their lost

110

year. With the endgame clearly at hand, both sides prepared for battle.[9]

On 19 May 1504, almost every fit man aboard the *Capitana* and the *Bermuda* left Columbus to muster on a hill above the village of Maime, a quarter league from the ship-fortresses. The Admiral sent a final offer of terms, but the impossibility of peace was obvious to everyone, and Porras began his all-out assault by attacking the messengers. The fight was short-lived, but its place in Hernando's mind is suggested by the lengthy and gruesome details he provides of the battle wounds. Foremost in his memory were those of Pedro de Ledesma, who had displayed heroism by swimming ashore to the besieged settlement of Belén, but had later joined the mutineers. Ledesma had fallen down a cliff face during the battle and lain there abandoned for two days and a night. He was found by the Taino, who, thinking him dead, poked at his wounds with a stick: his brain was open to the air, his arm hung by a thread, and his leg was cut near through. When the broken body spoke, the Taino fled, only to return later and tend to his wounds as he lay writhing in a sweltering and mosquito-infested hut. This brutal scene was what Hernando remembered of the battle, and his traumatic memories of Ledesma's suffering cast a pall over what the Admiral saw as another divinely sanctioned victory. The debilitated loyalists had triumphed, capturing Porras and putting the rest of the mutineers to flight. When, a little over a month later, the rescue ships finally arrived in Santa Gloria Bay, Columbus was once more de facto commander of his men, and ready to give the official account of what had happened on his latest voyage of discovery.

At this moment Hernando brought his father's life abruptly to a close. Though Columbus would live another two years, they were not happy ones, and Hernando's mercy to his father is to pass over in silence most of the indignities he suffered in his last days. The loyal son could not resist recording his fury at Governor Ovando, who greeted their arrival in Hispaniola "with a scorpion's kiss," feigning delight at seeing Columbus safe and lodging him in his house on the new Calle de

Fortaleza, but at the same time freeing Porras. Hernando's first stay in the town his family founded was to be dogged by the disdain of the overweening governor. A ship was prepared to take the Admiral back to Spain, but a later document records how Ovando made them pay for every last thing themselves. Even the two ships supplied at their own expense proved faulty, with the mainmast of one splitting two leagues out of port, and of the other when they were on the high sea, hobbling Columbus's final return voyage in the same way as his First.

The bedridden Admiral directed repairs from where he lay, and with a jury-rigged lateenyard mast made from the dismantled forecastle they landed at Sanlúcar de Barrameda on 7 November 1504. The news reached them shortly thereafter that Isabella, Columbus's most steadfast supporter, had just died in the palace facing the Plaza Mayor of Medina del Campo. Gaspar Gorricio had been at her side in her final days and taken down her will from her dictation. Peter Martyr, who accompanied the corpse from Medina to the Alhambra (where it would await the completion of the Chapel Royal), noted the skies opened as they traveled and neither sun nor stars were seen during all of this time. Columbus set himself anew to his perennial task of asserting the rights that had been granted to him in January 1492 outside the walls of Granada, acting now through his sons as proxies at the court. But this was a forlorn hope: the Admiral was broken, bedridden, and the money he felt was owed to him from his New World simply failed to make its way to Spain. He was abandoned by everyone other than a few fellow explorers, such as Amerigo Vespucci, who took turns sitting with him. Hernando's friend Bartolomé de Las Casas was later to comment on Hernando's silence over the insult offered to his father when the New World he discovered was named, by quirk of cartography, after this Amerigo, but perhaps Vespucci's loyalty during this period of abandonment reconciled Hernando to the injustice.[10]

In this desperate solitude Columbus clearly felt the weight of his earthly affairs and wrote repeatedly to his elder son, Diego, imploring him to cherish and protect his younger brother in later life. Columbus also added a new codicil to his will. Though he had included a legacy for Hernando's mother in his will of 1502, written before departing on the Fourth Voyage, this had left her a mere ten thousand maravedís a year—one one-hundred-fiftieth of what he bequeathed to her son. Revisiting this decision in his final days, Columbus wrote instead that his heir should give Beatriz the means for an honest life,

> as a person to whom I owe so much. I am doing this as bidden by conscience, because it weighs so much on my soul. It is not permitted that I should record here the reasons for this.

As Columbus mentions shortly beforehand that Beatriz is mother to his son Hernando, it cannot be their illicit union that weighs on Columbus's mind; more likely, perhaps, it was not their shared sin but Columbus's sole guilt at having abandoned the young woman to a world unforgiving of female indiscretion, in large part because she was an inconvenience at his moment of glory. The whole truth is likely lost forever, but provides some depth to the emotional legacy of the relationship between Hernando's mother and father.[11]

Hernando dutifully stayed with the court and received instructions from his father, who tried to keep up with the swift progress of the royal households, but couldn't. The great explorer last coincided with the court when it arrived in March 1506 in Valladolid, but it moved on and he was too ill to follow. He died there on 20 May that year. The hollow created in Hernando's life by the death of his father would become apparent in the decades to come, as he slowly removed the Admiral's weakness and madness from the historical record, allowing his own life to become like a New Testament to Columbus's Old, changing its patterns and its meanings. But to salvage his father's reputation as a maker of epochs, Hernando would have to embark on an era-defining project of his own.

PART II

A

LANGUAGE

of

PICTURES

VI

Shoes & Ships & Sealing Wax

On 15 August 1509, five years after leaving the New World, Hernando found himself once again at Santo Domingo, celebrating his twenty-first birthday in a room of the Governor's Palace on Hispaniola's first street. The house on the Calle de Fortaleza, which runs from the fort overlooking the River Ozama to where the administrative buildings were being raised, was the same one Hernando and his father had recuperated in from their Jamaican ordeal. Though many of the earliest structures of Santo Domingo have now disappeared, replaced by imposing stone structures as Spain attempted to make its rule a solid reality, Hernando's room has been preserved like a fly in amber by his compulsion to list. Looking around his quarters shortly after his birthday, he drew up an inventory of everything he had brought with him for his life in the New World, descending from his most prized possessions to the inexpensive but still precious goods he needed to prosper in this environment. This glimpse into the things that lay around in Hernando's room has few parallels from so far in the past: most inventories of this period survive in the form of wills, which list only those treasures the deceased felt worth passing on, and understandably overlook the vast majority of objects that came to hand in this world. But Hernando's vision, in this as in all things, gloriously failed to exclude things most people thought unimportant, and in listing them he has left us a still life of the early colonial Caribbean replete with clues about that world and the life he planned to live there.[1]

At the bottom of the list, written in Hernando's neat and minuscule hand, are: molds for making gunshot, eight pairs of canvas shoes, some blades with handles and sheaths, a helmet with faceplate, white and dun thread, a padlock with two keys, a large number of nails, and some tools (a hammer, a chisel, wood-turning instruments, an adze, an auger, and four hatchets, two large and two small). Strange as this assortment of ironmongery seems among the possessions of a gentleman, Hernando would have learned the value of the metal during the years of his first voyage, when he saw his father save even nails from worm-eaten ships before abandoning them. Though the Spaniards visiting the New World were obsessed with finding pure, soft gold, it was really the worked iron they brought with them that made the difference between life and death in the Caribbean. The image we get, from this end of the list, of preparing for hardship, danger, and a life constructed from the ground up, gives place as we work our way up the list to more refined instruments. We see: four dozen quills, a ball of fish resin the size of a small apple, strings for a clavichord, a chunk of sulfur and colors for painting, and some bowstring. It is unclear whether the bowstring was intended for defense or to make some small effort in the field of hunting—an arena in which Hernando never succeeded in interesting himself, to the chagrin of some contemporaries—but the other materials make clear he intended to cultivate in the New World not merely plants and profits but also his own artistry. Further to this end he also had in his quarters two paintings by "Viñola"—which seem to be the first recorded European paintings to be taken to the New World, likely by a member of the northern-Italian Vignola dynasty of artists—and three sheets of his own painting, as well as two booklets of models for painting.[2]

Hernando also records six booklets containing forty-seven pages of music (not counting blank ones); though we cannot be sure, there is

(*opposite*) A musical teaching device from the *Principium et ars totius musicae*, a copy of which was inventory number 3097 in Hernando's print collection.

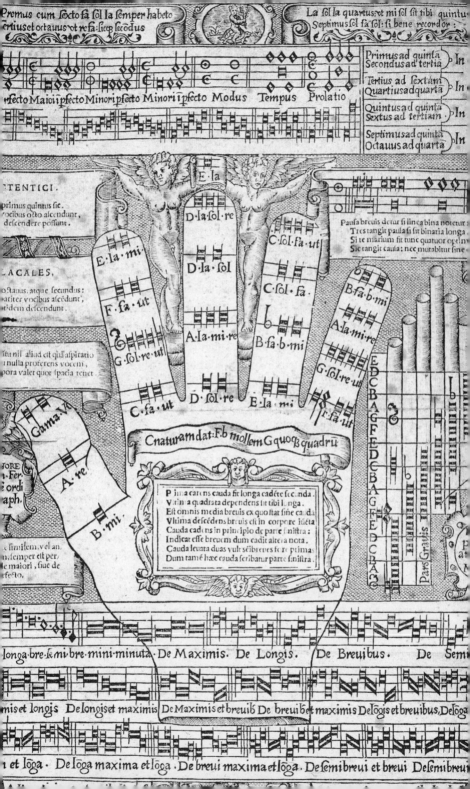

the mouthwatering possibility that this was an early version of the *Cancionero de la Colombina*, one of the two greatest songbooks of early modern Spain, which entered Hernando's collection at an unknown time. Next on the list is an array of papers, ranging from loose writings by the Jewish astrologer Abraham Zacuto (whose work had allowed Columbus to predict the eclipse in 1504), writings by the Spanish theologian Torquemada, as well as maps, writings on geometry, grammar, and heraldry, recipes for medical concoctions, and sheets upon sheets of verses, which may have been written by Hernando (who had already tried his hand at poetry for *The Book of Prophecies*) or copied from elsewhere. Pride of place at the top of the list, though, goes to Hernando's 238 books, contained (as was common for book storage in the period) in four chests with various identifying marks. Remembering perhaps the two years of his last voyage, during which he had little to read other than some astrological manuals and *The Book of Prophecies*, Hernando had come more prepared this time. These books undoubtedly constitute the first collection recognizable as a library in the Americas; they are the books Hernando believed indispensable to founding a civilization in a strange land.

No list survives of exactly which books Hernando took with him to Hispaniola—at 238 volumes the collection could still just about be kept in the head, and so perhaps he needed no catalogue. We can be fairly certain about a few of them, including *The Book of Prophecies*, as well as the cherished volumes his father bequeathed to him: the book of Marco Polo's travels sent to Columbus in 1497 by the Bristol merchant John Day, Pliny's encyclopedic *Natural History*, and two works of history and cosmography, the *Imago mundi* by the French geographer and theologian Pierre d'Ailly and the *Historia rerum* by Pope Pius II. These had been the core of Columbus's small collection of books, and on them he founded his ideas about sailing to the East Indies and about the shape of history. They remained Hernando's prize possessions, and over time his notes in their margins intertwined with his father's, but by now they were overwhelmed by his own collection, which despite the lack of a list we can reconstruct with a fair amount of confidence. Once again, we have his ever-increasing obsession with documenting the world around him to thank for this: while from the very beginning of his book buying Hernando had the habit of noting in each volume how much he paid for it and where he bought it, soon after the inventory of 1509 he also began noting the date on which he bought the books; it is reasonable to conclude, then, that most of those with a location of purchase but no date come from the period before he started recording dates. The hundred-odd surviving books in this category demonstrate the extraordinary variety of Hernando's interests, and how as well as being an ark of civilization in the New World the library was a field laboratory, a survival kit, and a scheme of immense ambition for expanding the intellect of its owner.[3]

Around a third of these books are spiritual aids—sermons, Bible commentaries, works of theology and religious meditation—which doesn't suggest any particular piety in a book collection of the period, but may add some slender evidence to later rumors that Hernando's mission in the New World was to further establish the Christian faith there. Almost as many volumes fall into the broad category of philosophy, with a heavy emphasis on the works of Aristotle and the medieval scholastics who drew on his thinking (Occam, Nicholas of Cusa, Giles of Rome). But there was plenty of the newly fashionable Platonic philosophy as well, including works by the Neoplatonists Marsilio Ficino and Pico della Mirandola as well as Cardinal Bessarion, the great scholar from Trebizond on the Black Sea, who had helped to ignite Renaissance humanism by bringing to Italy Greek learning that had been lost to Western Christendom for a millennium, perishing along with the fragile papyrus on which the Romans wrote but being preserved in the libraries to the east. Hernando seems to have hoped to spend his time among the Taino and the Carib peoples improving his knowledge of Greek, as in addition to two Latin dictionaries he brought with him Johannes Crastonus's monumental Greek dictionary, widely acknowledged as the most important tool for those who were serious about learning ancient Greek.[4]

As in philosophy, Hernando's tastes in literature were divided between the idols of the later Middle Ages, with large amounts of Ovid as well as some Macrobius and Boethius, and the authors beginning to be worshipped by more fashionable intellects back in Europe, with Cicero's orations and Horace's satires joined by the hilarious and irreverent comic dialogues of Lucian of Samosata, whose fame was growing even then as the pattern of style for the likes of Erasmus and Thomas More. But it seems certain many of the books in the four chests were intended for more immediate practical purposes: there are a dozen medical books in this group, gathering the best of classical and medieval physiology and pharmacology, and nine astronomical treatises, which cannot be separated from the handful of volumes that deal with farming and with geographical techniques, both of which would have relied heavily on a knowledge of celestial bodies. Two books he certainly had with him were the manuscript treatises on alchemy given to him by a fellow traveler on board the ship *Que Dios Salve* (which brought him to Santo Domingo), books intended perhaps to remedy the perennial shortfall of gold from the New World. There is also a small but significant group of zoological treatises—the works of Aristotle and Albert the Great on animals—which might help Hernando to extend the observations he had made on manatees, manta rays, peccaries, and spider monkeys during his first voyage.[5]

Yet it would be a mistake to draw too firm a line between practical books for use outside of the library and scholarly ones for use inside: the foundation of humanist thinking, which Hernando absorbed from his tutor Peter Martyr, was that all learning could be bent toward life in the world. Who is to say, then, whether the fifteen-odd works of (mostly Roman) history in this collection were designed to make him an expert in classical history or to guide him and his brother in constructing the new version of the Roman Empire their father envisioned spreading outward from Hispaniola? The truth is that Hernando, like many of his contemporaries, would not have made a distinction between learning and doing, and even dividing the 238 volumes of his first library into different subjects is something we do reflexively as users of modern libraries, and not something Hernando necessarily did himself. To begin with, it would have been unclear in which category a great many of the books belonged: Should books of astrology and medicine go together, given the influence heavenly bodies were believed to have on human health, or should astronomy go with mathematics and music, since all three relied on numbers and proportions? What about sermons and books of philosophy, which often dealt with the same questions about the nature of existence and the ethical way to behave? And perhaps tracts about the animal world should go with those as well, given that many argued God's plan could be read in the Book of Nature. It would make sense, then, that many of the works of classical literature should also be included in this category, since Cicero and Horace are also often concerned with ethics. Their value as sources on Roman history, however, probably meant they should go with the works of history, which should also include the books of law that were founded both in classical and church history. By this point it becomes clear all 238 books might simply belong in a single category, and it might be easiest to leave them together, as one can (for now) just about keep each of them in mind without having to use classification to help locate a single volume. Though Hernando and his contemporaries did have ways of dividing up knowledge—most notably into the seven liberal arts, as in the *Marriage of Philology and Mercury* by Martianus Capella, which Hernando had with him—this culture saw all things of the world as integrally linked and did not think of these as separate fields of thought. Indeed, an ideal was beginning to emerge in Italy, in the works of Angelo Poliziano and Pico della Mirandola, of a man who contained all knowledges within himself and *made himself universal* in doing so. As a model for this, Hernando would have read in his father's Pliny of Eratosthenes, an ancient Greek who had been the first to calculate the circumference of the earth and had produced a miraculous method—a "sieve"—for winnowing out prime numbers from all the rest. What was more, he had done all this while serving as librarian to the great, lost bookworld of antiquity—the fabled library of Alexandria. Little was known of this vanished kingdom of books, but both its vast ambitions and the tragedy of its disappearance loomed large over Hernando's own project, and fragments of the Alexandria catalogue could still be found in a great medieval encyclopedia called the *Suda* (which Hernando owned in its first printed edition).[6]

In the end Hernando had no chance to put his library to the test as a field kit to make himself and the world anew. On 17 September 1509, only two months after arriving in Hispaniola, he returned to Spain, leaving it seems with such haste that he did not even have the chance to pack: the inventory of his possessions was in all likelihood a list of the things that should be sent on after him. This second eastward Atlantic crossing was five years almost to the day since the last, and a great many things had changed. Hernando was no longer merely a passenger on the fleet returning to Spain but its *capitán general*, and Nicolás de Ovando, the governor of Hispaniola who had denied Hernando and Columbus shelter in the port their family built and then left them to rot on their ship-fortresses off Jamaica, was traveling with him as a subordinate. This must have given some satisfaction to Hernando, who decades later was still bitter at Ovando's temerity in welcoming him and his father back to Santo Domingo with open arms after leaving them to suffer a slow death aboard the worm-eaten *Bermuda* and *Capitana*. Greater satisfaction, however, would have come from the fact that Hernando's brother, Diego, was now governor in Ovando's stead, restored to their father's seat and to his title of Admiral.

The period from Columbus's death to this moment at which the family fortunes seemed restored had been anything but smooth. Before he died, Columbus had been attempting to gain further assurances from King Ferdinand regarding his rights over the New World and their hereditary nature, but in truth the matter was no longer entirely in Ferdinand's hands: with the death of Isabella in 1504 the throne of Castile had passed to her daughter, Juana, and Juana's husband, Philip the Fair of Burgundy. The kingdoms of Spain were no longer united, as they had been under the *Reyes Católicos*, and there was no prospect of their being united again under Juana: although she was her father's heir, Aragon functioned under Salic law, which meant that females could not inherit the crown. The Aragonese may have considered this something of a blessing, as it would have brought them under the rule of Philip, a foreigner, and Juana herself, who was accused (perhaps opportunistically) of inheriting the mental instability common in her mother's line, which would earn her the sobriquet La Loca, "the mad." Juana and Philip took eighteen months to arrive from the Netherlands, where they had left their children in the care of Margaret of Austria (the Infante Juan's widow, the course of whose 1497 voyage to Spain had been prophesied by Columbus); they had arrived in Spain just as Columbus lay dying.

Ferdinand, who despite his strong partnership with Isabella had always been amorously inclined and sexually active outside the marriage chamber, had soon remarried, to the eighteen-year-old Germaine de Foix, daughter of the Count of Navarre and niece of the king of France. Germaine reportedly fed him ox-testicle concoctions in hopes of restoring his youthful vigor and producing a rival heir, and Ferdinand left for Italy soon after marrying, to busy himself with his Aragonese possessions on that peninsula. It seemed the great union of Spanish kingdoms, which had been the project of Ferdinand and Isabella's joint reign, was at an end. But just as suddenly, another reversal changed everything: Philip the Fair died suddenly in September 1506, only a few months after arriving in Spain, and the distraught Juana gave rein to paranoia and hysterical grief, having his body mummified and later exhumed against the will of the Church before parading it around Spain. It is said she would not let his body lie in any nunneries along the way because she was jealous of the presence of other women around her husband. By mid-1507 Ferdinand had returned from Naples, and in August he took effective control of Castile back from Juana.

The return of Ferdinand could nevertheless not solve the fundamental problem facing Hernando and Diego: the hereditary rights they claimed were so immense there was no chance of their being secured by two youths, the elder entirely foreign and the younger not wholly legitimate, no matter who their father might have been. Hernando had a little money, such as the munificent sixty thousand maravedís paid to him in 1506 for each year he spent on the Fourth Voyage, but he was unlikely to collect on the vast sums promised in Columbus's will. In the hands of someone powerful enough to uphold it, of course, the Columbus claim was a very attractive proposition indeed. The right partner in the claim was found in the Duke of Alba, whose niece María de Toledo married Diego in the spring of 1508. Aside from being one of the most powerful nobles in Spain and an indispensable ally of Ferdinand's in keeping peace in the peninsula, Alba was also one of the few who had stayed by the king's side while most others flocked to Juana and Philip, so his wishes now carried significant weight. Improvements in the Columbuses' fortunes followed swiftly: on 9 August that year Diego was appointed governor of Hispaniola and Admiral of the Indies by Ferdinand. This was far from the full extent of what had been promised to their father—Diego was governor, not viceroy, and Admiral of the Indies, not of "the Ocean Sea" and all it contained—but a suit was lodged for the recovery of those rights as well and entrusted, during Diego's absence, to the Duke of Alba's agent.[7]

Ferdinand gave his new governor his instructions on 9 May 1509, and the newlyweds departed on 3 June on the *Que Dios Salve*, accompanied by Hernando and their uncles Bartholomew and Diego, as well as a hoard of silver plate and jewels, and a large number of gentlewomen attending on María de Toledo, who were intended to elevate the social scene in Santo Domingo. The Calle de Fortaleza was soon to be renamed the Calle Las Damas, as that was where María de Toledo and her ladies-in-waiting paraded their pristine Spanishness up and down a street between houses uncannily like those they knew in Valladolid and Medina del Campo. Diego's jewels—such as the angel-face pendant, surmounted by an emerald, bordered by diamonds, and with a pearl suspended beneath, which he later had Hernando pawn for him—show a taste for luxury that set him far apart from the rest of his family.[8]

The newfound air of confidence among the Columbus faction was belied by the precipitous nature of Hernando's return to Europe that September. Though the great historian of the Americas Bartolomé de Las Casas, who was in the fleet that brought Hernando over, suggests he was merely going back to continue his studies, Hernando's departure without even managing to ship his chests of beloved books indicates his return had more alarming motives. In part it may have been prompted by the arrival at Santo Domingo in late June of an expedition led by Vincente Yáñez Pinzón (who had accompanied Columbus on the First Voyage) and Juan Díaz Solís, claiming to have explored parts of the Central American isthmus not known to Columbus. Hernando refuted this, claiming they had merely visited the same regions of Veragua that he and his father had on the Fourth Voyage, and derided their maps as simply showing the same landmass twice so they could claim a discovery. In support Hernando cited the testimony of Pedro de Ledesma, the pilot on both voyages whose gruesome wounds had so fascinated Hernando during Columbus's last stand on Jamaica. But Hernando's mockery hid the danger this posed to the Columbuses' claim, part of which turned on whether the family had rights covering all territories in the Ocean Sea west of the Tordesillas Line, or simply those Columbus had personally discovered. If other navigators began to lay claim to their own new discoveries, this might seriously harm the family's fortunes.[9]

This was not, however, the only storm cloud hanging over the future of the Columbus clan. In the winter of 1507, even as marriage negotiations were under way with the Duke of Alba and it looked possible that Columbus's shaky claim would become one of the greatest fortunes in Europe, Diego had managed during liaisons to impregnate not one but two local women. One of these, Costanza Rosa, gave birth to a son (Cristóbal) in mid-1508, and the other, Isabel de Gamboa, to a second (Francisco) in October of the same year. Following the pattern of his father's proceeding with Hernando and his mother,

...distanced himself from the women while providing for the ...en they bore him—as long, in the case of Costanza Rosa, as she ...d prove the child was actually born in June or July of 1508, which ...ould match up with the dates of their liaison. But disastrously for Diego the other affair was proving altogether more difficult: as the will he drew up before leaving for Hispaniola made clear, Isabel de Gamboa's child was only to be provided for if she lost the suit she was currently pursuing against him in the diocesan courts of Burgos. The case alleged Diego had made a legally binding promise of marriage to her during their liaison and that therefore her child was legitimate. The significance of this can hardly be exaggerated: should Isabel's son be upheld as Diego's legitimate heir, no son of María de Toledo's could inherit the Columbus claim, turning the Duke of Alba in an instant from their most powerful ally to a cheated and humiliated foe. As would later become clear, part of the reason for Hernando's being back in Spain was to fight the fires his brother had created through his sexual incontinence, a tragic irony given Hernando was himself the product of a union disowned to make way for greater glory.[10]

But Hernando's plans were of an altogether more ambitious nature than simply cleaning up his brother's messes. While he did carry back to Spain a list of issues Diego wished to be represented to Ferdinand and spent the next eighteen months arguing family business at the itinerant court, he also made good use of his time in the king's presence. The climax came when Hernando was traveling with Ferdinand in late June of 1511, as the court moved northward from Seville to the remote and famous monastery at Guadalupe, which Columbus had visited in pilgrimage after the First Voyage and for which he had named an island on the Second. As they progressed through the high plain of Estremadura, Hernando communicated to Ferdinand his plan to undertake the first circumnavigation of the earth, one he soon set down in a detailed written proposal at the king's request. This extraordinary voyage, Hernando proposed, would be brought to completion by a veritable Argo consisting of the Columbuses (Hernando, Diego, and Bartholomew) and Amerigo Vespucci, as well as Vincente

Yáñez Pinzón and Juan Díaz Solís, who had just returned from exploring the Yucatán. The idea of this voyage had been hugely important to
Columbus, who was repeatedly frustrated in his determination to
return from the New World by sailing right around the world and
following the Portuguese route around the Cape of Good Hope. The
idea of circumnavigation was for Columbus a curious obsession, just
as it has remained for many since: a symbolic act of closure, completion, which may achieve nothing more than returning to the starting
point but nonetheless exerts a powerful hold. This hold was not only
felt by Hernando but even believed by him to be a craving common
to all mankind up to that point, and he told Ferdinand this voyage (if
successful) would be a gift to all the generations throughout the world,
who would then have physical proof of the roundness of the earth, its
potential to be circled, and of its being everywhere inhabitable—proof
that until then would remain tantalizingly elusive. The voyage had the
potential to draw a line around a world that would otherwise remain
worryingly open.[11]

For Columbus the project of circumnavigation had been filled with
millenarian overtones, promising to bring about the universal conversion that would set in motion the endgame of Christian history. Hernando was at least in part faithful to his father's vision and also
presented to the king the *Colón de Concordia*, a work in three parts
that, though lost, clearly revived the project of *The Book of Prophecies*.
As Hernando relates in a later account, the *Colón de Concordia* listed
prophecies and authorities to demonstrate that the circumnavigation
of the globe would occur in their lifetime, that it would bring about
universal conversion, and that the resulting universal empire would
come to Spain. But it seems Ferdinand had tired of hearing these
arguments, which also had fierce critics at the court, so Hernando
agreed to focus on the value of the voyage to human knowledge. He
prepares the ground by pointing out the relatively minor expense of
the enterprise—no more than 5 or 6 million maravedís, which (while
three times the cost of Columbus's First Voyage) he suggested was less
than it cost to feed a single town for a year—a sum (Hernando says,

Ferdinand) that would never have made Caesar or Alexander before the magnitude of their destinies.[12]

After rehearsing the reasons why he believed the voyage possible, Hernando proceeded to the real substance of his petition to the king by providing a detailed outline of the person needed to lead such an extraordinary venture. Though technically Hernando was presenting the petition on behalf of his brother, he is clearly talking about himself in his proposal rather than the courtier brother who had no ocean experience, making his description in effect a remarkable self-portrait of Hernando in his early twenties. He insists the circumnavigator would need to know the different types of ship intimately, given that each sea's currents and shoals require different ones, even down to the regions and seasons in which the wood for them should be taken; that the captain should be able to recruit crew and lay in supplies expertly for the intended voyage, for (*as sailors say*) by a single filament in a rope a whole ship can be lost; and that he should have the navigational, meteorological, celestial, zoological, cosmographic, and cartographic knowledge necessary, for which purpose he must be an arithmetician, astrologer, cosmographer, and painter. While the first eight points in Hernando's portrait of the circumnavigator cover these important technical skills, the final three focus on qualities of mind, passages in which Hernando's self-portraits are almost identical to the picture he would later draw of his father. He says that the person capable of completing this task must not be too reverent toward the authority of ancient cosmographers, whose ideas have been overturned by recent events; that he must not be too drawn to the attractions of ports, so as not to risk being stranded by fog or foul weather; and that the person must be of good upbringing and reputation, so as to be more zealous in the service of God, to bear more hardship, and

(*opposite*) A print of *The Ship of St. Reynuit* (also known as *The Ship of Mismanagement*), showing how great journeys (and great nations) succeed or fail depending on how well they are run. The print (c.1520–30), by an anonymous printmaker after Jan Wellens de Cock, was number 2808 in Hernando's image collection.

(most strikingly) to be more firm in virtue for fear of shame. In his design for the perfect pioneer Hernando reveals an unguarded conviction that his own mastery of minutiae, borne out by shipping manifests and a vast range of technical skills, would in combination with his inherited traits of self-belief and self-control provide for him a destiny equal to his father's. Hernando was, in no uncertain terms, laying claim to the *special genius* of his father, which combined meticulous observation with an inspired spirit to bring unthinkable feats—whether circling the world or enclosing its knowledge in one library—into the realm of the possible. This document also suggests the feats of almost superhuman determination that Hernando would later undertake were driven at least in part by the memories of shame that had scarred his early life—and that perhaps he believed this had also been a motive for his father, even if Hernando would always publicly insist on Columbus's higher and nobler motives.[13]

Hernando's heroic proposal makes clear that in rounding the world with a small group of companions there was no separating the pursuit of knowledge from the rewards of power and wealth this would entail. If he charmingly suggests the circumnavigation should be undertaken in part to break the tension of living in an uncircled world, he also sees the conquests of Arabia, Persia, intra-gangetic India, and Calicut as following almost inevitably from the success of the voyage, and enough wealth accruing from those conquests to put the rest of the globe under subjugation. For Hernando, closing the circle of the unknown world meant gaining the ability to control it. And though physically encompassing it was one way to achieve this, he was not averse to pursuing the same objectives on multiple fronts. While his book collecting showed no signs yet of aspiring to the universal, the year in which he proposed the circumnavigation to Ferdinand (1511) marks both a significant escalation in his purchasing and a more serious attitude toward his books, as suggested by the dated inscriptions in each volume that begin to appear in this year. In the characteristic formula he was to use for the rest of his life, for instance, we learn of the *Librum de fine* by the thirteenth-century Mallorcan sage Ramon Llull that "Este libro costo en Alcalá de Henares 68 maravedís anno 1511" (This book cost sixty-eight maravedís in Alcalá de Henares in the year 1511). Llull, an extraordinary figure who wrote more than two hundred works in a bewildering variety of categories and in three different languages (Latin, Catalan, Arabic), seems already to have been a favorite of Hernando's before 1511, with his great Romance *Blanquerna* and one of his philosophical treatises being among those books likely taken to Santo Domingo. But the volume purchased in 1511 was born of Llull's other great ambition: it was a plan for a crusade, proposing that, as a first step to conquering Islam, Christians must learn to speak the Arabic language—as Llull himself had done, by secluding himself with a Muslim slave for nine years. Perhaps inspired by Llull's ideas, Hernando had acquired a manuscript of the Qur'an in 1510, the beauty of whose calligraphy he noted though he almost certainly knew nothing of what it meant. The idea that the ultimate triumph of Christian culture could be achieved by unlocking the secrets of other languages came to obsess Llull, who would later focus less on learning individual languages and more on developing infinite translation machines. Hernando seems to have caught this bug, and in addition to purchasing several texts in Greek (Homer, Hesiod) during a stay in Seville in 1511—suggesting perhaps he had managed to make good use of his Greek *Lexicon* in Santo Domingo—he bought a number of Hebrew language manuals published in Paris by the pioneering French printer of Greek and Hebrew François Tissard. While acquiring Greek was fashionable for intellectuals of the day, Hebrew was if anything more esteemed as the language of the Old Testament and of Moses's revelation, and because of this there was a hint that, unlike the other languages of Fallen Man, which had been scrambled when God destroyed the Tower of Babel, Hebrew might provide access to eternal truths in ways that other, all too human languages could not. Evidence of this belief was to be seen in the growing interest in cabbala, the mystical Jewish practice of deriving hidden truths from the Hebrew Bible using occult, systematic decryption methods.[14]

But Hebrew was not the only language that held out the promise of unlocking the secrets of the universe if properly mastered. Another book that appeared in 1511, as Hernando followed the court around Spain, was the first modern European account of ancient Egyptian civilization, written by none other than Peter Martyr (Hernando's old tutor) and printed in the same volume as Peter Martyr's monumental history of Columbus's discoveries, the *De orbe novo decades* (Ten books on the new world). During an embassy to the court of the Mameluke Sultan in Cairo almost a decade before, Peter Martyr had visited the Sphinx and Pyramids at Giza on a side trip, even sending back the first reports of entering the chambers of the Great Pyramid. (Another European traveler had supposedly entered a few years previously, but was never heard from again.) Peter Martyr's was the first eyewitness report in modern Europe of Egyptian antiquities, but it was part of a wider and growing interest, which included the extraordinary volume of *Hieroglyphica* published by Europe's greatest printer, Aldus Manutius, in 1505, and which Hernando may already have owned in 1511. This volume, supposedly written originally by the last surviving member of the ancient Egyptian priesthood, Horapollo, and discovered on the Greek island of Andros in the early fifteenth century, offered a model of language in which words were linked unbreakably to the things they described and so were not subject to the worrying weaknesses of verbal languages, with their vagueness and ambiguity.[15]

Here Hernando would have read, if his Greek was strong enough, that *only Egypt is in the navel of the world*. Yet Egypt was not the only place where early modern Spaniards encountered hieroglyphs: the Taino also used a system of sacred pictograms in their petroglyph cave art, and Aztec manuscripts using pictographs were soon on their way back to Spain from Mexico. Recently discovered caves on the Isla Mona between Puerto Rico and Hispaniola—an island where Columbus spent some time in 1495, just before his log is broken off in one of his fits of blindness and delirium—show early Spanish graffiti alongside the sacred Taino markings, carved into the powder-soft limestone with the tips of fingers yet kept pristine in the depth of the caves. One inscription found by archaeologists—*plura fecit deus* (God has made many things)—provides eloquent witness to European attempts to make new experiences fit within existing frameworks. And around this time in the Jamaican settlement of Sevilla la Nueva, founded by Diego a stone's throw from where Hernando had lived on the ship-wrecked fortress, stone pillars were being carved for a church, paid for by Peter Martyr, in which the Renaissance motifs mingled with Taino iconography. While it suited European thinkers to erect a clean, lineal descent of their thought from the ancient Egyptians through the classical Greeks, clearly other sources existed for thinking about the language of pictures, which with Llull's infinite-translation devices played into the same idea: he who spoke the universal language held the keys to universal power. There is more than a little tragic irony in the fact that a pictographic language, close in many ways to the Taino and Aztec glyphs, was shortly to be developed in Seville by the Franciscan friar Jacobo de Testera, with the specific goal of getting the New World peoples to abandon their own sacred culture for that of Christian Europe.[16]

While Hernando investigated universal languages as a mode of conquest, however, the domination and exploitation of the world proceeded elsewhere through more mundane and brutal means. A stark reminder of this comes with Hernando's permission to travel to the New World in 1508 and his license to transport two stallions, two mares, and a black slave. His father had already desecrated his dream of an Edenic New World by setting in motion a trade in Arawak Indian slaves, though the unfitness of the Arawak for physical labor in the New World's mines soon prompted another trade through Mediterranean ports, in the black slaves that had been transported from northern and western Africa, a practice that had continued uninterrupted since antiquity. To add to the execrable practices they inherited, the governors of the New World had instituted the system of the *encomienda*, whereby many settlers were given charge of a certain number of indigenous inhabitants. While lip service was paid to the idea that these subjects should be treated humanely, the arrival of the Dominican order on Hispaniola in 1509 had, by 1511, led to a series of shocking and increasingly systematic expositions of the bestial cruelties inflicted by Spanish settlers upon the peoples of the Caribbean. Bartolomé de Las Casas, who had been with Hernando on the crossing to Santo Domingo in 1509 and who was later to become the greatest historian of the New World and champion of the rights of native peoples, was converted to this lifelong vocation during an excoriating sermon given by the Dominican Antonio Montesinos as the colonial elite of Santo Domingo prepared to celebrate Christmas in 1511. Hernando's position on the rights of non-European peoples is unclear: he sold his 1508 license for a black slave to a bookseller in Seville shortly after acquiring it—though it is not known whether this was driven by his distaste for slavery or his passion for books, or both—and during his life he repeatedly distanced himself from the ownership of other people. Las Casas, who was unflinching in turning a mirror to the insane cruelties of the settlers, showed a lifelong affection for Diego and Hernando, which may suggest that at the least they were relatively unbarbaric. Hernando was certainly to insist, as he began to shape his father's image, that the explorer held the rights of the people he had encountered dearly; and though clearly a lie, it suggests Hernando freely recognized it as desirable that his father should have thought this way. But Hernando certainly never launched himself into the cause of native rights in the way Las Casas did, and it cannot be forgotten that, at best, Hernando's astonishing ambitions to synthesize the knowledge of the world involved turning a blind eye to the atrocities on which the empire he served was built.[17]

Hernando's plans for a circumnavigation that would reduce the world to Spanish rule in a single, majestic swoop would have to wait. Ferdinand responded to his proposals vaguely, asking him to wait for further instructions in Seville or Córdoba. The need for fresh Columbus victories to renew the family fame may have seemed less urgent, given the resolution on 5 May 1511 of the suit that had been lodged regarding the rights of the Columbuses over the New World. The verdict recognized the right of Columbus's heirs to hold the viceroyalty of the Indies, but only over the areas Columbus had actually discovered, rather than the western hemisphere as a whole. They were also given the right to 1.5 million maravedís in perpetual income—though this was only as much as Hernando individually had been left in his father's will. Hernando instead was given the right to an *encomienda* of three hundred Indians, which he seems promptly to have sold on to someone else. But the storm that had been gathering over the Columbus fortunes had suddenly become even more onerous: the case that Isabel de Gamboa had been pursuing against Diego, asserting the legitimacy of their son—a bastard who might someday be viceroy of the Indies—had now passed from the diocesan court at Burgos to the highest court in all of Christendom: the Vatican itself. The fate of Columbus's legacy would be decided in the Eternal City, at the very center of the world, and the successful navigation of this affair was put into Hernando's hands. He prepared to go to Rome.[18]

If the task was of the utmost moment and could only have been daunting to the twenty-three-year-old who had never before been to Italy (much less trained as a canon lawyer), it must also have been thrilling beyond belief. Europe's print market was surprisingly fluid, and Spain's bookstalls were reasonably well stocked—allowing Hernando to buy as he traveled through Spain in 1511 books from Paris, Venice, and Cologne, as well as from all over the peninsula, including a guidebook of sorts for his trip, the *Roma triumphans* by the leading antiquarian Flavio Biondo (printed at Brescia). But visiting Italy itself was a different matter altogether: it was the beating heart of print, humanism, and Renaissance art, not to mention the center of Christendom and of the Roman civilization by which the age was so captivated, as well as being stuffed full of hieroglyph-inscribed Egyptian antiquities brought back by the Romans. If the world could be captured in a single voyage or a single language, it could also be captured in a single city, and that city was Rome: as Flavio Biondo put it, *Urbs terrarum orbis*—the World City.[19]

VII

The World City

Little could prepare travelers to Renaissance Rome for the panoply of marvels they would encounter. Approaching the city from the north, as Hernando likely did with other arrivals from the port of Cittavecchia, they would pass through the old city walls using the Porta del Popolo, constructed in 1475 over the remains of an old Roman gate. The sight that greeted them, as they looked south and east across the city, was unexpected to those who still imagined Rome as the bustling imperial metropolis of its classical peak: vast stretches of abandoned scrubland inside the Aurelian walls, the *disabitato*, given over to grazing animals and only broken by the crisscross of dusty cart tracks. The walls, which had been built to surround Rome when it was a place of a million citizens, now hung loosely around a city of fifty thousand. The Roman Forum and the Tarpeian Rock on the Capitoline Hill were popularly known as Campo Vaccino and Monte Caprino—the Field of Cows and the Mount of Goats. Though Rome was still the center of the early-modern imagination, the 150 years during which it had been vacated by the papacy and given over to local factions, ending in the mid-fifteenth century, had reduced it to a bedraggled state from which it was only just beginning to recover. The surrounding coastlands were still partly lawless and often visited by parties of Turkish and North African pirates, who had in 1511 (the year before Hernando's arrival) ransacked the papal hunting lodge at La Magliana. The Spanish historian Argote de Molina, writing at the end of the century, even suggests Hernando was briefly captured by Turkish pirates as he made his way to Rome. Whether or not this unsubstantiated story can be believed, it was clearly a common enough experience to make the journey a tense one.[1]

The Roman population of the day huddled densely together inside the bend in the Tiber, across the river from the Vatican edifices of St. Peter's and the Castel Sant'Angelo. As he passed through these streets on the way to his lodging in Trastevere—a neighborhood on the same side as the Vatican but somewhat downstream—Hernando would have seen the crowds of vendors vying for the custom of pilgrims, who came in the tens of thousands annually and tripled the size of the city in Jubilee years. If pilgrims could not afford to stay in one of the 1,022 hostelries recorded in the city at the time, having perhaps spent too much money on the souvenir *suadaria* (veronicas) made from mutilated ancient manuscripts, they always had recourse to the *paliarii*, who sold straw beds that could be slept on under the porticoes of St. Peter's. The Vatican, however, was far from the only attraction on offer: travelers purchasing (as Hernando did for a small copper quatrin on arrival) the classic guide to Rome, the *Mirabilia urbis Roma*, would find a bewildering mixture of classical and Christian relics housed in churches around the city. There was Aaron's rod, the tablets of the law given to Moses, a gigantic bronze Roman head and a bronze she-wolf on the Capitoline Hill, with recently added twins suckling from her teats; the entire house in which Mary was conceived and nurtured, and a phial of her milk ("of wonderful whiteness," according to Biondo); the manger in which Christ once lay, the table at which he ate the Last Supper, the gate he had passed through into Jerusalem on Palm Sunday, the stairway to Pilate's room of judgment; the *bocca della verità*, a statue that could reveal if a wife was unfaithful; the wooden sign that hung above Christ, "King of the Jews," the rope Judas had used to hang himself, the chains that had bound Saint Peter and the heads of Saints Peter and Paul. More recent arrivals included the *Vera Effigies*, an image of Christ that had miraculously appeared in an emerald cameo and had been sent to Rome in

1492 by Sultan Bajazeth II of Constantinople, accompanied by the Holy Lance of Longinus, which had pierced Christ's body on the cross.[2]

More recent guides to the city purported to sweep away the fables and falsehoods of the medieval *Mirabilia* by instituting must-see lists of approved monuments, such as Francisco Albertini's *Opusculum de mirabilibus novae et veteris urbis Romae* (Hernando also bought this on arrival, for the much-higher price of thirty quatrines), which detailed recent archaeological finds and modern wonders including

(*below*) The Eternal City, Rome, much as Hernando would have seen it on his arrival in 1512. This illustration by Pleydenwurff and Wolgemut for the grand *Nuremberg Chronicle* (1493) was number 433 in Hernando's image collection.

the Sistine Chapel. Albertini's other guide, the *Septem mirabilia*, proposed an itinerary of seven ancient and seven Christian sites:

The Aqueduct of Claudius	St. Peter's
The Baths of Diocletian	S. Maria Maggiore
The Forum of Nerva	S. Maria in Aracoeli
The Pantheon	Palazzo di San Marco
The Colosseum	Church of the SS. Apostoli
Hadrian's Tomb	Palace of the SS. Apostoli
Lateran Complex	S. Maria ad Martyres

Such attempts to separate out the city's classical and Christian heritage were wholly artificial: the Lateran site was both Roman and Christian, the Pantheon was the same place as the church of S. Maria ad Martyres,

and even the Colosseum hosted a *sacra rappresentazione* (a passion play) every year on Good Friday, the script for which was among Hernando's first purchases on his arrival in Rome. Further complicating matters, many of the classical monuments were, in a sense, "newer," having only recently been uncovered (such as the underground Domus Aurea, found in 1480, or the statue of Laocoön, dug up in 1506) and serving as the inspiration for the most fashionable artists of the day.[3]

The attempt to transform Rome's chaotic historical medley into a stately order took place in the streets as well as in the guidebooks. As Hernando progressed toward Trastevere, he might have taken the via Giulia, a broad thoroughfare lined with cardinals' palaces leading to the proposed site of the Ponte Giulio, which the current pope, Julius II, wanted as a third place to cross the river from the city to the Vatican. In an attempt to link Rome's imperial past to the Church's destiny at the head of a universal empire of the spirit, the papacy facilitated the clearing of humbler dwellings and the construction of imposing neoclassical residences by the cardinals, the majority of whom were scions of the wealthiest and most powerful Italian families. The architectural challenge thrown down by the cardinals was taken up by others, such as the Sienese banker Agostino Chigi, who spent part of the riches he accrued from his monopoly on alum in the Lazio region on building a colossal villa in Trastevere, which Hernando would have passed each time he walked upriver to the Vatican. A Frenchman visiting the city in 1518, after marveling at Chigi's forty-two-horse stable, remarked that the merchant's riches were truly otherworldly. Chigi was fond, in the manner of the dissolute Roman society host Trimalchio from the recently rediscovered Latin novel the *Satyricon*, of turning his banquets into performances. Guests were reputedly free to take the silverware home with them, and after one particularly lavish meal he had the costly table settings taken out in full view of

(*opposite*) Andrea Palladio's sketch of the Tempietto, a masterwork of neoclassical perfection designed by the great architect Bramante, which stands in the same monastery where Hernando stayed during his years in Rome.

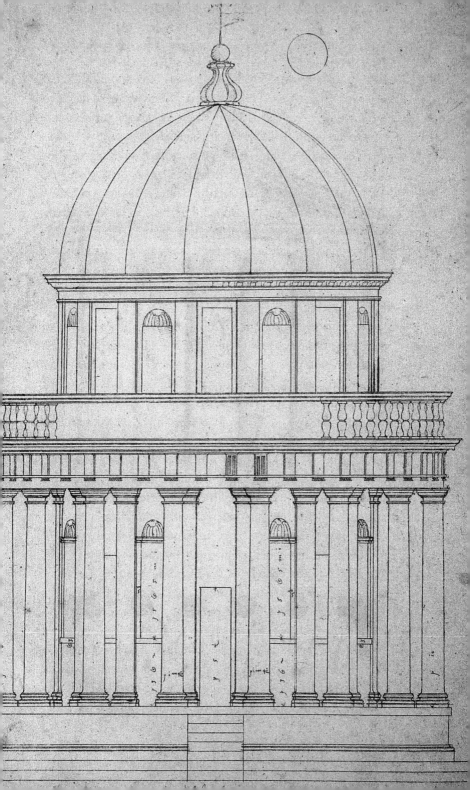

the guests and thrown into the Tiber, only later to reveal that the dishes had been caught in underwater nets. The frescoes of the palace, of Ovidian scenes by Raphael and Peruzzi and Sebastiano del Piombo, were soon on the itinerary of the city's main attractions.[4]

Hernando seems to have stayed, during his many years in Rome, with the Amadists (a branch of reformed Franciscans) at San Pietro in Montorio, a place of special importance to Ferdinand and Isabella, who had sought to make it a symbol of Spanish power in the Eternal City. At the top of a steep slope leading up from Trastevere, Hernando's base would have given him a commanding view of the city, with the immense new St. Peter's rising under the direction of the architect Bramante to his left and north, and the ancient and modern city stretching east in front of him. San Pietro offered a vantage point and seclusion from the bustle, but also allowed Hernando to live daily in the presence of one of Renaissance Rome's minor miracles, in the form of Bramante's recently completed Tempietto, commissioned by Ferdinand and Isabella in 1502 to celebrate the tenth anniversary of their annus mirabilis, when they conquered Granada and their Admiral discovered the New World. The diminutive perfection of this chapel, a marble cylinder surrounded by a loggia and topped by a cupola of exquisite sky blue, provided Hernando with a pattern of the forms, the simplicity, and the proportionality that was central to the revival of classical architecture. The Tempietto was also, fittingly, related to another of Hernando's obsessions: the ambition of the Spanish crown for a universal empire centered on Jerusalem, whose reconquest was cryptically figured in many of the chapel's features.[5]

After he had descended from San Pietro in Montorio, Hernando's official business in Rome would require him to turn left at the Tiber, walking past Chigi's villa with its orangery and apple orchard, to the Apostolic Palace. As well as being the papal residence, the Palace was also the seat of the Sacra Romana Rota, the highest tribunal in all of Western Christendom, which would now sit in judgment over the matter of Diego's affair with Isabel de Gamboa. Characteristically, Hernando had acquired and made assiduous notes on the two principal guides to the functioning of these courts, the *Stilus Romanae Curiae* and the *Termini Causa in Curia*, but even these could not have prepared him for the byzantine complexities of the Rota. The court met on Mondays, Wednesdays, and Fridays, but only during the terms of the legal year, with breaks over Christmas, Easter, and summer, and there was moreover a litany of church feasts during which the court was also not in session. On days when it sat, the court would hear arguments from advocates but also admit evidence from proctors, highly specialized functionaries whose job it was to make sure their clients knew how to abide by the conventions of the court. Without a proctor, Hernando may have missed the fact that business could also take place on Tuesdays, Thursdays, and Saturdays, but only with the specific notary who was overseeing the case, and often at the notary's own house. In an extraordinary stroke of luck, the notary's documents from Hernando's case survive—as less than a tenth of records from the time do—in a ledger a foot thick written in almost illegible writing and buried deep in the Archivio Segreto Vaticano, the private Vatican archive. Those with the stomach—and a knowledge of Latin, canon law, Vatican legal abbreviations, and Italian secretary hand—can follow the sclerotic and arcane grinding of the case through over two hundred pages of court records.[6]

Like most of the matters reaching the Sacra Romana Rota, the case between Diego Colón and Isabel de Gamboa would have been referred to the court after she appealed on the grounds that the defendant was too powerful in his home territory for there to be any hope of a fair trial. This was undoubtedly the case here: Diego Colón was not only the Admiral of the Indies, governor of Hispaniola, and viceroy of Hispaniola, but also nephew-in-law to the Duke of Alba; Isabel, on the other hand, was a widow with children from two previous marriages in addition to the child fathered by Diego. She was not, however, as entirely powerless as Hernando's mother had been in relations with his father. She was a lady-in-waiting to the rightful queen of Castile (Juana), which presumably was how Diego met her while at court in the winter of 1507; but more importantly, in this instance, she also had a relative, Berengario Gamboa, who was one of the powerful proctors in the Sacra Romana Rota. Diego, with a fecklessness that was clearly habitual, had chosen the wrong damsel to distress: he had jeopardized his marriage to the most powerful family in Spain by sleeping with a woman who might just be able to wrest the machinery of Western Christendom against him. Hernando made his first appearance in court on 28 September 1512 and settled in for a long and arduous process.[7]

But Hernando had no intention of allowing his time in the Eternal City to be swallowed whole by the court. As we know from his notes in the books he bought, which from September 1512 began to include the month as well as the year of purchase, Hernando must on most days have crossed the Ponte Sisto from Trastevere—instead of turning left toward the Vatican—and headed into the Parione district, home to the city's book emporia. These *cartolai* would have been fairly familiar in style to Hernando (if wholly unimagined in scope): most of the books would be sold unbound—a cover was added later, according to the customer's specifications—so the window of a shop presented a display of the title pages of the latest and most exciting works, with others inside on a browsing table known as the *mostra*. And just as book lovers today can spot certain kinds of books from a distance by their stylized covers, early-modern book lovers might be able to identify printers' marks on title pages, of which the most prestigious by far was the dolphin and anchor of the great Venetian printer Aldus Manutius, printer of Erasmus and resurrector of classical texts thought long lost. While some bookshops were divided into rough sections, usually simply separating out the expensive law and theology books from the rest, the trained Renaissance reader would have been able to navigate the shop in large part by looking at the size of the books: large-folio volumes for heavy scholarly tomes, thin quarto pamphlets for plays and poetry, and the diminutive octavo "handbooks" pioneered by Aldus Manutius, who made his masterpieces small enough to be carried by men of power out into the world. Hernando would have found the Roman bookshops not simply places of commerce but centers of intellectual life, where devotees of classical architecture would meet to share their observations from walks around the ancient ruins, and thinkers were encouraged to use the books in their discussions of the latest ideas, even if they hadn't bought them. Although Hernando must have known book collections in Spain, such as the library in Salamanca that had been frescoed with the signs of the zodiac on the orders of King Ferdinand, they were sedate places with strict policies on what got in and what did not, with the august volumes of theology and philosophy literally chained to heavy wooden benches. In the bookshops of Rome, however, he found a library alive with the newest publications, constantly shedding its skin and reinventing itself with new ideas and forms.[8]

It must have been difficult for Hernando to resist the temptations of the booksellers given that their district lay directly between his lodgings in Trastevere and the Studium Urbis, the Roman university that Hernando clearly attended in some capacity (official or unofficial) during his years in the city. While the university had been without a permanent home for the first two centuries of its existence, it had recently been given its own buildings near Sant'Eustachio. Though it was not the equal of the ancient University of Bologna, the elite of the Italian and European intelligentsia were drawn to it by the hope of finding patronage that might come from being near the Holy See. A rare surviving document from 1514 lists those lecturing at the time, and upon arrival in September 1512, Hernando stockpiled their books, in a fashion charmingly similar to the eager undergraduate of today. One of the lecturers Hernando might have been most excited to hear was Filippo Beroaldo, son of the famous scholar (of the same name) whose study of Apuleius's *Golden Ass*—a Latin novel about the mysteries of Egyptian religion—Hernando likely owned before he came to Rome, and whose commentaries on the Roman historian Suetonius he purchased on arrival. In December, Hernando was making assiduous notes while listening to lectures on the Roman poet Juvenal, perhaps by Beroaldo or Giovanni Battista Pio, another rhetorician, whose elegies Hernando had bought in September. And if Hernando was not already aware of his fame before turning up in

Rome, he would soon have heard the name of Tommaso Inghirami on everybody's lips—or, more likely, his nickname, Fedra, which he had earned after a legendary performance (in drag) of the title role in Seneca's play, staged at the palace of Cardinal Riario. Inghirami had published no great works, and it is even unclear what he would have been lecturing on at the Studium Urbis, but he was one of those familiar professors whose talent as a performer of genius diverts attention from any accusations of insubstantiality. His skills as an orator had paid huge dividends: he was widely seen as the heir to Pomponio Leto as the living spirit of ancient Rome, and since 1510 he had held the lucrative post of Vatican librarian, which did not necessarily demand much from its incumbent. Hernando also seems to have worked closely on Greek grammar and Greek and Roman history with Bartolomeo da Castro, a Spanish scholar of Aristotle who was in Rome at the time.[9]

Hernando did not, however, confine himself entirely to humanistic studies at the university: following the precepts of one of his first purchases in Rome, the *Panepistemon* of Angelo Poliziano, he showed an irresistible attraction to a more universal knowledge. He owned a volume by one of the medical lecturers, Bartolomeo de Pisis, and may have heard him speak on medical practice, and much of his time seems to have been given over to lectures on astronomy; several notes from the coming years record Hernando's work with Sebastianus Veteranus, under whom he studied the latest theories on planetary orbits, a subject with immense implications for the measurement of time and space and which would come to be a linchpin of Hernando's thought in the years to come. Given his later projects in his garden in Seville, Hernando may well have taken an interest in Giuliano da Foglino, who in 1513 was appointed to Europe's first professorship of medical botany. One celebrity he certainly took pains to follow was the famous mathematical lecturer at the Studium, the mathematical mentor to none other than Leonardo da Vinci, Luca Pacioli, whose recent treatise *De divina proportione*, which offered to teach its readers to speak the language of proportion through which God had designed the universe, was illustrated by Leonardo and bought by Hernando upon his arrival in Rome. Less thrilling, perhaps, but no less important in its impact upon the world, was Pacioli's other contribution made in his *Summa arithmetica*, which Hernando also bought that September: the first formal European treatment of double-entry bookkeeping. This accounting system, invented by the merchants of northern Italy, was designed to make the increasingly complex transactions of Renaissance finance manageable; yet it was such a powerful tool that it would come to shape profoundly the way in which Europeans saw the world, as a system of profit and loss, of credit and balance: life as a zero-sum game. It seems also to have suggested to Hernando a way to organize the hydralike monster of his growing library.[10]

It is an open question at what point Hernando's lavish expenditure on books begins to turn into the idea of a library. It is possible to own a large number of books without their becoming a library: the library only comes into being when the books are put in relation to one another and to books and things *not* in the library. Or, as a seventeenth-century scholar-librarian put it, *even fifty thousand books without order is not a library, any more than a crowd of thirty thousand undisciplined men is an army.* Rome would have presented Hernando with a number of prominent models of the library idea, including the Medici family collection, which had been brought to Rome by Cardinal Giovanni de' Medici in 1508. The blueprint created for this library, when it was founded by Cosimo de' Medici, was followed by many Renaissance libraries. After inheriting the books of the great Florentine humanist Niccolò Niccoli in the 1440s, the merchant-prince Cosimo had become captivated by the idea of the perfect library and had commissioned one Tommaso Parentucelli to design it for him. The list of books drawn up by Parentucelli, known as the *Canone*, consisted of volumes considered indispensable to a learned library— thus creating the first "canon" of great books. Parentucelli's list was groundbreaking in its inclusion of non-Christian learning, and it conceived of a library in broader terms than any before, explicitly including books in every faculty of the Renaissance university—an expanded horizon that caused many contemporaries to celebrate this library as equal to or even greater than the legendary Library of Alexandria—even if Parentucelli's *Canone* contained a relatively modest 260 or so titles. When Parentucelli became Pope Nicholas V in 1447, he used the same model to lay the foundations for what was to become one of the world's greatest libraries: the Biblioteca Palatina, or Palace Library, of the Vatican. It is unthinkable that Hernando would not have visited the public rooms of this library, as many other travelers did, given how much time he spent at the Sacra Rota in the same building. The library consisted of four rooms, though the public could only visit the first two—the Latin and Greek rooms, divided in the way Roman libraries were believed to have been—as the other two, the Secreta and Pontificia, contained the archive of the Vatican and were only accessible to members of the Curia (the Vatican establishment). The rooms were open to the public for two hours a day when the College of Cardinals was in session. The Latin room consisted of sixteen desks, in two rows of nine and seven, divided by a line of columns and presided over by a glorious fresco by Melozzo da Forlì of Pope Sixtus IV, who had given the library its physical space, and the first great librarian, Bartolomeo Platina. The Greek room was accessed through a door from the Latin and had a single row of eight desks. Each desk had an upper and a lower shelf, on which sat about fifty to sixty books, though the books had begun to overflow into a number of separate chests and cupboards.[11]

But while the Medici and Vatican collections offered Hernando models for his library, these were book temples that emphasized the sacredness of their contents by excluding all but the most prestigious texts—*perfect* libraries rather than universal ones, and perfect by means of this exclusiveness. The overwhelming majority of the books were manuscripts, and all but a small handful were in the classical languages of Latin and Greek: the newfangled products of the printing press, and books in vernacular languages aimed at a more common readership, were either ignored or consciously excluded. But Hernando's appetites were already showing themselves to be much less confined than this. Far from restricting himself to prestigious, classical texts, Hernando's appetite for everything Roman did not even confine itself to the formal bookstores and the rarefied environment of the university: for him, the library of Rome sprawled beyond the civilized displays of the *cartolai* and the Studium. Out on the street the street singers (*cantastorie*) would sing the latest ballads and sell copies of the lyrics from their baskets, and peddlers would hawk pamphlets alongside snake-oil cures, souvenirs, and trinkets. Hernando was later to express not just an acceptance of but a *preference for* little booksellers over the grand emporia who thought their own stock the be-all and end-all. It is not clear at what stage Hernando arrived at the radical conclusion these *obrecillas*—small, cheap works—were, if anything, *more* important than the heavy elite tomes collected by most bibliophiles and made plans to collect them systematically; perhaps to begin with he was simply indulging himself when he bought, in his first months in Rome, *The Story of the Blonde and the Brunette, or Love Conquers All* for a single quatrine, or the *Matters of Love* for five.[12]

Wandering the streets and buying from the hawkers would have immersed Hernando in the unending carnival of Rome's lowlifes: this was still a city in which, as Juvenal had said in his Third Satire, it was careless to go out to dinner without making a will. The contemporary underworld was captured in delicious detail in a Spanish fiction called the *Lozana Andaluza* (The lusty Andalusian), a picaresque tale that reflects Hernando's life as if in a fun-house mirror. The heroine of the story, Aldonza, is also born in Córdoba, the product of a love match, and similarly moves to Seville after being orphaned, before traveling the length of the Mediterranean and arriving in Rome at much the same time as Hernando. Unlike Hernando, however, Aldonza's beauty and friendlessness make her the prey to masculine lust, and her experience of Rome leads her through the city's cosmopolitan underbelly, doing her best with her body, her many languages, her cooking, and her drug making to navigate the communities of Andalusians, Castilians, Catalans, Genoese, Jews, and Turks who each in turn attempt to hang her out to dry. Touchingly, she and Hernando owned some of the same books—including one of the earliest printed cookbooks (by Platina, the great Vatican librarian)—and faced some of the same challenges as orphaned bastards, though there their similarities end. Hernando's copies of these books allowed him to participate in elite, male discussions about the nature of things, whereas in Aldonza's hands they were merely the tools of a lower-class woman.

The lines of separation between the street and the sanctuary were not always so neatly drawn. The elite of the city mingled with the poor during the endless civic festivals, when everyone was allowed masks (though they were enjoined not to bear arms or throw eggshells filled with water, a form of holiday game that lives on in the Dominican Republic as the *Juego de San Andrés*). Many courtesans like Aldonza leveraged themselves into positions of immense power, perhaps most famously the woman known as Imperia, a favorite of the likes of Agostino Chigi and the cardinals: her apartments were so luxurious that the Spanish ambassador, when paying a visit, felt obliged to spit in the face of his servant as it was the only thing present that wasn't worth a fortune. And erotic literature was not the sole purview of the street and the boudoir—one of Hernando's most expensive purchases, which set him back two hundred quatrines in September 1512, was the mystico-sexual fantasy *Hypnerotomachia Poliphili*, printed with lavish illustrations by Aldus in 1499. And, conversely, the poetry of the street was not all just bawdy fun. Just around the corner from the Studium Urbis a broken classical statue set up in the Parione district had become a landmark for political opposition, with the wits of the city pinning to the statue (nicknamed Pasquino) unflinching satires of the pope, his cardinals, and the city elite. An enterprising—though wisely anonymous—printer had in 1509 begun to collect and publish the best of the poems pinned to the statue. Hernando bought the 1509 volume in his first Italian months and was to become a loyal collector of these in the years to come.[13]

The pope at which these first "pasquinades" took aim, Julius II, was in every sense the man called forth by Renaissance Rome. Giuliano della Rovere was practically weaned onto papal power in the circle of Pope Sixtus IV, publicly called his "uncle" but widely rumored to be his father, at whose side he was while the first great della Rovere pope worked to restore the Vatican to its former glory and position of political influence. In addition to Sixtus's creation of an august space for the Vatican Library, his political appointments had swelled the College of Cardinals far beyond its traditional body of twenty-four, and he had instituted major works of building and renovation, bringing Botticelli, Luca Signorelli, Ghirlandaio, and Perugino in to work on the Sistine Chapel. But Giuliano's ambitions were to dwarf those of his uncle. After signaling (somewhat scandalously) his intentions by taking the papal name Julius, this Caesar of the Church set about rebuilding the military and cultural power of Rome and of the Church, launching himself into the wars that had been raging in Italy since the 1490s in an attempt to limit the growing power of Venice and to resist French encroachments on the Italian peninsula. At the same time, Julius had broken ground in 1506 on both the new St. Peter's and on the Cortile del Belvedere, two of the greatest building projects of the age. To meet the incalculable costs of these gigantic works, which were to earn their architect, Bramante, the nickname Maestro Ruinante (the Architect of Destruction), Julius issued a Jubilee Pardon in 1507, a document that promised forgiveness of the sins of those who purchased it, with the proceeds of the lucrative sales being used to plug holes in Vatican finances caused by these lavish projects. Rebuilding the center of Western Christendom almost in its entirety was not, however, enough to satisfy Julius: his *terribilità*—a new term that sought to capture at once the inspiration and domineering ambitions of Renaissance Rome—found its equal and its second self in the person of Michelangelo, whom Julius set to work building a tomb of immense proportions that was to be the crowning achievement of both sculptor and pope. A contemporary story told how, when Michelangelo pointed out that the roof of St. Peter's would need to be raised to accommodate the tomb at a cost of one hundred thousand crowns, Julius suggested they round the figure to two hundred thousand and make sure the job was done properly. Many of the satirists pinning poems to Pasquino must have felt, like their Roman predecessor Juvenal, that in such an age "difficile est saturam non scribere"—it was hard *not* to write satire.[14]

The presence of this warrior pope in the Vatican must have been a considerable draw for Hernando, and accounts from later in the century suggest he may have been carrying letters to Julius from Ferdinand, an ambassadorial role that would have given him the chance to observe the *terribilità* at close quarters. If Hernando might have had to spend much of his time at the court of the Sacra Rota in an attempt to save the family's fortunes from his brother's sexual incontinence, at least his route to the court lay through the building works in which the greatest artists of the age were giving free rein to their imaginations and ambitions. The Cortile del Belvedere had also begun to function, by the time Hernando arrived there, as a museum of the classical antiquities that were constantly being unearthed in and around the city, and passing through its corridors, he would have seen those figures of such intense perfection that even then had begun to bring European notions of beauty within their gravitational pull: the Apollo Belvedere, Hercules with the infant Telephus, and the sculpture of the walking woman, *La Gradiva*, which was later to inspire Freud and Dalí. As the Sacra Rota was not in session on All Souls' Day (1 November) 1512, Hernando was free to go to the Apostolic Palace that day to witness the unveiling of Michelangelo's ceiling frescoes in the Sistine Chapel, as the rest of Rome did (according to an eyewitness) "even before dust that had been raised from taking down the scaffolding had settled." It was said Michelangelo had been commissioned by Julius to paint the chapel at the prompting of Bramante and Sangallo, who were certain the sculptor would fall short with the brush and so lose his fame and his hold over the pope. Yet though Michelangelo had resisted and written a sonnet complaining at the discomfort of being suspended beneath the ceiling—"with my groin crushed into my gut /And my arse hung as a counterweight"—there was no mistaking the triumph when it was revealed. Michelangelo had taken up the challenge thrown down by the original wall paintings—in which Botticelli, Perugino, and others had shown (in the parallel lives of Moses and Christ) the fulfillment of the Old Testament in the New and the triumph of the New Law over the Old—and in response had proposed a schematic diagram of all Christian time laid out over the framework of the chapel ceiling. The thirty-three individual sections of the composition treat history from Creation through the Fall and the Flood to the ascendancy of Israel, flanked by portraits of the prophets who show that the same history would be repeated after the coming of Christ, ending with the ultimate victory of the Church Militant. The ceiling entirely overwhelms any attempt to take it in whole, and it is significant that Michelangelo's disciple Condivi, in trying to describe the composition, constantly has recourse to the grid created by the vaulting: like grid lines on a map, this framework allows Condivi to guide the reader around his master's painting, giving the coordinates of each image. Describing Michelangelo's ceiling, then, becomes much like plotting a course on a map.[15]

Hernando may just have been finding his feet in the tumultuous disorder of Rome—its pilgrims, popes, plutocrats, paupers, professors, ruins, relics, and rogues—when the spring of 1513, six months after his arrival, raised the pitch of chaos to another level of intensity. Carnival was always a time of license and release in the Christian West, but Rome went a step further by holding its traditional city festival (the Festa d'Agone) at the same time. So alongside the time-honored rituals uniting the city in a frenzied release of energy before Lent, there were the triumphal processions celebrating its glories and the achievements of its papal leader. For Carnival, there were races around the city with different handicaps—between youths, old men, donkeys, horses, buffaloes, and Jews and (a recent addition by the Borgia pope Alexander VI) a race of whores—as well as a barely concealed pagan sacrifice at Monte Testaccio. From the top of this hill made of broken pottery pieces heaped up by the ancient Romans, pigs and bulls were attached to carts and launched downhill to an awaiting mob, who smashed both carts and beasts to pieces. Other carts were brought on as floats for the Festa d'Agone in 1513, celebrating Julius as the Warrior Pope and showing the various provinces of Italy he had liberated in his many wars against the Venetians and the French. For a newcomer such as Hernando, it must have been difficult at times to tell the licensed hooliganism of Carnival apart from the brash pomposity of the Papal Triumph.[16]

On Ash Wednesday 1513 Hernando was in the Apostolic Palace for the sermon that began the Lenten season of austerity and repentance, noting in his printed copy that he had heard the Spanish preacher deliver a reminder of the dust from which the audience came and to which they would return. This somber note must still have been ringing in Roman ears when, a week later, Julius died. A satire that appeared shortly after his death, rumored to be by no less a figure than Erasmus, imagined Julius presenting himself at the gates of heaven, leading the army of vagabonds to whom he had promised blanket forgiveness of sins in return for fighting in his wars. St. Peter is unimpressed, to say the least.

> You've brought twenty thousand men with you, but not one of the whole mob even looks like a Christian to me. They seem to be the worst dregs of humanity, all stinking of brothels, booze, and gunpowder. I'd say they were a gang of hired thugs, or rather goblins of Tartarus plucked from hell to make war on heaven. And the more closely I look at you yourself, the less I can see any trace of an apostle. . . . I'm ashamed to say, and sorry to see, that your whole body is disfigured by the marks of monstrous and abominable appetites, not to mention that even now you're all belches and that you stink of boozing and hangovers and look as if you've just thrown up.

Julius's boasts of the great wealth and power he has won for the Church fall on deaf ears, and even he admits people were growing tired of the Roman Curia, accusing them of being "tainted by a shameful obsession with money, by monstrous and unspeakable vices, sorcery, sacrilege, murder, and graft and simony." If Julius's *terribilità* was a major force driving the resurrection of classical glory and putting it at the disposal of the Church, for many this magnificence was a mark of the luxurious damnation into which Rome was sinking.[17]

The court of the Sacra Rota, along with most other institutions of the Roman Curia, stopped all proceedings upon the death of a pope. The churning wheels of power and patronage fell silent as the College of Cardinals met in conclave, and the furious horse-trading to decide the next pope commenced behind closed doors. Although there was now present need for it, soon Michelangelo's work on the tomb that he and Julius had planned together also ground to a halt. Of this gargantuan work, which was to have over forty statues and to represent all the areas of human achievement that Julius stoked to unprecedented heights—the liberal arts, painting, sculpture, architecture— only a single sculpture remains. This statue, housed today in the church of the della Rovere family, San Pietro in Vincoli (St. Peter in Chains), is nevertheless a contender for the greatest artwork of an astonishing age and gives some sense of the crushing ambition of the project as conceived in its entirety. The giant figure sits enthroned and contemplative, the delicate folds of his robes and the wild tendrils of his flowing beard drawing attention to the massive solidity of his frame and his muscles. Under his arm he clasps a pair of tables, for all the world like an artist's portfolio. This is Moses, who sets the history of the world and the peoples of Israel in order, telling of their genesis and exodus, compiling their genealogies and the tables of their law: Moses, the maker of lists.

VIII

The Architecture of Order

Periods of indolence such as the Lenten conclave of 1513 provided Hernando with an opportunity to indulge another passion that was fast growing into an obsession, one that would by his death make him the owner of the largest collection of printed images in the world—3,204 to be precise, as Hernando's equally obsessive list making allows us to be. Printmaking had been around before Gutenberg's movable type made printed books a reality, and religious images roughly cut into wooden blocks for stamping on paper and parchment had been bought as pilgrims' souvenirs since at least 1400. But movable type had made print a major industry and had revolutionized the techniques and markets for picture making as well, with images of ever-higher quality becoming more widely available. The channels through which these printed images circulated around Europe were still in their infancy, however, and while Hernando may have found a small selection of prints in the Spanish trade fairs of his youth, he would have found the market in Rome, where some of the greatest printmakers lived and worked, of infinitely greater variety and higher quality. The lines carved into the surface of the printing block had become ever finer, until the masters of the craft had almost made them disappear from sight, to be replaced by a sensation of depth, texture, and movement that was astonishing to behold. Printmakers delighted in the ability this gave them, to bring the suffering of contorted saints to life, to show the muscles of hunters and warriors as they rippled, to show the water slick off naked bodies fresh from bathing. This was an art whose realism rivaled that of the ancients, a standard the Renaissance was obsessed with reaching. The power of this realism was nicely captured in Pliny's well-loved story of a classical painter (Parrhasius) and his triumph in a painting contest. Having applauded his opponent, whose still life of fruit was so real that birds had gathered to feast on it, Parrhasius invited the other painter to draw back the curtain on his own creation. The opponent had to concede defeat when he realized the curtain he was trying to draw back was *part* of Parrhasius's painting. The extraordinary level of detail in these images allowed printmakers not only to bring human and animal bodies to life on paper, but also to create maps of towns and countries so intricate as to give the viewer the sensation of being present there, and perhaps showing them more of the place than would be seen with the naked eye.

Printed images would have been for sale in the same places as printed books—in the bookstores of the Parione district, and from the peddlers wandering the streets—but also directly from the workshops of the printmakers themselves, such as that of Giovanni Battista Palumba, a master of the craft who was present in Rome during Hernando's time there and whose work Hernando seems to have collected carefully. Palumba's prints, signed with his first initials and a pictograph of a dove (*palomba* in Italian), are a tour de force of the printmaker's art, with richly forested or sharply craggy backgrounds falling away in deep perspective behind the classical figures of the foreground. In the *Mars, Venus, and Vulcan,* which Palumba produced from around 1505, the blacksmith's powerful back turns toward us as his hammer reaches the top of its arc, while the delicately armored and amorous Mars puts his hand on naked Venus's shoulder as she glances over it, touching one of the curves of her flesh that draws the eye around toward where they disappear from view.[1]

Although Hernando seems to have been drawn to those masters who specialized in printed images, in the same way as he preferred printed books to manuscript works, the Roman print market also allowed him to buy images drawn from the painters who were idolized in Renaissance Italy: the head of an ecclesiastic after a drawing by Leonardo, and engravings after Raphael by Marcantonio Raimondi and Ugo da Carpi, as well as the first engraving designed by the young Titian, a monumental *Triumph of Christ* on ten sheets of paper. There is even an exciting possibility that Hernando commissioned in this period the most famous portrait of his father, by Sebastiano del Piombo. There are no surviving depictions of Columbus from his lifetime, but del Piombo's painting is one of the earliest and most credible of those from the generation after; he was working with many Spanish patrons in Rome at this time, including on a commission at San Pietro in Montorio where Hernando was based, and Hernando is surely the most likely patron of such a work (as well as perhaps the only person in Rome who could have provided a model—in words or drawings—of his father's appearance).[2]

Hernando's desire to collect pictures by these celebrated artists may have been increased by the fact that both Leonardo and Raphael were, soon after Julius's death, at work in the Vatican. Those who may have hoped for a less extravagant, less worldly pontiff this time were to be sorely disappointed: on 11 March, less than three weeks after Julius's death, Cardinal Giovanni de' Medici was elected as Pope Leo X, and he was installed in a coronation ceremony of particular opulence a few days later, on the nineteenth. Though Leo had the good taste to delay the semipagan festival of *Possesso*—in which the pope took formal possession of the city of Rome—until the sobriety of Easter had passed, many might have wondered, when the ceremonies resumed in April, whether the party had ever really stopped. The *Possesso* made its stately, riotous way around Rome, with various ritual halts: Leo met with Rome's Jewish community at Monte Giordano, where he was presented with a copy of the Torah (as a book containing the Jewish law), which he ceremonially let fall to the

Hernando's immense collection of images, such as this print, *Mars, Venus, and Vulcan* or *Vulcan forging the arms of Achilles*, by Giovanni Battista Palumba (*opposite*), required a revolutionary method of organization to prevent the admission of duplicates.

ground in condemnation of the Jews' refusal to recognize Christ; he was enthroned in the *sedes stercatoria*, the "seat of shit," in the Lateran, a performance of his humility that involved his throwing handfuls of golden coins to the assembled crowds. If anything, Leo's habits of grandeur even outshone those of Julius and were less directed at church glory than at increasing the standing of the Medici family. In September of that year a festival (the Palila) celebrated the citizenship of Rome that the *Conservatori*, the city fathers, had granted to Leo's brother as well as his nephew Giulio de' Medici, who was one day (though perhaps not yet) to be a patron to Hernando. For the celebrations, overseen by none other than Tommaso "Fedra" Inghirami, a thousand-seat theater was constructed on the Capitoline Hill and tricked out in classical style, for entertainments culminating in a production of Plautus's *Poenulus*. It is not clear whether the performance of the play in Latin, with an all-male cast, was intended to allay or accentuate the scandal of this comedy about North African sex slaves. It probably didn't matter: the play was, after all, performed after a meal of ninety-six dishes, also served in the theater, whose surviving menu includes

> prunes
> figs confit in muscatel
> roast warbler
> roast quail
> prairie oysters
> roulades
> Greek pies
> cockerel's testicles
> kid's head, green sauce
> various salamis
> jellies
> calf head, lemon and gold
> vermicelli tart

pear pie & peach
a pastry wolf, suckling twins
dove pie
roasted—
    cockerels
    hens
    pheasants
    peacocks
    eagles
    kids
    venison
    boar
    calves
    hares
    falcons, chasing
    cormorants
—all sewn back into their skins, to appear living
capons in white sauce
marzipan
quail pastels
pheasants in royal sauce
forest goat pie
various pies
veal with mustard
cockscombs
sugared capons, gilded
duck pie
blancmange
pies, green
suckling pig
veal in pomegranate
fowls in soup
perfumed toothpicks

In addition, there were gilded pastry balls—a gesture to the Medici arms, the *palle*—filled with live rabbits and live songbirds under the napkins.[3]

It was fitting, and perhaps inevitable, that the counterpart to this mayhem of excess was a yearning for order, for some way of arranging the world that kept it from overwhelming with its plenitude. At the Studium Urbis, Hernando would have heard Luca Pacioli lecture on his grand theory of proportionality, which suggested that not just mathematical shapes but in fact all the world and all human knowledge could be arranged according to ideas of proportion, from the symmetry of basic shapes to the most complex structures. Hernando may not, however, have been the most attentive student: the evidence of his books from this period suggests he was beginning to have ideas of his own about the world and how to order it. When his tutor Bartolomeo da Castro was leading him through Suetonius's *Lives of the Twelve Caesars* in the summer of 1515, the intention was presumably that Hernando should be learning from the example of ancient Rome's most prominent men. Yet while Hernando's volume of Suetonius contains only a few notes drawn from his instructor, it does preserve an extraordinary product of Hernando's young mind: a twenty-page, three-column handwritten index, providing an alphabetical key to the book's people, things, and concepts. The level of specificity is astonishing: to take the middle of the letter *c* as an example, Hernando has not only recorded instances of the words *Corinth* and *creditors*, but also *cube* and *crepusculum* (moonlight). This was not an isolated incident: he was to do the same with the copy of Lucretius glossed by another lecturer at the Studium Urbis, Giovanni Baptista Pio, compiling lists of three thousand terms mentioned in the magnificent *De Rerum Natura*, from lips to wagging tails. Subject indexes such as these were still at that point fairly rare: they had only come into their

(*opposite*) Leonardo da Vinci's illustrations of complex shapes for *De divina proportione* of Luca Pacioli, a grand theory of how the world fit together.

own with the birth of print, and at this time relatively few books featured such a device. During the age of manuscript, when no two copies of a text were exactly the same, any index compiled would be good for just a single copy. The index of a printed book, on the other hand, should hold true for *every* copy—at least of that edition; a map was provided to lead the reader quickly through the concepts of the book to the parts in which they are most interested. It is particularly touching that one of Hernando's indexes provides just such a map to Lucretius: the Roman poet's extraordinary scientific epic, which argued that the world was made of minuscule atoms colliding with one another in a universe abandoned by the gods, was helping to prompt a reexamining of the world that would strike at the very foundations of its religious beliefs. These materialist ideas, which held that even the soul itself was a physical thing and not immortal, were proving so popular that in 1513 the Church felt it necessary to direct professors of philosophy throughout Western Christendom to refute them. If the world Lucretius portrays might be chaotic, Hernando's index at least manages to bring this revolutionary text under control.[4]

An alphabetical index was all very well for creating an ordered list of a book's contents, but how was Hernando to go about arranging his swiftly growing collection of printed images? As the number of prints he owned rose beyond the capacity of any individual, even one of prodigious memory, to remember them all, a system was needed, at the very least to ensure he wasn't simply buying the same images over and over. But whereas the words in a book can be placed in an alphabetical order agreed upon and familiar to all users of the Roman alphabet, no such shared language exists for images. A small minority of prints were signed by those who made them, and as often as not they were signed with pictograms such as Palumba's dove rather than with the full name of the artist, engraver, or printer. In response to this wordless world, Hernando devised an eccentric but ingenious method for putting his prints in order, first dividing them by the subject matter they portrayed, split into six groups:

humans
animals
inanimate objects
"knots" (abstract designs)
landscapes (including maps)
foliage

Within these categories, the images were then subdivided according to the size of the paper on which they were printed; the group containing images of humans, which was by far the largest, was further broken down by the number of people, sex, saints and secular, and clothed or nude. The catalogue would allow Hernando, when browsing among prints at the booksellers, to check whether he already owned an image or not. With Giovanni Battista Palumba's *Mars, Venus, and Vulcan* in hand, then, he need simply turn to

humans > folio-size prints > prints with four men > secular > naked

But because there might easily be more than one image of four naked people on a folio-size sheet, Hernando also noted some detail of the picture that was likely to be unique. For this print, then, he noted the following:

Vulcan who is working in a helmet with a forge, behind is an armed
cupid with a bow, an armed man touches the left of a naked woman,
there is a huge tree in the middle from which hangs a cuirass, a
guard, a knife, author IB 🦆 , Vulcan has the right foot higher than
the left upon a round stone, the hammer is in his right.

Bizarre though the catalogue is, it provides an almost foolproof technique for ensuring he never purchased the same print twice.[5]

That there was no accepted way of ordering these images would have confronted Hernando with the essence of list making in its purest form: namely, that all ordered lists must have both *sameness* and *difference*. The recognition that things are in some sense the same allows them to be put in a list together, a list that contains these items and not others—so, here, Hernando gathered in his list all of the printed images he purchased and did not include any paintings or books or leftover meals. While *sameness* allows things to be gathered together, then, *difference* allows them to be sorted internally, just as the different spelling of words allows them to be alphabetized. Hernando chose *subject* and *size* as the two central kinds of difference on which to structure his catalogue. It was fairly easy when looking at an image to know if it was a postcard-size octavo or a poster-size *marca real* (royal folio). Subject proved a little more difficult. What if the image contained both men *and* women, or men and animals, or naked people and clothed people? Hernando solved this problem by introducing a *hierarchy* of subjects: if the image contains even one human, it goes in the human category, even if the human is surrounded by animals; if it contains one man, it goes in the male category, even if surrounded by women, and so forth.

The indexes that Hernando created in his copies of Suetonius and Lucretius and the catalogue he produced for his prints are astonishing witnesses both to the experience of being overwhelmed by sheer numbers of things—ideas, facts, images—and to Hernando's first experiments in how to respond to this tidal surge. How does one act when confronted by a plenitude beyond one's own ability to grasp? How else but by creating tools to extend the natural abilities of the mind: if you can remember the word *Corinth*, the index can lead you to all the places it occurs in a book, and if you can count the number of men in a picture, the catalogue can remind you of all pictures with that number of men. Yet, amazing though they are, as the products of a young mind often acting without any models to copy, these early tools of Hernando's had serious and significant weaknesses. While the print catalogue allowed him to check whether a particular print already existed in the collection, it was more or less useless if one wanted to find all the pictures of (say) Venus among the 3,204 prints:

while you might find some of them by looking up women who were solitary and naked, many others might be (like Palumba's *Mars, Venus, and Vulcan*) in the male section. Similarly, Hernando's book indexes make no attempt to group similar words together, so you could use the index to find instances of *pride* in Suetonius, but entirely miss when the author was using another word—*vanity*, perhaps— instead. As he mounted his assault on the burgeoning world of printed information, Hernando would learn these lessons and improve on the results.

The example of Hernando's print catalogue also gives some indica- tion of the dangers involved in this kind of categorization. To begin with, any system you choose immediately makes other possible ways of organizing the world invisible. Even the very fact that Hernando chose to catalogue his printed images as a group, separate from, say, his books or his plants, meant a barrier had been erected between pictures and books that treated the same subjects. Someone who found a book on the city of Nuremberg on the bookshelves would have no idea a map of the city was in the print collection, and vice versa. More troubling than this, however, was the erection of hierar- chies. All systems of order involve hierarchy: one could not alphabet- ize without an accepted order to the alphabet, *A* first and *Z* last. But even if the hierarchy is arbitrarily selected—there is no *reason* why the letters shouldn't be in a different order in the alphabet—after a time it comes to seem natural, inevitable. Hernando's hierarchy of subjects, in which humans take precedence over animals and men over women, reinforces the sense that these hierarchies are also natural and inevi- table. It should be said they wouldn't have seemed remotely contro- versial to Hernando and his contemporaries. But soon he would confront other fields in which there was *not* an accepted hierarchy. And once these hierarchies are written into the tools we use to navi- gate the world, this step becomes ever harder to undo. Eventually, in fact, we often forget the hierarchy was imposed in the first place and no longer see anything other than a natural, inevitable, timeless order, from Alpha to Omega. If God was revealed, according to medieval theologians, in the order of the world, orders imposed upon it could come to seem godlike. *God* is the name we give to the possibility of order.

Once you begin to look—and there is no doubt Hernando was looking—expressions of this urge to categorize and order can be seen everywhere in Rome. In a room close to the Palatine Library in the Vatican, Raphael had (in 1511) completed a series of frescoes in which all of human thought was represented in four immense scenes, one on each wall of the cubic chamber, each labeled in a painted medallion on the ceiling above.

> *The Disputation of the Sacrament*
> *The School of Athens*
> *Justice*
> *Parnassus*

On the western wall, the painting known as *The Disputation of the Sacrament* depicts the knowledge of divine things; facing it on the east is *The School of Athens*, in which the causes of earthly things are delved into; to the north is *Justice*, showing the sources of the law; and to the south, *Mount Parnassus*, showing "things proceeding from inspiration" (poetry, music, and so forth). *The Disputation of the Sacrament* shows an arrangement familiar enough from traditional paintings of the heavenly hierarchy, though focusing here on the great figures of theology: beneath the Trinity are the four evangelists and the authors of epistles in the New Testament, and below them the Church Fathers, flanked by important latter-day theologians such as Thomas Aquinas and (peeking out from behind the crowd) Girolamo Savonarola. The other walls use this familiar structure to arrange the remaining branches of knowledge: in *The School of Athens* the key figures are Plato and Aristotle, with Plato pointing upward to suggest his dominance in metaphysics and Aristotle gesturing downward, showing his thought is grounded in observation of things of this world. On either side of this central pair are the philosophers who belong to each of their schools, with figures such as Epicurus and Heraclitus representing the metaphysicians on the left and Euclid and Ptolemy standing in for the empiricists on the right. This pattern, in which the structure of the painted composition is used to propose a structure for human knowledge, is continued in the other frescoes, with *Justice* showing law descending from the Four Cardinal Virtues before being divided into Church Law and Secular Law, while *Parnassus* depicts the arts descending from Apollo and the Muses before being split into two branches that descend on either side of the window that looks out onto the Cortile del Belvedere, with epic, historical, and comic poetry (Homer, Dante, Virgil) on one side and tragic, romantic, and sacred poetry (Horace, Ovid, Propertius) on the other.

Raphael's paintings were more than merely decorative: this was art as a grand proposition about the structure of knowledge. And this was far from a haphazard choice of subject, given that the rooms' original purpose was to house the pope's personal library. The saintly Pope Calixtus III, who had lamented the wasting of church funds on pagan manuscripts for the Vatican Library, would have been astonished to see pagan thinkers such as Plato, Epicurus, and Homer portrayed as prominently on the walls of the pope's library as the figures of the Church. But Raphael's division of knowledge into these categories— theology, law, philosophy, poetry—allows each its dignity within its own domain, while neatly avoiding the fact that the thought of Epicurus is incompatible with the thought of Saint Paul. Indeed, it is this very division that allows these contradictions to subsist—if the two are dealing with different subjects, then they are not in contradiction. It also erects a natural structure for each field of knowledge, in which later thought descends from a few original authorities in the same way that Divine Truth emanates from God.

Representing the structure of knowledge in a painting was one thing, but dealing with it in the form of books was quite another, as they were finding down the corridor in the rapidly expanding Palatine Library. Though the original library of Nicholas V was based on the fairly manageable list (the *Canone*) he had drawn up for Cosimo de'

Medici, by 1475 the library had over three thousand volumes and was beginning to seem uncontrollable. One valiant author, who attempted to write a catalogue of the library in verse, an epic tour of it in imitation of Dante's *Divine Comedy*, gave up halfway through, exclaiming

> Seeing so many books, I was speechless,
> then said to myself, "Oh, what an abyss is here—
> this will be a hard meal to stomach!"

The only way to make the books manageable was to categorize, divide, and order them. The library had begun by dividing books into Greek and Latin, and Parentucelli's list had provided further structure, following the practices of medieval monastic libraries in giving the Bible (and commentaries on it) pride of place at the top of the list, followed by works by the Church Fathers, and then works by later theologians, with everything else more or less lumped together. This may have been sufficient for the original nucleus of the library—Dante's *Divine Comedy* was the only vernacular text, after all, in Parentucelli's *Canone*—but as it expanded under the Renaissance popes, the undifferentiated category of "classical letters" became so large that it was necessary to borrow categories from university courses—law, philosophy, medicine, etc.—to further divide up the books.

Much like most collections, then and now, however, the great Italian libraries' most effective tool in creating order was a rigorous policy of exclusion. By drawing up relatively narrow criteria for the books that were allowed in, they ensured the structures they had created for categorizing the world weren't overwhelmed by a torrent of things that didn't quite fit. This exclusivity even found amusing expression in the Stanza della Segnatura: on the *outside* of the door leading into the library is a portrayal of a much-despised and widely ridiculed poet of the day, seen riding the pope's pet elephant, Hanno (Hannibal), in a mock-triumphal procession intended to deride his pretensions. Like this foolish poet, works considered lacking in dignity were to be shut out, the door slammed upon them in disdain. So while Hernando

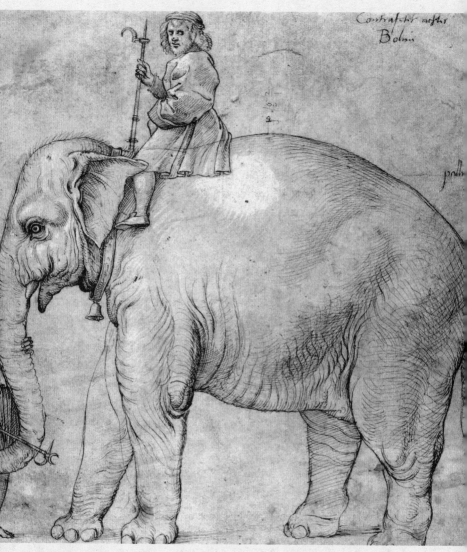

A sketch (c.1516) by Raphael of the pope's elephant, Hanno, a great celebrity during Hernando's stay in Rome.

must have marveled at the magnificence of the Vatican libraries, he must also have recognized that they did not offer much help as models for his own collection, which was more radically open to everything that was on offer, to the torrents of matter from the printing presses of Europe.

The arrival of the white elephant Hanno in Rome in March 1514, and his celebrated status in the public life of the city thereafter, must have served as a painful reminder to Hernando that his father's legacy still hung in the balance. While Peter Martyr's account of Columbus's discoveries was making its presence felt in Rome, with Leo reading the first *Decade* aloud to an assembled body of cardinals and members of his family, and major Vatican figures such as Giles of Viterbo echoing the Columbus line that the New World discoveries were the catalyst for a new age, the Portuguese discoveries had been making more of a splash of late. Hanno the Elephant was a present to Leo from Manuel I of Portugal, delivered by the explorer Tristão da Cunha along with forty-two other animals as part of a conspicuously lavish embassy designed to display the immense riches offered by their ventures in the East, in Goa, and (more recently) as they made inroads into the centers of the Eastern spice trade at Malacca in the Malaysian archipelago. The Portuguese may also have been bearing gifts of sumptuous palm cloth from the newly converted king of Kongo. Much to the delight of the Roman crowds, Hanno arrived for his papal reception at the Castel Sant'Angelo carrying two mahouts (elephant keepers) and a leopard: he trumpeted three times to salute the pontiff and sprayed the gathered crowd with water from his trunk, not omitting to douse the cardinals. While the forest elephant from the steeply sided woodlands of the Western Ghats in India was doubtless unimpressed by Rome, the city was entirely enthralled by him, which perhaps contributed to the success of the Portuguese embassy. In April, da Cunha was awarded the papal bull *Præclesæ Devotionis*, which threatened to tilt the balance between Portuguese and Spanish imperial ambitions, established at Tordesillas twenty years earlier, disastrously away from Spain. The Portuguese, this bull declared, could lay claim to any heathen lands they found while sailing east. This appeared to be a decisive blow for the interpretation of the 1494 Treaty of

Tordesillas to which Columbus had clung so tenaciously—allowing the Portuguese to claim only the parts of west Africa they had discovered by 1494, and not the entire eastern hemisphere—and which Hernando himself had hoped to set in stone when he proposed his trip around the world three years before. To make matters worse, Spain's influence was waning in Europe as well, in part due to the victory of French forces at the Battle of Marignano in September 1515, and Hernando accompanied Leo north to Florence as the pontiff went to seek terms with the victorious young King Francis I. Hernando may have filled in the background to these affairs by reading the first printed work of Niccolò Machiavelli, which he bought that year. In the room next door to the papal library Raphael began a new fresco in which Leo III was crowning Charlemagne as Holy Roman Emperor, though it was clear for all to see that these portraits were actually of Leo X and Francis I. Though the old Holy Roman Emperor, Maximilian I, was still very much alive, the wind of fortune was blowing toward France. Spain's dream of a *universal* empire, set in motion by the Columbian discoveries, was beginning to slip beyond reach.[6]

European politics was not the only thing threatening the Columbus legacy. Though the second phase of the case over Columbus's rights in the New World was still grinding through the Castilian courts, with the family attempting to extend the limited rights secured in 1511 to regain the broader powers over the western Atlantic promised to the explorer in 1492, things were beginning to move on regardless. Ferdinand's court was quivering with excitement over the newly founded region of Darién on the mainland south of Hispaniola, where it was believed the gold-rich regions for which they had all been searching had finally been found—just east of the area Hernando had explored with his father a decade before. The appointment of a governor for Darién in 1513 made no reference to Diego Columbus's government in Hispaniola: it was beginning to look as if Columbus's perennial adversary Fonseca was going to bleed Columbus's legacy dry by simply ensuring the Columbus base at Santo Domingo was bypassed by all the real wealth flowing out of the New World. As if

this weren't bad enough, in 1514 Diego was recalled to Spain in igno-
minious circumstances, after his administration in Hispaniola had
been brought to its knees by warring factions. Hernando returned to
Spain periodically from Rome, during the vacations when neither
court nor university were in session, but he could provide little comfort to Diego from Rome, where the case in the Sacra Rota, still far
from resolution, was continuing to cast a pall over the family fortunes.
During the return from one such trip, over Christmas 1514, Hernando made his first visit to his ancestral homeland of Genoa, and it
may have been then that he had the strange encounter he would
record in his biography of his father. Writing many years later, Hernando recalled how, in an attempt to verify his father's assertion that
their family had a long and distinguished maritime history, he stopped
in the Genoese neighborhood of Cugureo and spoke to two brothers
by the name of Colombo, who were the richest men in the region. But
Hernando was unable to gather much information, given that the
younger of the men was over a hundred years old. The achievements
and even the memory of his father's life must have seemed in these
years to be sifting through Hernando's fingers.[7]

His time in Rome, however, seemed to plant in Hernando an
awareness of a form of power different from that to which father and
brother laid claim, one to which his peculiar talents might give him
access and which might allow him to reestablish the family's deterio-
rating fame. This power consisted not in asserting dominion over
things—land, people, precious objects—but rather in making those
things disappear, abstracting from them information like a rare
essence, and one that could then be tabulated, categorized, manipu-
lated. Though Hernando's early exercises in this field—his print catalogue, the indexes he created for books—were limited and flawed,
they were part of a dawning realization that reducing the world he
saw around him to a set of figures and measurements gave him power
over them that was more than human. Like Pacioli's theory of proportions, which promised to unite a world of disparate things (polyhe-
drons, faces, columns) by uncovering their shared geometric patterns,

Hernando's tables gave him an artificial memory that could navigate enormous collections of words, ideas, or objects. What else in the world could be mastered by this strange alchemy?

Not for the first time in Hernando's life, a series of events followed that changed his prospects entirely. In January of 1516, when he was in Florence with the papal court for their rendezvous with Francis, Ferdinand of Aragon died after more than forty years at the center of European politics, history, and culture. Though his daughter, Juana, "La Loca," was still alive, she was relegated to the status of co-monarch while in practice the crown of Castile as well as that of Aragon now passed to her son with Philip of Burgundy—raised till then by Margaret of Austria in the Netherlands—who was crowned as Charles I on 14 March. Not only were the crowns of Aragon and Castile now united for the first time in the same person, but Charles brought with him immense and wealthy possessions in northern Europe and was also the grandson and heir apparent of the Holy Roman Emperor Maximilian I. Yet for Hernando and everyone else in Spain, Charles was something of an unknown quantity: it was to be eighteen months before he arrived in the south from his Burgundian homelands, and when he did, he was found to be a quiet youth, entirely controlled by Flemish counselors, most notably the Lord of Chièvres, Guillaume du Croÿ. If history was later to attribute an urbane cosmopolitanism to Charles—as the man who spoke *Spanish to God, Italian to his mistress, French to men, and German to his horse*—there was little evidence of this in the awkward adolescent who first appeared in Spain in 1517. Troublingly for Hernando, Charles was far removed from the shared histories that had made Isabella and Ferdinand at least somewhat loyal to Columbus and his sons, and the Flemish courtiers with whom he surrounded himself were detached from the Spanish circles of influence Hernando was used to navigating. Soon after acceding to the crown Charles had ordered an immediate review of the Columbus claims to the New World possessions, though mercifully he seems to have been distracted from it soon afterward.

Ferdinand's death closely coincided with that of Isabel de Gamboa, and without her driving the court case in the Sacra Rota, it also drew to a close during 1516. Hernando was free to return to Spain, accompanied by the thousands of books and prints he had acquired during his time in Rome, and armed with a series of ideas that would transform his curious obsession with words, images, and lists into tools at the center of remaking the world. A third death brought Hernando's time in the World City to a fitting close—the pope's elephant, Hanno, died on 8 June 1516. A poetic Last Will and Testament of Hanno earned the title "Master of Pasquino" for a young Pietro Aretino, then secretary to Agostino Chigi, but soon to be the darling of literary Italy. Hernando bid farewell, for now, to the cultured frivolities of Rome.[8]

No portraits of Columbus survive from his lifetime, but this 1519 painting by Sebastiano del Piombo may be the most authoritative and may have been commissioned by Hernando as part of his project to build his father's legend.

The only existing likeness of Hernando Colón, younger and illegitimate child of Columbus, curator of his father's legacy, and builder of the greatest library of the Renaissance.

▶ One of the earliest surviving maps of Hispaniola, showing ships arriving at the capital Santo Domingo. The map, likely in Hernando's own hand, was pasted into one of his books, and may represent his own voyage to the New World with his father in 1502–1504.

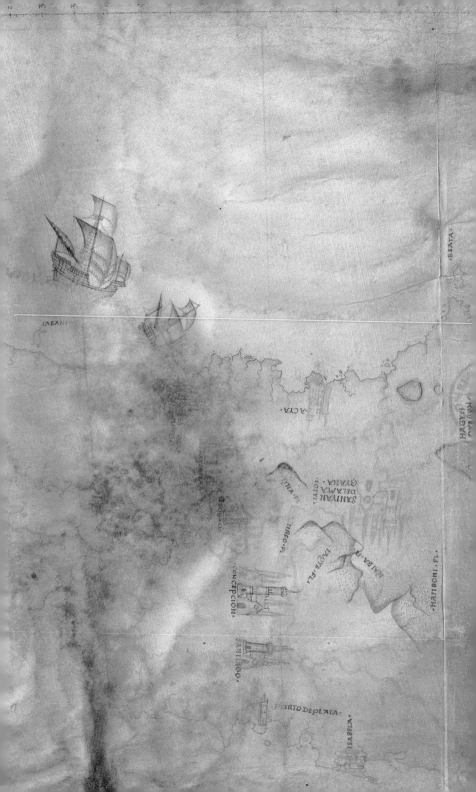

A fresco, once in the Vatican Library, showing the seated Pope Sixtus IV appointing Platina as librarian of this vast book collection. Standing beside Platina in this painting by Melozzo da Forlì is Sixtus's "nephew" (actually rumoured to be his son), who would one day be perhaps the greatest Renaissance pope, Julius II.

◄ A glorious manuscript illumination showing the court of Infante (Prince) Juan (*seated, center*), receiving a lesson from the great Spanish humanist Antonio de Nebrija (*seated, left*). Like the boy kneeling in front of Nebrija, Hernando was present at the center of Spanish power and learning from a young age.

A portrait of the great polymath Luca Pacioli—whom Hernando followed when in Rome—who introduced double-entry bookkeeping to Europe, and developed a grand theory of the geometrical foundations of the world.

A portrait by Raphael of another great polymath and Vatican librarian, Tommaso Inghirami, who was nicknamed "Fedra" after his memorable performance of that character in drag.

Karolus imparat

magnus Annus 14

A picture of Charlemagne by the celebrated painter Albrecht Dürer. The robes in which Hernando saw Charles V of Spain crowned Holy Roman Emperor were believed to be the same as those worn by Charlemagne at his coronation seven hundred years previously.

A sixteenth-century view of Seville, showing the bustling harbour of ships carrying New World cargo, and the library Hernando built to house his books, which can be seen just to the right of where the river disappears around the bend.

IX

An Empire of Dictionaries

Twenty-five years to the day after his father set out from Palos on his first voyage across the Atlantic, Hernando sat down in Alcalá de Henares, to the east of Madrid, and composed the following paragraph.

> *Monday, the 3rd of August 1517*
> *here begins the itinerary*
> Zaragoza, a large city in Aragon, is five leagues from Perdiguera, which is reached by crossing a river by boat a mile outside of Zaragoza—the Ebro—and you pass another river beforehand near Zaragoza by bridge. Perdiguera is a medium-size town of around 100 inhabitants, and from there it is four leagues to La Naraja. . . .

This note, which records the size of towns along the route from Zaragoza to where Hernando was sitting in Alcalá de Henares, as well as the distances between them, is the first of at least 6,635 entries that were compiled in this cosmographical register over the coming years, which he called his *Description of Spain*. The surviving notes, covering over seven hundred densely written folio sheets on both sides and with almost no space left at the margins, bustle with figures relating to population and distance, bewildering any attempt to read this "field journal" like standard prose. Yet at a different level of focus, from this mayhem of information emerges a picture of Spain in extraordinary detail and with minute precision. Unlike most attempts to represent places, which (then as now) start from a broad outline and then fill it in with significant features, Hernando's cosmographical notes work toward the final impression by bringing together an infinitude of seemingly insignificant local observations—as if one were to describe a beach one grain of sand at a time.[1]

Hernando's aim in gathering this hoard of information went further than simply creating a repository covering Spain in its entirety. Of the many designs he had for these cosmographical notes, among the most ambitious was the creation of maps of superlative detail, and capable of infinite reproduction without any loss of precision. This was to be achieved by laying the map out on a grid, beginning with lines of latitude and longitude and then further dividing those squares with lines at every mile of each degree. The concept was so new, however, that Hernando had no name for this kind of grid, and instead resorted to a comparison to get his idea across: *the lines should cross the map as they do on a chessboard, so that from the original picture others can be derived easily.* Just as chess reduced warfare to a series of standardized actors, moves, and directions, allowing its games to be recorded, precisely and re-created identically if necessary, so Hernando's chessboard of Spain would allow his maps to be re-created in previously unimaginable detail. The intended effect, as was later recorded, was to allow someone looking at this image to know the country as if they had been there themselves, or indeed perhaps *better* than if they had been there, as the significant things can be better seen in a drawing than in real life.[2]

The seemingly rather vague term that Hernando chose for this project—usually calling it a "description" of Spain—was in fact a bold statement of allegiance to a series of ambitious ventures that he would have encountered during his time in Italy. These drew their inspiration from the ideas of Ptolemy, the second-century Greek author whose compendium *Geography* came back into European culture in the early fifteenth century after being lost for a millennium. Hernando may have inherited a copy of the *Geography* from his father and had acquired his own copy early on, buying a third shortly after he arrived in Rome, and a fourth before he left, with additional tables of geographic information. While Ptolemy's survey of classical knowledge about the world became widely influential and was central to Columbus's vision of what he would find in the "Indies," it was Ptolemy's ideas about mapmaking that were to have a longer-lasting effect. Central to these were the use of coordinates for fixing locations on maps, which he advocated in the part of his treatise dealing with cartography. Among the projects inspired by this was that of Leon Battista Alberti, whose ambition to resurrect the glories of classical architecture required an accurate survey of Rome's remaining monuments, which would allow him to reconstruct the plan of the ancient city. To achieve this he put aside his spare time, while serving as papal secretary in Rome, to take the bearings of the ancient monuments from the Capitoline Hill using an astrolabe-like instrument, drawing on the techniques used by maritime navigators. Alberti then wrote two treatises deriving from this project, the *Descriptio urbis Romae* (description of the city of Rome), giving his measurements, and the *Ludi rerum mathematicarum*, which outlined a series of mathematical "games" (*ludi*), derived from Euclid's geometry, that could be used to produce a map out of the measurements he had taken. Ironically, the difficulty in fixing Ptolemy's polar coordinates meant Alberti—and Hernando after him—resorted to techniques more similar to those of surveyors than of cartographers.[3]

The term *descriptio*, then, as used by Alberti and by Hernando, meant less a verbal account of a place and more a map or plan, though both compiled written tables of data as a first step in constructing their maps. Alberti did not limit his ambitions to the observation of classical monuments: the rediscovery by Poggio Bracciolini of a manuscript describing the network of Roman waterways led Alberti to reconstruct part of this ancient system—the *Aqua Virgo*, letting out where today's Fontana di Trevi stands—as a monument to the power of Pope Nicholas V; and Alberti's great tract on architecture (inspired by the manuscript of Vitruvius also recovered by Poggio) advocated the resurrection of classical monuments on a much more massive scale. In service of this, Alberti would develop Ptolemy's ideas on how to project maps of the spherical earth onto a flat surface—central to the effectiveness of paper maps—drawing on the help of none other than Paolo dal Pozzo Toscanelli, the Florentine cosmographer whose secret letter expounding the "narrow Atlantic" hypothesis had partly inspired Columbus's First Voyage. Following in Alberti's wake, a range of undertakings sought to make ever more precise records of classical monuments as a first step toward the restoration of the glory of Rome: Flavio Biondo's *Rome instaurata*, which undertook a topographical survey of all the classical monuments known of in the city, Leonardo's attempt to reconstruct Trajan's port of Cittavecchia under the patronage of Leo X, and Raphael's proposal (also to Leo) to produce accurate drawings of all the classical artifacts in the city, as part of an early archaeological project.[4]

A major driver behind these Spanish and Italian cosmographical projects was the notion of *translatio imperii*—the "movement of empire"—which obsessed Renaissance culture. This was the belief that power in the world moved, like a torch in a relay race, from one nation to the next, with only a single empire holding sway at any one time. Though centrally inspired by the history of classical Greece and Rome, the idea also had a biblical underpinning in the interpretation of Nebuchadrezzar's dream by the prophet Daniel: the king's vision of a statue—head of gold, shoulders of silver, torso of bronze, legs of iron, feet of clay—was revealed as prophesying a succession of empires, ending when the final, clay empire was smashed by God and history would be brought to an end. There were many contending theories about exactly *which* empires were represented by the gold, silver, bronze, and iron—Saint Jerome thought they were the Babylonian, Persian, Greek, and Roman empires—but the central idea of a single, dominant world "superpower" was widely accepted (then as now). The most intriguing question regarded which nation would be the next to carry the torch of empire, and it was widely believed the nation that resembled the empires of the past—mirroring their cultural riches and technological achievements—would eventually triumph over the others. The artistic patronage of popes and monarchs was not, then, entirely disinterested, but rather sought to put them in the running for even greater glory. The same was true of the archaeological, surveying, and architectural projects of Alberti, Biondo, Leonardo, and Raphael: a first step toward the rebirth of Roman glory was the compilation of topographical records—tables of information, maps, and plans—at the same or (if possible) at a greater level of accuracy than those of classical authors, providing a framework through which to describe, capture, and control the world around them.[5]

This cultural arms race was very much on Hernando's mind when he was undertaking his *Description of Spain*. He was later to comment that every other Christian nation had detailed surveys of even smaller towns, allowing those who had not been to Rome, Jerusalem, Babylon, or Paris to know these places intimately; only Spain, he lamented, was lacking in such records. The project appears to have begun as nothing more than a sideline, with Hernando simply recording the populations of the towns the court moved through on its slow progress around northern Spain and the distance between them. It seems clear, however, that the project soon began to take up more of Hernando's attention, leading him on outings for the sole purpose of gathering topographical information. An early part of the *Description* charts a series of triangular treks from Alcalá de Henares to the villages of the surrounding countryside, darting out and across and back again, like a spider building a web, and recording distances along the way. Hernando wasn't taking bearings as Alberti had done from the Capitoline Hill—a task beyond the rudimentary surveying techniques available, especially given the lack of telescopes—but by using the longitudinal coordinates for the major cities established by Arabic astronomers and promulgated by Alfonso X, Zacuto, and Nebrija, the rest could be figured out using the distances between minor cities and a basic knowledge of trigonometry, as Alberti had noted in his treatise on mathematical games. The lines drawn by these rapidly multiplying measurements laid out over Spain a network wonderfully reminiscent of Luca Pacioli's diagrams showing the geometry of a human face: the landscape, like everything else, can be broken down into a mosaic of basic shapes.[6]

Though none of the individual elements in the *Description* were Hernando's inventions, in combination they created an unprecedented way of seeing this world. Medieval mapmakers had distorted the physical dimensions in their work to make places of special historical and spiritual significance stand out. A wonderful example of this is the Catalan map (traditionally dated to 1375) that arranged its image of west Africa around the figure of Mansa Musa, the Malian king who had spent so freely on hajj to Mecca in 1325 that he made the value of gold drop in Egypt. These maps were only partly a picture of the physical characteristics of the earth, and partly a memorial to great things that had happened; they were also a monument to God's plan for the earth as a whole. Hernando's *Description* departed from this tradition and sought to capture Spain as it was observed in the present and to set these observations within the dispassionate, objective space of the grid. The numbered lines implied the world portrayed was in the realm of mathematical proportion, scale, and measurement, and not subject to the blurring effects of human experience.[7]

Yet while the level of Hernando's rigor and ambition in this undertaking is astonishing, it must be said the greatest charm of the *Description* lies in its failure to maintain a strict focus on the geometrical relations between towns. The medieval philosopher Nicholas of Cusa had imagined an ideal cartographer as like one who, sitting in a walled city, sends messengers out of its five gates to report on the surrounding countryside: the gates represent the five senses, to each of which Cusa's ideal mapmaker must be alive in order to fully capture the world. Little by little, Hernando slips back into this medieval cartographic mode; the purity of the Euclidean plane becomes permeated by the other arresting qualities of the landscapes and settlements, as if a graph were to take notice of the textured paper on which it is drawn. To begin with this allows for the presence of rivers and the modes of crossing them, together with a note of how distant they are from a particular town—distances often roughly noted as "a crossbow shot" or "a stone's throw" away. Then cursory notes of the kind of terrain that is crossed between towns—plain or coastland—soon admit a more descriptive vocabulary, recording that the land is harsh or barren or fertile. Before long the list of words has multiplied to include pebbled beaches, sweet-water inlets, clear rivers, treacherous hillsides, forests of chestnut and of oak, vineyards, a hot spring that rolls boiling in summer or winter. The abstract space is also invaded by the seasons: the route inland from Sanlúcar, where Hernando had landed with his father in 1504, has lagoons that turn into marshes in winter and must be waded through knee-deep; the Galician town of Porriño has delicious turnips as big as pitchers, and nearby in Sancroy they have a technique for saving their vines by digging up their roots and stems and planting them again the next year. At Santo Domingo de la Calzada, Hernando has noted the presence of rabbit warrens and has left drawings in the margins of his notebook. The character of the towns also begins to seep through and blend with the statistics. At Ourense there is a miraculous cross that was found in the ocean and which is said to make hair and beards grow, and at Madrid, the tomb of Saint Isidore, which was built with the help of angels. The town of San Sebastián de los Reyes was founded in living memory when the residents of Alcobendas abandoned their homes in protest against their harsh seignorial master. Touchingly, these observations even record the existence of tiny settlements, such as the dilapidated Riaza on the slopes of the Sierra de Pico Cebollera, which has only five inhabitants. Perhaps most wonderful are the occasions when the land and the bodies within it act upon each other, turning this abstract space into a realm of lived experiences, as when Hernando notes that at Monterrey the wine is so strong it cannot be drunk unless mixed with water, or that at Bobadilla the soil is said to be a cure for fevers. These delightful notes remind us discovery is not the sole preserve of those traveling in distant lands but could take the form of a discovery within, unpacking the unknown densities of apparently familiar countryside.[8]

These observations, at first slipping into the entries of the *Description* almost by mistake, quickly added another dimension to Hernando's project. Though he seems from the outset to have imagined an encyclopedia of Spanish towns to accompany the maps, listing each settlement alphabetically with its vital statistics, the plans eventually included not only its location and its surroundings and its hereditary lords but *everything memorable about the place*. The expansion of Hernando's ambitions also, however, meant there was no possibility of completing this Herculean labor without assistance. Within months of starting the project, he had recruited a team of assistants who would be sent throughout the realm of Spain to record information for the *Description* on his behalf; returning, they compiled their findings into a central register that started to expand at an even more rapid rate, and eventually this multitude of individually walked itineraries would be turned into a cosmographical table and map of Spain. After compiling the first sixty or so pages of information himself, different hands begin to appear in Hernando's manuscript, describing in detail the journeys taken by these emissaries. In a pattern he was to follow for the rest of his life, Hernando formed around himself something that was less like the normal pattern for scholars in the Republic of Letters—a network of like-minded equals comparing their findings toward shared ends—and more like a ship's crew, acting like extensions of their captain's body, giving him eyes and ears and limbs beyond the capacity of a single individual.[9]

Even with a group of surveyors to help him, the logistics of the project would likely have been impossible for a private individual to undertake, and the costs of employing a team of educated assistants to gather and transcribe the information may have been beyond Hernando's means, given he was still surviving on the modest sum accorded to him in the 1511 settlement of the Columbus case. Whether through good fortune or necessity, then, the project took on a more official character as it expanded its scope and ambition. Though most of the new king's actions, after his arrival in September 1517, showed his slight regard for his Spanish subjects—such as

Charles's galling appointment of the nephew of his favorite, Chièvres, to Spain's most prestigious bishopric at Toledo—he seems to have taken favorable notice of Hernando at an early stage. The surveyors gathering information for the *Description* were provided with royal letters, instructing local officials to cooperate with them in the exercise, suggesting perhaps Hernando had already encountered the obstacle of irate magnates suspicious of this strange man who was pacing their land and asking questions. The prospect of a detailed and methodical survey of these kingdoms must have been attractive to Charles and his advisers, who were wrangling both with the bewildering patchwork of Spanish government and with strong resistance to his attempts to import trusted Flemish officials into key positions. Whereas Charles's grandfather Maximilian I had reputedly been able to draw maps of his dominions from memory, the uncharted nature of Spanish territory must have greatly contributed to the frustrations of the stranger king. This grant of royal patronage was a major coup for Hernando's project, not only signaling a certain amount of prestige at Charles's court, but ensuring the credibility of the information gathered as the project left Hernando's personal control. It was evidently a great concern to Hernando that his emissaries maintain the same meticulous standards as he had during the initial phase of the project, and to achieve this Hernando designed an ingenious double-lock system to ensure the facts taken down for the *Description* were trustworthy: the emissaries would record the testimony of the local officials, and their findings would in turn be certified by the local notary before being brought back to the central repository. This meant the emissaries were kept honest by having to gather testimony from local dignitaries—rather than simply producing their own, unsubstantiated observations—and the local dignitaries were kept honest by having their words witnessed as a legal document. Fascinatingly, Hernando not only allowed for but positively expected his representatives to retread the same territory: only by comparing several independent reports could they be sure the information was entirely exact. Hernando's great engine for mapping Spain was, in effect, a gigantic sieve that worked through repetition and verification to weed out human error.[10]

Charles's admiration for the robustness of Hernando's methods seems to have been so great that he not only gave the *Description* his blessing but also considerably expanded Hernando's remit, ordering him in May 1518 also to work on an official map to guide Spanish ships to the Indies. Though the Casa de Contratación in Seville, charged with the administration of all of Spain's overseas ventures, had produced an official map of the Atlantic shipping routes—the *Padrón Real*—as early as 1507, it was widely agreed this was vastly inferior to the charts used by their Portuguese rivals. One of Charles's first acts upon arriving in Spain was to appoint Sebastian Cabot, son of the Italian explorer John Cabot, as *pilót mayor* (chief navigator), in charge of all technical aspects of Spanish shipping, from the making of maps to the training of pilots and the certification of all nautical instruments. Though the family name, and the ambitious design of the *Description*, doubtless contributed to Hernando's appointment to assist Cabot, it may have been a manuscript dialogue circulating at court in 1517–18, likely written by Hernando, that sealed his nomination. The dialogue, which takes the form of a conversation between the young "Fulgencio" and the learned "Theodosio" about the dire state of Spanish mapmaking, accuses the old Casa de Contratación of a conspiracy of incompetence, in which the *pilót mayor* only signed off on maps by his cronies, who in turn knew nothing other than what they were told by the pilots, who themselves were trained by the same mapmakers to begin with. This cozy arrangement was perpetuated, it seems, because the *pilót mayor* took a cut from the sales of maps produced by the mapmakers he knew. As a result of this corrupt system, Theodosio laments, Spanish pilots are often up to six degrees out in their measurements—a distance roughly equivalent to the entire breadth of Spain. This hopeless situation was compounded by the fact that no one at the Casa de Contratación understood either magnetic variation—the different relation of the compass needle to true north at various points on the globe, which may have been Hernando's own discovery—or the arcane way mapmakers used to try to correct for this anomaly, which employed two different systems for degrees of latitude in different parts of the globe. The Portuguese, by contrast, could sail six thousand miles without going a single degree wrong in their calculations, and this level of technical superiority was sure to handicap Spain in its quest for global dominion. Theodosio's solution to the problem was similar to the one Hernando had employed in the *Description*: the Casa de Contratación should compile all the information received from the hundreds of ships that sailed between Spain and the Indies every year and use an average of these findings to reach a progressively refined picture of the Atlantic waterways.[11]

Envy of Portugal's superior navigational techniques may well explain a cryptic entry in the notes for the *Description* from November 1518. On the twenty-fourth of that month, one of Hernando's emissaries arrived at his house in Seville to find his steward and the rest of the household in residence but Hernando himself absent, gone to Portugal, it seems, *defraçado*—"incognito." If Hernando's mission was an act of cosmographical espionage, as the secrecy and later revelations would indicate, then it was part of a larger arms race between the two nations that was souring relations between Manuel I and his nephew Charles. Prominent among the defections this year was that of Fernão de Magalhães—better known to history as Ferdinand Magellan—who had arrived at the court in Valladolid in March 1518 and offered to put himself in Charles's service. Following a path similar to that of Columbus, Magellan had come to Spain after his proposals had fallen on deaf ears at the Portuguese court.

Magellan's proposed voyage, sailing westward to the Moluccas, had more modest ambitions than the scheme of Hernando's that had been rejected in 1511—it was not, indeed, clear that Magellan intended to circle the globe at all—though what he offered might achieve the same end of global domination by slightly different means. This voyage, Magellan argued, would establish once and for all that the Molucca islands, fount of the Eastern spice trade, were less than 180° west from the Tordesillas Line and thus lay indisputably within the dominion granted to the Spanish by the treaty of 1494. In his bid to play king-maker by diverting the flood of Eastern wealth toward Spain, Magellan also had a trump card that Hernando had lacked: Magellan claimed to have seen, in the possession of the king of Portugal, a map showing the location of the long-sought-after strait that would allow access from the western Atlantic through the Americas to the great "Southern Sea," the first European sightings of which were reported by the Spaniard Núñez de Balboa in 1513 after an arduous crossing of Darién (Panama). Repeated Portuguese protests against the Spanish harboring a defector and even capitalizing on his treachery had little effect, and by September 1518 Magellan was sufficiently forward in the preparations for his voyage to simply respond to emissaries from Portugal that there was now no turning back.

The major remaining obstacle to Magellan's voyage was the fact that his gambit about the strait on the king of Portugal's map seems to have been a bluff. No such strait is shown on the map of Martín de Behaim, where the chronicler of Magellan's voyage claims he saw it, nor does one appear on any other surviving map of the period. It may well be, then, that Hernando's clandestine mission to Portugal in November of 1518 was an attempt to substantiate Magellan's claims, and that his efforts were directed not at the pilfering of maps themselves, but rather at coaxing one or more Portuguese mapmakers into defection. Two key cartographers appeared in Seville for the first time in late 1518 or early 1519: Diogo (or, in Spain, Diego) Ribeiro, who was recorded in Spain as a maker of maps and instruments for Magellan's voyage, and who would work closely with Hernando at the Casa de Contratación over the coming years, and Jorge Reinel, scion of the greatest family of Portuguese mapmakers, whose father Pedro Reinel was forced to follow and bring him home before his treachery went beyond what his youth could excuse.[12]

Hernando had noted in March 1518, in the volume of Seneca's *Tragedies* that was his frequent companion, that this period found him "distracted with many tasks and much travel"—something of an understatement, given that he was presiding over the *Description* and perhaps continuing to gather geographical information himself, attempting to salvage the family fortunes in the court of Charles and in the law courts, working toward a navigational chart of the Atlantic, and perhaps engaging in stealing state secrets from Portugal. For all this, he chose this hectic moment to embark on yet another immense task. He left the court at Zaragoza and retired to Segovia, at the northern foot of the Sierra de Guadarrama, where in November the heat of the summer would just have been abating and returning some of that town's alpine feel. Segovia is a curious palimpsest of Castilian history, from the Roman aqueduct, at once both impossibly elegant and indestructible, to the stirring perfection of its Romanesque churches—San Millan, San Martín, San Esteban, and Veracruz. Though they are called Romanesque, their domes and patterned, rounded arches remind us these are memories less of Rome than of Byzantium. Alongside these are the convent of Corpus Christi, scarcely hiding its former status as the town's main synagogue, and the Moorish and Mudéjar elements of the much-reconstructed Alcázar, the triangular fortress that juts its bow out into the V where the rivers Esmera and Clamora meet. The Romanesque capitals, with their biblical kings who have become crusader knights, and their griffins, centaurs, and grotesques, speak less to Rome than to these other diasporas from the Levant. The private houses testify to the Segovians' awareness of their town as an architectural menagerie, from the punk-Gothic Casa de los Picos, faced by 617 granite spikes, to the symmetrical foliage on the façade of the Palacio del Conde Alpuente. At the top of the hill, the Gothic elements of the Romanesque cathedral—its cloister, choir, and portal—heralded links to France and Germany in the north, part of the Castilian assertion of an Old Christian heritage against the inescapable reality of its mestizo past.[13]

One morning Hernando began by writing the exact time (eight in the morning, on 6 September) and then the following definition:

A: the first letter both for the Greeks and for other nations, either because they imitate the Hebrew letters from which they all come, or because it is the first sound the newborn makes, or because in pronouncing it is the first sound one makes. . . .

This is the opening entry of almost three thousand entries that cover the 1,476 pages of Hernando's *Vocabulario* or Latin Dictionary, and it is followed by a nine-page entry on the word *ab*. While Hernando's ambition and stamina must be a matter for amazement, his decision to move from mapping and tabulating places to the art of dictionary making would not have been as surprising then as it is now. The foremost Spanish humanist, Antonio de Nebrija, had, after all, paired cosmography with his main occupation of philology and had seen no distance between the two, famously pronouncing in the preface to his great Castilian grammar of 1492 that "language is the instrument of empire," and that if Ferdinand and Isabella wanted their burgeoning empire to last as long as the Romans, then they would need a language as precisely constructed as Latin. Language would have to be fixed, like coordinates on a map, if it was to be used to build an empire in the real world.[14]

Interestingly, however, Hernando chose to begin a dictionary not of the Spanish language but of Latin, perhaps because even Latin, as the foundation for all the Romance languages, was itself only crudely documented by this point. For all the dignity attributed to Latin in European culture, Hernando had not yet found a satisfactory dictionary of the master tongue of Renaissance thought. The great dictionary of the Middle Ages, the thirteenth-century *Catholicon* of Giovanni Balbi of Genoa, was no longer felt to meet the high standards of humanist scholarship in the classical languages. In an attempt to remedy this, Hernando began to synthesize a vast range of existing language treatises that drew together examples of how each word had been used by the best writers of antiquity. This was—though not consciously defined as such—a dictionary on historical principles, one that did not so much set out to create an authoritative definition for words as an attempt to map how those words had been used by authors in the past. This excitingly allowed not only for variety in how words were used, but (more important) for a notion of historical development to emerge: a map of language alive to the organic creature it was treating, a creature that is constantly evolving and can only be charted in its movements, rather than pinned down to a particular set of meanings.[15]

Yet as the opening entry on the letter *A* suggests, something was at stake here greater even than the power of Spanish culture relative to the other empires-in-waiting of Europe. Hernando's definition of the first letter of the Latin alphabet is not merely telling us what it means, but rather making an argument in various forms that its place in the alphabet is *natural*, rather than arbitrary: this may be because it descends from aleph, the first letter of the Hebrew alphabet and therefore of the language closest to the original tongue given to Adam by God, or because both phonetics and the history of language prove that it belongs before the other letters, either as the most basic sound that can be made by the human mouth or as an interjection, the most basic part of speech. In addition to the many other tasks it may have set itself, then, Hernando's dictionary belongs in the long history of attempts, stretching back to Plato's dialogue *Cratylus* and beyond, to establish language as something with a solid and definite relationship to the world of things, rather than simply being a conventional tool that only works because we all agree on what each word means. Language and the tools used to fix and order it, such as the alphabet, were worryingly unstable foundations on which to ground human knowledge, and any attempt to organize the world using language needed first to tackle this basic problem. Just as the *Description* sought to put Spain on the path to empire by fixing its geographic features, so the linguistic tools of Europe needed to be put on a firm footing if they were to serve the universal empire Hernando had in mind.[16]

The need for Spain's tools of empire to be at the ready was given fresh urgency when, in February 1519, news reached Charles at the Monastery of Montserrat that his grandfather Maximilian I had died in early January at his seat of power in Austria. While Maximilian's death immediately added the Archduchy of Austria to Charles's titles, it more importantly meant the throne of the Holy Roman Emperor was now vacant. This was not an honor that Charles would inherit automatically: the selection of the new emperor lay in the hands of an unpredictable group of seven German princes and churchmen—the Electors—who appointed a king of the Romans, who then had to be crowned emperor by the pope. While the House of Habsburg, of which Charles was the scion, had held the post for much of the past century, the current election was far from a done deal. As Raphael's fresco in the Vatican suggested, the French king, Francis, also had ambitions, as did Charles's uncle by marriage, Henry VIII of England, and while Henry's hopes were founded on little more than the schemes of his right-hand man, Wolsey, Francis had realistic hopes of gaining the votes controlled by the pope. In large part, this was because Leo didn't want to see Charles as both king of Naples and Holy Roman Emperor, something that would bring immense power too close to the doorstep of the Vatican.

This election contest seemed to rouse in the indolent young Spanish king the first evidence of determination and skill at political brinksmanship. The extraordinary lengths and great expense to which the candidates went to further their bids, when placed against the fairly limited powers that came with being emperor, makes clear the symbolic power this nominal empire brought with it: if a nation's cultural riches and the dignity of its language could improve its chances as the next torchbearer of global empire, being crowned by the pope with the iron crown of Charlemagne provided the most important ritual and material confirmation of this inherited role. In the end, the outcome turned on the will of the bankers: both Francis and Charles relied on the Fuggers of Austria to lend them ready cash to bribe the electors, and the Fuggers, feeling a sudden national loyalty to Charles's German descent, cut off Francis's credit. The election duly fell to Charles on 28 June.[17]

Charles's triumph nevertheless created its own series of problems.

After having spent less than two years in his Spanish dominions, he abruptly announced his intention to return to his northern lands for his investiture as king of the Romans and, adding insult to injury, asked the Castilian Cortes (parliament) to bear the enormous expense of both his election and his triumphal progress north, having already blown through the six hundred thousand ducats they gave him in 1518 (and, in a further insult, having spent much of it in the kingdom of Aragon). To make matters worse, he overplayed his hand by insisting the Cortes be summoned to attend his pleasure at distant Santiago de Compostela, and then still farther up the road at the Galician port of La Coruña, from which he was busy preparing a fleet for departure. Charles seemed hardly to notice the level of outrage felt in Spain at this foreign visitor who many doubted would ever return, though his fixation on the north was perhaps understandable, given reports that the runners-up in the imperial election—Francis I and Henry VIII— were preparing an alliance against him. After making the minor concession that he would appoint no further foreigners to positions of power in Castile—and doing so in a convincing performance of the Castilian tongue, which he had been learning—Charles took his subsidy and promptly appointed the dour Dutch cardinal Adrian of Utrecht as regent in his absence, before turning his back on a Spain that was breaking into open revolt even as he set sail for England.

Hernando's reading in Seville during the autumn of 1519 showed signs of his assiduous preparation to be of use to the emperor-elect as he accompanied Charles on a victory lap through his Burgundian and German lands. After returning to a summary of Roman history he had set aside a few years earlier, Hernando spent the rest of the summer making his way through the thick wad of pamphlets that were bound together with it. We can follow his progress through his characteristic notes that record the dates on which he read each of them. These eighteen works, mostly of a dozen pages or less, had been purchased in Rome in the autumn of 1515 and probably bound together soon afterward, to preserve them from the disintegration that was their usual fate. Hernando's choice to buy and keep these flimsy pamphlets, at which most collectors would have turned up their noses, would have struck many as odd, and his decision to study them among the thousands of works he now owned may have seemed even stranger. But this miscellaneous haul from the Roman *cartolai* gave Hernando a sweeping view of global affairs and their historical context, one that anticipated by a century and a half the invention of newspapers, even though it served much the same purpose. Hernando read in these pamphlets of the Portuguese victories in north and east Africa—at Azamor in Mauretania and Kilwa and Mombasa on the Swahili coast—as well as of the taking of Malacca (in modern Malaysia) by the Duke of Albuquerque, who as Admiral of the Indian Ocean was the Portuguese counterpart to the Columbuses. Then there was a series of reports on military ventures in which the French were engaged, from the campaigns of the Italian Wars to the Auld Alliance with Scotland and its punishing defeat at the Battle of Flodden in 1513, and news of a major battle between the Ottoman Sultan Selim I and Shah Ismail, Sofi of Persia, which represented a turning of the Ottoman war machine east, away from its century-long onslaught on the eastern edges of Western Christendom. To the north of this, however, was news of the Hungarian peasants' revolt in 1514 and a major victory late that year for Polish and Lithuanian forces over the Muscovites at Orsha. Though Hernando's volume of cheap print—which mostly covers events five years distant and even stretches back to the fifteenth century and also included Roman history and saints' lives—hardly counts as breaking news in our digital world, it connected him, in a way few other royal counselors could rival, to the chatter of the globe over which Charles sought to rule. This global vision was partial and primitive, but Hernando may have begun to realize his library could be a resource with few parallels, an eye in a kingdom of the blind.[18]

Yet the momentous political and historical climate in which Hernando would be submerged as he traveled north may not have been the foremost thing on his mind. If his childhood had taught him to look toward Rome as the center of the world, his time in the city would have alerted him to the competing and perhaps superior claims of the north. While Hernando would have been familiar with Flemish architecture from a young age, and Isabella's collection of paintings by van Eyck and Rogier van der Weyden would have given the Spanish court a distinctly Dutch feel, his move to begin collecting printed images put him in a terrain where the north's dominance was plain. The prints he had collected in Rome, by the likes of Giovanni Battista Palumba and Ugo da Carpi, were mere prentice work when set against the woodcuts and engravings of the Dutch and German masters, Israhel van Meckenem and Lucas Cranach, and of course the uncontested genius of the printed image, Albrecht Dürer. Indeed, according to the great art biographer Vasari, Dürer's trip to Venice in 1505 was not to learn from the Italians but to secure legal protection against the incessant pirating and plagiarism of his work. Dürer's dominance in the world of the printed image was rivaled and perhaps even surpassed in the world of printed words by the towering figure of Erasmus: both men had mastered the revolutionary techniques of the Italian Renaissance, in pictorial realism as in classical scholarship, but had added to these a powerful awareness of the possibilities of print itself. Unlike the geniuses Hernando had met in Rome, who playacted the glories of the ancient city in hopes of tricking it back into life, Erasmus and Dürer were cannily attuned not just to what the past had to offer them but also to how the present might be reshaping it. Even as Magellan sailed west with the aim of encircling the world, and Hernando's team of cosmographers crawled Spain to fix its dimensions, Hernando himself headed north, approaching what some might call the ground zero of modernity: the unprecedented sense that the present might be entirely different from—perhaps in some senses superior to—the past.

This intense excitement at what lay in wait to the north may go some way to explaining Hernando's actions at the rocky Galician seaport of La Coruña in May 1520, as he waited for the fleet to set sail. His brother, Diego, was also there, finally headed back to Hispaniola after being reinstated as governor and an absence of more than five years. This was the result of continual lobbying, undertaken in large part by Hernando, particularly during an audience with Charles at Barcelona early in 1519 in which (according to Bartolomé de Las Casas) Hernando had made a forceful case for his brother's reinstatement and presented an audacious vision for the future of the Americas, one that would expand the Spanish presence through a series of posts for trading and exploration, but avoid the evils of conquest and subjugation. (Las Casas also suggests Hernando—ever his father's son—also scuppered this plan by asking that the Columbus family be given perpetual control of these posts.) But while a document drawn up by Diego at La Coruña mentions Hernando's tireless efforts on the family's behalf, both at the Spanish court and during the long years spent clearing up Diego's mess in Rome, and announces Diego's intention to award Hernando a lifetime pension of two hundred thousand maravedís, all this merely serves to cover up the real function of the agreement: to deprive Hernando of any direct claim to his patrimony, making him not one of Columbus's heirs but merely a pensioner in his brother's entourage. In truth, the family estates had never been equal to paying the lavish bequests Columbus had given his beloved younger son, but even the fraction of his inheritance Hernando was granted in the 1511 settlement seems to have gone unpaid, replaced instead by debts and empty promises from Diego on which Hernando could never collect. While some who knew Diego—including Bartolomé de Las Casas and Oviedo—left testimonies of his character suggesting he was simple rather than malicious, he certainly showed little compunction in casting aside the brother who had worked unstintingly for him for much of his life, and whom his father in his dying months had begged him to protect. Hernando probably signed away his legal status as one of his father's heirs at La Coruña because, as always, he put the interests of the family ahead of his own; but this moment made even starker the division of Columbus's inheritance, by which the elder son held all of the worldly goods and the younger all of the sublime spirit that had allowed their father to change the shape of the world.[19]

PART III

An

ATLAS

of the

WORD

X

The Devil in the Details

In the thickly detailed diary he kept of the years 1520–21, Albrecht Dürer records a visit he made on 27 August 1520 to the Town Hall in Brussels. There he saw objects newly brought to Europe from the coast of Mexico, where the Emperor Moctezuma had sent them from his inland capital to Hernán Cortés. Two rooms were filled with Aztec armor, weapons, shields, sacred costumes, bed coverings, and assorted instruments, the touchable things of an otherworld. The most striking exhibit was of two disks, each six feet broad: a "sun" made of pure gold and a "moon" of pure silver, of the type thought to have served the Mexica as calendars. Hernando would already have seen these objects in Spain, perhaps when they were first displayed at Valladolid in March earlier that year, when they were accompanied by five Totonac Indians kitted out with gloves against the Spanish winter; this unveiling had drawn breathless descriptions from Peter Martyr, Bartolomé de Las Casas, and the assembled ambassadors of Europe. But the response to them by a maker such as Dürer is particularly touching, as he knew better than most what went into their creation: "I have never in my life seen anything that gave my heart such delight as these things," he wrote with unusual emotion, "for I saw among them marvelously skillful objects and was amazed at the subtle ingeniousness of people in foreign lands. I cannot find words to describe all those things I found there." This was Europe's first introduction to the Aztec culture, and reports would soon afterward reach Spain of Moctezuma's city-in-a-lake Tenochtitlan, a new island in the European imagination that the conquistadores had nicknamed Venice the Rich. Moctezuma's capital was duly accorded an entry in Benedetto Bordone's compendium of island places, the *Isolario* of 1526.[1]

Dürer had made the trek from his home in Nuremberg (along with his wife) in hopes of seeing his imperial pension renewed, which had been frozen since the death of Maximilian the previous year; the minutiae of his daily life, recorded in his diary, wonderfully mixes the price of red chalk and roast chicken with near-miraculous encounters—meetings with Erasmus, a viewing of a lost masterpiece by Rogier van der Weyden, and the gift of a ring once owned by the recently deceased Raphael, brought to Dürer by one of the disciples among whom the artist distributed his worldly goods. The venerable and celebrated artist grumbled constantly at the tolls collected at each corner as he crossed the fractured German lands, using his fame to gain free passes where he could, and otherwise using his own prints as currency, exchanging them or selling them as necessary.

Hernando had arrived in the Low Countries six weeks before Dürer, appearing first at Antwerp in mid-June, where he began once again to purchase books on the scale that he had last done at Rome. Fittingly enough, his first acquisition in these northern climes was the *editio princeps* (first printed edition) of Saxo Grammaticus's great *History of the Danes*, in which Hernando might have read the story of the unfortunate Prince Amleth (later more famous as "Hamlet"). It seems likely that on the way to Antwerp Hernando had accompanied the main imperial party during their six-day stop in England, where Charles was eager to preempt Henry's fledgling dalliance with the French king. In a characteristic display of his chivalric virtue, Henry rode all night to meet Charles when news of the Spanish fleet arrived; writing to Erasmus, Thomas More said it was impossible to describe Henry's delight on hearing that Charles was coming to England. The

(*opposite*) A map of the great Aztec city Tenochtitlan from Hernando's copy of the report on the city by Hernán Cortés.

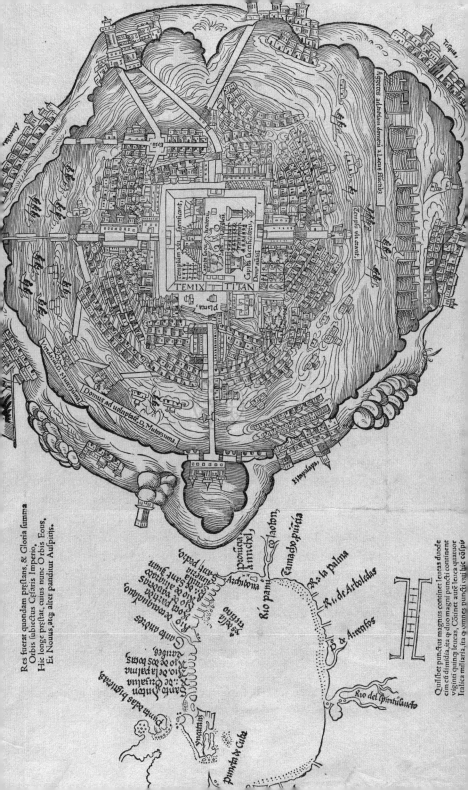

two kings later signed at Canterbury an agreement to continue the friendly relations that had long existed between the two royal houses. But the rendezvous could not last long: Henry was due, only days later, to meet Francis outside Calais for a diplomatic pageant that became known as the Field of the Cloth of Gold, though he promised Charles to meet with him again soon afterward at Calais. Henry was evidently enjoying his ability to tilt the balance between the two great powers of Europe. The imperial party was not going to allow Henry or the French to have everything their own way, however, and at Antwerp (barely a hundred miles from the Field of the Cloth of Gold) Charles was greeted with a triumphal entry of his own, processing through four hundred arches, forty feet broad and two stories high, topped by performers enacting tributes to the emperor-elect. That these tableaux included "living statues" of naked young women apparently delighted Dürer but greatly embarrassed Charles.[2]

In the time between the festivities surrounding Charles's arrival and the coronation itself, for which Hernando made his way to Charlemagne's cathedral at Aachen in October, the Low Countries offered a plethora of marvels for visitors like Hernando. In Antwerp there were the prized bones of a giant, who once collected tolls from travelers on the river Scheldt, and from whose hand—severed by Brabo, nephew of Julius Caesar's—Antwerp was reputed to have sprung. (Later in the century the Dutch antiquarian Johan van Gorp identified the giant's bones as the remains of an elephant in his *On Giant Slaying—Gigantomachie*.) At Brussels, Dürer noted having seen the jawbone of a whale six feet across, and visitors to the city could see *The Garden of Earthly Delights* by Hieronymus Bosch at the town house of the Count of Nassau. Hernando added to these swirling impressions by his choice of reading, purchasing on 29 August and at once beginning to read the *Magnus elucidarius* of Konrad von Mure, a medieval compendium of mythical knowledge that he annotated heavily as he went. In much of

(*opposite*) A sketch of Antwerp harbor by the great artist Albrecht Dürer, made while he and Hernando were staying in that city in 1520.

the art of the Low Countries, and especially in the paintings of Bosch and the prints of Dürer, Hernando would have found a crowded density completely unlike the spare and dignified classicism under whose spell he had seen the world at Rome (though perhaps reminiscent of the riotous Flamenco-Spanish Gothic of his youth). Unlike the Italian Renaissance, whose response to the messiness of life was to oppose it with the majesty of neoclassical order, the art of the north in the same period embraced chaos as its raw material. It required its viewers to excavate meaning from the thicket of symbolic images with which they were confronted, to read the image as they would a text. It comes as no surprise that Dürer was a devotee of Egyptian hieroglyphs, and he had illustrated a translation of the *Hieroglyphica* by his friend Willibald Pirckheimer with images not unlike the sacred Aztec disks he saw at Brussels. Hieroglyphs offered a picture language, drawn from nature and perhaps offering a way past the weaknesses of the spoken word. This was not a vision of a world bereft of order—far from it: instead, it showed order as emerging from chaos for those with the right gift, as Christ stares out from amid the crowds of sneering and grotesque faces in the late passion scenes of Bosch and Dürer.[3]

This tension, between almost excessive copiousness and a desire to impose order, also characterized the thought of the north. This was nowhere better seen than in the career of the leading light of northern humanism, whom Hernando met that autumn—Desiderius Erasmus, whose early works were of such riotous hilarity that he was widely suspected of being the secret author of *Julius Excluded from Heaven*, the indictment of that pope's debauchery that had titillated and scandalized Rome during Hernando's years there. Though he never admitted to writing the satire, Erasmus did allow that it sounded a lot like his style, especially in his rather edgy early works—the satiric dialogues of Lucian that he translated with Thomas More, and *The Praise of Folly*, in which Erasmus had trotted forth the foolishness of every group in society to subject it to witheringly ironic praise (Hernando had bought his copy in Rome in November 1515). The worst of Erasmus's scorn is reserved for the folly of the Roman Curia, whose shortcomings he ruthlessly exposes in terms reminiscent of *Julius Excluded from Heaven*. Following Erasmus's lead, the presses of northern Europe poured forth satires of social abuses—mostly directed at the Church and its failings—that combined humanist learning and classical wit with traditional forms of bawdy stories and scurrilous jokes: Sebastian Brant's *Ship of Fools* and tales of the German trickster Till Eulenspiegel, as well as the stories coming out of Thomas More's household that mocked the ways of greedy and lustful monks. But from the beginning, Erasmus's delight at this almost riotous excess was balanced by a belief that it must be purged and order restored. In a clever inversion, Erasmus had ended his *Praise of Folly* by showing he was not (in fact) joking about praising foolishness: it was, in a sense, a good thing to be a fool, but only if you were a *Christian fool*, who was foolish in the things of this world because you were focused on the hereafter. That, he suggested, was a kind of folly that purged the rest of the foolishness of the world. The same thing went for the celebrated Erasmian literary style, which encouraged *copiousness*— reveling in classical thought and in imitation of classical style—but only if kept under control by the person using it and turned toward serious ends. Copiousness without order was dangerous. The overwhelming plenitude of the world must be subjected to order, lest it engulf the one who seeks to use it.[4]

When Hernando met Erasmus in Louvain in early October 1520, stopping on the way from Brussels to the coronation at Aachen, the Dutch humanist was at the peak of his career. In the years following *The Praise of Folly*, Erasmus had turned his prodigious linguistic and scholarly talents to a project that showed the extraordinary power of this new form of learning: he had produced, in 1516, an edition of the Greek New Testament he claimed was more accurate than that used by Saint Jerome for the Vulgate, the Latin Bible that had stood at the heart of Christian thought, law, and life for over a thousand years; soon afterward, Erasmus produced his own Latin translation, intended to replace Jerome's. Erasmus had undertaken his edition and translation in a spirit of devout piety, but the Church had every reason to fear the destabilizing effects of humanist classical scholarship: after all, the Italian humanist Lorenzo Valla had used his knowledge of Latin's historical development to demonstrate that the Donation of Constantine— the foundation of the Church's claim to political as well as spiritual power—was not a genuine document from the fourth century but a later forgery. Valla's explosive document, long circulating only in manuscript, had recently seen a rash of printings, and Hernando snapped up a copy during this tour of the north. Any number of Church practices, whose authority had been established over the centuries using Jerome's Vulgate, might now be open to question. And the town of Louvain, where Hernando met Erasmus, was the home of an institution that threatened to multiply the Church's problems in this respect: the new Collegium Trilingue, or College of the Three Languages, which strove to make yet more Erasmuses by teaching Latin, Greek, and Hebrew to the highest standards of humanist scholarship. Soon there would be a generation of students with the tools to analyze the ancient Greek and Hebrew texts and to contest the interpretation of these words by the Roman Curia. On another level, the Collegium Trilingue was a symbol of resistance to a narrow definition of learning, which would exclude anything that was not Christian and Latin, a sentiment Erasmus most forcefully expressed in the volume he presented to Hernando when they met. The *Antibarbarorum*—"Against the barbarians"—was a rallying cry against the self-congratulating ignorance of the barbarians *within* Christian Europe, who were closed off to any thought they deemed "unchristian":

> If we are forbidden to use the inventions of the pagan world, what shall we have left, I ask you, in the fields, in the towns, in churches and houses and workshops, at home, at war, in private and in public? To such an extent it is true that we Christians have nothing we have not inherited from the pagans. The fact that we write Latin, speak it in one way or another, comes to us from the pagans; they discovered writing, they invented the use of speech.

This spirit of radical openness—believing knowledge was a good in itself and should be made widely available—drove the program of Erasmus and other humanists to hunt down the best writings wherever they could be found. This not only involved tracking down lost books in the most surprising places—as when in 1516 Erasmus charged a friend to search the land of the Dacians for a fabled tower of ancient books—but then also working with the great printers of the age to make them available in robust editions—greatly handsome and precise, but also made to go out into the world and be used. Hernando, in his library open to *all books in all subjects from within Christendom and without*, and in the tools he would use it to produce, would build on these foundations in ways Erasmus could not have begun to imagine.[5]

Hernando left a fitting monument to Erasmus in one of the crucial building blocks of his library, which certainly existed in an early form by this point. This was his *Abecedarium*, or alphabetical list of authors and book titles contained in the library. In the final version of the *Abecedarium* Erasmus is one of only two modern authors to have a section of their own separate from the main list, where in the back of the catalogue Hernando records 185 separate works by Erasmus contained in the library (the identity of the second author will become important in due course). In a sense, given that Hernando sought to acquire *every* book he could find for the library, this is less a personal tribute to Erasmus than a simple witness to his presence in the world of the early printed book: the great humanist, a million copies of whose writings are estimated to have been printed during his life, had simply overflowed from his place in the alphabetical lists, forcing Hernando to remove him to a separate supplement. If on the one hand Hernando's catalogue is simply recognizing Erasmus as a prolific author, however, it is also true (in another, rather counterintuitive sense) that the very notion of an "author" is *created* by lists such as Hernando's. As the number of books available to collectors grew, and new ways of organizing them became necessary, a list of authors in alphabetical order probably seemed a fairly unproblematic place to start. This kind of list, after all, is only using a memorable and seemingly innocuous fact about a book—the name of the person who wrote it—to differentiate it from other books, like a unique set of coordinates on a map. This obviously makes it difficult to list any work whose title isn't in the Roman alphabet, and Hernando's 1513 copy of the first printed book in the Ethiopian language of Geez (mistakenly believed to be a form of the biblical Chaldean tongue) would have presented a challenge were it not given a Latin title page. But the major problem is that this kind of list requires the book actually to have a named author: if too many books are anonymous, as a vast number of medieval works were, the list simply doesn't work—there would be an endless "Anon" section, and little way of navigating within it. Similarly, the list only really works if each book has a single, agreed-upon author, rather than being the product of many people who revised or translated or added to it or changed it over time. So the alphabetical list forces the librarian, and the users of the library, to attribute each of the books to a single, named author, in a sense "inventing" the notion of the author (or at least its centrality) as a matter of necessity. Over time, something else would happen: the character of the authors and the character of the works assigned to them began to become inseparable. Our sense of who an author is derives in large part from the works assigned to that author, and (on the contrary) we tend to come to works with preconceptions, preconceptions derived from what we know (or think we know) about the author. This inevitably leads to two kinds of mistakes: authors having works falsely attributed to them, giving us the wrong impression of who they were, and works *actually* written by the author being declared fakes, removing part of the author's life that the author (or we) would rather not see. As the greatest author of the age, Erasmus was involved in both kinds of deception, perhaps even at the same time: Was *Julius Excluded from Heaven* falsely attributed to him, making him more of an agent provocateur than he really was, or was it falsely excluded from the list of his work, distancing him from the violent ruptures that were just over the horizon?[6]

The influence of northern humanism may also be behind another curious decision the bibliomaniac Hernando made at this time. Beginning in 1520, he began to include in his purchase notes the exchange rates between the local currency and the money he used at home. This slightly odd, pedantic habit actually suggests Hernando was in tune with one of the most exciting strains of thought emerging in the period, pioneered by Erasmus's great friend Guillaume Budé. Budé had gained fame with the publication of a learned treatise on Roman coinage, weights, and measures—a slender claim to celebrity, it would seem, until one realizes it brought to life countless passages in ancient works that until then were all but meaningless. It is all very well, for instance, to say Dürer valued the treasures of Moctezuma at one hundred thousand gulden, but that means little unless one knows exactly how much one hundred thousand gulden is. For instance, one might mention it was the same as the dowry of the Queen of Hungary or the worth of the province of Friesland. Budé's interest in the *realia* of ancient life, the nitty-gritty everyday details of how much stuff cost in classical Rome, was not merely pedantry but a realization that the great ideas and artworks of the past were meaningless unless you understood the world in which they were produced and to which they referred. But it was also an insight into the nature of currency, of money as a medium of exchange with which we confer value upon an arbitrary object. Hernando, who at fourteen had deduced from the great value the Guanaja tribe placed on cocoa beans that they must serve as a form of currency, was clearly attuned to this from an early age; the age of exploration was to provide countless other examples of this, as in the shell currency the Portuguese encountered in the King-dom of Kongo. Far from precious metals being the only thing that could be used as currency, *anything* could be used for money as long as it was scarce enough that people couldn't just pick it up off the ground and so flood the market with it—and the Kongo used a par-ticular shell found only on one island controlled by the king. All that remained then was to confer upon your coin, bean, or shell an agreed value. The realization would dawn only slowly that this really had to be an *agreed* value, though: just as language works only when both people agree what a word means, money works only when both parties agree what it is worth—it was useless to insist, as the precious metals of the New World began to flood Europe, that they were still worth as much as when they were scarce, though this concept of inflation caught on too slowly to save many early-modern nations from disaster. Hernando's notes on exchange rates, then, which always give the value of the local currency (*craicers, pfenigs, quaternos, julios, florines*) in Spanish *ducados*, are (when properly used) a form of time machine: like Budé's study of Roman coinage, they resurrect a lost world of trade networks and fluctuating relationships between societies, recorded in the language of currency exchange.[7]

On 23 October 1520, Charles lay facedown on the floor of Aachen's cathedral, his arms stretched out in the form of a cross. Hernando would have been one of those in the crowd who shouted, in response to a question from the archbishop of Cologne, that they were eager to serve Charles as king of the Romans and emperor-elect. They then looked on as Charles's chest, head, shoulders, elbows, wrists, and hands were smeared with holy oil and he was wrapped in coronation robes believed to be over seven hundred years old; they had supposedly first been wrapped around the Emperor Charlemagne. The robes, captured in a painting by Dürer a few years previously, were every bit as sumptuous as Hernando might have expected: a cascade of gold cloth, only occasionally interrupted by scarlet embroidery and the black silhouettes of the imperial eagle. The regalia also included an orb, scepter, sword, slippers, and crown, which once held at its center the orphan stone, reputed to shine in the dark and protect the honor of the empire, but likely lost by 1520. In a world where power was still deeply linked to ritual displays of magnificence, few spectacles can have equaled this

(*opposite*) A souvenir print (c.1470–80) of the imperial treasures of the Holy Roman emperor, which Hernando would have seen at the coronation in Aachen. The print is number 2959 in Hernando's collection.

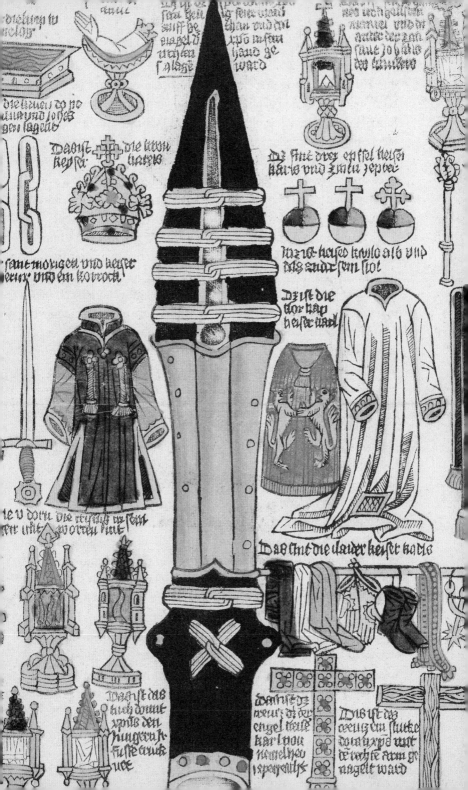

one. Such a display was desperately needed, because even as Charles was receiving the adulation of his newly expanded territories, news reached him of the widespread revolt gripping central Castile, with many of the chief cities of the kingdom advertising their disdain for this foreign king and declaring instead their allegiance to his mother, whom they hoped to control more easily. Charles had made a mistake by not only leaving his kingdoms before they were secured, but leaving them in the care of a pious Dutch cardinal with little head for statecraft, let alone war.[8]

As he made his way from Aachen toward Worms, where the Imperial Court would spend Christmas, Hernando began to prepare for the next great tumult to grip Europe. At Cologne and Mainz in late November he bought his first works by Martin Luther and the philosopher of Luther's movement, Melanchthon, part of a once-massive haul of Reformist works in Hernando's collection that have since been almost entirely destroyed, either removed by the Inquisition after his death or lost in one of the disasters that lay ahead, but records of which can still be found in his catalogues. Luther's harangue against the corruption of the Roman Curia was part of a long history of protest against clerical abuses, and his charge sheet of ninety-five theses, published in Wittenberg in 1517, included familiar complaints about the indulgences issued to cover the eye-watering costs of building St. Peter's (theses nos. 82 and 86), echoing similar complaints in *Julius Excluded from Heaven* and the Roman satires pinned to the statue of Pasquino. The Saxon monk's critique of these indulgences followed a logic strangely reminiscent of monetary inflation: If Leo could simply print indulgences (documents forgiving sins) to raise money for his building projects, why shouldn't he forgive *all* people their sins as an act of love? The unspoken answer was obvious: because if he did, the Vatican would have flooded the market with its currency—letters of indulgence—and made them worthless. This addiction to indulgences suggested to Luther (and increasingly many others) that the Church was no longer a place of charity but a den of money changers. Leo tried repeatedly to bring Luther to heel, but the protection of Frederick the Wise of Saxony, and the amplifying effect of the printing press, soon saw Luther's protest movement gaining in confidence and breadth. Leo declared in a papal bull of 1520 that forty-one of the theses were heretical enough to have earned the monk and his disciples excommunication, and Luther's works were burned in the Piazza Navona as part of the Agone festivities shortly thereafter; Luther responded by burning the bull of excommunication outside the city gates of Wittenberg later that year.[9]

It is unclear whether Hernando's impressive collection of Reformist writings purchased in these years is evidence that he was drawn to Luther (at least at this stage) along with Dürer and much of Germany, or if he was simply sweeping the bookstores for all of their most important wares as his ambitions grew toward the universal. Certainly he had spent long enough at Rome to know Luther's accusations had plenty of substance, and Hernando undoubtedly revered Erasmus, whose faith (like Luther's) was focused on internal spirituality and who was highly suspicious of external religiosity. But Luther's critique of the Roman Church was even now quickly diverging from a broadly supported list of reforms to Church practices and becoming a vision that stood to raze the traditional understanding of what the Church was. In essence, this was a vision of the incommensurateness of man and God. A revelation had struck Luther, namely that God was so infinitely powerful we could not possibly barter with Him for forgiveness, using the currency of indulgences and pilgrimages and building churches. You cannot pay someone with cocoa beans or shells when for them those things have no value. So infinite was the gulf between the things of God and those of Man that only unconditional surrender—faith—could have any value to Him, and thus man's interior relationship with God was infinitely more important than any external object or act. Though Luther held back from the full consequences of this logic, keeping a place for the Church in fostering this faith by preaching and the administration of sacraments, it was hard to avoid the conclusion to which this led: in this world of unconvertible currency, there would be no place for the Church as a bureau de change between man and God, turning the coin of this world into something that had value in the next.[10]

Luther was a subject of Charles's as Holy Roman Emperor, and the support for the schismatic monk by Frederick of Saxony—who had tipped the balance in favor of Charles during the imperial election—made it diplomatic for Charles to give Luther a hearing on the matter. The monk was duly summoned to address the Imperial Diet (parliament) at Worms when it gathered early in 1521, where after being uncharacteristically lost for words on 17 April, he expounded his doctrines and declared he was standing his ground. By the time he made his stand, however, Hernando was long gone from Worms. On 19 January, the financial constraints imposed by the agreement with Diego at La Coruña had suddenly been alleviated when Charles presented Hernando with a gift of two thousand ducats—more than his pension from Diego would amount to in three years, assuming it was paid—for services already rendered, as well as a salary of two hundred thousand maravedís a year, to be drawn from the treasury of his family's seat of power, Hispaniola. The grant does not specify for which services Hernando was being rewarded—the *Description*, the navigational chart to the Indies, or simply adding luster to Charles's entourage as witness to the New World his father had discovered—but Hernando clearly had plans for where to spend it. Having arranged, before the award was even official, for agents of the Genoese Grimaldi banking family to receive the salary in Hispaniola and pay it out to Hernando in Europe—minus a healthy fee, of course—Hernando was bound for Venice, the city-state in a lagoon that, of all the islands of the European imagination, was the one most central to Hernando's obsession—books. Venice had used its history of craftsmanship and international trade to reach the top of the pile of early print centers, and Hernando was headed toward this unimaginably delectable emporium.[11]

Leaving Worms, Hernando traced the main arteries of the Renaissance book trade: up the Rhine through Speyer, Strasbourg, and

Sélestat to Basel, another city-state whose strategic position—wedged between Italy, France, and Germany but relatively independent of all of them—already gave it an outsize influence in the trade, allowing Erasmus to spread his books from there to the rest of Europe with unprecedented speed. From Basel, Hernando seems not to have taken the easier route, eastward to Innsbruck and from there down to the Veneto, but rather to have taken the Simplon Pass through the Bernese Alps down to Lombardy, tracing in reverse the path taken by Italian book hunters as they scoured the monastic libraries of Switzerland and southern Germany for manuscripts of classical texts. An account from later in his life suggests Hernando undertook most of these journeys on horseback, becoming hardened during years in the saddle both to the discomforts of long treks and of the miserable inns of central Europe, of which Erasmus left a biting satire, denouncing them as execrably stuffy and filled with mud from the boots of traveling merchants. In Lombardy, Hernando stayed at Milan, Pavia, and Cremona, on his way to visit Genoa, pausing only briefly at each of these places before he reached his final destination at Venice. Rumors were arriving there, at the same time as Hernando, that Luther's plea to Charles had failed, that the heretic was now outlawed as well as excommunicated, and that he had been kidnapped, perhaps assassinated, after leaving Worms. Hernando may have heard reports that Charles had finally summoned the gravity required by the situation and responded by pouring scorn on the notion that *a single monk, trusting to his private judgment, has opposed the faith held by all Christians for a thousand years and more*, before swearing *to defend this holy cause with all my dominions, my friends, my body and my blood, my life and my soul*. Despite Charles's censure of the schismatic, Hernando continued to buy Lutheran and anti-Lutheran books in large numbers in Venice, where their plentiful supply suggested the dangerous mixture of print and protest in that town; but now, in the spiritual homeland of the printed book, Hernando's mind was beginning to turn from individual volumes to the idea of the universe of books.[12]

Hernando arrived in Venice just in time for the Sensa, the traditional Venetian celebration of the Feast of the Ascension, in which the doge, seated aboard the official barge or *bucintoro* with a ceremonial sword-bearer, "married" the city of Saint Mark to the lagoon in which it lay, ritually asserting the republic's dominion over the Adriatic beyond. This may have seemed a touch hubristic that year, given the hand dropping the traditional wedding ring into the water belonged to the sickly and increasingly frail octogenarian Doge Leonardo Loredan. Under Loredan's leadership the Venetian Republic had suffered a number of heavy military losses, most significantly to the French at the Battle of Agnadello in 1509, when the Venetians lost all the lands they had taken from Rome a few years earlier, and Loredan had (in the eyes of many) shown himself a coward by refusing to go to the front. Hernando had observed much of this feud from the point of view of Rome, and its two warlike popes (Julius and Leo), who were determined to hold back the influence of the island city-state. Yet for Venice the diplomatic and military maneuvers against it were evidence of the unchristian treachery of the popes: these peninsular wars, it was felt, distracted Venice from its main task of halting the advance of Ottoman power westward through the Mediterranean. The pamphlet Hernando had read when preparing to accompany Charles north, which suggested the Ottomans were turning their attentions east toward Persia, had proved a false dawn. Days after Hernando had arrived in Venice, a long-delayed embassy was dispatched to the Ottoman court with official congratulations to the new sultan, Suleiman (not yet "the Magnificent"), who had succeeded Selim I at his death late in the previous year. The ambassador's *relazione* describing the embassy would report that Suleiman, a paleskinned, dark-haired youth in his mid-twenties whose mysterious air was heightened by the turban he wore low over his eyes, was more belligerent than his father and a greater foe to the Christians and the Jews within his realm; but by then the ambassador was merely reporting what everyone already knew. Belgrade fell to Suleiman four months after Hernando arrived, giving the Ottoman Empire access to the Upper Danube and threatening the Venetian territories in Dalma-

tia. This added further to the woes of the Serenissima, whose mercantile dominance had faced challenges in the preceding decades from
the rise of a Portuguese sea route to the east and the Genoese expansion to the west.[13]

By the time Belgrade fell in August, however, Doge Loredan had
died, and Hernando had the chance to witness one of the most byzantine and extraordinary political processes in all of Europe. Rumors
of Loredan's death had already seeped through the city before it was
officially announced on 22 June, though the secrecy was being preserved not as part of a conspiracy, but rather to give his family time to
move out of the Ducal Palace, so the official state funeral could keep
a healthy distance between the doge as political figurehead and as
man of flesh and blood, with family relations and private possessions.
Separating the doge from his family life was important because, unlike
almost anywhere else in Europe, the leader of Venice was not hereditary but elected, and the Serenissima had devised an immensely complex machinery to keep it that way, preventing any one family or
faction from turning the post into a form of monarchy. The doge lay
in state in the Sala di Piovegi, then, for three days, as the deceased
father of the republic rather than the patriarch of the Loredan family,
before putrescence brought on by the warm weather, and the distor-
tion of his face that made it a fright to behold, forced the removal of
the body to the church of Giovanni e Paolo (or rather San Zane Polo
in the proudly distinct Venetian dialect).

This observance done, the election of the new doge could
commence—though perhaps *selection* is a better word for the long
series of lotteries and ballots put in place to safeguard the process
from corruption. Venice was a republic, yet its electoral process was
far from wholly democratic: only members of the Great Council, consisting of twenty-five hundred or so male members of ancient Venetian families listed in the so-called Golden Book, could participate.
From this body thirty were chosen by lottery, of whom none could be
related, and then these thirty were further winnowed by lot to a Committee of Nine; the Nine elected forty more, who were reduced to a

Committee of Twelve by lot and given the chance to elect twenty-five more; they in turn were reduced by lot to nine and elected forty-five, who were reduced by lot to a Committee of Eleven. The Eleven chose forty-one, none of whom could have been on the previous electoral committees (the Nine, the Twelve, and the Eleven), who (finally) elected the doge. At each of these stages each of the candidates had to carry a healthy majority of the vote. The design of the system made it incredibly difficult to rig, because of the lotteries and the rules to prevent any one person (or family) from participating at different stages of the process, and also because it was so complex that it would be hard to know where to start. All the same, a proposal was floated during the election that Hernando witnessed in 1521 to *double* the number of electoral steps, just in case. This was the mode that Venice, the mercantile republic par excellence, had developed to inoculate itself against the monopolization of power.[14]

That we know the Venetian Republic in such intimate detail in this period—in fact, our knowledge of the period as a whole, far beyond Venice—is in large part due to the efforts of a single man, who was cut very much from the same cloth as Hernando and was later to play a central part in Hernando's projects. Marin Sanuto was a member of one of the lesser Golden Book families, and he had held some minor administrative posts during his career, but he had early on discovered that (like Hernando) his true passion was for creating compendiums of information, mostly about his beloved city. After compiling a guide to the ancient gods and goddesses at the age of fifteen, Sanuto went on to write a description of the lands of the Veneto, a compendium about the lives of the doges up to 1494, and an encyclopedic tract about the city that began by detailing each of the magistracies of the republic but ended up including lists of "churches, monasteries, schools, bridges, ferry crossings, prisons, feast days, ceremonies, sights to show foreigners . . . moneys minted, fresh fish." Sanuto's masterpiece, however, begun in the wake of the French invasion of 1494, was a detailed log of all the chatter he picked up by hanging around the Brolo gardens (near the Ducal Palace) and the Campo San Giacomo (near the mercantile hub of the Rialto Bridge). With one ear to the political world and one to that of trade, Sanuto compiled fifty-eight manuscript volumes over forty years, filled with the most detailed reports of the day on statecraft, diplomacy, finance, exploration, scandal, culture, spirituality, and warfare, funneling them from the public places of this metropolitan hub into his study, where he composed his notes. Unlike the model of discovery pursued by Hernando and his father, in which the field of knowledge is expanded by the heroic individual crossing oceans, circumnavigating the earth, dispatching cartographic emissaries, engaging in foreign espionage, and searching the book markets of the world for information, Sanuto's model was resolutely stationary. He deeply resented any move that might take him away from Venice, and indeed when Hernando arrived, Sanuto was still nursing a grudge against the anonymous traitor who had had the gall to put him forward for the lucrative post of maritime inspector, a threat to remove him from his listening post that he deeply resented. Sanuto had, in effect, made literal Nicholas of Cusa's metaphor of the ideal cartographer: sitting in his study, surrounded by a library, Sanuto used the traffic of the city as his sensory organ, feeling the wider world through its reach. His model reversed the idea of exploration: instead of venturing forth, the agent placed himself at the center of a network, connecting to as many nodes as possible, and simply recorded history as it flowed over and through him.[15]

The importance of Sanuto's undertaking was recognized, to a limited extent, by the Venetian government, including the new doge, Antonio Grimani, who urged him to continue with his important task. While Venice was a pioneer in the world of diplomacy, creating an international network of *orators* (proto-ambassadors) who reported back in detail on current events abroad, only Sanuto's archive gave this diplomatic nervous system a brain in which to store its findings, one made possible in part by the new cheap medium of paper, which had become available in the West as late as the fourteenth century. But Sanuto and the thin-meshed net with which he trawled the world were never fully absorbed into the machinery of state, and he was repeatedly passed over for the post of official historian in favor of humanists trained in a more traditional mode, who could provide an account of the nation focused on high politics and the destinies of state. What, after all, were the official engines of the republic to do with Sanuto's detailed description of daily life, such as the story of a woman named Bernadina who, during Hernando's stay there, murdered her abusive husband, Luca, "the Jew," from Monte Negro and buried him beneath the stairs? Sanuto records in detail her exposure after forging a letter from her husband that claimed he was away on business at Rome, which aroused the suspicions of his family, and her failure to find a discreet accomplice to move the stinking corpse; then how she was paraded along the Grand Canal to her home, where her right hand was severed and hung from her neck, before being beaten senseless in between the pillars of San Marco to prepare her for quartering; and finally how she continued to crawl forward even as she was stabbed in the chest and the throat. Yet all of these things made no sense in the official archive of the state, which could not yet see the connection between the powers of the republic and Luca's rights over his battered wife. Sanuto's omnivorousness would save for posterity the lived experience of Venice that was filtered out of the official archive of the Serenissima.[16]

The same channels of communication that made Venice a perfect spot for Sanuto to lie in wait for information had made its book trade one of the most important in Europe. On the other side of the Rialto from the Campo San Giacomo, clustered around the German warehouse at the Fondaco dei Tedeschi, the print district had emerged with the new technology that had been brought south by emigrating German craftsmen. Venice had been important since the early days of print, with its status as a long-standing entrepôt between Western and Eastern Christendom attracting many of the Byzantine scholars fleeing the Ottoman expansion, bringing their knowledge of Greek and its texts with them. But while these things allowed Venetian printers to capitalize on the hunger for fresh discoveries from the ancient world, it was Venice's canny businessmen who enabled the city to emerge triumphant as the leading center of print. While the new technology spread rapidly all over Europe, it became clear the market simply wasn't big enough yet for a large number of printing houses, leaving only the best-resourced operations to survive the drought that followed. After the dust had settled, Venice and a few other cities across Europe had virtual monopolies on large-scale printing, led by families such as the Giunti of Venice and the Kobergers of Nuremberg. This gave these places—and these families—extensive power over what Europe knew and how it thought. Yet sustaining this power required that they secure markets for their products, which they did by cloning existing trade networks and financial links to create vast and fluid channels to spread their printed materials throughout Europe (and eventually beyond). The same channels also brought back books from foreign markets, as suggested by the fact that Hernando could walk through the streets of this Adriatic port and buy the latest writings of Luther and his colleagues in distant Bavaria. This had allowed Sanuto to collect a library of 6,500 volumes without ever leaving Venice, and Hernando followed suit during his six-month stay, entrusting no fewer than 1,637 books to the merchant Octaviano Grimaldi for shipping back to Spain when departing from the island city in mid-October, having also borrowed two hundred ducats from the Grimaldi to pay for this treasure of books. From its bookshops he had not only been able to acquire the jewels of Venetian printing, but had also bought tomes from Germany, Switzerland, and the Netherlands. From Sanuto and from Venice he was learning the lesson that universal reach did not necessarily require you to be everywhere: instead, one could simply place oneself in the thoroughfares and let the world come to you.[17]

XI

No Place like Home

B y Easter 1522 Hernando was back in the Low Countries, where in late March he was in Brussels and reading the copy of Thomas More's *Utopia* that he had bought two years before. He had arrived back laden with purchases, as even though he had left his considerable Venetian spree behind for shipping home, he continued to amass vast quantities of books on the return journey, beginning with seven hundred titles bought in Nuremberg during the month he spent there over Christmas. Between Nuremberg and Frankfurt, he took time to visit Würzburg, where the bibliomaniac Johannes Trithemius had left his library, an extraordinary monument to the kings of Germany, though beneath Hernando's ambition, given its limited focus on learned works from Christendom and its disdain for print. In his travels through the German lands, Hernando may have heard of another figure who had ambitions for a kind of superhuman knowledge: the itinerant necromancer and magician named "Doctor Faustus," around whom a legend grew up (of diabolic partnerships and punishments) that reflected the deep fears of the age, of how one might in striving for these forms of the universal be passing into forbidden territory. From Würzburg Hernando had passed through Cologne, buying two hundred more books in three days, and Mainz, where he bought a further thousand in a month. The pace of his acquisitions was quickening; it had now long surpassed the point at which he could possibly have given individual consideration to each purchase and was becoming something different entirely, a kind of mad and desperate bid to spin his passion for print into a scheme of unprecedented proportions.[1]

Reading More's *Utopia*, as the imperial fleet prepared to sail to England, Hernando must have felt as if he was looking in a mirror that showed all the pieces of his life so far, even if in a slightly unusual guise—voyages of exploration, maps, printing, language, the search for forms of perfection hitherto unknown. The feel of *Utopia* would have been familiar to Hernando: it presents itself as a report of a recent voyage to a newly discovered island on the other side of the world, one that More claims to have taken down from the mouth of the explorer—a Portuguese mariner called Raphael Hythloday—during a conversation in a garden in Antwerp. Hernando may even have wondered whether he knew Hythloday, given that this man claimed to have been a part of Amerigo Vespucci's crew before setting off on his own. The island that Hythloday claimed to have discovered, however, was far superior to anything Vespucci or Columbus had come across: on it is found nothing less than the perfect society, in which all things have been designed to produce the ideal form of life. Cities are planted at equal distances, in a grid, to ensure they are just close enough to travel between, yet not in competition for resources; property is communal (though competition still exists, in forms of civic pride such as gardening); couples intended for marriage see each other naked first to ensure sexual compatibility; even abattoirs are banned from the city limits to ensure the citizens of Utopia do not become too accustomed to blood and violence. But there was one problem: the exact location of the island seems to have been lost, and all because someone in that Antwerp garden coughed at the precise moment when Hythloday was revealing the whereabouts of this perfect paradise.

Hernando probably had enough Greek by this point—after years of work to improve his command of the language—to realize More's *Utopia* was a kind of learned prank, a spirited humanist game along the lines of Erasmus's *Praise of Folly*, and an act of homage to another fictional country dreamed up by a great philosopher, Plato's *Republic*. As part of this, More was making fun of the Age of Exploration with its unlikely travelers' tales of new Edens, as well as the navigational incompetence that was all too often a feature of that age. The game was given away to those whose Greek was good enough: the name *Hythloday* means "speaker of nonsense," *Utopia* means "no place," and even the Latin version of More's name (*Morus*) means "fool" in Greek. Not everyone was in on the joke, and the preface tells of the poor soul who put in to be bishop of Utopia. But if *Utopia* was meant to be playful, it was not simply a joke: instead, it revealed the profound importance of exploratory voyages for European thought, in giving them a way of considering the advantages and disadvantages of various social customs. If the world contained an infinitude of islands each with a different society, as it must have seemed to on Hernando's voyage of 1502–4, then surely *one* of them must be perfect—and what would that society look like? The idea that the perfect society could be created not by personal piety and God's grace but rather by engineering it through particular rules and practices was radical and profoundly important. Hernando would take the idea to heart in designing his library: as a form of the world in miniature, it would also succeed or fail on the basis of the rules he put in place to govern it, rules that were increasingly beginning to obsess him.

The perfect society designed by More in *Utopia* could be summed up, in a sense, like one of those old jokes: what the Renaissance humanist wanted was English landscape, Greek culture, and Roman government. (In the end, the colonies More and his countrymen would build unfortunately gave the world English culture, a landscape formed by Roman-style slavery, and Greek government.) It quickly becomes obvious that Utopia is, really, just England, with its capital Aumorote (shadow city) and chief river, Anydrus (without water), providing a distorted reflection of London and the Thames. Yet that is part of the point: it suggests the perfect society need not be discovered on some far-off island, but could be built right here at home. Key to this is to dispense with a pigheaded attachment to the way things have always been done, and Hythloday delivers a withering attack on those who fear to be found wiser than their forefathers. The perfect society should be founded on principles derived from reason, not tradition. More is, however, enough of a humanist not to want *everything* to be wiped clean and derived from first principles following logic: rather, he arranges it so that a shipwreck twelve hundred years ago brought Egyptian and Roman culture to Utopia in a pure state, and the perfect Utopians take to classical culture like fish to water. Hythloday and his companions can add only one cultural achievement to this perfect world, this paradise of civic reason and classical culture: they give the Utopians a printing press. The perfect humanist society, then, was a Europe resurrected in a classical guise and transplanted to the New World, but thriving on the new energies of the printing press.

The idea of a world made perfect by its rules was not the only thing Hernando would have found interesting in More's work. The edition of *Utopia* that Hernando was reading in Brussels was the 1518 Basel edition, which he had bought in Ghent in 1520 and left behind in the Netherlands during his trip to Venice. A recently resurfaced copy of the 1516 first edition of *Utopia*—published in Louvain and edited by Erasmus—was probably also owned by Hernando, but it is no surprise he bought the second edition as well, as this one contained several additions designed to draw in readers from across the continent: a map of the fictitious country designed by Ambrosius Holbein (brother of the more famous Hans), and two texts in the Utopian language—an alphabet and a short poem by the founder and first king, Utopus. Maps and alphabets were common features of early printed books on exploration, as they gave the reader a way of imagining the newfound lands and some artifacts of the culture. For instance, Bernard von Breydenbach's book on the Holy Land, which Hernando owned both in Latin and in Spanish translation, provided the alphabets of Arabic, Hebrew, Greek, Chaldean, Syriac, Armenian, and "Abbasinian or Indian" (though these get more fanciful in the latter parts of the list). The Utopian alphabet was another scholarly joke intended to add to the "evidence" that this patently fake island existed; but it was also an important joke, as suggested by the fact that the printer Froben had gone to the considerable expense of having movable type cut in a nonexistent language. It was an important joke because, to many Renaissance thinkers, the perfect *people* must have the perfect *language*, and (like the Egyptian and the Taino hieroglyphs) the perfect language was one that escaped the ambiguity and slipperiness of language in the world of sinners, one that (in the words of one historian of utopias) "led the spirit to its goals by the most natural and perfect paths." It was also an important joke for Hernando because it was perhaps around this time that he first started developing his own set of hieroglyphs, a secret alphabet to describe the books in his beloved library, and his biblioglyphs (book symbols) bear a striking resemblance to the alphabet of the Utopians.[2]

Hernando's system of signs is described in detail by his library assistant, Juan Pérez, and is designed to allow the viewer, at a glance, to learn a vast amount of information about the book being described. The basic component is a shape that tells the size of the book—folio, quarto, octavo, duodecimo. On to these, marks are added that tell us how long the book is (one page, up to five pages, up to ten . . .), whether it is in columns, whether it is divided into chapters, whether it has an index, whether it is in poetry or prose, in manuscript or print, is complete or faulty, perfect or damaged, in the original language or a translation, is a response to another work or not, is presented in the author's name or under a pseudonym. So the symbols for More's *Utopia* would be ⊕ ⬭, showing that it is a quarto volume in Latin, with prefatory poems, in one column but with no index. The components of Hernando's sign system, like the Utopian alphabet, consist of variations on a few basic shapes—circles, squares, and triangles—which are bisected or quartered to form other characters.

(*opposite*) Two scripts designed to convey the perfect language: Thomas More's Utopian alphabet (*top*) and a table of hieroglyphic signs Hernando used to describe his books (*below*).

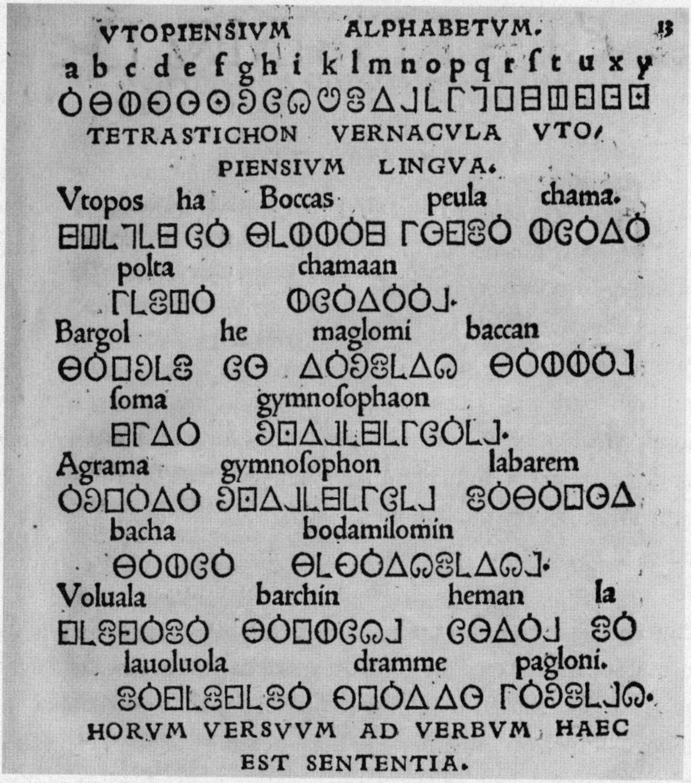

a b c d e f g h i k l m n o p q r f t u x y

ⒺⒽⒸⒹⒸⒼⒼⒼⒼⒼⒼⒼⒼⒼⒼⒼⒼⒼⒼⒼⒼⒼⒼⒼ

TETRASTICHON VERNACVLA VTO⁄

PIENSIVM LINGVA.

Vtopos ha Boccas peula chama.

polta chamaan

Bargol he maglomi baccan

foma gymnofophaon

Agrama gymnofophon labarem

bacha bodamilomin

Voluala barchin heman la

lauoluola dramme pagloni.

HORVM VERSVVM AD VERBVM HAEC

EST SENTENTIA.

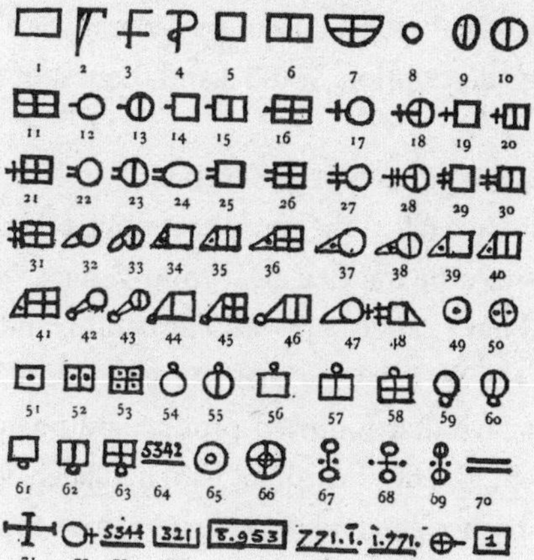

Like Luca Pacioli's theories of divine proportion or the Ptolemaic maps laid out on a grid, it seemed the surest way to fix a face, a landscape, or a language was to link it to the pure and simple universal truths of geometry.

During his Christmas in Nuremberg, Hernando may have learned that its most famous citizen, Dürer, was coming to the same conclusions: not only was he putting the finishing touches to his own book on human proportion and the mathematics of the human body, but he was completing a grand allegorical painting for the town hall of Nuremberg showing how pictograms and hieroglyphs offered a triumphant path past the frailties of normal language. Dürer's lost mural, which survives only in his drawings for its design, shows the slander and deception of common language being opposed by truth in the form of a cryptic symbol: a blazing sun, identical to the sun he had used to illustrate the *Hieroglyphica* and perhaps also rather like the lost Aztec calendar he had just seen in Brussels. Picture languages—pictograms, hieroglyphs, symbols—offered a route past normal speech to voice the great universal truths that lay just beyond the grasp of Renaissance thought. The creation of this alphabet of biblioglyphs was another piece in the emerging puzzle of Hernando's universal library: It was all very well to gather a vast quantity of books together, but what then? How was one to even speak about these books in any but the vaguest and most general ways, and could one be sure that one's description would stand the test of time?[3]

Even as Hernando's library began to take shape, events across the Continent must have given the sense that political matters were also coming to a head. As he traveled away from Venice, word of the death of Leo X would have caught up with Hernando, and perhaps of the celebrations in the Serenissima that had greeted news of the pope's death. The conclave that followed produced an astonishing result: Adrian of Utrecht, the dour cardinal who had been serving as regent in Charles V's absence and had thus presided over the near-loss of his Spanish lands to the revolting Comuneros (only to be saved by a few noble families loyal to the king), had been appointed pope. Though it transpired that his election was a ruse by Giulio de' Medici, who, having failed to secure the necessary votes for himself, thought to win favor with Charles while putting an old man in the post as a place-holder, it must have seemed to Charles that everything was finally falling into line: first the empire, and now a pope he could reasonably expect to control.

Hernando left Calais with the imperial party on 26 May, and they were greeted at Dover by Cardinal Wolsey and Secretary More, with King Henry joining shortly afterward, having arranged for his visit to be unannounced so that it could seem to be prompted by spontaneous affection for Charles. They made their way together to Greenwich, where Charles's aunt (Queen Catherine) and cousin (Princess Mary) were waiting, and where on 4 and 5 June a magnificent entertainment was staged, with Henry emerging from artificial gold and silver mountains to joust in golden costume, accompanied by nine knights dressed all in yellow. A series of masques and revels followed, designed by the court composer William Cornish—which celebrated the Anglo-Spanish alliance by portraying an unruly French horse tamed by the heroism of England and Spain—and then three days of talks between Henry and Charles. Hernando, who never had much time for the business of chivalry, must have breathed a sigh of relief when the imperial party left Greenwich for London. After another round of triumphal entertainments to welcome them to the city, he was free to explore the bookshops around St. Paul's, where during the month of June he bought a further eighty works for the library. This seems a rather small number after the hauls of hundreds and thousands from Venice, Nuremberg, Cologne, and Mainz, but in fact it is a testimony to the health and cosmopolitan nature of the London bookshops that Hernando was able to find so many books there—from two dozen cities across the Netherlands, France, Italy, and Germany, as well as ones printed in England—that he had been unable to find anywhere else. Included among these was a manuscript volume of Italian humanist comedies and letters, many of which are unknown elsewhere: the networks created by humanist friendships and the printing press meant that, for all it was in many ways a rather peripheral and unimportant place, England was in other ways a vibrant part of European culture.[4]

As well as the London bookstores, the other thing that left an impression on Hernando during his visit was the English beer, and charmingly his memory of it reconfigures how we imagine his travels through Europe. Many years later, when writing the biography of his father, he repeatedly remarked on the uncanny similarity between the maize wine made by the natives of Guanaja and Veragua and the beer drunk in England, just as he compared the covered canoes of the Guanaja to the gondolas of Venice. Yet Hernando had never actually been to England or Venice when he traveled through the Caribbean. In truth, then, in Europe he was seeing things that reminded him of what he had experienced on the other side of the Atlantic; for him, in a sense, this world was new while that of his youth was old. English beer tasted just like the Veragua ale, and the Venetian gondola looked the same as the Guanaja canoe.[5]

The imperial fleet left Southampton on 4 July and arrived at Santander on the northern Spanish coast on 16 July, probably following on their return voyage a route designed by Hernando and presented to the emperor before departure, and which Hernando later recalled as among the services he had done the emperor. In his proposed route, Hernando was probably simply reproducing, perhaps with modifications, the document his father had produced in 1497 for Ferdinand and Isabella, to guide the fleet of Princess Margaret— Charles's aunt—down from Flanders to Spain for her wedding with the Infante Juan. If so, it was another instance of Hernando's making what he could out of the trove of old documents that was the only legacy he still retained from his father. He was bringing back with him to Spain, however, the foundations of a new Columbian legacy: forty-two hundred books that he had purchased in northern Europe— the Low Countries, Germany, and England—and which, when added to the 1,674 he had acquired in Venice and the books he already either had, inherited, or bought in Spain and Rome, would give the thirty-three-year-old Hernando one of the greatest private libraries in all of Europe.[6]

It is fascinating that one of Hernando's clearest memories of this moment of triumph, returning to Spain with the newly crowned king of the Romans, and bearing the treasures of Europe's bookshops with him, was of an argument with a mule driver, whose name—Juan de Aransolo—he was to recall on his deathbed. One of the mules rented by Hernando, probably to carry part of his enormous freight of books on through Spain, had fallen and broken a leg, and he considered this to be the mule driver's misfortune and no concern of his, though evidently there was reason to question this judgment. Hernando's recollection of the event seventeen years afterward, leaving a ducat for prayers for the soul of Juan de Aransolo, is eloquent testimony both to his tender conscience and to the power of shame to tie threads between our mind and events in the past, threads that retain even at a great remove the power to tug at us. These threads from the past would, in Hernando's declining years, exert an ever greater pull on his mind.[7]

The Spain to which the imperial party returned in mid-1522 was vastly changed from the one it had left two years previously. The revolt of the Comuneros had by now been quashed, but the great market town of Medina del Campo that Hernando had visited almost annually during his youth had been destroyed, as had the Romanesque cathedral of Segovia, in whose shadow he had begun his dictionary in 1518, and the uprising had revealed deep fractures within Castilian society. Yet if the emperor needed distractions from the tensions at home, he had them in the news arriving at Spanish harbors. Reports had already trickled through during the tour of the north of how Hernán Cortés had traveled inland through the kingdom of the Mexica, against the wishes of Moctezuma, but had nonetheless been met by that delicate-mannered prince on the causeway leading across the lake into his capital Tenochtitlan; and of how Moctezuma, who (later accounts say) took Cortés for a reincarnation of the plumed serpent-god Quetzalcoatl, had lovingly lodged the Spaniards in a palace across from his own, only to be taken captive by his own guests, who feared they would not be welcome for long. Cortés had written of how the Aztec emperor, with whom the Spaniard had a strange relationship as god but also increasingly as an intimate friend, had submitted to Charles and agreed to be his vassal. As in so many versions of this scene in colonial history, though, it is unclear that Cortés and Moctezuma had the same understanding of what this meant, especially as the two men communicated through double translation: Moctezuma spoke Nahuatl to Cortés's mistress "Marina," who then passed on the message in Mayan to Jerónimo de Aguilar—a priest who had learned the language during seven years as a shipwrecked Mayan captive before being found by Cortés—who in turn spoke Spanish to the conquistador. Despite Moctezuma's submission, one of Cortés's deputies had (in his commander's absence) invited the Aztec nobility to a feast and slaughtered them en masse, hoping to make Tenochtitlan easier to control. Moctezuma himself had been stoned to death shortly afterward by surviving members of the nobility, and Cortés had fled the city to regroup before returning to besiege it. News had reached Spain on 1 March that Cortés had captured Tenochtitlan, and Hernando bought a printed version of Cortés's report in December, three weeks after it had been brought out by the great German publisher Juan Cromberger.[8]

The emperor had also received reports while in the north of the dire state of Magellan's expedition. A party of mutineers who arrived back in May 1521 with one of Magellan's ships, the *San Antonio*, were able to report that they had not yet been able to find the elusive strait leading through the American mainland to the Southern Sea; instead they were waylaid on a frigid coast south of Brazil, populated by giants. It must have seemed likely that the circuit of the globe would remain uncompleted, and that Magellan and his men would disappear into the American interior as so many expeditions had before over the last decades. It was a matter of astonishment, then, when news arrived at court in Valladolid that on 6 September 1522 a single ship from Magellan's original five, the *Victoria*, had arrived back at

A sixteenth-century image of Franciscan monks destroying Aztec treasures, including sacred maps and books.

Sanlúcar de Barrameda, having completed at last the circumnavigation of the world that had for so long obsessed the European mind. It transpired they had indeed found a strait that released them into the Southern Ocean, shortly after the departure of the mutineers, in a land they named Patagonia after a fictional country in one of the most popular romances of the day. Finding themselves amid the wonderful calm of the great ocean, which they named the Pacific, they had skirted the western flank of the continent before striking out across the ocean, a stage of twelve thousand miles that they believed would never be accomplished again; they reached the islands south of Japan in March 1521, shortly before the mutineers were arriving back in Spain to report on the expedition's failure. Magellan himself was not in the party that had returned to Spain, having died in a foolish display of chivalry in the Philippines, and only 18 men of the 265 who had left Sanlúcar in 1519 were on the returning ship, importantly including the voyage's chronicler, Antonio de Pigafetta; the ship was now captained by an obscure Basque named Juan Sebastián de Elcano. He was simply the most senior sailor left alive when the expedition returned and was duly rewarded for the feat when he arrived in Valladolid, including being given a coat of arms that featured the globe and the motto *Primus circumdedisti mihi* (You first encircled me), just as the Columbus arms featured islands and recorded the gift Columbus had made of them to Isabella and Ferdinand. Hernando had reason to be grateful, on seeing the devastation wrought on Magellan's expedition, that he himself had been prevented from attempting this act of epic madness.

Not all the news arriving at the ports was so miraculous. Early in 1523, while Hernando was still in Valladolid, a list of grievances against Diego's conduct in Hispaniola arrived, drawing censure from Charles and another summons back to Spain to answer the charges. Diego's reinstatement had barely lasted three years. Later that year, the king himself would be frustrated by the death of his papal ally Adrian VI, who died after hardly a year in Rome, to be replaced by Guilio de Medici, who accomplished his ambition in donning the papal tiara as Clement VII. Hernando also learned, shortly after his return in 1522, that the 1,637 books he had entrusted to Octaviano Grimaldi in Venice had gone down with the ship that was bringing them to Spain. The loss of these precious volumes must have been utterly devastating. Not only was it an extremely expensive consignment—Hernando had spent much of the two thousand ducats from Charles on books during his shopping spree, including the advance of two hundred ducats he had borrowed from the Grimaldi that would fall due in October of 1523—but it also meant the destruction of Hernando's harvest from his seven months spent at the very epicenter of printing, the annihilation of what may well have been his most triumphant encounter so far with the world of the printed book. These hundreds of beautiful volumes, mostly unbound and probably stored in sealed barrels for safekeeping, joined the sleeping and ancient cities of the drowned with which the Renaissance imagination populated

An illustration for Cicero's *Officia* showing two men clinging to the wreckage of a ship. The figure at left is dressed as a fool. Hernando suffered a second catastrophic shipwreck just as his grand project got underway, a tragedy that shaped the final form of his library.

the seafloor. Besides the loss of the books themselves, the episode of his life that they represented, and the investment of wealth that he could not afford to replace, the destruction also meant something else: the extraordinary catalogues, which he had created to organize the collection, were now obsolete. Never fearing loss on such a tremendous scale, Hernando had forged ahead, entering the Venetian purchases not only in his alphabetical list of authors, but also in another catalogue he had developed. This was a kind of register, roughly in the order of acquisition, in which he had begun to assign each volume an identifying number and to make notes about each unique piece in minute detail, recording, as well as the author and the title, details of the opening lines of each book, where it was printed, where he had bought it, and how much he had paid. The books lost on the return voyage from Venice represented entries number 925 to 2,562 in the second of these four volumes. In this catalogue, for the first time, he had begun to sketch out how the books of the library might be divided by subject matter, sorting them into crudely defined fields: Theology, Astrology, Humanities, Grammar, History, Alchemy, Logic, Philosophy, Cosmography, Law, Medicine, Geomancy, Mathematics, Music, Poetry, Tuscan Verse, Greek, Chaldean, and so forth. But there was now a hole in the collection, sucked into the waters of the Bay of Naples along with the hundreds and hundreds of books these entries described.[9]

It was not the only one of Hernando's projects to run aground in this period. On 13 June 1523, letters under the king's name were sent out to the emissaries trawling Spain for Hernando's *Description*, ordering an immediate halt to the project. They probably caught up with these information foragers in the region between Seville and Córdoba, as it was to Córdoba that the order to cease and desist was sent. Local authorities were instructed no longer to cooperate with Hernando's assistants and were instructed to remove the letters of authority they carried with them, by force if necessary, and to confiscate the cosmographic notes found on their persons. It is unclear exactly what prompted this sudden and rather draconian end to the project; Hernando's only surviving mention of the affair gestures cryptically to the "jealousy" of the Consejo de Castilla, though he does not say of what precisely they were supposed to be envious—that a project of this scope and importance was being undertaken by a private citizen, or of the enormous power that might accrue to the holder of this information? In all probability, the obstacles were the same as those that met similar projects across Europe in the decades to come: landowners and local magnates felt these surveying projects to be invading their property and roping them into a centralized, national system, a system that knew the land with unprecedented exactitude and was able therefore to tax and control it in ways previously unimaginable. The Revolt of the Comuneros in 1520–21 had been provoked by precisely these kinds of administrative impositions, which some Castilian communities were incensed to have foisted upon them by this foreign king and his Teutonic entourage, and Hernando's *Description* may have been among the many ways in which Charles had gone too far, one of the sparks that lit the touchpaper of revolt. The Spanish were not to try anything similar again until fifty years later, when Philip II's *Relaciones topográficas* represented a fundamental change in the relationship between the crown and its subjects.[10]

Hernando's second great project from the years of the *Description*, his dictionary of the Latin language, also came to a halt, ending partway through the letter *B* on the word *Bibo*, "I drink." If one is tempted to laugh at his failure to get any further than the second letter, it is worth remembering that by that stage he had covered 1,476 pages in closely written script and had racked up perhaps three thousand entries. It is possible the project was drawn to a close by a dawning realization of the scale of the task: if the first letter and a half were in any way representative, the final dictionary would span tens of thousands of pages and cover fifty thousand definitions, well surpassing the forty thousand that would appear in Samuel Johnson's monumental dictionary a century and a half later. Hernando's retreat from the field of lexicography may also, however, have been prompted by his having been beaten to the punch: Ambrosius Calepino had already, as early as 1502, completed a dictionary that made up for many (if not all) the perceived shortcomings of the medieval Latin dictionaries. Calepino's would become the standard dictionary and would see 211 editions between 1502 and 1779; Hernando's stopped where it was and would be largely ignored from then on.[11]

Many people would have been prompted into a spiral of despair by defeat on so many fronts at once, with his shipwrecked books, his brother in disgrace, his *Description* and his dictionary in ruins. There is no evidence that Hernando paused for a moment, though it does seem that from this time forward he would focus his attention, as much as he possibly could in the swiftly moving world in which he found himself, on the single and singular project of his library, with its rich profusion of books and images and music. It would be impossible to save the alphabetic catalogue he had drawn up, seeded as it was throughout with the ghostly presence of the books that had been lost in the sea, so he began a new one. The register that described each of the books in detail was also now fatally compromised, as it contained a large section, a whole volume almost, of books no longer physically present in his collection. Rather than attempting to cut this section out of the old catalogue, he began another, better one, which this time would include not only the descriptions of the books but also the hieroglyphic language he was developing. The only part of the old book-register he kept was the very section that detailed the books at the bottom of the sea, which he intended to replace, volume by volume, until the library was once more complete. To this orphaned volume, this memento of the departed, he gave the exquisite name of the *Memorial de los Libros Naufragados*, "The catalogue of shipwrecked books." Not only was this the first catalogue Hernando made of his collection, but its title resounds with the poetry of his life, of the bringing together of books and shipwreck, of the struggle for memory in the face of fast-eroding loss. The sunken consignment had taught him an important lesson: his was not an imaginary library, such as the storied one at Alexandria, which could exist as an idea but need never worry about how it would live in the world. It was a library of flesh and blood—or rather paper, ink, and vellum—and needed to be housed, guarded, ordered, and arranged, tended to like a garden that must be restrained from the wildness to which it always wishes to return. For the first time in his itinerant life, Hernando needed to put down roots, to find a place where his books could be safe; and one whence the library could begin to work its magic upon the world.

This, however, would have to brook one more extraordinary delay. For the arrival back at Sanlúcar de Barrameda of Magellan's crew, even without Magellan himself, had precipitated a political crisis thirty years in the making. The circumnavigation had indeed reached the Moluccas, as planned, and the local king had even obligingly renamed the island Castile and made the standard pledge to be a vassal of the king of Spain. It may even have made matters somewhat easier that Magellan had died *before* they reached the Moluccas, as it meant these transactions could be clearly separated from any complications arising from Magellan himself (like Columbus) not being Spanish. The submission of Rajah Sultan Manzor, king of the Molucca island of Tadore (now Castile) meant little; the burning question still remained whether the islands rightfully belonged to the Spanish or the Portuguese under the terms of the 1494 Treaty of Tordesillas. Were the Moluccas more or less than 180° of longitude going west from the Tordesillas Line? This question could only be answered by determining the size of the world, and a summit was duly convened between the Spanish and the Portuguese to thrash the question out. Each delegation consisted of a team of navigators, astronomers, and lawyers. Hernando, despite being none of these, was chosen to lead the Spanish side; though technically included in the Spanish quota of astronomers, he was in reality one of the few people in any position to understand all of the mathematical, nautical, political, historical, and diplomatic issues involved. But with his immensely varied skills, Hernando brought a wealth of baggage to this task. The result of the summit might not only be crucial to allowing Spain's empire to compete with Portugal's in the future; it also represented a breaking point for his father's legacy, for what that inspired or insane voyage across the Ocean Sea would finally mean for Spain and for the rest of mankind. Hernando was being asked to determine, once and for all, the size and shape of the world.

XII

Cutting Through

During the Christmas season of 1523–24, which he spent in the ancestral home of the Dukes of Alba at Piedrahíta, Hernando returned once more to the volume of Seneca's *Tragedies* that he had last been annotating in 1518, but which had been put aside while the *Description*, the dictionary, the nautical chart, and his tour of Europe's greatest book towns made greater claims on his attention. Seneca was more valued in the Renaissance than he is today, beloved for his stately declamations and political themes, but the place he held in Hernando's life had more to do with one particular passage—the passage in the *Medea*, stored in *The Book of Prophecies*, in which the chorus foretells that

> During the last years of the world,
> the time will come in which Oceanus
> will loosen the bounds, and a huge landmass
> will appear; Tiphys will discover new worlds,
> and Thule will no longer be the most remote land.

Against this passage, Hernando has written, in a note only partly legible today, "A prophecy . . . by my father . . . Christopher . . . admiral . . . the year 1492." Yet for all the pride captured in this note, which linked Hernando through his father to both the great feats of exploration and the glories of the classical world, it may well have seemed the beguiling prophecy had now revealed itself as a lurking and treacherous riddle. It was no longer as clear that Tiphys, discoverer of new worlds, represented Columbus; many others now contended for the title, and Diego's presence in Spain—at his in-laws' castle at Piedrahíta—to answer charges of misgovernance suggested that the family's foothold in the New World was slipping. While the discovery that Thule was not the most distant land may once have seemed a glorious revelation, it was obvious now that it was also a cruel trick: If not Thule, what *was*? Where did one reach the other side of the world and start to turn back, getting closer again instead of farther away? In the end the obsessive quest to establish the roundness of the earth by circumnavigation had simply given way to another instance of the maddeningly obscure, in which the true measure of the earth's circumference retreated ceaselessly beyond grasp. If his father was undoubtedly the one who had loosened the bounds of Ocean, to Hernando fell the far trickier task of putting them back again.[1]

With a delicate sense of the diplomatic symbolism involved, the towns of Badajoz and Elvas, which faced each other across the Spanish-Portuguese border at the Río Caya, had been chosen for the meeting point. The document naming the deputies was signed by the emperor on 21 March 1524 in Burgos, where Hernando joined the rest of the Spanish delegates to present to the Consejo de Castilla their strategy for the impending encounter. To keep the conference from getting out of hand, each sovereign had been allowed to nominate a team of nine experts to represent him: three pilots, three jurists, and three astronomers. While the jurists were career bureaucrats and possibly unknown to Hernando, he would likely have known the astronomer from Salamanca (Dr. Sancho Salaya) and the mathematician from Valencia (Fray Tomás Duran), and certainly Pedro Ruiz de Villegas, a cartographer from the Consejo de Indias. Though he was technically included in the delegation as one of the Spanish astronomers, records of Hernando's involvement show him drawing together arguments from every side—legal, cartographic, political, historical, and geometrical. In addition to the official delegates, a constellation of others were at Badajoz to assist in an unofficial capacity: Sebastian Cabot and Juan Vespucci, two other members of exploration dynasties with whom Hernando worked at the Casa de Contratación, as well as their fellow mapmaker Diego Ribeiro, who had been lured to the Spanish side perhaps to help with Magellan's expedition. The Spanish team had two more trump cards to play at the conference: the testimony of Sebastián de Elcano, the last man standing from Magellan's circumnavigation, and Simón de Alcazaba, a Portuguese pilot with experience of the very region under discussion who had turned witness for the Spanish.[2]

Hernando set himself apart from the rest almost as soon as they met, first pressing them to get started on rehearsing their case (while the others favored waiting for the emperor) and then, in presenting written arguments, suggesting a gambit that wholly departed from their instructions. While the emperor had intended the team to establish, by means of astronomical and cartographic demonstration, that the Moluccas were within the half of the world set aside for Spain in the Treaty of Tordesillas, Hernando wanted to go further, reviving his father's old belief that the papal bulls gave the Portuguese not half the world east of the Tordesillas Line, but merely the tiny segment between the line and the farthest extent of their discovery by that point—namely the Cape of Good Hope. After all, as Hernando pointed out, the pope had conceded to Spain all territories to the west of the Tordesillas Line *as far as the Indies*—which included all of the territories between the line and India going west, such as the Moluccas, even if this was simply taking advantage of the fact that (in 1494) it was believed the territories Columbus had discovered *were* the Indies. This was a point, then, not of astronomy or cartography, but of legal interpretation of the treaty, one that stood to win for the Spanish not simply the fount of the spice trade but the better part of the world. The majority view, however—indeed of everyone but Hernando—was for sticking to the remit they had been given by the emperor.[3]

In response to this, Hernando patiently outlined the flaws in this plan. The division of the globe depended, he pointed out, on an accurate measure of its circumference, which could be done in one of two ways: either by physically measuring the globe itself or by extrapolating from measurements of celestial bodies. As for the first method, short of actually taking the measurement with a string, estimates would have to be based on distances sailed and so would have to take into account not just wind speeds and currents, but also the drag on the ship of the freight, whether the hull was free of impediments or not, whether the ship had old or new sails, and whether it was freshly caulked or riddled with damp—and that was without even beginning to factor in magnetic variation and other things affecting the bearings taken. There is a disorienting frankness to Hernando's observations, drawing attention to the uncertain nature of all their measurements. The second method, using celestial observation, was more promising, but still far from guaranteeing universal agreement, as suggested by the wide variety of estimates on how many miles were in a degree of longitude. In the end, no one had achieved an indisputable demonstration of this, and each cosmographer fell back upon whichever authorities he most credited: this was, in other words, a game of rhetorical arguments rather than mathematical proofs. When pressed for his own opinion, Hernando stayed faithful to the small-earth hypothesis of his father, which (drawing on Tobit and Alfragano and Pierre d'Ailly) put the world's circumference at 5,100 leagues, as opposed to the 5,625 of Ptolemy, the 7,875 of Strabo, or the 12,500 of Aristotle.[4]

But even if one *could* agree on the size of a single degree of longitude, one would still need to measure how many degrees lay between two places, a task fraught with difficulty. Hernando proceeded to lay out five different methods for measuring longitude, each with its attendant problems, coyly adding that he intended to enumerate them

(*overleaf*) One of the first great world maps made using new mapping techniques, produced by Diogo Ribeiro under the supervision of Hernando in his post as *pilót mayor*, 1529.

Carta Vniuersal En que Se contiene todo

CIRCVLVS ARCTI

CHINA

MARE SINAR

TROPICVS   CA

LINEA   EQVINO

TROPICVS   CAPRI

CIRCVLVS

so the gentlemen of the Consejo could tell him if he missed any. These methods included

> sailing in a straight, diagonal line between two
>   latitudes
> by the use of a "fluent instrument"
> a waterwheel to measure distance
> the observation of eclipses
> the observation of fixed and unfixed stars

Although he discounted the first method, given the difficulty of sailing in a straight line while at sea, and the last two are dismissed on the basis that eclipses are too rare and observations of celestial bodies too hard, the idea of measuring longitude using time differences in different parts of the globe, drawing on the method used by Nebrija and others that Hernando used in the *Description*, is more intriguing—in part because this is precisely the method that would solve the puzzle of longitude more than two hundred years later. Hernando's "fluent instrument" is, essentially, a clock of sufficient accuracy to allow one to measure the different times of high noon in each spot and anticipates by decades a similar suggestion by Gemma Frisius, who is often given credit for having come up with the idea. But the problem was—and would remain for two centuries—that the clocks available were simply not accurate enough. Hernando concluded it would be impossible to force the other side to accept one's conclusions using any of these methods, allowing anyone who wished to (in his lovely phrase) to *tergiversate*—to object endlessly and play for time.[5]

The opening of the conference showed Hernando's predictions were entirely correct. After a ceremonial meeting on the bridge between the two towns in early April, the Portuguese caused an immediate delay, moving to strike Simón de Alcazaba from the Spanish delegation on the grounds that he was a Portuguese subject and that his presence as a Spanish witness was an insult to King João. Much to Hernando's annoyance, Charles accepted this request and

Alcazaba was duly removed from the panel. Then there was further contention, before any start could be made, over exactly where was the Tordesillas Line: the treaty set it down as 370 leagues west of the Cape Verde islands, but had not thought to specify *which* of the Cape Verde islands was the starting point. The Spanish insisted it should be the most westerly (the Isla de San Antonio), while to the Portuguese it was clear it should be the easternmost Isla de Sal. Each degree farther west the line went, of course, dragged the corresponding line on the other side of the world further west as well, holding out the hope for the Spanish that they could give up more of the empty Atlantic in return for encroaching upon the Far East. When on 23 April they were finally to meet to decide on this point, as well as on two other fundamentals—whether to draw the line on a flat map or on a globe, and on the precise longitude of the Cape Verde islands—the Portuguese lodged a further objection over the distance *between* the eastern and western tips of the Cape Verde islands. Because of all these issues, the starting points of both sides were more than 60° of longitude apart—a sixth of the world. Discussions were thus further delayed until 4 May, though it must have seemed almost certain they would forever be mired in intractable quibbles. A charming story that did the rounds at Badajoz gives a sense of the absurdity of this quest to fix lines on maps: the Portuguese commission, wandering by the Rio Caya, were confronted by a small boy whose mother was washing clothes and who, exposing his buttocks, asked the Portuguese if the line between them might be the one they were looking for.[6]

In the absence of a solid base of evidence, Hernando and his team were thrown back upon the only tactic they had left: turning the very testimony of the opposition back against them. First, Hernando pointed out that the Portuguese had, at one point, produced a map on which they had moved the Tordesillas Line from 370 leagues west of the Canaries to somewhere *east* of those islands; that another of their maps showed only a few locations in the Indies and not the full extent of their discoveries; and that they had even presented a globe showing the Cape Verdes precisely where the Spanish had claimed them to be, only to withdraw it rapidly when realizing it put the Moluccas in the Spanish zone. All of this, Hernando argued in his report to the king, showed they were acting in bad faith, in the knowledge that if they showed their full hand, it would prove the Spanish right. While it was more likely that the Portuguese did not want to divulge classified nautical information during the negotiations, they were forced to fall back on claims that the confusion arose from the sheer number of lines crisscrossing the map—black, green, and red plumb lines giving the cardinal compass bearings. In the end, the Portuguese insisted that maps and globes were insufficient to determine such a point and suggested the two sides move on to astronomical arguments.

Determined not to be waylaid again by intractable disagreements—especially when the talks had been allowed a maximum of two months—the Spanish instead followed Hernando's advice and steered away from astronomy and back toward the evidence of authorities ancient and modern. Once again, given that either side could cherry-pick evidence to suit its case, the emphasis was on making the other side argue the Spanish case for them, an area where Hernando's growing and increasingly powerful library came into its own. In addition to evidence from travel narratives by the Venetian Alvise Cadomosto and a letter to his father from Jerónimo de Santistevan, Hernando produced a printed translation of Portuguese travel reports and pointed to the precise chapter in which they themselves gave the measurement from Lisbon eastward to Calicut as thirty-eight hundred leagues (almost 270° away on Hernando's "narrow earth"). The Spanish also submitted that, despite the great Portuguese secrecy over maps, which (the Spanish suggested) was designed to avoid acceptance of Spain's rights, "certain Portuguese and Castilians" had nevertheless managed to bring these strictly guarded maps out of Portugal. Possibly a veiled reference to Hernando's clandestine mission to Portugal in 1518, it was also a way of embarrassing two members of the Portuguese delegation—the master cartographers Pedro and Jorge Reinel—who had been in Seville in service of Magellan's voyage and who probably were instrumental in giving up the secrets of the Portuguese maps. A further series of pilots and mapmakers was marched out to testify that, in their experience and knowledge, the Portuguese maps shortened the distance east to the Moluccas by at least 25°. Lastly, but most damningly, perhaps, the Spanish showed that a member of the Portuguese delegation itself—Pedro Margalho, a professor of philosophy at the premier Spanish university at Salamanca—had recently published a volume in which he openly stated the Moluccas were within the Spanish half of the globe.[7]

Though it must have been clear that there was little chance of the other side conceding, Hernando had warmed to his theme. He produced editions of Pliny and Ptolemy printed in 1508 that included modern measurement tables not only agreeing with the Spanish placement of Malacca in Malaysia (a key reference point) but suggesting the Strait had been visited by Europeans before the expedition by Diego Lopes de Siqueira, a member of the Portuguese delegation at Badajoz who claimed the distinction of having been there first in 1509. Hernando also pointed out the Portuguese were out of step with the rest of the world, who largely followed Ptolemy in putting a degree of longitude at 62.5 miles, whereas the Portuguese used a figure of 70 miles. This, Hernando said, would gain them 2,600 miles in a complete circuit of the globe, or forty-three Ptolemaic degrees—almost precisely the amount they differed from the Spanish count. In fact (Hernando suggested), the situation was even worse, as the Ptolemaic mile was only eight *stadia*, the *stadia* being the measurement of distance a man can run without breathing. Hernando then produced a passage from Pliny in which a messenger from Alexander the Great walked twelve hundred *stadia* in nine hours and pointed out that if the Portuguese notion of a *stadia* was correct, the poor man would have had to maintain a walking pace of almost seventeen miles an hour for the entire distance—an impossible speed, he drily noted, to walk for a single hour, much less nine in a row. (The fastest modern marathon runners manage just under thirteen miles an hour, and then for just over two hours.) Until accurate methods for measuring longitude could be developed, the greatest weapon in the fight for universal empire—as Hernando's withering point-scoring on the Portuguese delegation made clear—was an ability to navigate and make use of the library, where that world was represented in miniature.

Needless to say, when the conference broke up in mid-May, it had achieved no progress whatsoever in resolving the issue of the Moluccas. Hernando wrote repeatedly to the jurists nominated by Charles, and to Charles himself, arguing the legal case for Spain to reduce the Portuguese claim to west Africa alone, and insisting on the Spanish right and destiny to conquer Persia and the Holy Land. The emperor thanked Hernando for his advice and efforts and dispatched a number of further expeditions in an attempt to secure accurate measurements of the longitude of the islands, but the matter would have struggled for the attention of the emperor and his council: not only were large sections of the German Habsburg lands now in open revolt, but the Ottomans looked set to advance into central Europe after conquering Hungary in 1526, and early in 1525 the perennial struggle with France for control of northern Italy took a surprise turn. The pact between Charles and Henry VIII to quell the ambition of Francis I, which had been sealed during the imperial visit of 1522 and had since seen a number of small victories in Lombardy, gained an unexpected coup at Pavia, where France was not only routed but King Francis was taken prisoner and brought to Madrid, a feat that allowed Charles to impose the harshest terms in return for the French sovereign's eventual release. Charles married his sister to the king of Portugal in the year after Badajoz, and with his mind on the balance of power in Europe, he soon afterward let it be known he was willing to concede Spanish claims over the Moluccas in settlement of Catherine's marriage portion, something he could better afford than ready funds needed for deployment in Germany and Italy. The islands were finally recognized by the Spanish as belonging to Portugal by the Treaty of Zaragoza in 1529, and the political drive to establish an accurate measurement of the earth's circumference evaporated.[8]

It is as well that accurate longitudinal measurements were never made: even measuring from the version of the Tordesillas Line most favorable to the Spanish, the Moluccas are in reality a good 25°—more than fifteen hundred miles—within the half of the globe claimed by the Portuguese. But there was no way of knowing this at the time, and Hernando was right from the outset that, in the absence of agreed measurements, the issue could only be contested by demonstrating the argument of the opposition to be contradictory and duplicitous. To this end he had produced printed evidence that suggested one of the Portuguese party was lying about being the first European to visit Malacca, that another had published a work that supported the Spanish case, and that the Portuguese accounts of their own voyages lent weight to Spanish arguments. What was more, the technology of print lent this claim a particular force. That Hernando could point to the specific edition of the work to which he was referring, and to the exact sections in that work, meant the Portuguese could not claim he was falsifying evidence: anyone in Europe who cared to check could simply locate a copy of the book and verify what he was saying—printed evidence was in the public domain and beyond recall.[9]

This way of proceeding was not foolproof—indeed, the chapter number Hernando so triumphantly cited was wrong, owing to a printer's error in the copy he was using. Early printed books could—and did—not only have faults but also differences within the same editions. But it becomes clear in reading Hernando's reports on the conference that the real weapons he took with him to Badajoz were the catalogues of his library. Here it was not so much the alphabetical list of authors, or the registry of books, which was crucial—after all, these could only provide him with titles and publication dates—but rather his newest project, which made him such a formidable adversary. The catalogue in which he noted his departure for Badajoz on 25 March would become known as the *Book of Epitomes*, and it represented yet another leap forward in Hernando's ambitions and in his inspired confrontation with the world of books. The alphabetical catalogues to the library had become necessary once the number of tomes expanded beyond the ability of any person to remember, forcing the creation of an external memory that could easily be navigated by the user. But if Hernando could not even remember the titles and authors of each of his books, how would it be possible to remember their contents?

The feeling of being overwhelmed by the flood of books issuing from the printing presses of Europe was widespread: in an addition to his *Adages* published in 1526, Erasmus was to ask plaintively, "Is there anywhere on earth exempt from this swarm of new books? Even if, taken out one at a time, they offered something worth knowing, the very mass of them would be an impediment to learning." Hernando's proposed solution to this, begun around 1523, was to distill the contents of each volume in his library down to a slender *epitome*—a Greek word meaning "to cut through." The idea of the epitome was not new—it had been common practice since the second century to provide shorter summaries of longer works, and Hernando may have been directly inspired by the model of his compatriot Isidore of Seville, the great medieval encyclopedist—but no one had attempted to manufacture them on anything like this scale before. Just as with the *Description*, the scale of the task facing Hernando led at an early stage to the employment of a number of *sumistas*, scholars employed for the specific task of cutting through the immensity of the library to produce these distillations. By 18 January 1524, the *Book of Epitomes* already had 1,361 entries. Most of these managed to compress the ideas in the volume to hand into seven or eight lines, though sometimes a little more was required, as in the thirty-page entry (#1444) that summarizes the works of Plato—even then, something of a miracle of compression.[10]

Hernando's epitomizing project had both practical and visionary elements. Just as some of the earliest catalogues had been developed to ensure the same books and printed images were not duplicated in the rapidly expanding library, so the *Book of Epitomes* was in part designed to circumvent a fatal flaw that had been introduced by the market for printed books. Owing to the peculiar nature of books—which are ingested over days, weeks, and months and cannot be effectively trialed during a trip to the bookshop—unscrupulous printers and publishers had from an early period realized that the sale was more to do with what the title page promised than what the book contained. Without a journalistic press to review books—a seventeenth-century innovation that was itself corrupt almost from birth—customers had to take the claims of the title page at face value. "There are many books," Hernando's librarian would later recall, "with grandiose and swollen titles that afterward treat nothing of what they promised, something the printers do to increase their profits." Hernando's *Book of Epitomes*, however, would allow those in the library to bypass the vainglorious names given to these books and get to the heart of the matter, meaning less time would be wasted on irrelevant material. In moving from the surface appearance to the interior, he was putting into practice the lesson he had learned from the manatee off the coast of Hispaniola, which hid its mammalian secrets in its entrails.[11]

Although the stated purpose of the *Book of Epitomes* was to extract the ideas of each volume by summarizing the arguments, it is delightful that (as with the geographical notes for the *Description*) this desire for objectivity is quickly hijacked by expressions of the experience of reading, making the *Epitomes* a form of early book review. Among the list of terms used to describe various authors' styles are

> wordy, learned, to-the-point, conversational, clean, ornate, compendious, diffuse, diligent, elegant, not-unlearned, not-unuseful, delicate, resplendent, pedestrian.

The *sumistas*, doomed forever to digest the world of print for the greater good, would have known better than most that there was no separating an author's thoughts from the manner of saying them. But Hernando's ambitions were not limited to foiling the schemes of duplicitous publishers. As Erasmus had suggested in his *Adages*, the very volume of printed material was in itself an enemy to understanding: even if one were to weed out all of the detritus of the publishing world, the industry had no means or motive to converge on a single, definitive account of any one subject. Instead, the book market was incentivized to pump out endless iterations of the same thing, each with minor variations but also grand declarations that the former versions were now obsolete. As Hernando's collection grew, he seems to have conceived a misery familiar to all lovers of learning: the feeling that for every step one advances, a million paths to further understanding open up—a world of opportunity, of course, but also something that makes a mockery of the pathetic progress you have made so far. The *infinite* library (like the one imagined by Jorge Luis Borges in a famous short story) is worse than no library at all: it will have an infinite number of (ever so slightly different) biographies of Hernando Colón by people named Edward Wilson-Lee, for instance, meaning you could never master even that one topic. The universal library to which Hernando aspired was perhaps not quite so impossible to navigate as the infinite one imagined by Borges, but it may often have seemed there was little difference. Yet Hernando was not one for surrendering, even against seemingly insuperable odds. While his librarian's memoir noted that it weighed upon his employer that there were so many books of law and medicine in the world, Hernando nevertheless believed it possible to create one book of medicine designed to cure all illnesses, one primer with the perfect method of teaching grammar, and one book of laws—or at the most, say, four—capable of ruling the world. The *Book of Epitomes* was the first step toward this, reducing each book to its essentials so that theoretically the books could, in turn, be grouped together by subject and distilled further until one had a single book that treated that subject in its entirety.[12]

The *Book of Epitomes* was also the first sign Hernando was beginning to think about the universality of his library in terms of shape as well as size. It was all very well for the library to grow to gigantic proportions by the constant acquisition of books, but beyond a certain point its size stood to make it less, rather than more, useful. The mission to epitomize the books in the collection—and the desire beyond this to reduce each subject to a single book—was a very different vision of universality, one in which the sum total of human knowledge was confined within a limited space, growing *denser* rather than larger over time. Like the globe under debate at Badajoz, an unbounded world, of indefinite size, was a terrifying thing that crippled attempts to navigate within it: only once the circumference had been fixed could it then be further reduced, divided, and charted, replacing an ambition to extend the bounds of knowledge with one that sought to grasp what was there more firmly. The plan, however, had something missing from it. If one were to reduce the knowledge of man to a small number of encyclopedic volumes, what would the title of these books be? What are the subjects into which the sum total of knowledge can be divided? And where do you draw the bounds of each subject? It was easy enough to talk about a single book of medicine or law, but even in the small collection Hernando had taken with him to Hispaniola in 1509, the boundaries were hard to discern—medicine bled into astrology on one side and botany on the other; law needed history as a foundation, which in turn required a knowledge of the *realia* of those historical periods: their grammars and vocabularies, their coinages and weights and measures. Choosing where to cut through knowledge was of the utmost delicacy and gravity, as dividing in the wrong place could from thenceforth sever some essential means for understanding things on either side of the divide. This conundrum would occupy Hernando for the fifteen years that remained of his life.

The furious pace of Hernando's activities was, as ever, counterpoised by the fraught and desperate state of his family's affairs. In September 1524, a formal list of charges was issued against Diego, accusing him among other things with overreach in the execution of his role in overseeing both civil and criminal suits on Hispaniola. Hernando once again summoned his energies to defend his brother and the legacy of which he was now the sole custodian, preparing a legal brief in which Hernando asserted the natural right of the Admiral and vice-regent over judiciary matters in his domains. It is unclear whether he was aware that his brother, upon returning to Spain the previous year, had added a codicil to his will noting that he and Hernando had had some "differences" in interpreting what their father intended to leave his younger son in his will, and that while Diego meant to do right by his brother during his lifetime, he absolved his heirs of any obligation to continue to provide Hernando with anything at all from the family estate after his death. In the same codicil, Diego names Hernando as the executor of his will, a move some have seen as a mark of the continuing affection and love between the brothers, but which is surely rather an act of quite unthinkable cruelty: Hernando was to be called upon to enact the wishes of his closest living relative in the days after his death, down to the very clause in which he was finally excluded from any claims at all upon the legacy of his father. While he remained at court for much of 1525, battling for the family's rights, Hernando's constitution finally gave way in November. He wrote to Charles from Seville on the twenty-sixth, excusing himself for having left the court at Toledo, begging time to recover from "certain *quartan* fevers" that were afflicting him daily, as well as the work from which he had never known a day of repose. He signed off by wishing Charles that God might bless him with Lordship of the Universal Empire, a thought that now as ever was at the center of the Columbus obsession. Hernando seems still to have been in Seville when Diego died on 26 February 1526 near Toledo, leaving his brother nothing more than the poisonous remembrance in his will. But by then Hernando was pressing onward with wholly other things.[13]

XIII

The Library without Walls

Two weeks before his brother died on the other side of Spain, Hernando bought a plot of land in Seville on which over the next three years he built a home for himself and (more important) his books. The plot may not have seemed much to some: it was a *muladar*—literally, a "dung heap"—outside the city walls at the Puerta de Goles and within a broad meander of the Guadalquivir. But it was the first place Hernando had settled with anything like permanence since he had left his mother's house in Córdoba at the age of five. In the intervening years, thirty-two of them, he had lived in the itinerant court, on board ships and shipwrecks, in a government house in Santo Domingo and a Franciscan convent in Rome, and in the endless junkets set aside for those accompanying the Imperial Court. Though he seems to have owned several houses in Seville before this, they left little trace upon his life. The house at the Puerta de Goles—the "Hercules Gate"—was different: not just a place to live but the materialization of an idea, fabricated out of the many places and things that had made up his life, and designed like More's Utopia to shape the life of those who lived within it. It is often said houses are either rambling, organic expressions of the personalities that built them, or ordered, systematic attempts to impose order on the lives within. With Hernando, however, it could only ever have been both, and all the evidence points to the Casa de Colón as growing out into the world from his internal orders, built around his growing ideas about how to arrange the many thousands of books and pictures in his collection, and the archives of words, maps, geographical data, and music. Yet, as ever with Hernando, the search for a perfect order always contended with the gravitational pull of his father's memory. The *muladar* at the Puerta de Goles was not just a random location in Seville, but rather on the bank of the Guadalquivir that looked directly across to the Cartuja de las Cuevas, where in the Capilla de Santa Ana Columbus's body had rested since it was moved there in 1509.[1]

Keeping his father in sight may have been a central motivation for Hernando, but his foundation at the Puerta de Goles was also in conversation with other places more distant in time and space. Like the great villas Hernando would have known in Rome—Johan Goritz's and Angelo Colocci's little academies, founded in the *desabitato* region inside the city walls—Hernando's open stretch of riverbank offered the perfect location for a humanist idyll, at once urban and rural, allowing him to combine contemplation with the active life. The humanists, who were mostly born into a medieval landscape of open countryside and

A perspective of Seville from the *Civitates orbis terrarum*, showing Hernando's great library (the Casa de Colon) on the banks of the Guadalquivir.

dense towns, held strongly to the idea that classical thought did not just take place in Cicero's Tuscan villa or in the Gardens of Sallust by accident, but were in a sense produced by these surroundings. More's *Utopia* not only unfolds during a conversation in an Antwerp garden, but imagines a world in which every house has such a green place into which to retreat and in which everyone is a better person for it. Like Thomas More's own home in the London borough of Chelsea near Westminster, which he moved into this same year, the suburban house allowed its dweller the *otium* (leisure) of the countryside without having to lose touch with the *negotium* (business) of the city.

Though the house Hernando built for his books has long since disappeared, sixteenth-century descriptions allow us to re-create it with a fair amount of accuracy. The house presented a broad front of 198 feet and was 78 feet deep, and a drawing of 1572 suggests it was built to face across the river to the Cartuja de las Cuevas, rather like Agostino Chigi's villa in Trastevere. Also like Chigi's house, Hernando's had two floors of cube-shaped rooms, with the public rooms on the ground floor and the private suites above. From all of these there was a grand vista down to the river and across to Las Cuevas, hard-won by an extensive landscaping project that began with the construction of covered ditches to drain the land and proceeded to the movement of large amounts of earth that would otherwise have obstructed the view. On one side of the house were stables and service quarters, while on the other was the magnificent walled garden, the Huerta de Colón, which Hernando acquired from the adjacent church of San Miguel, in exchange for a house he owned on the Calle San Blas. Some idea of the capaciousness of this garden is suggested by a description from 1570 where Hernando is said to have planted five thousand trees there. The façade of the house, from its archway supported by Corinthian pillars, with dolphins supporting the Columbus arms, to the program of window casements formed of pilasters and tympanas, busts and floral motifs, advertised the neoclassical character of Hernando's project: this was not a Mudéjar courtyard building like the noble houses of the city, but a classical villa in the humanist style. The façade was created by two sculptors from the Columbus homeland of Genoa, one of whom— Antonio Maria Aprile de Carona—had already made his mark in Seville by building the sumptuous tombs for the Ribera family at Las Cuevas and at the University Church, and who was at the same time working on the entrance to the Ribera Casa de Pilatos across the city, from which surviving structures we can get some sense of the external appearance of the house Hernando built for his books.[2]

If the architecture of his house imitated the finest models in Italy, the gardens that surrounded it were without parallel. In his will Hernando was to speak of his gardens as the finest he had seen in all his travels through Christendom, and reports from later in the century speak of thousands of plants from around the world, but evidence regarding Hernando's creation of what would seem to be Europe's first botanical garden is fragmentary. The inventory of his papers drawn up by his executors contains what seems to be a catalogue of his plants and gardens, but sadly this is lost. What does survive is an extensive

(*opposite*) Though Hernando's groundbreaking botanical garden no longer exists, this image of another early collection (at the University of Leiden, from 1610) shows what it may have been like—the wild world of exotic life, reduced to orderly arrangements.

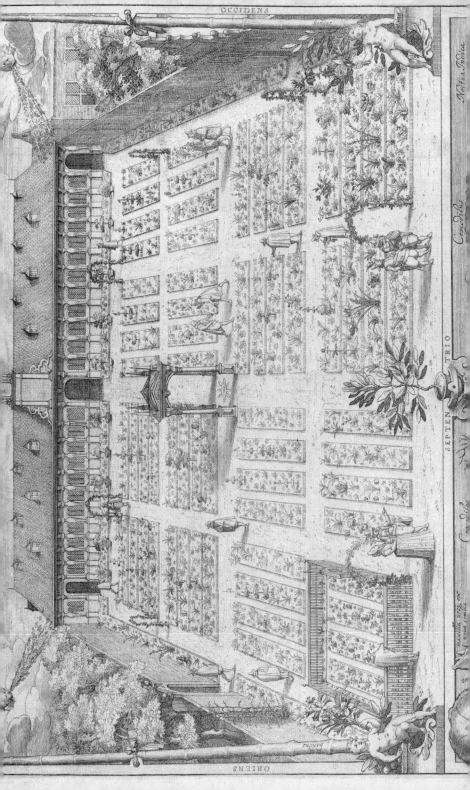

set of instructions given to his gardeners—one Alonso de Zamora and his wife, Maria Rodríguez—in 1528, instructing them to water the trees every five days, to create a precise irrigation system for the planting beds, and imposing heavy fines on them if they allowed grazing animals into the garden (tethered or not). While this document does not go into detail about what trees the garden contained, Seville is filled today with New World plants that are said by local legend, almost without exception, to have been planted by Hernando, something that increases its uncanny likeness to its architectural twin Santo Domingo, though now by means of a botanical colonization going the other way. Prominent among those foreign plants putting down roots are the extraordinary ombús at the Cartuja de las Cuevas and elsewhere—a South American treelike plant, actually formed from the fused stems of a giant grass—as well as the ceibas that are littered around Seville, and the bizarre Indian laurel in the Plaza de San Leandro, which seems like a waxwork forest melting in the midday sun.[3]

It seems clear from Hernando's writings that he had a strong and early interest in plant life, perhaps first prompted by the botanical marvels reported by his father on the early voyages. Prominent among these were the tree Columbus saw on the island of Fernandina, which had five or six different types of branch that grew ungrafted from the same stock, and the fruits on Dominica on the Second Voyage that drove the settlers mad and made their faces swell. Hernando also possessed the most detailed description of Taino culture, by Raymon Pané, including the *cohoba* they sniffed as part of their spiritual and medicinal regimen. Several botanical volumes were among Hernando's early purchases, and his sections of the *Description* regularly record grafting and viticulture techniques. His own observations on New World plant life would also feature frequently in the narrative of the Fourth Voyage that he later wrote as part of his biography of his father, from the tooth-rotting leaf (cocaine) chewed by the tribes near Belén to the applelike paradise plum (*Chrysobalanus icaco*) they found at Caxinas point.[4]

That Hernando's interest in these plants was largely medical is wholly in keeping with the botanical culture of the time: rather than classifying plants morphologically (by physical form), as later scientists would do, early Renaissance plant science focused on what different plants did to the humans who ingested them, driven by an increased interest from doctors and apothecaries in the vegetal life from which their drugs derived. While the ingredients for "simples" and "compounds"—drugs with either one or many components—had traditionally been gathered by herb wives and other unlettered people with knowledge of local plant life, early botanical gardens grew out of a feeling that pharmacology needed to start with the plants themselves rather than with purchased ingredients, especially now that many of the plants came from exotic places and were unknown to traditional plant lore. They also, from the mid-fifteenth century, began putting their drugs in labeled ceramic jars, a practice that meant the willful and chaotic world of organisms could be placed on shelves and reduced to order, though—like the books in the library—the number of new species flooding in from around the world quickly put paid to the idea of a universal garden. But for all this professionalism, these early pharmacologists were often heavily reliant on the existing knowledge of the herb wives, and this seems to have been the case with Hernando, whose instructions to his gardeners goes to extraordinary legal lengths to include Maria Rodríguez in the contract to look after the gardens, suggesting it was her knowledge (rather than her husband's) that Hernando was after. The extent of Hernando's own medicinal practices is unknown, though the same inventory of his writings records a note regarding recipes for medicine.[5]

Like the Venetian listening station of Marin Sanuto or the central repository for the *Description*, the botanical garden would become the place where the world's plant life could be studied without going to the expense of travel. From the early 1530s onward, the Sevillian doctor Nicolás Monardes became the European expert in drugs derived from New World plants without ever leaving the city, simply by gathering the reports and samples from there that passed through the city and spreading them through his published writings. Hernando himself may have gleaned some of the wisdom of Arabic medicine from a recently converted potter whom he knew, who also practiced medicine in the Triana district across the river from Hernando's house (though the potter refused to use any Arabic terms for fear of recrimination). Much of the time Monardes and his peers were actually collecting traditional prescriptions from non-European herbalists to cure the illnesses colonists brought home with them, such as the *guayacán* (lignum vitae) tree from Santo Domingo that became the main cure for the pox (syphilis). But given that these plants were not local, Monardes and others often had to experiment by planting seeds sent to them from the New World and observing the results. A major difference between the old medical practice and the new, then, was simply a matter of scale and the systems developed in response: whereas both drew upon traditional plant lore, collectors such as Hernando and Monardes had a global reach, meaning they had to cultivate exotic specimens locally and sift conflicting reports in search of consensus on what could be learned from the indigenous knowledge of distant people.[6]

The method of classifying plants by their effects was the same system Hernando used for his next step in ordering his library, one taken to remedy a serious fault in the existing catalogues. While the alphabetical list of authors and titles could help you to find a specific volume, and the *Book of Epitomes* saved you the trouble of reading the whole thing to discover its contents, these catalogues made the assumption you already knew which book you were looking for. Hernando's librarian recalled him describing libraries without adequate guides, where you simply had to go through each book until you found the right one, as "dead." But a library that could be navigated only when you knew the author or the title of the book you were looking for was scarcely any better, a sort of undead collection with some appearances of life but none of its essence. Readers entering it

(*opposite*) A scene of instruction in an apothecary's shop (c.1512). Renaissance botany tried to tame the wilderness of the world's plants by arranging them in shelved jars, like a library.

with a question about syphilis or architecture would be entirely lost unless they already knew to search for Monardes or Vitruvius. The *Libro de materias*—the *Book of Materials* or *Subject Matters*—sought to remedy this by extracting from each book the main subjects treated therein, and arranging them in an alphabetical list. This was, then, rather like the indexes Hernando had added to some of his individual books—his copies of Suetonius and of Lucretius—but now expanded to cover the collection as a whole. So, as Hernando's librarian suggests in his account of the library, Erasmus's *Lingua* ("The tongue"), a treatise on the dangers of poor and the benefits of good language, would receive entries under "bad language, dangers" and "good language, benefits," as well as under subtopics treated in the same book, such as "the asp, nature of." This would allow anyone wishing to gather knowledge on language or poisonous snakes to be guided toward Erasmus's work, without having to know where to look beforehand. It was, in effect, a universal index of subjects, which broke down the barriers between books and constructed a network that linked similar materials throughout the library, allowing the user to gather at will an immense amount of information on any given subject from a wide range of different volumes. Hernando and his team of *sumistas* were furiously at work on it in the same year that he began construction at the Puerta de Goles, covering 802 pages with entries of two or three lines each, rough notes that would later be transferred into the alphabetical index.[7]

As ever, this invention brought with it new challenges. To begin with, they faced the challenge of deciding which term to use in the index: should the asp in Erasmus's *Lingua* go under *asp*, or under some other word—*snake, serpent, viper, adder*? Searching an index is all but useless unless you know the term you are looking for, and in the instructions Hernando left for his assistants he directed them to use the most *common* term for the subject in question, as well as putting it under more than one heading when in doubt. So anything treating the Incarnation, for instance, should also be put under both *Christ* and *Jesus Christ*. This is largely a practical measure—the index would be useless if the entries weren't intuitive and didn't use the term most people would think of for a given subject—but it represents a profound departure from how language was thought of by most of Hernando's contemporaries. While the various quests for perfect languages at the time (hieroglyphs, More's Utopian, Hernando's biblioglyphs) wanted perfectly unambiguous terms even if they had to be ones no one used or understood, the *Book of Materials* turned this on its head. Now the standard for language was to be the way people used it rather than some abstract and elusive perfection, and the *Book of Materials* acknowledged that a single thing might be referred to in many different ways. The desire to make the colossal hoard of information in the library *useful* meant Hernando and his librarians had to think about how people might use it—the words that would occur to them in any given context. Even if this step was taken for purely practical purposes, it was a step down a path that would lead to radical changes in how language (and, by extension, knowledge) was conceived: not as a thing capable of being fixed in one perfect state, but a growing, organic thing, born out of the everyday negotiations we enter into when we use language.[8]

Hernando must have been relying heavily on his *sumistas* for the work on the *Book of Materials* as, in addition to continuing work on the *Epitomes*, directing construction at the Puerta de Goles, and acting as executor to his brother's will, Hernando had in 1526 taken over as Spain's chief geographical officer. After the conference at Badajoz had ended inconclusively, Sebastian Cabot (the *pilót mayor* who headed Spain's Casa de Contratación) had been dispatched on an exploratory venture designed to acquire new evidence on the longitude of the Moluccas. Some months after Cabot's departure, in October 1526, the emperor directed Hernando to set to work on a new version of Spain's central navigational chart—the *Padrón Real*—and from the following August made him the acting *pilót mayor* in Cabot's absence. While Hernando's initial geographical venture, the *Description*, had been halted, and his efforts at Badajoz had come to little, he now had the chance to work on what was in some ways an even more ambitious cartographic venture. For the *Padrón Real* was not meant to be just a map but rather the central instrument of Spanish navigation, and its technical sophistication could give Spanish ships an advantage over their competitors from Portugal and any other pretenders to colonial ambitions. Hernando's first step in this venture was wholly characteristic: on 16 March 1527, Charles issued an order that all Spanish pilots on the shipping routes to the New World should keep daily logs recording their measurements and deposit these diaries upon their return with Hernando at the Casa de Contratación, where they would be collated into the new shipping chart. This manner of proceeding was the same as the one Hernando had used for the *Description* and had seen Marin Sanuto use at Venice to write the history of his city, as well as being the central recommendation of the dialogue (probably by Hernando) between Fulgencio and Theodosio criticizing the way the *Padrón* was created: rather than relying on any one authoritative model or source of information, a flood of data was used to refine understanding progressively, converging toward an ever-more-precise representation of the world.[9]

We are fortunate to be able to follow in some detail the sequence that Hernando and his fellow cartographers went through in making a map because one of the best surviving descriptions of this art comes from the pen of Alonso de Chaves, who was appointed on Hernando's personal recommendation in 1528 to work with him and Diego Ribeiro on the chart. Hernando appears to have overseen the cartographic and nautical activities of the Casa de Contratación not at the Casa itself but in his house at the Puerta de Goles, as a letter of 1528 describes the instruction of pilots in the use of nautical instruments (another of Hernando's duties) taking place there. Chaves's *Espejo de Navegantes*—"A mirror for navigators"—recounts how the cartographical process began with the laying out of a net of fine lines on the blank paper or vellum: first the rhumb lines, emerging from the compass rose to striate the surface with the major bearings, then a second web of perpendicular lines, providing a grid of latitudes and longitudes and marking out the equator and tropics. Once the surface had been prepared with this fine mesh, the mapmaker was to choose a starting point with an established latitude and work from there to nearby points, combining the latitude measurements—which could be trusted with some confidence—with readings of distance and bearing accrued from reports. Once this spread of points was laid down, the coastlines could be filled in between them in detail from pilots' reports. The system worked like a connect-the-dots drawing, using the experience of pilots (as in the old *portolan* maps) to join up a network of locations established by more technical measurements of latitude, distance, and bearing. Finally, the mapmaker could populate the map with topographical detail, from the names of ports, written at right angles to the shore and often crowded thickly along the coasts of these maps, to warnings of sandbanks (shaded in with dots) and underwater dangers (marked by crosses). Although the official maps were likely drawn by the professional mapmakers Ribeiro and Chaves, evidence of Hernando's own cartographic skills can be seen in the books of his library, such as the 1513 edition of Ptolemy's *Geography* in which he has corrected the maps and filled in place names in his own hand, as well as labels such as the *"insula anthropophagorum"* (Island of the Man-Eaters) above the *Isla de las Once Mil Virgenes* (Virgin Islands). Another contemporary cartographic manual describes how copies would be produced from these blueprints, to make the charts that every Spanish pilot was supposed to carry aboard with him: an outline was created by soaking thin paper in linseed oil, before the lines of the blueprint were traced, and then retraced, on top of paper smoked on one side to create a carbon transfer sheet.[10]

The maps created in this workshop of soot, oil, paint, and paper at the Puerta de Goles were working documents, intended for the use of pilots at sea, and so like all other nautical charts of the era have perished through use. Even the blueprint maps of the *Padrón Real* were destroyed once a new version made them obsolete, so little can be said about these nautical maps with confidence. A number of presentation maps from the period of Hernando's tenure as *pilót mayor* do survive, and though the credit for these groundbreaking creations usually goes to Diego Ribeiro and Alonso de Chaves, by whom they were signed and who have been fêted by map historians, this idea of the map-maker as solitary artist wholly ignores the realities of how maps were made at the time: as collaborative efforts drawing on a wide range of reports, inheritances, and technical skills. Four maps survive from Hernando's years as Cabot's substitute, two of which are held today in Weimar, one in the Vatican, and the last (perhaps from after Hernan-do's time) in Wolfenbüttel. These maps are less practical instruments than display pieces, designed to give the viewer the full visual sweep of the world opening to Spanish explorers, and were decorated with exquisite illustrations of those instruments—the astrolabe, celestial sphere, and quadrant—that underwrote the technical sophistication of the maps, featuring also the same instructions for using these instruments as Hernando was helping to teach pilots during these years. The maps also continued the diplomatic wrangling that had been left unresolved at Badajoz, significantly placing the Moluccas on the far left—and thus within the western, Spanish, hemisphere—despite that by then Charles had all but conceded the islands to Por-tugal, and populating the ocean with images of Spanish fleets and flags, taking possession of the world like so many toy armies. The use of these maps for political bargaining was to lead the English geogra-pher Richard Hakluyt later to joke that the cosmographers and pilots of Spain and Portugal put the coasts and islands of the world wherever it suited them best.[11]

Hernando's duties as *pilót mayor* spread well beyond the business of making maps and instructing pilots: the post also required the examination of all pilots in navigational skills and the inspection of all technical instruments intended for use at sea, allowing Hernando the chance to improve upon another of the shortcomings of Spanish navigation lamented in the dialogue between Theodosio and Fulgen-cio. The *pilót* had the additional duty of developing Spanish artillery, as the skills required for the effective use of cannon were dependent more on techniques and tools used by mapmakers and surveyors—

accurate measurements of distance, bearing, and inclination—than on traditional military tactics. Hernando seems to have taken an early interest in Spain's outdated arsenal, noting, in a pamphlet describing the Battle of La Motta in 1513, the ineffective use of bombs by Spanish troops, and in 1528 Diego Ribeiro was updating the Consejo de Indias on the bomb-making techniques being developed at the northern outpost of the Casa de Contratación at La Coruña in Galicia. If Hernando had cherished any hopes of the Casa de Goles being a bookish sanctuary, sheltered from the business of the world, they would have been disappointed in these years, in which the house seems to have been filled with cartographers and cosmographers making charts and delivering instructions, and pilots delivering reports and hearing lectures and taking exams. Later descriptions suggest Hernando's house had at that time become a kind of mathematical academy, re-creating the villas of the Roman humanists but substituting a love of technical data and systems of measurement and order for the Roman obsession with the culture of the classical past.[12]

Re-creating Rome on the banks of the Guadalquivir could only have been a bittersweet occupation, given recent events in the Italian peninsula. The capture of Francis I at the Battle of Pavia had startled even those fighting with Spain by tipping the balance of power too heavily in Charles's favor, causing a series of imperial allies—Henry VIII, Pope Clement, the Venetians, and even the Sforza Duke of Milan whom Charles had installed—to throw in their lot with France, forming the League of Cognac in hopes of counterbalancing the emperor before he became simply unstoppable. Charles, disgusted that Francis would so casually go back on the parole he swore when released from Spanish captivity, didn't mince his words, refusing to take any ransom payments from the French king: *He has cheated me; he has acted neither as a knight nor as a nobleman, but basely,* Charles said witheringly, suggesting Francis could redeem himself only by surrendering again as prisoner or fighting Charles hand to hand. As there was no chance of either of these things happening, Charles's commanders in

Italy recruited mercenary German *Landsknechts* to replace the Venetian and Florentine troops they had lost, swiftly retaking Milan; and when the French troops failed to materialize, Clement sought a truce. The imperial commanders were, however, no longer fully in command of their soldiers of fortune and had no money to pay them off and so were carried along by a surging and unruly force toward Rome. On the morning of 6 May 1527 the Spanish and German troops entered the Eternal City, with Pope Clement fleeing from the Vatican along the Leonine Wall to the Castel Sant'Angelo.[13]

The sack of the city that followed, in which the cultural, artistic, and spiritual sanctuary of Christendom was the scene of frenzied violence and brutality, scarred the conscience of Europe in ways that are hard to express. The full extent of the atrocities is uncertain: one man testified to having (himself alone) buried ten thousand corpses on the north bank of the Tiber, and having pushed another two thousand into the river, and uncountable rapes were committed as the soldiers swarmed the city; no house was spared from looting, down to Chigi's villa and the papal palace, where among the frescoes by Raphael and Peruzzi German graffiti can still be seen today. But the fullest measure of the *Landsknechts'* wrath was directed at the fabric of the Roman Church: the *sanctum sanctorum*, as the chronicler Luigi Guicciardini reported, was turned into a brothel, and after desecrating the relics—football with the heads of Peter and Paul, the Holy Lance of Longinus used as a bayonet—they paraded in front of the Castel Sant'Angelo, in a carnival mocking the lavish citizenship ceremony for Clement that Hernando had watched in 1513. The Veronica, believed to be the only authentic image of Christ, also went missing during the sack. In the ultimate insult, the *Landsknechts* demanded Clement submit to Luther, whom they hailed as the new pope. Rome, went the common cry around Europe, is no longer Rome. To many throughout the Continent, this was another Fall of Jerusalem, and the Temple was once more destroyed. The event became, almost at once, one of those epochal moments Europeans found it hard to think beyond: it served as a tragic ending to countless narratives in the century to come and has variously been used by historians to mark the end of the High Renaissance in Italy, the beginning of Mannerism and the Baroque, the close of medieval Christendom and the start of the Counter-Reformation, and the end of the papacy as a significant political player.[14]

As is so often the case, the anger of the looters seemed particularly intense when they were faced with books and libraries; sensing in these inanimate things the spirit of the city, they attempted to annihilate the learned traditions that had so long been a focus of antipapal scorn. Great humanist libraries such as Angelo Colocci's, at his academy on the Quirinal, were destroyed entirely, as was that of Giles of Viterbo, along with the manuscript of his *Historia XX saeculorum*, in which he had presented history to Leo X as entering its last phase through the Columbus discoveries. Some recognition of the Vatican Library's immense value was shown when the Prince of Orange was set on guard over it, but even he could not prevent the marauding troops from raiding the library, where they ripped the precious bindings off the manuscripts and, scorning the contents, left the exposed pages to disintegrate. Many would have seen in this a repetition of the destruction of the libraries of classical Rome by the Ostrogoths in the sixth century, or of the storied destruction of the Library of Alexandria. Large portions of the Archivio Segreto in the fourth room of the library were lost, and a cataloguing project in the aftermath of 1527 found great swathes of the library were missing. The stone had been cast and broke the clay-footed kingdom of Rome, and for better or worse the Spanish Empire—and Hernando's library—were now without rivals.[15]

The vanquishing of all Charles's foes meant, however, that Hernando's endless occupations—the maps and the *Book of Materials*, the epitomes and pilot's exams, the Casa de Goles and the library—would again have to be put on hold so the final scene in Charles's imperial pageant could be played out. While Charles had been crowned the king of the Romans at Aachen in 1520, the volatility of northern Italy, and the unpredictability of papal politics, had so far prevented the enactment of the final rite. With both Rome and the Vatican now unquestionably subdued, he could proceed to Italy to be crowned as Holy Roman Emperor by Clement himself, becoming the full ritual and spiritual heir to the Roman Empire and, by extension, the rightful inheritor of the imperial torch held by only one nation at a time.

It was unthinkable that Hernando, who with his father had been tireless in his efforts to position Spain as the necessary home for this universal empire, should miss this climactic event. But the coming to completion of the rituals of empire also lent a new urgency to Hernando's work. If Spain was to be a universal empire, it would need at its core a universal library, a memory bank in which the thought of the world was stored, and one moreover that was not a lifeless repository but a working organ, capable of making connections through the fog of the printed world, of forming a single picture of the world rather than simply reflecting it in a mirror with unnumbered faces. Indeed, universal empires of territory and of knowledge were deeply linked, as suggested by the many geographical metaphors used to describe the world of knowledge: Hernando's library would cover all of the possible *fields of knowledge*, making all *terrains* one. His book and picture registers had ensured the library was not full of duplicates, his alphabetical lists had allowed particular books and authors to be found, the epitomes would help the reader to move through the shelves at greater speed, and the *Book of Materials* could guide researchers to the right place once they had a particular topic in mind. But how was one supposed to move from these particular things—authors, titles, ideas—to a greater understanding of the framework in which it all sat, of its coordinates in the world of knowledge? What was adjacent to any given subject, in what region did it lie? What was the ultimate form of this library? What were its boundaries and its divisions, its meridians and degrees, which would allow one to glance upon it and say, This is the picture of the world and the natural shape of knowledge? When he left for Italy in August 1529, Hernando was forty-one years old and not a young man by the standards of the age. His health was faltering and his financial situation precarious, to say the least, dependent on the caprice of his brother's widow and the attention of a ruler mobbed by the cares of empire. But he was on the threshold of bringing something extraordinary into being, something truly different from anything before it, and something that would mark him out as the heir his father deserved. All that was missing were the final arrangements.[16]

PART IV

SETTING
THINGS
in
ORDER

XIV

Another Europe and the Same

Exactly two years after leaving Spain, in the autumn of 1531, Hernando was returning from the Low Countries in a small party that would pass back across France to Spain. As the party moved from Louvain and Antwerp to Cambrai and on to Paris, they made a remarkable gathering: Hernando, the seasoned traveler on horseback, was joined by two Dutchmen he had recruited to help him in his library—Jean Vasaeus, and the corpulent and jovial Nicholas Clenardus, who quickly gave both themselves and their horses painful sores by sitting awkwardly in the saddle, using neither their feet in the stirrups nor their hands on the crupper to displace their weight. Though Clenardus, whose letters recount the journey in vivid detail, admits it was usually his lolloping and wincing that drew attention as they entered the towns, he recalled with some amusement the time his companion Vasaeus had stolen the show, becoming so unsteady in the saddle that he had been forced to cling to the horse's mane with his teeth. At Paris they were joined by Jean Hammonius, a French legal expert who was also recruited for the library project, making up a party of ten or so, which also included Hernando's companion Vincentio de Monte, who was hired in Rome early in the journey, and who would be with him for the rest of his life.[1]

Hernando had met Clenardus in Louvain, at the Collegium Trilingue, where Hernando had gone to look for those with the necessary skills to help him bring order to the growing chaos of the library.

Communicating his requirements to a Portuguese humanist at the college, André de Resende, Hernando had promptly been taken to the room where Clenardus was lecturing on a Greek text by John Chrysostom to a group of students. Though Clenardus had only been made a doctor by the Collegium a few years previously, he was already winning a reputation as a revolutionary teacher of language, and not simply because of the flamboyant hats he had taken to wearing after a period of living in Paris. Clenardus was pioneering an Erasmian approach to language learning, determined to prove language was best taught not by sitting bent over dense books of grammar and vocabulary, but rather through conversation and play. He claimed to be able to teach even the dullest child a classical tongue in a matter of months, simply by making Latin or Greek part of their daily conversational habits, though he would later also introduce to his classrooms two "Ethiopian" slaves (more likely from west Africa), to whom he had taught Latin and who would perform dialogues for the astonished students. The two language-learning manuals, for Greek and Hebrew, that he had published in Paris during a year teaching there were already becoming runaway successes, and he was gaining a popular reputation as a teacher at the Collegium in Louvain. Hernando approached him as soon as the lecture was finished, and the two soon came to terms.

Clenardus was later to write to Hernando expressing admiration for his patron's endurance of the scarcely bearable privations during his recent travels through Europe, and though Clenardus does not go into detail, it is possible to put together the pieces of Hernando's odyssey across the charred and altered landscape of the Continent. He followed the same crescent-shaped route he had a decade earlier in 1520–22, from northern Italy to Basel and up the Rhine through lower Germany to the Netherlands. The similarities between this voyage and the earlier one must have brought the differences even more starkly home. Lutheranism was no longer a sporadic protest movement against an overmighty Rome, a spiritual energy that Hernando could sympathize with or ignore as the feeling took him. It was now in the ascendant through much of Charles's German lands, and indeed in many areas the grounds of Luther's arguments had been taken to their logical conclusions, far beyond the comfort of the fathers of the movement. If, as Luther—and, in the view of some, Erasmus before him—had argued, the only crucial thing was a spiritual relationship with God through faith, then surely there was no need for the mighty princes of the Church (popes, cardinals, and bishops) to act as intercessors between man and God; no need, perhaps, for a Church at all. In the spiritual map of the universe, as in the new maps being made by Hernando, all points were equidistant from God. Indeed, while Luther had helped his own cause with the German princes by insisting that true believers should leave all political matters to their sovereign leaders, the poorest sort in some parts of Germany were easily persuaded by charismatic preachers that the revolutionary logic applied to secular rulers as well as the heads of the Church. In 1524 the radical preacher Thomas Müntzer, who captivated the Saxon mining town of Allstedt with his message of open season on the wicked and the rich, had preached before a gathered audience of inspectors a new interpretation of Nebuchadrezzar's dream of the statue of gold, bronze, iron, and clay. The smashing of the clay feet did not, he proclaimed, symbolize the beginning of a Last Kingdom but the end of *all forms of government*. Though Müntzer himself did not survive long after this, tortured and killed as the Peasants' Revolt got under way, a more stable (though hardly less antiauthoritarian) movement emerged in the Anabaptists, and Hernando would have had a taste of their ideas during his stay in their temporary home, Strasbourg, in late June 1531.

This was a very different vision of the End of Days to that conceived of by Columbus and Charles and Hernando, one in which the consolidation of universal rule in a single, supreme emperor was replaced by the flattening of all earthly hierarchies, with a difference being recognized only between the Elect and the Damned. It was also not a vision Charles could choose to ignore, even if his temptation might have been to focus on the more traditional threat to the east, where Suleiman's Ottoman forces had returned to continue their advance through Hungary and had laid siege to Vienna in September 1529, just as the imperial party was crossing over to Italy. So great were the joint threats in Germany and Austria that Charles had been forced to abandon, in the end, plans for a triumphal coronation ceremony at St. Peter's in Rome, settling instead for Bologna, which was closer to these theaters of action even if it was a poor substitute in terms of imperial symbolism. Charles's advisers had hurriedly prepared a case that the imperial coronation was valid no matter where it took place, as long as the pope was present, and (to further diminish the embarrassment) Bologna was decorated to look as much as possible like the Eternal City, with a wooden set of triumphal arches sporting images of Roman emperors, and the Basilica of San Petronio dressed up to look like the Vatican. Charles may have found some consolation for these half measures by choosing for the date of the coronation 24 February 1530, the fifth anniversary of his defeat and capture of Francis I at Pavia.[2]

If Charles's thoughts were elsewhere, so were Hernando's, and he may have departed before the coronation itself after seeking an audience with Charles. At this audience Hernando made a rather astonishing announcement: after opening by reminding the emperor he had now been in service with the royal household for almost forty years, he declared he had never sought reward for his employment because he had always assumed that one day the suit concerning his father's rights would be resolved, and his livelihood would be finally guaranteed. Seeing as he did now that the case was, in his lovely turn of phrase, *immortal*, he had decided because of age and poverty to take up holy orders, in part because the current pope had always had him in mind for such a path. Hernando begged the emperor not to stand in his way, but to allow him to spend his last thousand florins in traveling to Rome.[3]

It is hard to believe this was much more than a ruse on Hernando's part. Although Columbus had included a cardinal's hat among his demands upon his return from the first voyage in 1493—meant for

Diego rather than Hernando and ultimately unsuccessful—and a career in the Church was a common choice for younger (and especially illegitimate) children, little mention is made in Hernando's writing either before or after about joining the Church. His petition to Charles may suggest Hernando had got to know Giulio de' Medici reasonably well during his years in Rome, but it is hard to find evidence that he pursued a life in the Church with any conviction. His pleas of poverty may also have rung false in the ears of a sovereign who paid Hernando a pension of two hundred thousand maravedís a year, even if this may have been his only source of support and was quickly depleted by his ambitious projects.

If Hernando ever did intend to join the Church, the idea did not last long, and his supposed poverty seems to have been short-lived as well, as by September he was once again purchasing books in huge quantities, first at Rome and then up through northern Italy at Perugia, Milan, Turin, and Venice. He seems to have resolved his financial difficulties in part by deciding, after a lifetime of begging his portion from his brother, to turn the tables on his brother's family, repeatedly drawing loans from the Grimaldi merchant-banker family and telling them to present the bill to the family estates in Hispaniola and the widow Virreina María de Toledo, whose agents denied they had funds of Hernando's with which to pay the creditors. This was something of a dangerous game, but evidently by now Hernando felt the need to buy books, and the fear of leaving his great library incomplete, more keenly than the threat from the great and powerful merchant-banker families of Europe. Perhaps this desperate ploy was provoked in part by the sight of Marin Sanuto, the historian-recorder of Venice, whom Hernando found (during a visit to Venice in April 1530) reduced to dire poverty and forced to sell many of the books from his magnificent library—some of which Hernando bought, out of either charity or book lust, with the funds he borrowed from the Grimaldis.[4]

Sanuto had once again been passed over for the post of official historian of the city, this time in favor of Pietro Bembo, and was living off a pittance paid to him by the state in return for his making his life's work—scores of volumes recording each detail of the city's affairs—available to Bembo for his use. In the will he drew up shortly after Hernando's visit, Sanuto pitifully describes the catalogue of his "rare and beautiful" books—replete, like Hernando's, with details of cost and date of purchase—with the following note: "Those marked with a red cross I sold in my time of need." The sight of Sanuto's famous library being sold off to pay debts can only have provoked sympathy in Hernando for that particular horror, familiar to the impoverished bibliophile, combining both the sharpness of parting from books and the sadness that things so prized by the collector should fetch such a meager price. The bibliomaniac Walter Benjamin recounts that even the *thought* of having to sell his books drove him to buy more to soothe the pain he felt, and Hernando's acquisitions in these years have something of this flavor. The Biblioteca Malatestiana, which he must have visited when passing through Cesena in October 1530, offered something of a consoling vision. While in so many ways this library, founded by the local magnate and given to his city, was unlike Hernando's—stocked mostly with manuscripts from its own scriptorium and filled with book pews to which the volumes were chained—it nevertheless managed at once to be a public library and to maintain a policy on lending so strict it lost only six volumes over the next five hundred years. This could not be a direct model for Hernando: his library contained so many books that one could not possibly chain each of them to a desk. But it may have set him thinking about how to safeguard his own collections without turning a key upon his library and turning it into a sepulchre for books.[5]

Hernando had not come to the Collegium Trilingue in Louvain at the end of his sweep through south-German book territory to look for Erasmus himself: the idol was no longer to be found in that sanctuary. As the Reformation had advanced, perceptions that Erasmus's ideas had led to Lutheranism (and its more radical successors) had hardened. As the common joke went, "Erasmus laid the egg that Luther hatched." This became less of a joke when the Inquisition in Spain and the Faculty of Theology in Paris reviewed Erasmus's works and condemned sections of them as unorthodox; while defending himself against these charges, Erasmus had nonetheless withdrawn from the European scene, first to Basel and then (when the Reformation followed him there) to Freiburg, which Hernando visited in June 1531. But if Erasmus was no longer at Louvain, it was still a stronghold of Erasmian thinkers, and Hernando had come there in search of assistants for his library. In part, this may have been driven by the loneliness of his work, but the library presented Hernando with greater needs than this, as suggested by his first recruit, Nicholas Clenardus.

Clenardus's readiness to leave Louvain and cross the Continent with this stranger shocked many of his colleagues, especially given that Hernando was not able to offer him better terms than he had at the Collegium. But the two clearly sensed in each other a kindred spirit, and Hernando knew exactly how to tempt the Dutchman. During his doctoral studies Clenardus had come across an edition of the Psalms that printed each of these sacred songs in five languages—Latin, Greek, Hebrew, Chaldean, and Arabic—and he had fallen in love at first sight with the swooping, fluid curls of the Arabic script. The language was entirely unknown in Flanders at the time, and while Clenardus claims the impressive feat of having decoded the Arabic alphabet (by looking at how proper names were written in that script), there was no way for him to progress further in his love affair with the tongue. Hernando had only to dangle in front of Clenardus the Arabic riches of Spain—both the fluent speakers who could be recruited to teach him, and the treasury of Arabic manuscripts locked away in Spanish libraries, including the dispersed remains of the famous Umayyad library in Córdoba (and a few in Hernando's own)—to induce this glossophile to up stakes and follow him into the unknown.[6]

The recruitment of Clenardus promised to solve for Hernando a growing problem of the library—namely that as his ambitions grew from merely an unparalleled library to a truly universal one, and he set his sights on the world outside Christendom as well, there would inevitably be innumerable books in languages he could not read.

Although they were few in number, there was already a problem with transferring the Arabic volumes in his register over to the alphabetical list, for the simple reason that they were in a different alphabet. To all intents and purposes, these books simply disappeared when they entered the library, as there was no way of putting them on the map. And there was no chance of including these titles in the *Epitomes* or *Materials*, given that their contents were a mystery to his *sumistas*. This problem could only expand: Hernando had already bought books in Greek, Hebrew, and the Ethiopian language of Geez, and many more were beginning to appear in Armenian and Arabic, with some now even being printed in north Africa and beyond. While as early as 1484 the Ottoman sultan had prohibited Turks from using the printing press, Jewish refugees from Europe had nonetheless taken the technology with them and begun printing in the Levant. In addition to the growing number of printed books, there were also the treasure hoards of manuscripts brought back to Spain as the spoils of conquest, such as the two thousand volumes rumored to have been brought back to Spain after the capture of Tunis in 1536. Between these foreign scripts and the growing number of invented languages—such as the pictographic books being developed in Seville by Jacobo de Testera to aid universal proselytization—it was clear the alphabetical lists for the library might soon become obsolete. Worse than this, large parts of the library might become unreadable to *any* extent by the librarians, making them unsortable, unshelvable, and threatening ultimate chaos. This was not only a danger for non-European languages: that Hernando had almost no books in English, despite his visit to London, is likely because few even of the most learned outside of the British Isles understood anything of the language. Clenardus's coming promised to stem the flood, at least for the time being, by making the Greek, Hebrew, Chaldean, and Arabic tomes more manageable, and perhaps to provide a longer-term solution, given his interest in finding a universal key to language, looking for the common ground that underlay them all.[7]

This threat facing the library is wonderfully captured in a book that first appeared in these years and was purchased by Hernando soon after. It does not appear under its author's name in the alphabetic catalogue, perhaps because the name—Alcofribras Nasier—appears to be one of those Arabic words that caused a problem for that mode of order. Yet the *title* of the book does appear—*Pantagruel, Son of Gargantua: His Deeds and His Prowess*—alerting us that, though unknown at the time, the arabesque name on the title page is actually an anagram of the author's real name: François Rabelais. Rabelais's uproarious tale, addressed to the "Illustrious Drinkers" of Europe, recounts the adventures of the giant Pantagruel, son of the king of Utopia (Gargantua), who reverses the direction of European travel narratives by coming from afar to Europe in search of knowledge. At Paris he finds the Library of St. Victor, a magnificent collection whose extensive (and imaginary) catalogue Rabelais provides. The list, which contains both real books and made-up volumes, is a parody of the contemporary book market, as this small sample of titles suggests:

> *A Testicle of Theology*
> *The Mustard-Pot of Penitence*
> *On Farting Discreetly in Public*, by Mr. Winegarden
> Tartaraeus, *On Ways to Shit*
> Pasquino, Doctor of Marble, *On Eating Venison with Artichokes during Lent*
> Bede, *On the Excellence of Tripe*
> *Fourteen Books on Serving Mustard after Dinner*, by Our Master Rostocostojambedanasse
> *On the Arses of Widows*
> Ramon Llul, *The Bumtickle of Princes*
> *A Perpetual Almanac for Sufferers of Gout and Pox*
> *The Foolishness of Italian Things*, by Mr. Firebreaker
> *The BO of the Spanish, Distilled by Brother Inigo*

. . . and so on, for many pages. While hilariously puncturing the insufferable pomposity of contemporary writers and scholars, Rabelais is echoing Hernando's more serious point that book titles are often gibberish, telling us almost nothing about their contents, and so providing a list is no better than putting together a compendium of nonsense. Luckily, however, Pantagruel meets soon after this his soul mate and companion for life, Panurge, who wins his heart by greeting him with scurrilous and lewd speeches in fourteen different tongues: German, Hispano-Arabic, Italian, Scots, Basque, "Lanternese," Dutch, Castilian, Danish, Hebrew, classical Greek, Utopian, Latin, and (finally) French. It is entirely possible Rabelais had the polyglot and glutton Clenardus—wearer of remarkable hats—in mind when creating this character. Panurge, a whorehound and bon viveur, is a glorious parody of the Renaissance universal man, who (after escaping from Turkish captivity) has a career as an urban planner and as a humanist, designing new city walls for Paris out of the genitals of its ladyfolk and defeating an English scholar who has developed a *perfect language* of gestures by waggling his codpiece at him. Panurge offers to Pantagruel, as Clenardus did to Hernando, the promise of cutting through the linguistic fog of the world, and doing so with a certain flair.[8]

Hernando and his party had no possibility to visit England on his way back, as he had a decade before. Relations between England and Spain, which were difficult enough when Henry sided with France after the Battle of Pavia, were now at an even lower ebb, given that Henry was attempting to divorce Charles's aunt, Queen Catherine. To make matters worse, the emperor's control of Pope Clement following the Sack of Rome meant there was little chance of Henry's getting rid of his wife through the traditional channels of the Church. Wolsey had fallen after failing to deliver the divorce, and Henry had begun to listen to those who argued the pope had no authority over the English

(*opposite*) A satire on gluttony by Hans Weiditz (number 1743 in Hernando's picture inventory). During his tour of Europe in 1529–31, Hernando recruited the corpulent and jovial Nicolas Clenardus, a wearer of extravagant hats, to work in his library.

king's marriage arrangements. Henry, whose 1521 tract against the Lutherans was a treasured text in the Vatican Library, was not yet breaking with Rome, but he was starting to sound a lot like those who had. Though famous throughout Europe as the author of the radically skeptical *Utopia*, Thomas More now found himself overtaken by events and increasingly isolated in his public defense of the traditional powers of the Church. And Juan Luis Vives, the Spanish humanist who had been sent to England to give Princess Mary an Erasmian education, was expelled from the country after a brief house arrest for siding with his countrywoman Catherine.

If visiting England was not an option, France was now open to Spanish travelers for the first time in Hernando's adult life. The 1529 Peace of Cambrai had ended the thirty-five-year war that played out between France and Spain in northern Italy, and Hernando could finally travel through the country he had circled during much of his life. Clenardus narrates the journey through France to Spain, with Hernando and his other new recruits, with his usual charisma and focus on things of the body. The well-fed Dutchmen were horrified by the hostelries along the way, which Clenardus claimed were infinitely worse than those of which Erasmus had complained in southern Germany, especially when they reached Spain, where they found (after the good French dinners) virtually nothing to eat. They were forced to form scavenging parties to scrape together enough bread, wine, fish, and raisins to make up a homely meal, and struggled to find a single stick of kindling to light a fire against the frozen winds of northern Castile. They were also shocked to find they often had to share a single drinking glass among the whole table—and sometimes even with a neighboring table of complete strangers. On one occasion, near Vitoria, the communal glass slipped out of Vasaeus's hand and shattered on the floor, and after that they were forced to drink their wine "in the manner of Diogenes"—from their own cupped palms. With wonderful gallows humor, Clenardus took this as a prompt to label Hernando their Prophet—a playful title by which he addressed him thenceforth—because Hernando had, after all, warned them before arriving in Spain that a time would come when they would lack even vessels from which to drink.[9]

After passing through Burgos and Valladolid, which were wholly frozen, against all of the Dutchmen's expectations, they arrived at the court in the slowly regrowing Medina del Campo, where the sumptuous household of the Dowager Virreina, María de Toledo—still almost sovereign of Hispaniola during her son's minority—provided at long last sufficient comfort for Clenardus's taste. Hernando had evidently reached some accommodation with his sister-in-law by this point, though the party departed soon after on urgent business to Salamanca, where for the time being Hernando agreed to leave Clenardus to study the Arabic manuscripts held there. In a letter written to Hernando soon after, it is clear Clenardus had become something more for him than an amiable companion and a linguistic wonder: the Dutchman appears to have been the first truly to understand what Hernando's library meant to the world and to its owner. In his letter, Clenardus remarked that, in drawing from the most distant corners everything that authors had to the present produced, Hernando had, like his father, reached beyond the limits of our world to make another: just as Columbus had, *by a prodigious act, planted Spanish power and civilization in another world, so he Hernando had gathered the wisdom of the universe to Spain. Sons often resemble their fathers in appearance,* his new Dutch friend remarked, *but some also bear a resemblance in spirit and moral qualities.* High praise indeed given that the first part of the letter argues Columbus's deeds had made him like a god among men. It is, Clenardus concludes, just this resilience inherited from his father that has allowed Hernando to build in Seville the greatest library of all time. Unlike his father, Hernando had made few grand claims for his master project, and Clenardus's reaction is the first on record. It is hard not to share the broken gratitude and swelling pride Hernando must have felt when, after a lifetime struggling in the wilderness, someone finally saw what he was doing and spoke openly of it.[10]

Clenardus's fulsome praise of Hernando and of his father may, however, have been prompted by something more than friendship or admiration; it may have been meant to provide comfort for Hernando in a time of great difficulty and pain. In part, this was caused by Hernando's growing awareness that his father's reputation was being formed out there, in the world of print and public conversation, in ways hardly complimentary to the man he loved so much. In fact, it may have been Clenardus who first drew Hernando's attention to this: the Psalter in five languages, which the Dutchman had spent so many years poring over in detail to learn the basics of the Arabic alphabet, contained one of the first biographical descriptions of Columbus to reach print, in the form of a note to Psalm 19 that spreads over five pages, written by its editor, Agostino Giustiniani. Columbus had used this psalm to prop up his claim that his discoveries were not just random events but rather a key part of God's plan, but now his interpretation was part of the official fabric of Europe's most sacred text, contained in one of the most prestigious editions of the Psalms being read across Europe: Columbus's discoveries had become the *meaning* of this psalm, the fulfillment of its prophecy. Here the life of the explorer was being used to explain the psalm's words about God's message having traveled to the Ends of the World. Yet for all that it made Hernando and his father's *Book of Prophecies* part of mainstream European thought, the account of Columbus's life in the note on Psalm 19 was riddled with errors and (worst of all) opened with the damaging allegation that Columbus was *vilibus ortus parentibus*, "born of low stock." The *Psalterium* had been published as long before 1516, and this note had appeared separately as a short pamphlet on Columbus, but this crucial document seems to have passed Hernando by in the flood until around this time.[11]

However, the version of Columbus's life in the Psalms was hardly Hernando's biggest problem. The "immortal" case between the crown and the Columbus family over New World rights had taken a surpris-

(*opposite*) A copy of the psalms in five languages (Hebrew, Greek, Arabic, Chaldean, and Latin), which played a key part in the spread of the Columbus legend.

(Arabic)	(Aramaic/Hebrew Targum)	Latin version	Latin commentary (right margin)

Central Latin column:

i p̄ſetia mea. Filii populorū cōsumētur
& migrabunt de pretoriis suis. Viuit
DEVS ipse, & benedictus fortis,
quoniam ante eum dabitur mihi
fortitudo & redemptio, & exaltetur
DEVS fortis redemptio mea.
DEVS qui vltus est me,
& proſtrauit populos, qui exurgunt
ad offenſionem meam ſub me.
Eripuit me de pronis inimicitie mee,
iſup pluſq̄ illos q̄ exur. vt noceat mihi
valetiore me efficies, ab gog at & ab
pplorū rapaciū, q̄ ſt cū illo (exercitibᵒ
eripies me. Propterea
laudabo te in populis
DEVS & nomini tuo laudes dicam.
Magnifico vt faciat redemptionem
cum rege ſuo, & facienti bonum
MESSIE ſuo Dauidi,
& ſeminie eius vſq̄ in eternum.

XIX. In laudem.

Laudatoria Dauidis.
Qui ſuſpiciunt celos enarrant
gloriam DEI, & opera manuum eius
annunciant qui ſuſpiciunt in aera.
Dies diei apponit, & manifeſtat
verbum & nox nocti
diminuit & nunciat ſcientiam.
Nōeſt verbū lamentationis, & nō ſunt
ſermones tumultus & non
audiuntur voces eorum. In omnem
terram extenſi ſunt effectus eorum,
& in fines orbis omnia verba eorum,
ſoli poſuit tabernaculum,
illuminatione aūt i illos. Et ipſe i mane
tanq̄ ſponſus procedēs de thalamo ſuo
pulcherrime, & dum diuiditur dies
letatur vt gigas, & obſeruat
ad currendam in fortitudine viam
occaſus veſp̄tini. Ab extremitatibus
celorum egreſſus eius,

Right commentary column:

F. Libro midras te-
hilim in calce
pſalmi
(Hebrew text)
(Hebrew text)
Et quod eſt caſtrum,
uel uel eſt turris, que
facta eſt eis? Rex
MESSIAS, qua ad
modum dictū eſt tur-
ris ſalutis, & ſcripſi
eſt turris fortitudinis
nomen DEI in ipſum
currit iuſtus & ſuſtol
letur.

A. Secundum ex ſe
ptem nominibus qui
bus hebrei celum ſi
gnificant, impoſita ue
rius ab extendendo
quam à firmando.

B. Non auditur uox
eorū, Iuxta illud. Nō
enim uos eſtis qui lo
quimini, ſed ſpiritus
patris ueſtri loqui
tur in uobis. Et hic li
teralis ille ſenſus, qui
cum ſpiritali coinci
dit, uel ſcripſit Faber
principio comentatio
num ſuarum.

C. In omnem terram
exiuit filum ſiue linea
eorū. coi intellectu quo
linea p̄prie ſignificat
filum illud, quo mate
riarii ut utitur fabriad
ſignandam materiam,
perinde ac ſi dixiſſet
propheta. exiuit ſtru
ctura ſine edificio eo
rum.

D. Et in fines mundi
uerba eorum, Saltem
teporibus noſtris q̄b̄
mirabili au ſu Chriſto
phori columbi genu
enſis, alter pene orbis
repertus eſt chriſtia
norum q̄cetui aggre
gatus. At ueroquoni
am Columbus freque
ter p̄dicabat ſe a Deo
electum ut per ipſum
adimpleretur hec pro
phetia. non aliena exi
ſtimaui uitam ipſius
hoc loco inſerere. Igi
tur Chriſtophorus co
gnomento columbus
patria genuenſis, uili
bus ortus parentibus,
noſtra etate fuit qui
ſua induſtria, plus ter
rarum & pellagi ex
plorauerit paucis me
ſibus, quam pene reli
qui omnes mortales
uniuerſis retro actis
ſeculis. Mira res, ſ̄ ta

ing and potentially catastrophic turn. An agent in the case, Villalobos, acting for the emperor, had dramatically asserted that Columbus did not have the right to be called the sole discoverer of the New World— because parts of it had been discovered by Martín Alonso Pinzón, the captain who had accompanied Columbus and who had raced him back to Spain in an attempt to claim the glory all for himself. This was an entirely cynical ruse on the part of the emperor, as the Pinzóns had long since sold to the crown any rights they might claim over the discoveries in return for a small consideration up front. In addition to these attempts to chip away at the Columbus claim, wild rumors were circulating that several pilots had sighted the same islands years before he had, and that he was acting on their information when he sailed; the rumors would have meant little if they hadn't potentially played into the interests of the emperor. But even this was not the worst in store: Charles, it seems, had also been pursuing another line of inquiry, following up on a theory that Columbus not only was not the sole discoverer of the New World, but could claim none of it at all—that he had been beaten to the punch by *sixteen hundred years*. The theory, the main proponent of which was none other than Gonzalo Fernández de Oviedo—Hernando's fellow page at the court of the Infante Juan, who had written so scornfully of those he felt were of too lowly birth to be there—claimed Columbus's Indies must be none other than the Islands of the Hesperides, mentioned by the classical author Statius Sebosus as being "forty days sail west of the Gorgonas Isles." Oviedo further asserted that these islands had been conquered by an ancient Spanish king, Berosius, and were therefore *already* a Spanish possession when Columbus went there in 1492, meaning he had discovered nothing at all and had no claims whatsoever. This story was backed up by claims, first published in the 1533 history of Spain by Lucius Marinaeus Siculus (another figure from the court of the Infante Juan), that in the gold mines of the Americas coins had been found with the image of Augustus Caesar, which had been sent to the pope as proof of contact between Europe and those parts in classical times. Staggeringly, the courts agreed with the arguments of the crown, and on 27 August 1534 they issued the *Sentencia de las Dueñas*, stripping the Columbuses not only of their right to the title of viceroy of the Indies but also of any right to a share in the gold and other goods of those lands.[12]

Hernando's world was in pieces. Before his eyes, the image of his father was slowly being transformed into a shrunken and grotesque parody of the one Hernando had always kept in mind. His certain sense of the events of his childhood, when forty years before his father had found a new world and triumphed over mutiny and ingratitude to live to see himself vindicated, was crumbling away, assailed by contending and slanderous accounts, in which the lands his father had wrestled out of myth and legend into the light of day were slowly disappearing back into these mists. Everything that Hernando had spent his life learning, from ancient history and the labyrinth of the law to the use of ancient coins and inscriptions for understanding history, was now being turned against him. Faced with the annihilation of all he held dear, he turned to the only weapon he had left—his library, and in it the papers left to him by Columbus—in an attempt to make solid the father who was quickly slipping from his grasp.

XV

The King of Nowhere

How does one make a life out of words and paper? Capturing the essence of another person using the crude tools of narrative is a challenge at the best of times: out of the myriad events a pattern must be discerned, a structure created in which the life makes sense, and words must be found that resurrect the subject, conjuring for the reader the experience of being in their presence. How much greater, then, the challenge faced by Hernando in these years: to write about a father of whose memory he was infinitely jealous, and to do so with that father's fate, of fame and of fortune, hanging in the balance. Hernando began this task as he did almost all others. He gathered about himself the papers he would need, those he had inherited from his father, the letters and charters, logbooks and collections of notes, and all the books in which his father had written as he read. Making a life out of paper is infinitely easier if the subject has already begun to cross over into the written world by himself. The physical features of these documents are tantalizingly present as Hernando writes about his father: he mentions the phrase Columbus used to test whether his pen was working properly—*Jesus cum Maria sit nobis in via* (Jesus and Mary accompany us)—and the moment at the end of June 1494 when, even as his father was writing in his log, the ship ran aground on a shoal south of Cuba. These absentminded marks of the Admiral's pen—the words he wrote without thinking, the jag of his nib as the

ship shunts into the sand—transport us to the moment of their creation, like a needle tracing the tremors of that world. They are eloquent
testimonies to the arduous task of the biographer: using only pen
strokes, to break down the distance between language and the world;
to turn the paper and words back into something real.[1]

The reverential attachment to Columbus's writings that can be seen
in Hernando's biography has something to do with the son's devotion
to his father and something to do with his profound affinity for written things, but it is also a product of the special circumstances in
which Hernando was writing. As the opening chapters make clear, the
immediate and practical reason for Hernando writing is to respond to
the assertions—about Columbus, about the New World discoveries—
that were swirling around Europe and the law courts of Spain as well
as among the entourage of the emperor. Giustiniani's slander regarding the Admiral's parentage, the claims to equal credit made for the
Pinzón family, and Gonzalo Fernández de Oviedo's strange assertions
about ancient contacts with the western Atlantic threatened, singly or
collectively, to blot Hernando's father's name from the Book of History, to bankrupt his family, and to put paid to Hernando's plans for a
library the likes of which the world had never seen. Yet Hernando's
life, with years at the Sacra Rota in Rome and leading the Spanish
delegates to Badajoz, had amply prepared him for high-stakes games
of assertion and counterassertion. And, as at Badajoz, his library gave
him an immense advantage: within its holdings he could find the
books Oviedo was citing and all of Giustiniani's publications. He
could use them to show Giustiniani's account not only contradicted
the Columbus version of events but even contradicts itself, while
Oviedo has misunderstood what he was reading because of his poor
command of Latin. Each of these arguments could be checked, by
anyone who cared to, against any of the copies of these same works.
The library formed the perfect witness: objective in the fullest sense
of the word, of nearly faultless memory, and open to simple verification. The appetite with which Hernando pursued his advantage over

these adversaries was occasionally unattractive and may hint at some lingering disdain for his schoolmate Oviedo, but was wholly understandable given the circumstances.[2]

While the farragoes of Oviedo and Giustiniani were easily dismissed, the claims of the Pinzón family were not so simple. Hernando could, and did, reproduce the text of the *Capitulaciones de Santa Fe*, and the confirmation of these terms from 1493, always reminding the reader he was copying documents word for word that could be checked against official archives if necessary. These documents made clear that Columbus had rights over everything discovered on the expedition (and not just discovered *personally*), and that this extended from the Tordesillas Line westward to the Indies—as Hernando had asserted—rather than simply halfway around the world. But the lengths to which Hernando goes to show Columbus not only captained the first expedition across the Atlantic, but was the first person to see the fire lights on the island of Guanahani on the night of 11 October 1492, makes clear Hernando knew this was about something more than mere legal technicalities. It was Columbus, in Hernando's words, *who saw the light in the midst of darkness, in token of the spiritual light that he would bring to these benighted lands.* As we move from the question of Columbus's legal rights to his role in ordering the world, we enter the realm of biography proper.[3]

Hernando's library held many models for biography, many volumes telling the life stories of various kinds of people highly prized by European culture. There were saints' lives, in which the blessedness of the individual is marked out by precocious piety, inhuman feats of endurance, a disregard for earthly things, calm in the face of pain and death, and miracles surrounding the saint's remains; there were biographies of authors, written as prefaces to their books, which sought to flesh out the person who had written the works that followed—such as the life of Pico della Mirandola, written by his nephew and translated by (among others) Thomas More. Then there were collections of lives, mostly of political figures, such as the *Lives of the Noble Greeks and Romans* by Plutarch or Boccaccio's *On the Fall of Illustrious Men.*

Some political leaders merited separate biographies, including the life of Agricola by Tacitus or the life of Richard III that Thomas More had written but not yet published. Yet though life writing presents itself as focusing on the actions and motives of an individual, biography is a literary ruse, a sleight of hand that uses the personal story to say something about the world beyond that person, to arrange (in a sense) the world around them. The saints prove the existence of heaven by their special awareness of it and the divine rewards they reap; the literary biography explains the author's writings according to the manner of life he or she is shown to have led; the life of a political figure demonstrates the workings of society and history by revealing what kinds of character and policy succeed or fail within it. The point of a life is to make sense of the world in which it is lived, and Hernando's biography of his father is just such a project, an act of ordering and interpreting that strikingly—and perhaps inevitably—bears close relation to his obsessive thought about order in his library.

The relation of Hernando's *Life and Deeds of the Admiral* to the world belongs to one of the most powerful and enduring versions of biography: the assertion of *primacy*. Who was the first to discover, invent, create? Primacy is such a powerful and fundamental way of structuring the world that we rarely pause to examine its underlying assumptions, to question why it should matter if someone was first or the thirty-first to do a thing. Beneath these claims to primacy lies a notion of the world as sequence: it matters who did something because everything afterward follows from that, not just in the sense of being later than but also of being caused by. When God speaks to Job out of the whirlwind, His assertion of omnipotence is founded precisely on His being there *before everything else*: he is the first cause, the Prime Mover. Although this goes against one of the first principles of logic—*post hoc non est propter hoc* ("after" is not the same as "because of")—it is nonetheless a fundamental part of how many cultures understand the world. The deep European attachment to this principle was shown in Clenardus's letter suggesting Columbus was a god among men, and that Hernando could be one, too. In this

Clenardus was following a popular way of understanding pagan religion in the Renaissance, which argued (after the classical writer Euhemerus) that the pagan pantheon was simply homage to famous ancestors, and that the great inventors and discoverers of the past had slowly been transformed into gods as their mortal forms and lives faded from memory. If Columbus was the first discoverer of the New World, he was a god, a figure in the pantheon of history; if not, he was nothing, one of those to whom history had merely happened. Chronological lists of those who have invented, found, or discovered things provide us with one way of ordering the world.[4]

This method of arranging the world on the basis of primacy presented one of the first means of ordering the new libraries of the Renaissance. In the 1490s, Johannes Zeller of Tritheim (Trithemius)— whose library in Würzburg Hernando may well have visited in 1522— had created a list of around a thousand writers, placed in chronological order, drawing on even older, medieval models. (Hernando had owned a copy of this list since his trip to Florence in 1516.) Trithemius's work was part of a broad and complex project of chronology in the Renaissance, which engaged all available evidence to try to establish exact dates for historical texts and events. If confidence in major historical dates is something we largely take for granted, this is because of the painstaking and horrendously complex efforts of scholars such as Trithemius, who spent lifetimes sorting through a thicket of contradictory evidence about when precisely key events had happened—centrally, the birth of Christ, and everything else radiating out from this. The task became so maddening that in later life Trithemius took to inventing chronicles allowing him at last to put the unsettling lack of certainty to rest, eventually causing his exposure and disgrace. But even secure chronology has obvious limitations when one begins to apply it to the books in a library: books will appear to be bizarrely unrelated to books written the year before or the year after them, or even in the same year; books will not appear next to the titles to which they are responding or to which they inspired in turn—they won't even appear next to their own sequels in a properly chronological list of titles. Any attempt to be properly chronological quickly fails: other categories—form, genre, geography—must be introduced to make sense of it all, and before long chronology is not the major principle of order.[5]

The limitations in ordering the library chronologically are much the same as for thinking of history in that way: just because something is first does not mean that what comes after follows from it. Arguments can be made for Hernando's own primacy in various fields: the first to record magnetic variation; head of the first team to undertake a map on modern, "scientific" principles; the first to conceive of and attempt to create a truly universal library. Indeed, one might even suggest his life of Columbus is the first modern biography—not an exposition of theology (like a saint's life) or of national history (like the chronicles of kings), but taking a private individual as its subject, and attempting to understand not the example he provides for others but rather his uniqueness, and doing so moreover not using received traditions but documentary evidence and eyewitness report. The credibility of these claims, however, always rests on how they are framed—what do we consider evidence of "recording," what is "scientific" and "universal," what is the essence of a "modern" biography? More interesting, perhaps, is the question that will increasingly pose itself in the final parts of Hernando's life: What relationship do invention and discovery have with that which comes after?

The impossibility of proving *definitively* that his father was the first to cross the Atlantic meant Hernando had another, infinitely subtler task: to move beyond the establishment of simple primacy to the assertion of a *natural order*. He needed to demonstrate his father's extraordinary feat was in keeping with Columbus's character, something that convinced by its *probability* where he had failed to do so by proof. This is the focus of many modern biographies: it would not do for the great achievements of a celebrated figure's life to seem to come from random happenstance, so they must proceed inevitably from that person (and only ever from that person). In biographies written after the Enlightenment, this would take the form of narrating the events that led up to the crucial moment: if the mind was a blank slate, written upon by the world in which it lived, then the person was necessarily the sum total of the experiences leading up to that moment. Without this notion of internal development, however, the event must have some *external* cause: it is just as important, then, that we know nothing of the childhood of Jesus or of Galahad, because they were not formed into the Messiah or the Grail Knight by experience but were chosen for it by Providence or Destiny.

This distinction, between ways of ordering the world that are internal, that come from within us, and those that exist outside and simply await discovery, lay at the heart of another possible way of organizing the library. Just before returning to Spain from the Netherlands in 1531, Hernando had purchased at Antwerp a new book, *On the Disciplines* by Juan Luis Vives, the Spanish follower of Erasmus who served as tutor to Princess Mary Tudor until his stance on Henry VIII's divorce saw him expelled from England. In this book, Vives proposed a way of seeing knowledge that was entirely different to the thorny and abstract ideas of theologians and scholastic philosophers. Placing man himself at the center of things, Vives suggested the natural structure of knowledge is the one that comes from the order in which real people learn things. To explain what he means, he tells the story of a primitive man who leaves his dwelling and narrates the things he encounters: he must find food, learn to protect himself against his environment, and develop relationships with other human beings; eventually, he will have time to consider things such as beauty and to contemplate the heavens and the origins of things. Each of these things properly understood, Vives argues, is a field of knowledge, a discipline—agriculture, military science, politics, the liberal arts, theology—and meant that even the humblest men could know as much about the world as philosophers, given that all knowledge began in and was built from basic experiences. This, in a sense, reversed the ordering in medieval monasteries' libraries, in which the Things of God came first and everything else followed after. It is also

similar to, though not the same as, the chronological way of organizing the library: instead of placing the books, and the thoughts they
contain, in historical order—the sequence in which they occurred to
humanity as a whole—Vives suggests we should place them in the
order that they would occur to a particular person, as he or she builds
from basic experience to complex constructions. This *psychological*
way of ordering knowledge—though Vives would not have used that
term—fits the order of the world within the span of a human life.[6]

The decision whether to portray Columbus as someone who grew
into his knowledge of the world, or one of those who gained it by
inspiration from above, was (in a sense) made for Hernando because
his father did not *have* an early life that led up to the years of discovery. It is unclear whether to give credit to the strange and painful
confession Hernando makes early on in the biography, namely that he
did not know many of the details of his father's early life, having been
too full of filial piety during their years together to pry into a past that
was not volunteered. In truth, even if Hernando had known, he would
have been forced to draw a veil over the youth of his father. What we
know now of Columbus's early life—descended from humble weavers,
unlearned if not unlettered, caught up in the expansion of Genoese
shipping networks as they pushed west to make up for the rise of the
Ottomans in the East—would not combine, in most sixteenth-century
minds, to produce a major player in the history of the world and of
mankind. In response to this need, Hernando chose for his father a
form of life similar to that provided for other figures of destiny, such
as Jesus or Galahad. Hernando even suggests Columbus consciously
chose to be vague about his parentage and early life—so as to be like
the other Apostles, or like Christ himself, who, despite being
descended from the royal line of Jerusalem, preferred to be known as
the son of Mary and Joseph.

But Hernando also found for his father, buried in the library, an
origin story out of the pages of chivalric romance. The volume that
helped him to stitch this together still survives in his library today and
provides us not only with proof that Hernando wrote the biography,

but also with clues as to when and how and why. He records that he began reading the *Enneads* by the historian Sabellicus in 1534, on 3 August—that eventful date in the Columbus story, which marked both the beginning of his father's First Voyage and the start of Hernando's dictionary. On the page of this epic history that records Columbus's First Voyage, Hernando has marked out a passage in a way he reserved for those about his father: with a delicate and detailed drawing of a hand, its index finger pointing to the section in question, and the label "Christopher Columbus, my father." This symbol, known as a manicule, was commonly used by Renaissance readers to identify passages in text they thought important, but Hernando hardly ever used it. He has drawn another, similar mark a few pages earlier, however, next to a passage dealing with a man who shared his father's name: "Columbus junior, the Illustrious Archpirate."

From the pages of Sabellicus Hernando drew a wholly new story of Columbus's arrival in Portugal, at the beginning of his career as an explorer. Columbus (Hernando writes) was prompted to leave Genoa and take to the sea to join up with another man bearing the Columbus name, a member of the family who was a corsair in the western Mediterranean involved in the daring capture of four Venetian galleys off the coast of Portugal. Hernando writes for Columbus a role in this sea battle and departs from his usually fastidious accounts of the explorer's life to insert a scene of pure romance: it tells of how, when the ships closed on one another, hand-to-hand combat broke out, of such ferocity and daring that from morning until the hour of vespers the sailors fought without pity using sidearms as well as bombards and other explosives. At the climax of the battle Columbus's ship is set alight by one of the Venetian vessels, and the flames grow so quickly that those aboard can more easily bear the thought of drowning than the torment of the fire, and they leap overboard. Columbus, being a great swimmer and seeing land only two leagues distant, avails himself of an oar that fate presents to him and reaches shore, from where after many days of recovery he makes his way to Lisbon in the confidence that he will find others there of his Genoese nation.

God, the biography suggests, preserved Columbus that day for greater things.[7]

This description is so starkly different from the rest of the serious, documentary biography that it has left many Columbus experts with the conviction it could not have been written by his son. Indeed, if Hernando had not marked these passages in their source and drawn a link there between Columbus the Pirate and his father (who in reality were unrelated), it would seem out of keeping with his usually reserved and fastidious character. But in the light of this evidence, the scene reveals itself as central to Hernando's personality, though perhaps a part he kept hidden almost all his life: a moment in which the boy who lost in his father the source of his pride finds a secret place of fantasy to give that father a little more life. Resurrection is among the most powerful narrative devices ever invented, and this, I suppose, is just such a thing.

If Hernando could not *prove*, using documentary evidence, that his father was the first to discover the New World and could not provide him with a life that led naturally toward the act of discovery, what was left to him? The answer to this is related to a third way of organizing the world of knowledge, one to which we are led by the increasing diminutions of scale we have been following: from the chronological order, which arranges things on the scale of history, to the psychological, which takes the progress of a human life as the foundation of order, to the *physiological*, which takes the human body itself as the best model for how to understand the structure of the universe. Hernando had always been intensely interested in the body and in medicine, as is suggested by the large number of medical books among his early purchases, and this may have been part of the reason why during this climactic period of his life he traveled to France, where as well as visiting Montpellier (a center of medical science) and buying thousands of books, he sought out and met at Lyons the only modern author to join Erasmus in having his own section at the back of the alphabetical catalogue: Dr. Symphorien Champier. Champier is barely known today even among specialists of the period, but in his time he was a celebrated author on philosophy, history, and the occult sciences, the mystical attempts of which to unearth a hidden structure to the world drew strenuous objections from Champier. His main interest, however, was in medicine, and he presided over the medical college at Lyons alongside—among others—François Rabelais. Rabelais had lovingly mocked his senior colleague in *Pantagruel*, including in the chaotic Library of St. Victor many volumes by Champier, as well as in the episode in which the author takes a journey into Pantagruel's innards after being sheltered during a rainstorm by the giant prince of Utopia's tongue. Rabelais's jocular suggestion that the real worlds awaiting discovery actually lay *within* the human body was part of a fundamental concept at the time; namely that the body reflected the same structure as the world outside—it was a microcosm, or small universe, reflecting the big one. Erasmus himself had translated several short treatises by the leading figure of classical medicine, Galen, and was a close supporter of many of the leading medical figures of the day, including Paracelsus (a pioneer in using cadavers for teaching and research, opening the secrets of man's insides to the same scrutiny Hernando had given to the manatee) and Champier himself. Given the relation between microcosm and macrocosm, Erasmus reasoned, the true physician was also a philosopher. The reverse was also true: anyone interested in philosophy, in how knowledge *works*, would be mad not to take as their road map the human body, giving one as it did a local laboratory in which to investigate that God in whose image man had been created. In an oration, *In Praise of Medicine*, which Hernando had bought in Bruges at the end of his first European tour, Erasmus had declared that medicine *comprises not one or two branches of science but an encyclopedic knowledge of all the arts*, that it brought together "countless disciplines, an infinite knowledge of things," and, quoting Galen, that the physician was *a man of universal knowledge.*

On just these grounds Hernando founded the central claim of his biography of Columbus. Time and again during the *Life and Deeds of the Admiral*, he suggests his father had succeeded where others failed because of his superhuman discipline, endurance, and self-control, which allowed Columbus to ignore the many signs in the ocean that his crews were scrabbling to interpret and to focus instead, calmly, on the threefold argument that had convinced him he would find land in the west—reason, the authority of ancient writers, and the reports from other sailors in the Atlantic. Hernando considered the proof of this levelheadedness to be the logs his father so assiduously kept, meticulous records demonstrating that the path to discovery was through the slow and methodical compilation of measurements, records, and observations. In his biography Hernando even sets up an antagonist, a rival who represents the opposite approach—none other than Martín Alonso Pinzón, who in Hernando's telling is endlessly scheming, paranoid, and capricious, and who (as his reward) dies of a broken heart when Ferdinand and Isabella deny his attempt to announce the discovery.

This image of Columbus, which has, since Hernando created it, been central to the legend of the explorer, required Hernando to perform considerable acts of historical revision to make it work. Gone from Hernando's life of his father are Columbus's beliefs that he had in 1492 reached the Far East—Cipangu and the outskirts of Cathay—and many of the wilder theories about the places he had visited, which survive in his letters to the *Reyes Católicos*. *The Book of Prophecies*, with its argument that Columbus's discoveries were part of God's plan for mankind, with its divine revelations that Columbus and Hernando used to guide them on the Fourth Voyage, is nowhere mentioned. Hernando is also silent on the series of visions his father experienced from 1498 onward, which were felt by Columbus to be guiding him in his ventures and to be proof of his election by God for the task. Hernando similarly fails to mention his father's attempt to make his discoveries profitable by starting a trade in Arawak Indian slaves, and instead emphasizes the great affection Columbus had for the New World natives and his attempts to save them from Christian brutalities. As with so much in Hernando's biography of Columbus, this narrative constructs the character that was needed in the 1530s—when it was clear America was not part of the Asian continent, when the providential character of Columbus's discoveries was less clear, and when the railing of Bartolomé de Las Casas had begun to open European eyes to the atrocities of the conquistadores—and bears little resemblance to the Columbus who comes out of his own writings. If anything, the Columbus portrayed in the *Life and Deeds of the Admiral*—the calm and methodical compiler of information, sympathetic to the ideas of Las Casas—looks a lot more like Hernando himself.[8]

Hernando's extended tour of southern France, where he was once again amassing large numbers of books—particularly medical tomes and the printed music for which Lyons was beginning to be famous— was cut abruptly short when, in mid-1536, he was summoned from Avignon to the Spanish court at Valladolid. That the queen had ordered comfortable lodgings to be prepared for him against his arrival may have alerted him that the tide, flowing for so long against the Columbus family fortunes, had finally turned in their favor. Ten days before he was summoned to court, the judges who had been assigned to arbitrate between the Columbus family and the crown had pronounced their verdict, one that reinstated Diego's son Luis as hereditary Admiral of the Indies and also conferred upon him the titles of Marquis of Jamaica and Duke of Veragua. Though the verdict did not reinstate the Columbuses to the governorship of Hispaniola or the vice-regency of the Indies and denied them the vast financial claims over the riches of the New World promised to Columbus in the *Capitulaciones de Santa Fe* in 1492, it nevertheless awarded the heir the not inconsiderable annual pension of ten thousand ducados, as well as a series of smaller pensions for other members of the family. The judges seem, mercifully, to have overlooked Hernando's self-inflicted wound when he gave away his rights to his patrimony at La Coruña in 1520 and awarded him a pension of a thousand ducados for life, to which the emperor added a further five hundred gold pesos to help with the work on the library.[9]

While we cannot be certain what role Hernando's biography had in this final victory for the Columbus legacy, its timing and its direct address to the case against his father suggest the *Life and Deeds of the Admiral* was designed to play a decisive part at a key moment in the history of his family and of Spain. Whatever the immediate effect upon the Columbus fortunes, Hernando's biography of his father was to have an immense and lasting impact upon European history, both through the image of his father that arose from it and by creating a model for future narratives of European superiority, narratives founded on the qualities of discipline and technical mastery Hernando put at the center of his portrait. Like the *Life and Deeds of the Admiral*, these narratives would quietly ignore the religious zealotry and pure serendipity that often drove European expansion. But for the moment Hernando must have swelled with the knowledge that the onslaught on his father's reputation, which had continued almost without pause for nearly forty years, was finally in retreat and had been put to flight in large part by his own efforts.

With Columbus's legacy now more secure than at any other time since Hernando was a boy, he was able at last to turn his mind to perfecting his own creation. For this mammoth and unprecedented task, time was running short, and Hernando could no longer rely on the help he had scoured Europe for during his tour of 1529–31: the Burgundian doctor Jean Hammonius had been ill-suited to the heat of southern Spain and had quickly succumbed to a fever upon arriving in Seville, dying shortly afterward; Clenardus was too entranced by the Arabic riches on offer elsewhere to be tied down to Hernando's library in Seville. Soon after Hernando left him in Salamanca, Clenardus had also lured away his friend from Louvain Jean Vasaeus to join him there, before setting off himself to Portugal, from where he would plan a linguistic crusade into North Africa, using his beloved Arabic to set in motion a universal conversion of the Barbary Muslims. Hernando helped his friend occasionally during these years, scouring the markets of Seville with him in search of a Moor to help with his studies of Arabic. In the end, though, Hernando would have to face his library and its gargantuan challenges alone.[10]

XVI

Last Orders

With the settling of the family suit, Hernando could finally turn his full attention to his masterwork, though it was gradually becoming clear he was working against the clock. He seems to have suffered constantly in his final years from mysterious fevers similar to those that deprived his father of sight and of sense; his books increasingly record him being read to rather than reading himself, and his choice of titles shows a mind turning more and more toward Last Things. If his own fragile health were not enough to sharpen his focus on the imminent end, something else soon provided a definite and swiftly approaching moment of closure. In June 1537 Charles gave permission for Columbus's remains to be exhumed from the Capilla de Santa Ana at las Cuevas, where they had lain since 1509, and for them to be reinterred in the new cathedral nearing completion in Hispaniola. It is doubtful Hernando even paused before deciding to accompany his father's remains to this final resting place, and soon he was acquiring the relevant permits for this crossing. Among these documents are many indications that he did not imagine he would ever return from the New World: not only did he gain permission to transport four black slaves as the foundation of a household in Hispaniola, but the will Hernando drew up made specific provision for his remains should he die at sea or in foreign lands, and he even wrote an epitaph for himself that mentioned *three* voyages to the New World. This renewed funeral procession, thirty years and more after the Admiral's death, was to be a kind of pilgrimage in reverse: a journey that would make the destination more sacred and would bring Columbus and the world he had discovered together, creating a center on what had once been the edge of the world.[1]

The journey would end in the cathedral of Nuestra Señora de la Encarnación in Santo Domingo. In the town Bartholomew Columbus named for their father, the grid of streets had slowly been encompassed with stone, moving inland from the earthworks at the river Ozama and the Calle de Damas, which was now strung with stout Castilian mansions between the Fortaleza and where it ended in the Alcázar de Colón, a New World palace like those in which Hernando and Diego had been billeted as pages of the court. The cathedral was a block farther from the shore and had been under construction since 1523, under the direction of Alessandro Geraldini, who had left his post as confessor to Catherine of Aragon to serve as bishop of Santo Domingo. The original wooden structure had been replaced by a Gothic nave in dressed stone, where, in a crypt under the altar, the Admiral's body would lie. As the only Gothic building in the New World, the cathedral with its ribbed vaulting and stone tracery is an isolated memory of the Europe from which Columbus had set out, an island forgotten in the river of time. It was, in a sense, the perfect resting place for Columbus's remains, with its willful attempt to make the New World in the image of the Old, even as the Caribbean trees erupting into the square outside protest in silent eloquence against this fantasy.

The prospect of this journey seems to have convinced Hernando, who was ever the master of beginnings but not of endings, that the time had come to make final the form of his library. By this point, at over fifteen thousand volumes, it was by far the largest private collection in Europe and also contained the largest collection of printed images and printed music in the world; yet it was far from satisfying Hernando's ambitions. He had been putting together elements of his design throughout his life—in the travels he had made across Europe and to the New World, in the libraries and bookshops he had visited, in the parts of the Caribbean he had traveled and the things he had seen there; in a sense, the design is no more or less than a summary of his life. But only in these final years could he bring himself to describe what had been gathering in his mind for so long. In four documents—a letter to Charles V, his last will and testament, and notes left by his executor and librarian—we begin to see the lineaments of this thing, born of a lifetime spent in the print markets of Europe. As he reveals his plan, it becomes clear the Biblioteca Hernandina (as he wished it to be known) would be not simply a building or a set of books but an engine for extracting the writing of all mankind, an organism adapted to living in the new world of print. "It is one thing," he wrote in his letter to the emperor, "to build a library of those things found in our time: but entirely another, to order things in such a way that all new things are sought out and gathered forever."[2]

Hernando's design began with a root system that tapped into the core of print, using existing trade networks to draw books to the library. The major arteries would start in five cities central both to print and to Hernando's life: the great Italian book cities of Rome and Venice, where Hernando's project had first taken shape, and through which flowed new works from Greece, Byzantium, and the missionary ventures; Nuremberg, Dürer's city, where Hernando first began to amass tomes from the German kingdoms and the lands to their east; Antwerp, the great book emporium for the Low Countries, Scandinavia and Britain; and Paris, the center of French publishing, to which Hernando had only gained access late in life after decades of warfare. Each year in April, a bookseller chosen in each of these five cities would send twelve ducados' worth of newly printed books to Lyons— itself a center of musical and medical publishing—where a sixth bookseller would gather them and add a further twelve ducados' worth from his own city. All these books together would then be sent overland by a merchant to Medina del Campo, at the time of the May fair Hernando knew so well, and from there on to Seville and the library at the Puerta de Goles. Every sixth year, an agent from the library, carrying with him the catalogues of the Hernandina, would sweep through a series of smaller cities, seeking out titles that had been missed. The itinerary, which Hernando lays out in detail, is a voyage through his own memory, following routes he knew intimately: starting in Naples, the book hunter should then take the Sunday *percacho* (stagecoach) to Rome, proceeding from there to Siena, Pisa, Lucca and Florence, Bologna, Modena, Arezo (i.e. Reggio Emilia), Parma, Piacenza, Pavia, Milan—all cities (he notes) a half day's journey from each other—Lodi, Cremona, Mantua, Venice, and Padua. The harvest from these places would be gathered at Venice, where the Genoese merchants could send the books on to Cadiz.

Hernando's next instruction would have been astonishing to other collectors of the day: he ordered that they should not seek to recruit the help of grand booksellers in these cities, because these places would never deign to look outside their own stockrooms for the pamphlets and one-sheet ballads that Hernando was determined to have in his library. Owners of small bookshops, he reasoned, were much more likely to go out into the city and learn what was on offer there. In fact, the instructions for buying were exactly the reverse of those followed by other famous libraries of the day. The humble bookseller chosen to gather books in each of the six major cities should *first* buy as many of these ephemeral pamphlets as he could with the twelve ducados, only then moving on to larger printed books, and finally—if anything remained after all of this—buying those manuscript works that were the objects of lust to other librarians of the day. The buyers were, furthermore, forbidden from paying more for manuscripts than they did for printed books, and even the more expensive printed books were not to be bought but merely noted in a list sent to the library for further consideration. At the heart of Hernando's extraordinary instructions is a profound intuition, one that almost no other person yet shared—namely that the invention of print had upended the world of information, replacing one in which a few authoritative and venerable manuscripts held sway with one flooded by an endless supply of the new. Each of these novelties by itself might seem slight and of little value, but taken together they made up the giant mass of what the world had committed to writing. No engine had yet been conceived to harness this flood of words, to make this plenitude knowable to individuals rather than simply a source of confusion and revulsion. That Hernando believed he had succeeded in doing so is reflected in the verses he asked to be inscribed near the door of the library:

> The wise care little for widely held views
> As most people are easily swayed
> And that which they throw from their houses
> Is later thought to be of highest value.

The meaning of this inscription, he says, *is that I have founded my house upon the shit that others once threw upon the dunghill.* The wry humor with which Hernando draws attention to this fact—that his house is both built upon a dunghill and filled with things thought by many to be of little worth—is born of the supreme confidence of the visionary, who no longer cares that others aren't seeing what he is. Whether or not he knew it, Hernando had by his last days succumbed in some measure to the visionary madness he had removed with such painstaking care from the record of his father's life.[3]

If Hernando's contemporaries would have been baffled by his decision to favor cheap print, many might have been scandalized by what came next. In a phrase he repeated often in these final documents, Hernando stated the library would collect *all books, in all languages and on all subjects, which can be found both within Christendom and without.* While it is not entirely clear how he hoped books from outside of Christendom would arrive at the library—though he might reasonably hope global trade would bring them through his book hubs at Seville, Venice, and Antwerp—his refusal to privilege particular languages, subjects, or even the knowledge of Christian authors represents a radical transformation of how knowledge was understood to work—what, in a sense, knowledge was understood *to be.* The focus of most medieval European libraries on works by Christian authors was driven by the simple idea that the highest kind of knowledge was revealed by God, and that therefore you must be dealing with the right god for true knowledge to be revealed—everything from other gods would simply be false revelation. Medieval and then Renaissance humanist readers, enraptured by the thinking and writing of ancient Greek and Roman writers (and, less often but no less importantly, writers in Arabic and Hebrew), managed sometimes to bring them into the libraries of monasteries and universities, though their arguments that these authors had a partial form of revelation, allowing them to contribute to the understanding of God's world, did not always convince everyone. The humanist libraries Hernando would have known in Rome and Venice replaced the authority of Christian knowledge with that of classical knowledge, using the notion of "the translation of empire" to argue a resurrection of classical knowledge would bring with it a return of the glories of the classical empires. But *all* of these libraries, whether Christian or humanist, retained a hierarchy of knowledge: some knowledges were simply better than others, and the library should put its energies into collecting those. The same is true for languages and subjects: without exception, other libraries of the day privileged some languages and some subjects over others, usually reflecting their social status—the languages used by elites (the classical tongues, and increasingly Italian and French) were more valued than less well established vernaculars, and the literature of elite occupations (theology, law, medicine) was favored over writings that dealt with more mechanical crafts. The idea that Hernando's library would not be bounded by language, subject, or religion once again marks a profound shift in European conceptions of knowledge. This does not, it should be said, mean his idea of knowledge was without prejudices of class, nation, or faith—far from it. Nothing in these documents indicates he had stopped thinking of the library, in these final days, as a counterpart of the universal, Christian, Spanish empire he believed his father had set in motion, and which he hoped would one day submit to Charles V and his heirs. But the notion that the power to subdue the world might come not from a few, privileged sources of knowledge, but from a distillation of all that the world had to offer, regardless of origin, represents an imaginative leap of immense proportions.[4]

If the channels flowing into the library were more voluminous and diverse than any previously imagined, the arrangements made for the materials once they arrived at the library were scarcely less surprising. The single, enormous room that Hernando was intent on constructing for his books may not have looked that different from some of the great libraries of Europe—similar, perhaps, to the great Laurentian Library that Michelangelo was even then constructing for Pope Clement in Florence—even if the bookshelves lining the walls would have been an unusual sight, with their books standing vertically and displaying their call numbers and titles on their spines. More striking, however, would have been the metal grate standing six feet from the bookshelves and trapping the readers in the center of the room, like divers in a shark tank. The gauge of the crisscrossed metalwork was designed to be large enough for readers to stick their hands through to turn the pages of books, which librarians would place in front of them on lecterns, but too small for them to pull the books back through. Hernando expected many readers would object to this bizarre and draconian arrangement, but on this matter he was insistent. Perhaps still flinching from the fate of the Roman libraries during the sack of that city, he mused that even a hundred chains were not enough to keep a book safe. And the grate was not the only measure taken to ensure the collection's safety. Hernando set down a strict code of penalties to be imposed upon the librarians—who were to live in the library, and whose accommodation was specified down to their bedding—if any books were to go missing. He also ordered a monastery should be found—perhaps las Cuevas across the river—where in a sheltered place any duplicate titles could be kept in large wooden chests, set upon runners to keep them from the dampness of the floor. These chests were to be opened two or three times a year, and the books turned to prevent their warping, but would otherwise be kept safe as insurance for the library against the violence of man and nature. Readers who protested against being kept at arm's length from their books were to be told the library's primary purpose was not for it to be used by the public. They might, at least, console themselves in the shop of unwanted books, stocked with titles that the library had in three or more copies—which would still, Hernando expected, be the greatest bookstore in all of Europe, drawing as it did from such a huge network of suppliers.[5]

That the library was not for public consultation did not mean it was not meant to be useful to the public. Part of Hernando's jealousy in guarding the collections was to ensure a place existed in which all writings could be kept safe forever, a doomsday vault that would prevent human culture from being lost again on the scale it had at the end of the classical period. This central, read-only data bank would also guarantee there was somewhere in which matters of great doubt could be resolved: a complete library, with a copy of every book by every author, would allow assertions to be checked against the originals, rooting out contradiction and error as Hernando had done at Badajoz and in his biography. Yet it would be wrong to assume Hernando thought of the library primarily as a place of last resort, a sanctuary that guarded against the loss of books by making them inaccessible. Confusing as it initially sounds, Hernando declared the library's central purpose to be the compilation of the three great catalogues that served as guides to its collections—the *Book of Epitomes*, the *Book of Materials*, and the final project, the *Table of Authors and Sciences*, the form of which will become clear shortly. This sounds at first like madness—the gathering of these infinite collections only to lock them away and make lists of them—until it emerges that Hernando intended copies of these catalogues to be distributed throughout Spain. As the testimony of his last librarian shows, the imagined reader of the *Book of Epitomes* and the *Book of Materials* is not sitting in the library at all, but in some remote location, without access to many books. The distribution of these catalogues would allow an unlimited number of readers to navigate through the collections of the library from a distance, using the *Book of Materials* to search for key words and the *Book of Epitomes* to digest many volumes at a sitting, sorting relevant material from irrelevant. As a counterpart to his global memory vault, Hernando had created a search engine.[6]

It is hard to capture fully the excitement of Hernando's creation. Whereas many libraries of the age—and of the ages directly succeeding this—were little more than boxes for holding the books of their founders, Hernando had engineered a system to draw the knowledge of the world to the banks of the Guadalquivir, to process it into indexes and epitomes that would make it useful, and then to redistribute it, creating a network that could access the immense realm of print. Extraordinary as this was, though, Hernando realized these measures helped only those who already knew which book they were looking for, enabling them to search for a title in the catalogue or a key word in the *Book of Materials*. Using the library to discover new things, however, was a different matter altogether. This requires an act of browsing, which may seem like the most casual and undirected of acts, but is in truth where the library works most powerfully upon the mind of the reader. It both suggests certain categories and links they have little choice but to accept and puts other things far apart, out of sight and out of mind. In these final years, Hernando and his assistants were busy rearranging his library to conform to the *Table of Authors and Sciences*, his last catalogue, which provided a subject order that attempted to divide the library into manageable sections.

The underlying architecture of this was simple enough, following the basic divisions of medieval knowledge into the Trivium (grammar, rhetoric, logic), the Quadrivium (arithmetic, geometry, music, and astronomy), and the three professional fields of medicine, theology, and law. But these categories were no longer enough to navigate the world of print—many already contained, as they began to be arranged on the shelves of Hernando's library, hundreds if not thousands of titles, and the problem would only get worse as the network he had designed began to draw books to the collection. The category of rhetoric, for instance, covered every sort of writing (in verse and prose) that did not belong to other categories, from works of ancient history to bawdy ballads and reports of recent battles. Within these larger categories, then, Hernando began to divide the books, to assemble the things that belonged together in his mind: rows of orations and saints' lives, a section of sermons and another of Roman history. The logic of these gatherings, which have never before been reassembled, is not always clear: often it is like staring at a tablet in a lost language, beautiful but wholly impenetrable. After following Hernando through his life, however, many sections are instantly recognizable as reflections of his own experiences. The first section of his library is given over to dictionaries, tables, and catalogues; he puts geographical writings with philosophy but also with chess, after spending a lifetime trying to know the world by plotting it on a grid. The library and the librarian cannot help but reflect each other, endlessly forming and being formed in each other's image.

If the order of the books seems in danger of solipsism, of telling us nothing about the world outside the library but only about the librarian himself, the *Table of Authors and Sciences* had one last trick to perform. Unlike the other catalogues designed to guide the book hunter through the collection, the *Table* was not a thick and weighty tome. In fact, it was not a book at all. Rather, the *Table* consisted of more than ten thousand scraps of paper, each having an "annotation" including Hernando's book hieroglyphs, which gave access to a vast amount of information about the book at a glance, as well as a wealth of other details, from title and author to subject matter and publication details. What is instantly recognizable to us as a form of card catalogue would have been an inexpressible mystery in a world where decades would pass before this system began to be used elsewhere. We should not let our own experience of card catalogues—of filing cabinets exuding the vanilla odors of decaying paper, long since neglected for the computer terminals nearby—distract us from the wonder and the novelty of this thing. For the promise heralded by this card index—the *Table of Authors and Sciences*—was essentially one of infinite orders, of a catalogue that could eternally rearrange itself to suit the needs of the searcher, shuffling and sorting to make first one thing and then the next the main principle of order. It was a century and a half before the philosopher Gottfried Leibniz, attempting to organize the Royal Library at Hanover, was similarly struck by how "a single truth can usually be put in many different places," creating a machine he called a note closet that allowed him to rearrange his index cards at will to suit the purpose of his present chain of thought.[7]

Yet even as Hernando's miraculous library reached its greatest moment of triumph, a storm was building on the horizon. Although the first ten thousand books had been ordered, sorted into subject categories and subcategories, the system begins to break down in the numbers above ten thousand. With the rising sea of books, it may have become impossible even to *look at* each one for long enough to understand what it was about, to know where in the library to put it. Above ten thousand, the books begin for the first time to be divided by language—long runs of books that share nothing more than being written in Italian or in French. While the sections of the library up until that point had blended the languages together, aiming to order all the gathered knowledge of humankind without regard to where it came from, the sheer scale of the task seems to have forced certain compromises on Hernando and his assistants toward the end. Perhaps there was not time to do anything more than simply glance at the title and the first few pages before putting the book with others in the same language. This seems an eminently practical solution, and a choice made in good faith—maybe even something they might have hoped to correct at some time in the future, even though the number of books was likely to continue to expand at an alarming rate. It was, however, a solution that was to have disastrous historical consequences.

The problems of scale were being compounded by the problems of finance. Who on earth was going to *pay* for this gigantic thing, this enterprise that grew exponentially in size and complexity? Hernando's letter to the emperor, explaining the form of his library and the marvelous benefits it promised to its enlightened patron, was merely a preamble to a request that the pensions Hernando had been allocated for life be allowed to outlive him, to be granted in perpetuity to the upkeep and expansion of the library. Even if the wealth Hernando could himself claim was sufficient to make a start—and there is reason to doubt it was—it was nevertheless tied up in a complex set of annuities and debts owed to him for various things, many in the New World, assets he had struggled to lay his hands on during his lifetime and that would almost certainly be even more elusive after his death. The fabric of the library was far from complete: outside his window two "blacks" were still employed with their beasts, dredging the waterlogged earth after the massive landscaping Hernando had undertaken, creating a vista of the place where his father's remains were being prepared for departure. Fifty days before his death, and knowing the end was not far away, Hernando began to draw up a final inventory of all the things around him, right down to the pewter mugs and cups of his household, just as in his days as a page with the *Book of Everything* at the court of the Infante Juan. A price was put on each of these things, the accumulated detritus of a life, in a document to be appended to his will. The estate was to be made over, in its pieces and its entirety, to his nephew Luis, Diego's son and heir, along with 15,370 books, over 3,000 printed images, the Casa de Goles, a garden of plants never before seen together, the maps and papers of Columbus, and the most sophisticated piece of information technology ever designed. In return for his life's work and the legacy of their great progenitor, Hernando asked that the young Columbus scion commit one hundred thousand maravedís a year to the upkeep and expansion of the library—a mere fifteenth of what Hernando had once been promised as his inheritance.[8]

For all the singularity of Hernando's purpose in his final days, seeking to ensure his beloved library would be safe after he left it, the will he drew up shows that lives cannot be so easily and neatly tied together. Many things still clearly weighed on his mind as he prepared to die: the Basque mule driver he had mistreated on his return from England in 1522, a tile maker from Triana in Seville with whom he was in dispute, the relatives of Jean Hammonius, who had joined him in Paris only to die quickly and in strange circumstances. In a break from the silence of the preceding decades, when his father's name alone was on his lips, Hernando does ask for his mother to be remembered in his funeral prayers. In this light, among the many minor bequests he made, one perhaps stands out more than others: a bequest to one Leonor Martinez, daughter of an innkeeper in Lebrija—a town between Seville and the seaport at Sanlúcar—explaining the payment of three thousand maravedís only by saying it was "for the discharge of his conscience." These words might mean little if not for the fact that it was the same phrase his brother had used when offering to pay off his mistress Isabel de Gamboa, and that his father had used when leaving a pitiful inheritance to Hernando's mother, Beatriz Enríquez. Hernando's compulsion to list every detail may have betrayed him into revealing that, along with his father's singleness of purpose, he had inherited Columbus's blindness to all other claims upon his life. But even with his characteristic completeness in this last list, his will, Hernando struggles to sum the pieces of his life, confined as it is to a list of credits and debts. Who knows what may have lingered in his conscience to the end, but have been beyond the scope of this list, like the girls who came aboard the ship in Cariay, naked but for the gold pendants over which his father obsessed, and whose bravery he admired so much.[9]

But even to the end, the father he had lost (as he noted precisely) thirty-three years before held the place of honor in his mind. The funeral monument he designed for himself, which interrupts the dense writing of his will with a glorious illustration, is a striking symbol of this: it centers on Columbus's coat of arms, with its picture of islands, and his motto

A Castilla y Léon
Nuevo mundo dió Colón

To Castile and Leon
Columbus gave a New World

Yet the supporters of the shield—which in heraldic terms are the pillars of the dead man's fame—transformed its meaning. While these would usually be heraldic beasts or symbolic figures representing the virtues of the deceased, Hernando has placed the four principal catalogues of his library as his claim to a place in history equal to his father's:

The Book of Authors
The Book of Sciences
The Book of Epitomes
The Book of Materials

At eight o'clock in the morning, on 12 July 1539, Hernando called for a bowl of soil to be brought to his bedside and painted his face with the mud of the Guadalquivir, from which his father was being removed on the other bank.

XVII

Epilogue: Ideas on the Shelf

The glorious world that Hernando had woven out of the strands of his life began to unravel shortly after he died. Luis Colón, Diego's son, who was now Marquis of Jamaica and Duke of Veragua as well as the third Admiral, showed little interest in the library left him by his uncle; the only further role he would play in Hernando's story was when, late in life and imprisoned in Oran (North Africa) on charges of bigamy, he may have given (or sold) Hernando's biography of Columbus to a Genoese merchant, who financed its publication in Venice. After five years of abandonment, in 1544 María de Toledo had the books transferred to the monastery of San Pablo in Seville, where during the following decade Bartolomé de Las Casas used them to write his monumental histories of the New World discoveries and of the brutal genocide inflicted upon its native inhabitants. After a legal challenge by the Cathedral of Seville—Hernando's second choice to inherit the books—the library was moved there in 1552, where it has remained to this day.

Yet the cathedral proved anything but a sanctuary. Many of the books fell prey to the Inquisition, which identified certain of them as proscribed, including the works of Erasmus, next to whose name, in the volume he gave to Hernando, is written the phrase "*auctor damnatus*"—a condemned author. In 1592 the Spanish historian Argote de Molina was to lament that the library was now "incarcerated in an attic room off the nave, and used by nobody." The custodian who at the beginning of the eighteenth century looked after the library along with the candles and wall hangings of the cathedral would record that, when a child, he and his friends used to play among the books, leafing through the illuminated manuscripts to look at the pictures. Though an interest would again begin to be taken in the library at the end of the nineteenth century and (still more so) at the end of the twentieth—around the fourth and fifth centennials of 1492—almost five centuries of neglect, poor storage, and pilfering have reduced the collection from its original glory to a state that, though still infinitely precious, is also a painful reminder of how much has been lost. Of the original fifteen thousand to twenty thousand volumes, fewer than four thousand remain. Some of the rest can be found scattered among the world's great antiquarian book collections, instantly recognizable by Hernando's characteristic notes on where he bought the book and how much he paid; many more simply decayed to pulp and dust. Hernando's collection of images, the greatest of the Renaissance, has disappeared in its entirety, likely destroyed by water damage and simply thrown away. The originals of Columbus's logs, recording the discovery of the New World, have vanished, leaving historians to rely on transcriptions by Bartolomé de Las Casas and accounts by Hernando. Hernando's card catalogue to his library, containing the final order of his library and the potential to make his collection infinitely sortable, is likewise lost. The remaining portion of the library continued to be damaged by flooding, with significant disasters in 1955 and again in the 1980s. Miraculously amid this destruction most of the catalogues survive, providing us with a map of his collection at a level of detail unparalleled for its day. And even during the writing of this book, new discoveries give fresh hope that more of Hernando's library can be resurrected: the priceless *Book of Epitomes*, which summarized thousands of books from the library, including many that now exist nowhere in the world, has been found in an archive in Copenhagen after going missing for more than four centuries.[1]

Hernando's dream of a universal library, bringing together every book without distinction of creed or language or subject matter, similarly went with him to the grave. Though others in the age to come also recognized the need to harness the powerful flood of information they saw around them, none had the maniacal ambition Hernando had inherited from his father, and all those who followed in Hernando's wake set much narrower bounds for their projects. The great Swiss polymath Conrad Gesner, who in addition to making important contributions in botany and zoology attempted to sketch a complete map of knowledge in his *Bibliotheca universalis*, nevertheless confined himself to learned works in classical languages and satisfied himself with making catalogues without ever attempting to actually gather the books together in one place. Francis Bacon imagined a place of universal knowledge (in his utopian *New Atlantis*) that may have been modeled on Hernando's vision for the Casa de Contratación, and though this "House of Salomon" served as a blueprint for London's Royal Society, it was by then cut off from the idea of collecting books and images on a universal scale. In the mid-sixteenth century several European countries—Spain, France, England—founded (or attempted to found) national libraries, and Philip II's Escorial library may have taken materials and ideas from Hernando's creation, including building the oldest surviving bookshelves on Hernando's model. With a few exceptions, the great library projects in the following centuries did not collect the flimsy pamphlets that captured contemporary events and popular culture, leaving later collectors to scrabble to save what could still be found of these precious things. The national libraries, and the national bibliographies that went along with them, were also increasingly focused on building collections that captured the publications and spirit of the nations that built them, and had no aspirations toward the universal. The solution Hernando had been forced into during his final years, of dealing with the excess of printed information by sorting it into different languages, became widespread, effectively walling the thought of one culture off from another and giving the impression that each had a unique and independent existence. More often than not books from different languages and cultural traditions were simply excluded, as European nations responded to the cornucopian world by turning their backs and stopping their ears. Perhaps unsurprisingly, from the bowels of these libraries antiquarians emerged, in the late eighteenth and the early nineteenth centuries, to articulate ideas about distinct (and superior) national characters, ideas that were to become increasingly hard-set during the rise of nationalism in the late nineteenth century and its attendant horrors in the twentieth.[2]

Similarly, just as the thought and writing of different nations became increasingly separate within the space of the library, so the disciplines into which books were divided became more distant from one another, making it harder and harder for anyone to work in fields as varied and disparate as Hernando did. The later Renaissance and the Age of Enlightenment presented many examples of polymaths— Conrad Gesner, Athanasius Kircher, Gottfried Leibniz—but in many ways these men embodied a fantasy of universal knowledge in a world to which the possibility of knowing everything was lost, a world in which labor was increasingly divided and knowledge increasingly specialized. This fantasy, which lingers today, is prompted in part by the alienation brought on by the fragmentation of knowledge, one that asks each mind to be content with knowledge of only a few small pieces in the whole puzzle.

Some of Hernando's ideas were to be taken up later, by other people in ages better equipped to carry them through to completion. Emperor Charles's son, Philip II of Spain, was in the 1570s to set in motion a project to survey Spain (the *Relaciones Topográficas*) that bore a striking resemblance to the *Description* Hernando had been ordered to halt in 1523. The concept of magnetic variation or magnetic declination, which Hernando may have been the first to record in his arguments for the Badajoz conference and in his biography of his father, were later to be put on a firmer footing by Edmund Halley in the eighteenth century when he produced a map showing the contours of magnetic variation. The eventual solution to the problem of accurately measuring longitude, when it came in the form of John Harrison's marine chronometer, bore a certain resemblance to what

Hernando had imagined in his *instrumento fluente* in 1524. But Hernando's grandest ambition—to create a repository of all of the written knowledge of the world, searchable by key word, navigable through short summaries, and sortable by different criteria, all accessible from points widely dispersed in space—represents an extraordinary premonition of the world of the internet, the World Wide Web, search engines, and databases that was to emerge almost five centuries later. While Hernando's efforts were astounding and his plans were a marvel of conception, the project he envisioned was in truth not possible without digitization, the ability of machines to read and transcribe texts, and search algorithms that could be run through the Boolean logic of computers. When these technologies did become available, the information behemoth Google was able in the Google Books project to complete in a few short years much of the work that had been stalled for the five centuries since Hernando's death (even if that revolutionary project was again quickly mired in legal difficulties over copyright and to this day remains half-hidden).

If Hernando's dream of a universal library was for him impossible to realize, his tireless labors are nevertheless immensely instructive to this generation, which has the same dreams and faces the same challenges. Confronted with the constant and exponential growth of information in the digital age, the digital search companies seeking to chart this sphere know (as Hernando did) that all this information is useless—*dead*—unless it can be divided up, sorted and searched effectively. Understandably, much effort has been focused on attempting to predict what the wanderer in the library (or the internet) is most likely to want, and presenting this in response to his or her queries. This, perhaps, is to some extent inevitable, as people will necessarily be drawn to a map that leads them to what they desire. But it also leads, inevitably and perhaps inexorably, to a world in which the library provides nothing more than an infinite series of mirrors, giving people back that which they already know and already think. Hernando clearly saw this problem with his initial catalogues—that they only worked if you already knew the author, title, or subject you were looking for—and he was, at the time of his death, working to provide a universal schematic of the library (and, by extension, of knowledge) that would allow people to wander in places they did not know, perhaps had not even dreamed existed. There is, as yet, no such map to enable us to wander in unfamiliar realms of the new information age, and without it we are in danger of hemming ourselves into ever smaller enclaves, increasingly oblivious to the infinite and varied worlds that we simply no longer see. As with the walling off of national cultures in different sections of the library and the nationalism that followed, this shortcoming will likely have vast and almost certainly catastrophic consequences.

Some comfort can be taken from the fact that, even when worlds very different from ours are obscured by new information revolutions with their new sorting tools—so hidden that we can no longer see how they are similar as well as different—these worlds are not entirely lost to us and can (like Hernando's) be dredged up from where they have long lain. The great Renaissance historian Flavio Biondo—whose guidebook to Roman antiquities Hernando read as a youth—likened this process, of bringing hidden parts of the past back into view, to the act of bringing up planks from a shipwreck, making visible what once was drowned in oblivion, submerged beneath the waters of time. Though most of Hernando's great vessel has been wrecked, the pieces we are able to gather tell a story of someone who set out before us into the unknown. They are relics of a vision that is with us once again.[3]

ACKNOWLEDGMENTS

My first debt of gratitude must go to my colleague, collaborator, and dear friend José María Pérez Fernández, with whom I began working on Hernando and his library many years ago and have spent countless hours discussing them since. Working with him on this project has been one of the great pleasures of my life, and this biography of Hernando would have been much the poorer without his input and companionship during the time it was written.

I am also deeply grateful to the president and fellows of the British Academy, who awarded me a Mid-Career Fellowship during which much of this book was written, and to the master and fellows of Sidney Sussex College, who allowed me time off from teaching to take the fellowship year.

In writing this book I have been supported in innumerable ways by my wonderful editor from William Collins, Arabella Pike, and the superb team with which she is surrounded, including Marianne Tatepo, Alison Davies, and Iain Hunt; as well as Colin Harrison, Sarah Goldberg, and the team at Scribner to whom I am extremely grateful for a glorious American edition. I am also very thankful to work with my excellent agent, Isobel Dixon, and her talented colleagues at Blake Friedmann Literary Agency.

I have been lucky enough to have many immensely talented friends and colleagues read through the manuscript, in whole or in part, at various points during its composition—Trevor Dadson, Kevin

Jackson, Mark McDonald, David McKitterick, Joe Moshenska, José María Pérez Fernández, and Kelcey Wilson-Lee. I have also benefited from extremely helpful advice from a wide number of specialists in many fields, including (but by no means limited to) Alice Samson, Iain Fenlon, and those who attended the workshop on Hernando at the Parker Library in 2013 hosted by Christopher de Hamel: Brian Cummings, Vittoria Feola, Andrew Hadfield, Ana Carolina Hosne, Tess Knighton, Alexander Marr, Miguel Martinez, David McKitterick, Andrew Pettegree, and Jason Scott-Warren. All of these people have saved me from innumerable slips and oversights, and any that remain are entirely my fault. Claire Preston and Trevor Dadson were kind enough to write in support of this project during funding bids.

The research for this project has involved extensive periods in libraries and archives, during which I have been supported by many excellent people. I am grateful to the staff of the following institutions for their kindness, hard work, expertise, and assistance: the Biblioteca Capitular and Colombina in Seville (especially the director, Nuria Casquete de Prado); the Archivo de Indias in Seville; the Archivo Histórico Provincial de Sevilla; the Archivo General de Simancas; the Biblioteca Nacional de España; the Archivo y Biblioteca Capitular in Salamanca; the Archivio Segreto Vaticano and the Vatican Library; the Fundación García Arévalo in Santo Domingo; the Museo del Hombre Dominicano in Santo Domingo; and, as always, the staff of the Rare Book and Manuscript Rooms at the Cambridge University Library. Professor María del Carmen Alvarez Márquez was of great assistance during research in Seville. Patrick Zutshi was an excellent guide to the resources of the Vatican, and Dra. Christine Grafinger at the Vatican Library and Professor Kirsi Salonen from the University of Turku were of invaluable assistance during my work in Rome. Maya Feile Tomes offered extremely helpful advice on the afterlife of the Columbus legend. My excellent student George Mather built a database of Hernando's library for me that was indispensable to my research and writing. Steve Csipke prepared a superb index for the book, giving this study of lists a perfect ending.

As ever, I am grateful to my colleagues at Sidney, in the English faculty, and more widely throughout Cambridge and the world, who have made life brighter and easier with innumerable little kindnesses. I was also given much encouragement and support from friends in Dharwad during a period at Karnataka University Dharwad, during which part of this book was written. I am grateful as ever to Ambrogio Caiani, with whom I have discussed this book often, and whose friendship is one of life's great pleasures.

This book is dedicated to my wife, Kelcey, who has put aside her own writing on many occasions to read mine, whose insights have improved the book immeasurably, and who has patiently borne the many lengthy absences occasioned by research. Though dedicating the book to her by no means discharges my conscience in the matter (as Columbus and Hernando would put it), I suppose it's a start.

A NOTE ON THE *LIFE*
AND DEEDS OF THE ADMIRAL

This appendix is provided to summarize some of the historical controversies surrounding the *Life and Deeds of the Admiral*; while discussion of the biography occupies chapter 15 of this biography, this outline is intended for those wishing to know the historiography in greater detail.

Hernando's biography of his father was first published in Venice in 1571 as the *Historie del S. D. Fernando Colombo . . . della vita, & de fatti dell'Ammiraglio D. Christoforo Colombo, suo padre*, printed by Francesco de' Franceschi Sanese and translated by the Spanish humanist Alfonso de Ulloa. The prefatory letter by Giuseppe Moleto informs the reader that the manuscript of the biography was given by Luis Colón, the third hereditary admiral (Hernando's heir and nephew), to the Genoese merchant Baliano di Fornari, who in turn passed it on to another Genoese patrician, Giovanni Battista di Marino, to see through the press under the guidance of the humanist Moleto and the translator Alfonso de Ulloa.

The text was, for more than three hundred years, accepted unproblematically as a biography of Columbus by Hernando. In 1875, Bartolomé de Las Casas's monumental *Historia de las Indias* was published, having until then remained in manuscript, and the parallels between the two texts quickly came to light, with many scholars noticing Las Casas's heavy reliance on a biographical work by Hernando that he cites or refers to at least thirty-seven times. The fantastical imaginings often prompted by historical figures of great significance, however, led in the early twentieth century to various theories that Las Casas had in fact falsified the biography (or at least its source) to serve as a foundation for his work. These conspiracy theories were slowly and methodically disproved by the work of scholars including Rinaldo Caddeo, Miguel Serrano y Sanz, and (finally) Antonio Rumeu de Armas, whose magisterial *Hernando Colón, Historiador del Descubrimiento de América* (1972) remains the authoritative work on the subject (and from whom this account of the earlier scholarship is largely drawn). While Rumeu painstakingly outlines the overwhelming evidence that the vast majority of the biography was written by Hernando, he nevertheless posits that those parts of it not about the voyages (but rather about Columbus's life before the First Voyage) were not by Hernando but rather by a pseudonymous impostor. While otherwise Rumeu is entirely methodical, his argument in this regard is wholly impressionistic, based largely on a conviction that a scholar and humanist such as Hernando could never have engaged in the vituperative rhetoric and opportunistic fudging of the historical record that is witnessed in this part of the biography (Rumeu, 71–73). This is a strange conviction, not only given that humanists as a group frequently did engage in vituperative rhetoric (and historical fudging) in their pamphlet wars, and that Hernando himself can specifically be shown to have done so in many of his unquestionably authentic writings (in Rome and for Badajoz, for instance), but also given the likely sources available for the biography outside the voyages and what was at stake in writing it. Yet most significantly, Rumeu considers the decisive passage the (purely fictitious) scene in the biography linking Columbus to a Mediterranean pirate and a sea battle off Lisbon, a scene, he insists, that Hernando could never have written (Rumeu, 99–103). As detailed in chapter 15, however, marginalia in Hernando's library not only shows that he was reading the source for this scene (the *Enneads* of the historian Sabellicus) at the time the biography was believed to have been written (1534), but also places two identical manicules (the only ones in the volume, and a device he used only rarely) next to two scenes—one describing his father, and the other describing the Mediterranean pirate and the sea battle. This newly discovered evidence (as well as more circumstantial evidence laid out in chapter 15) seems to remove the last remaining reasonable doubts that the biography of Columbus was in all parts substantially written by Hernando, for all that one must allow for the vicissitudes in translation and printing.

NOTES

Abbreviations
The following frequently used sources are referred to using the abbreviations listed below; any other works by these same authors are given as standard references.

Bernáldez—Andrés Bernáldez, *Memorias del Reinado de los Reyes Católicos*, ed. Manuel Gómez-Moreno and Juan de M. Carriazo (Madrid, 1962)

Caddeo—*Le Historie della Vita e dei Fatti di Cristoforo Colombo per D. Fernando Colombo suo figlio*, ed. Rinaldo Caddeo, 2 vols. (Milan, 1930)

Cartas—Juan Gil and Consuelo Varela, eds., *Cartas de particulares a Colón y Relaciones coetáneas* (Madrid, 1984)

Descripción—*Descripción y Cosmografía de España por Fernando Colón*, facsimile of the edition by the Sociedad Geográfica (1910) (Seville, 1988)

Fernández-Armesto—Felipe Fernández-Armesto, *Columbus* (Oxford, 1991)

Guillén—Juan Guillén, *Historia de las Bibliotecas Capitular y Colombina* (Fundación José Manuel Lara, 2006)

HoC—*The History of Cartography: Cartography in the European Renaissance*, ed. David Woodward, vol. 3, pt. 1 (Chicago, 2007)

Obras—Tomás Marín Martínez, "*Memoria de las Obras y Libros de Hernando Colón*" *del Bachiller Juan Pérez* (Madrid, 1970)

Rumeu—Antonio Rumeu de Armas, *Hernando Colón, Historiador del Descubrimiento de América* (Madrid, 1972)

Rusconi—Roberto Rusconi, ed., *The Book of Prophecies*, ed. Christopher Columbus, trans. Blair Sullivan, *Repertorium Columbianum*, vol. 3 (Oregon, 1997)

Testamento—Hernández Díaz and Muro Orejón, eds., *El Testamento de Hernando Colón y Otros Documentos para su Biografía* (Seville, 1951)

Textos—Cristóbal Colón, *Textos y documentos completos*, Prólogo y notas de Consuelo Varela (Madrid, 1982)

In addition, the following abbreviations are used when referring to the main archival sources:

AGI—Archivo General de Indias, Seville
AGS—Archivo General de Simancas
ASV—Archivio Segreto Vaticano, Rome
BCC—Biblioteca Capitular y Colombina, Seville

Following established convention, and for ease of understanding, I have used these terms to refer to Hernando's main *repertorios* (catalogues) in the notes: *Registrum B* for the Índice Numeral de los Libros (Colombina 10-1-14); *Abecedarium B* for the *Índice General Alfabético* (10-1-6); *Descripcíon* for the *Itinerario o Descripción y Cosmografía de España* (10-1-10, 10-1-11); *Materias* for the *Libro de las Materias o Proposiciones* (10-1-1, 10-1-2, 10-1-3); *Diccionario* for the *Diccionario o vocabulario latino* (10-1-5). The *Memoria de los dibujos o pinturas o Registrum C* is referred to using the catalogue of Mark P. McDonald, and the other catalogues (where used) are given as full references.

Prologue

1. The deathbed scene is recorded in an eighteenth-century copy of a letter to Luis Colón (AGI, Patronato, 10, N.2, R.3, fol. xx), attributed to the Bachiller Juan Pérez by Harisse and Jos; see *Obras*, 27n; it is transcribed in Fernández de Navarrete, *Noticias para La Vida de D. Hernando Colón*, in *Documentos Inéditos para la Historia de España*, vol. 16 (Madrid, 1850), 420–24. Columbus's landing at Cadiz in chains on 20 November 1500 and his deathbed request is noted in Caddeo (2; 173), though he questions whether Columbus kept the chains about him during the rest of his life. The prophecy, discussed below at pages 69 and 248, is taken from Seneca's *Medea* and is recorded in the *Book of Prophecies* (59v, in Rusconi, 290–91), but also mentioned in other Columbian writings, most importantly the *Lettera Rarissima* or *Relación del Cuarto Viaje*, a report on the last voyage written on 7 July 1503 (*Textos*, 323).

2. The most authoritative edition of the will is Hernández Díaz and Muro Orejón, *El Testamento de Hernando Colón y Otros Documentos para su Biografía* (Seville, 1951), which collects all the *protocolos notariales* (notarized documents) concerning Hernando from the Archivo Provincial in Seville. The probatory copy of the will occupies pages 123–61, and it is followed by a facsimile of the document; another copy is in Seville Cathedral, though it has a number of errors (Guillén, 132). As is conventional, the will begins with a description of the circumstances in which the will is read, "quel dicho señor don fernando colon puede aver una ora mas o menos que fallescio desta presente vida" (the said gentleman Don Hernando Colón having left this life more or less an hour ago), as well as giving details of those present at the reading of the will. Instructions for the library begin at page 144 and occupy most of the rest of the will. Hernando's intentions for the contents of the library are repeated in various places, most succinctly in his executor Marcos Felipe's clarificatory document (*Testamento*, XCII, 227), but also in greater detail in the will itself and in the "Memoria" of the Bachiller Juan Pérez. Evidence for the various claims regarding the size of the library, picture collection, and garden is discussed below on pages 158, 262, and *Obras*, 595–610. The library at Celsus in Ephesus was independently endowed, as recorded by its inscription (James Campbell, *The Library: A World History* [London, 2013], 49–51), but its ruins were not reconstructed until the end of the nineteenth century; I have not been able to find similar endowments from the postclassical period.
3. The bookshelves are described in the will (*Testamento*, 148), which also mentions Hernando's plans for ordering the books on the shelves, discussed below on pages 322–23; the claim that these are the earliest modern bookshelves is first made in Anthony Hobson, *Great Libraries* (London, 1970), 14; see also Campbell, *Library*, 23 and 113, on the "stall" system and the "wall" system and the histories of their development.
4. The instruction that Marcos Felipe and Vincenzio de Monte should open the chest only when together is in the will (*Testamento*, 160); the inventory of these documents is also given in *Testamento*, XCIII, 262–66, and is followed by a facsimile of the document. Marín Martínez (*Obras*, 171–72) suggests that the "Bocabulario" here relates not to Hernando's Latin dictionary but to the topographical vocabulary projected as part of the *Cosmografía*.

5. The outline of Hernando's travels, drawn from his book annotations as well as legal records, is available in Klaus Wagner, "El Itinerario de Hernando Colón según sus Anotaciones: Datos para la biografía del bibiófilo sevillano," *Archivo Hispalense* 203 (1984): 81–99; digital databases of Hernando's surviving work have, however, allowed some details to be added to this. As Wagner writes (83), that Hernando specifically notes the few occasions on which he sent someone else to purchase a book allows one to infer that the other purchases were made by him personally.

I. The Return from Ocean

1. See Caddeo, 1:259. The most detailed description of the scene is given in the letter of Guillermo Coma (*Cartas*, 182–83), but see also the letter of Dr. Chanca (*Cartas*, 155) and Columbus's own report in his letter of 30 January 1494 (*Textos*, 146–62). The estimate of thirteen hundred men comes from Fernández-Armesto, 102; the *Life and Deeds* suggests fifteen hundred, and Bernáldez gives twelve hundred (279).

2. The *Historie* estimates the crew of the first voyage as ninety (Caddeo, 1:124), though Fernández-Armesto gives the most likely number as eighty-eight (72).

3. Hernando's copies of the letter are listed in his *Abecedarium B*, col. 369, where he lists the 1493 Catalan edition (now surviving in a single copy) and the Basel edition of 1533, as well as listing "de insulis nuper inventis" but without attributing it a registry number. See also Bernáldez, 251–56. Hernando may well have learned of the discoveries first when another letter from Columbus was read out in the Cathedral of Córdoba on 22 March 1493; see Guillén, 108.

4. See *Textos*, 139–46, as well as Caddeo, 1:176, and Bernáldez, 272.

5. For lists of what Columbus brought back on the First Voyage see Fernández-Armesto, 89, Bernáldez, 277–78, and the account of the First Voyage in the *Historie* (Caddeo, 1:121–245). On the collection of Jean, duc de Berry, see Guiffrey, *Inventaire de Jean, Duc de Berry* (Paris, 1894–96), and Umberto Eco, *Art and Beauty in the Middle Ages* (New Haven, 1986). There is some disagreement over the exact number of indigenous people Columbus brought back with him to Spain on the First Voyage and their eventual fate: Bernáldez (278) records that Columbus brought ten in total, leaving four in Seville and bringing six to Barcelona as a gift to the Monarchs; but Dr. Chanca suggests that seven were taken on the Second Voyage, with five dying during the

Atlantic crossing (*Cartas*, 171); Las Casas, on the other hand, records seven being lodged with Columbus in Seville on his return from the New World (Guillén, *Hernando Colón: Humanismo y Bibliofilia* [Seville, 2004], 34–35). On the fate of one of these captives, who was rebaptized Juan de Castilla, see below on page 36.

6. Fernández-Armesto, 93; Pedro Mártir de Angleria, *Cartas Sobre el Nuevo Mundo* (Madrid, 1990), 25; Bernáldez, 269–70. According to Marín Martínez and Ruiz Ascencio, *Catologo Concordado de la Biblioteca de Hernando Colón* (Seville, 1993), 1:203, Bartholomew Colón later lived with Bernáldez. As Peter Burke points out in *A Social History of Knowledge* (London, 2000), shipbuilding and navigation were also considered "mechanical" arts, so it is unclear that Hernando was saving his father from this charge by outlining his nautical past.

7. We are largely reliant on Columbus's own later claims that he had been sailing for twenty-three years before attempting the crossing in 1492, and that he had visited among other places the Greek islands, Tunisia, Guinea, the Canary Islands, England, and "Thule" (possibly meaning Friesland or Iceland). There is often little corroborating evidence for these claims, which are sometimes hard to fit into the chronology of his life, and he almost always had an ulterior motive for mentioning them, a need to prove his authoritative knowledge of something or other. His familiarity with Greek mastic allows him to attest to its presence in the New World; boasts about his part in a sea battle off Tunisia show his ability as a soldier; his visit to the Portuguese fortress of La Mina in Guinea backs up his assertion that people were indeed able to live in the torrid zones, which were once thought too hot for human settlement.

8. On the Perestrelos/Palastrelli, see Hugh Thomas, *Rivers of Gold* (London, 2004), 47–48. The transcription of the Toscanelli letter in the *Historie* can be found in Caddeo, 1:55–63, with the description of Zaiton on page 58. On Toscanelli's life and reading of medieval travelogues, see Rumeu, 263–87. See Fernández-Armesto, 30, for a discussion of the likely date of Columbus's acquaintance with Toscanelli's writings.

9. Caddeo, 1:91–95; Fernández-Armesto, 46; assertions of opposition to and support for Columbus's claims are also complicated by later narratives of those who wished themselves to be seen as early supporters of the project. As Fernández-Armesto suggests, the later legend that traces Columbus's support to an early and fateful meeting

with the queen's confessor Fray Juan Pérez at the monastery of La Rabida is wholly unsubstantiated, even if there is evidence for the part of La Rabida in the immediate run-up to the voyage.

10. For the summary of these arguments see *Historie*, chs. 6–9 (Caddeo, 1:61–80); Rumeu, 296. Manzano Manzano, *Cristóbal Colón: Siete años decisivos de su vida* (Madrid, 1964), 193–213, provides further details of a meeting in 1489 in Jaen; see also Fernández-Armesto, 190. Columbus drew heavily on the early-fifteenth-century work *Imago mundi* (The picture of the world) by the French theologian Pierre d'Ailly, from which he was able to extract the arguments of Marinus of Tyre, Strabo, Ctesias, Onescritus, Nearchus, Pliny, and Ptolemy that the Eurasian landmass extended for two-thirds of the circumference of the world (or fifteen of the twenty "hours" in another measuring system), leaving only one-third to be sailed going west from Lisbon toward the Indies (i.e., India and China). This distance had been closed farther by the Portuguese exploration of west Africa and by the discovery of the Canary Islands off Africa's western flank. For all the weight of this argument, however, it simply displaces the question: If only a fraction of the world, between the west of Europe and the east of Asia remains unexplored, how big exactly *is* that fraction? The difficulty of estimating the circumference of the earth given the methods available at the time was crucially to make arguments about this distance, during Columbus's lifetime and even more so during Hernando's, a matter for rhetorical ingenuity as much as scientific measurement. Drawing on Portuguese reports, emerging from Bartholomeu Dias's successful rounding of the Cape of Good Hope in 1488, about the southern extension of Africa, Columbus made the case that the distance between the Canary Islands and Cipangu (Japan) off the east of the Eurasian continent had been reduced to a mere 45°. He also willfully rejected the claims of Marinus of Tyre and others that each of the 360° of the earth measured 66⅔ miles at the equator, instead siding with the Arabic cosmographer Alfragan (al-Faragani) that the real figure was 56⅔ miles, and arguing by extension that they could expect to find Asia at 700 to 750 leagues west of the Canary Islands. To back this up he was able to cite Aristotle, Averroës, Seneca, Strabo, Pliny, Solinus, Marco Polo, John Mandeville, Pierre d'Ailly, and Capitolinus in support of the idea that the eastern lands were no more than a few days' sail away from Spain.

11. Mark P. McDonald, *The Print Collection of Ferdinand Columbus (1488–*

1539): A Renaissance Collector in Seville (London, 2004), 19, places Filipa Moniz's death around 1484. There are differing testimonies on the exact date of Hernando's birth in 1488; most sources give 15 August (Guillén, *Hernando Colón*, 25; Rumeu, 5n1; the Repertorium tome of the *Historie*, 2:8), while Fernández-Armesto, usually infallible, gives November (52), though the source of this variant date is unclear. Importantly, however, Marcos Felipe's notarized clarifications to Hernando's will records (which show signs of following Hernando's direct instructions) that he was fifty years, ten months, and twenty-six days old on the day of his death, and that his birthday was 15 August 1488; this, it seems likely then, is at least what Hernando believed his birthday to be (*Testamento*, 92:229). On Columbus's meeting with Beatriz Enríquez, see Paolo Taviani, *Christopher Columbus: The Grand Design* (London, 1985), 185–86, and Fernández-Armesto, 52. On Diego and Hernando in Córdoba in 1492–93 under the protection of Beatriz, see Caddeo, 1:223, and Rumeu, 114.

12. For the letter see Navarrete, *Documentos Inéditos*, 1:363–64; on the copying process see Rumeu, 127.

II. In the Chamber of Clean Blood

1. The *Historie* puts the arrival of Hernando and Diego at court as occurring in March/April 1494, as it says the dispatch of Diego (on 14 April) was "no sooner than they had arrived" (Caddeo, 2:16); this is echoed by Bartolomé de Las Casas, *Historia de las Indias*, ed. Augustín Millares Carlo, 3 vols. (Mexico, 1951), 1:402. *Descripción*, 1:34; this is in the part of the *Cosmografía* in Hernando's own hand. See *Obras*, 205n, 211.

2. Hieronymus Munzer, *Viaje por España y Portugal: 1494–1495* (Madrid, 1991), 53–57; see Fernández-Armesto, *Ferdinand and Isabella* (London, 1975), 58–59, for a list of prominent figures in Juan's court.

3. The *Memoria* mentions specifically that Hernando did not spend his time and money on hunting, though others expected this of him; see *Obras*, 50.

4. On Deza, see Las Casas, *Historia de las Indias*, 2:269, 3:82.

5. Munzer, *Viaje por España*, 275.

6. Fernández-Armesto, 56–58; Caddeo, 1:284–85; *Cartas*, 152–76; Paolo Taviani, ed., *Christopher Columbus: Accounts and Letters of the Second, Third and Fourth Voyages* (1994), 12–32. Among those returning in the first fleet along with Chanca and Antonio de Torres are Fray Boil, the

NOTES

lead missionary, Gorbalán, Pedro Margarit, and Juan de Aguado (though there is some disagreement over who returned in this first convoy). On this and future occasions Columbus chose to send (rather than, or as well as, a letter) a trusted emissary with a list of news to be communicated and petitions to be submitted orally. The advantage of this mode of operating was that not only did it provide a checklist to ensure that individual requests were not lost in a thicket of prose, but the items on the list could be rearranged or omitted in response to the evolving narrative in the court in Spain.

7. A digitized nineteenth-century copy of the list of inhabitants of La Navidad can be found at the Archivo Histórico Nacional, Diversos-Colecciones, 41, N.19; the original is ES.41091.AGI/10.5.11.583// CONTRATACION, 5575.

8. Munzer, *Viaje por España*, 45.

9. Rumeu, 216; Caddeo, 1:308–9.

10. Umberto Eco, *The Infinity of Lists* (London, 2009), 133. See also Anthony Pagden, *European Encounters with the New World* (New Haven, 1993), ch. 2; Stephen Greenblatt, *Marvellous Possessions: The Wonder of the New World* (Oxford, 1991).

11. Caddeo, 2:34–54; Eco, *Infinity of Lists*, 153–54.

12. On the complaints of Father Buil, the lead missionary on the Second Voyage, and Pedro Margarit, as well as the dispatch in October 1495 of Juan de Aguado, see Caddeo, 2:55–56, Fernández-Armesto, 104–14.

13. Bernáldez, 376–77.

14. *Textos*, 307; Poliziano, *Panepistemon*, which was among Hernando's purchases in September 1512 (Colombina, 15-6-8). See Christopher Celenza's introduction to Angelo Poliziano's *Lamia* (Leiden, 2010).

15. See J. Manzano, "La legitimación de Hernando Colón," *Anales de la Universidad Hispalense* 21.2 (1960): 85–106. As Hugh Thomas points out, the *mayorazgo* also required the heir to look after younger brothers: *Rivers of Gold*, 38. On rates of inheritance for the Spanish gentry, see José María Monsalvo Antón, *Torres, Tierras, Linajes* (Salamanca, 2013), 171–72.

16. Caddeo, 2:162–63; Emiliano Jos, *Investigaciones sobre la vida y obras iniciales de don Fernando Colón*, Anuario de Esturios Americano, Tomo 1 (Seville, 1944), 527–698.

17. It is unclear whether Bobadilla was actually going further than his instructions here, as the *juez de residencia o de visita* was specifically charged both with gathering written accusations and

providing a forum for spoken accusations against the official being audited. A first inquest into Columbus's governorship was led by Juan de Aguado in 1495, with inconclusive results.

III. *The Book of Prophecies*

1. Rusconi, 5, 8. As Rusconi points out, the title *Book of Prophecies* is first used by Hernando in the "memorial de las cosas que hay que de hazer y dezir en Castilla," though he assumes that this was drawn up in 1526 rather than 1509 upon Hernando's return from Hispaniola. On the correct dating of this to 1509, see Rumeu, 6, and Guillén, 117. My account of the book in most respects follows here the account provided by Rusconi in his excellent edition and study.

2. Fernández-Armesto, 150; Caddeo, 2:173–75.

3. Caddeo, 2:80–81, 92, 98–101; *Textos*, 236–38. The figure of sixty-five leagues west is provided in the account of the Third Voyage extracted by Las Casas (Taviani, *Accounts*, 90). For the letters, see *Textos*, 224–42, 270.

4. *Textos*, 213–18; Fernández-Armesto, 129–31.

5. Rusconi, 18; Fernández-Armesto, 132; *Textos*, 243, 263, 270.

6. *Textos*, 171–76; Rumeu, 80. See also below Hernando's continuation of this argument, in his arguments to the king on 1511, and in his *Declaración* after the Badajoz conference.

7. *Textos*, 308, 360.

8. Rusconi, 120. It is worth noting that at the beginning of the manuscript a note from Columbus records his intention to collect references to Jerusalem with a view to later looking them over and "ponerlas en rrima," though scholars disagree about whether this means that he intended to write a verse epic using them ("to put them in rhyme/ verse") or simply to put them in order (as in the sense of "number"). Though Columbus did undoubtedly write verse (Fernández-Armesto, 180), the lack of further evidence means this question will likely remain unsettled.

9. Rusconi, 60–62, 66–67, 140–41. The spelling of *lunbre* here seems to be part of Columbus's idiosyncratic version of the Castilian language, which is on display throughout *The Book of Prophecies*.

10. Rusconi, 64–65.

11. Ibid., 20–21, 120, 124–31. As Marín Martínez notes (*Obras*, 358), a manuscript version of Rabbi Samuel of Fez's "de adventu Messie in hispanico" was entry 1584 in the *Libro de Epitomes*.

12. Rusconi, 18, 70–73.

13. Ibid., 290–1; see also Caddeo, 1:49–50; *Textos*, 323.

14. Rusconi, 28, 337–47. I am grateful to Andy Niggemann for his help with the Hebrew here.

15. Ibid., 197, 249.

16. Ibid., 316–17, 108–9.

17. The lost "tragedie en español de mano" appears in *Abecedarium B*, col. 1616, and is *Registrum B* entry 3291; a surviving, mid-fifteenth-century Latin manuscript contains the *Medea* (Colombina 5-5-17), which a previous librarian has confused with the Spanish translation, recording there in a note that the Spanish translation was likely an early gift or an inheritance from Columbus. In a later edition of Seneca's tragedies, the 1510 Venetian edition by Philippo Pincio (Colombina 1-4-19), Hernando has written against this passage, "prophecia . . . per patre[m] . . . cristoforo . . . almirante . . . anno 1492" (fol. XCII^v, sig. q ii^v), and it is possible that he was copying this note from an earlier, superseded edition.

18. Rusconi, 354–57.

19. Ibid., 9. Rusconi attributes this intervention to the historian Ambrosio de Morales and dates it to the late 1560s, though the ultimate source of this attribution is the rather uncompelling, offhand assertion of Bartolomé José Gallardo in 1866 that the writing "appeared" to him to be that of Morales. Given that the "inventorial note" on the first folio, used to identify Morales's hand, uses the shelf reference developed by Hernando for his library (7816, the number given for *Registrum B* number 2091 in *Registrum B*, fol. 200), it seems certain that this entry—and therefore the note about the removal of the missing leaves—was made while this shelf-referencing system was still in place, i.e., before *The Book of Prophecies* left Hernando's house in 1542.

20. Ibid., 6–7; *Textos*, 323. The passages on the eclipse of 29 February 1504, recorded in the book (Rusconi, 292), may well have been written at the time of the eclipse; this is on the same page of the book that contains the passage from Seneca, suggesting that these passages were added after Gorricio's work, perhaps during the voyage itself.

IV. Rites of Passage

1. On the names and naming of the ships, see the note in Caddeo, 2:188; the supplies for the voyage are contained in the *Memorial a los Reyes* (*Textos*, 275–76). For the conversion of early modern Spanish measures

of volume and weight I have relied on the *Diccionario de la Lengua Española* definitions; I have used the Aragonese *cahiz*, as this seems most likely to be what was meant here. The presence of *oruga* (rocket) on the list likely describes a paste made from the leaves.

2. Caddeo, 2:181–82.

3. Ibid., 1:142. As Caddeo points out (2:182), Columbus's *Lettera rarissima* puts the crossing at sixteen days (*Textos*, 316), a figure repeated in later writings.

4. *Textos*, 232; Taviani, *Accounts*, 82; Rumeu, 156; Fernández-Armesto, 78–80. See J. H. de Vaudrey Heathcote, "Christopher Columbus and the Discovery of Magnetic Variation," *Science Progress in the Twentieth Century* 27/105 (1932): 82–103. Hernando himself provides an excellent summary of the problems with dead reckoning in his "Parecer que dio D. Hernando Colón en la Junta de Badajoz sobre la pertnencia de los Malucos" (AGI, Patronato, R.48, 16), which is also transcribed in Navarrete, *Expediciones al Malucco*, vol. 4 of the *Colección de los Viages y Descubrimientos* (Madrid, 1837), 333–39.

5. It is possible that Matinino was not modern Martinique but rather St. Lucia (see Caddeo, 2:182n).

6. Ibid., 2:182–85; *Textos*, 317; Fernández-Armesto, 163–64. For Ovando as part of the household of the Infante, see Thomas, *Rivers of Gold*, 37, and the *Libro de la Cámara Real del Príncipe don Juan*, ed. Santiago Fabregant Barrios (Valencia, 2008), 83.

7. Caddeo, 2:187: "E, anchor che l'Ammiraglio nel sui interno sentisse quell'istesso dolore . . ."

8. Rusconi, 228–29; Caddeo, 2:190. Caddeo (2:186n) points out that a schedule of 1505 suggests that Roldán, at least, was not among those to have perished in the storm.

9. Caddeo, 1:191, "il primo fu un pesce chiamato schiavina, grande come un mezzo letto . . ." Caddeo declines to provide an identification for the *schiavina*, but in Taviani, *Life and Deeds*, 272, it is translated as a ray.

10. On Aristotelian zoological classification, see for instance *Historia Animalium*, Book VIII, §589. Gesner, in his *Historia Animalium*, still classified aquatic mammals with the fish (in Part IV, order XII), following the hexameral scheme of medieval zoology (sorted into the six days of creation), rather than with the viviparous land animals of Part I.

11. Caddeo, 2:192–97; Taviani, *Life and Deeds*, 274; Thomas, *Rivers of*

Gold, 196. See Matthew Restall, "Maya Ethnogenesis," *Journal of Latin American Anthropology* 9/1 (2004): 64–89, for details on the formation of a discrete Mayan identity under colonial influence.

12. Caddeo, 2:197. For a comparison, see the Portuguese observations of the shell-based currency in the Kingdom of Kongo: Malyn Newitt, *The Portuguese in West Africa, 1415–1670: A Documentary History* (Cambridge, 2010), 62, 103.

13. In addition to Benedetto Bordone's famous *Isolario* of 1528, there was also a manuscript *Isolario* by Alonso de Santa Cruz, though possibly from after his period of overlap with Hernando at the Casa de Contratación. See George Tolias, "*Isolarii*, Fifteenth to Seventeenth Century," in *HoC*.

14. Caddeo, 2:195. The map in question may be one of those included in the *Claudii Ptolomei . . . Geographi[a]e opus* printed in Strasbourg in 1513 (Colombina 15-8–19), which Hernando has annotated heavily, including adding the label "insula anthropophagorum" to the Islas de Las Onze Mil Virgenes (Virgin Islands).

15. Caddeo, 2:198–216.

16. *Textos*, 318.

17. Caddeo, 2:220–25.

18. Ibid., 2:243–44.

19. *Textos*, 322–23.

V. A Knowledge of Night

1. *Textos*, 325–26; Caddeo, 2:199.

2. See Michael R. Waters et al., "Geoarchaeological Investigations of St. Ann's Bay, Jamaica: The Search for the Columbus Caravels and an Assessment of 1,000 Years of Human Land Use," *Geoarchaeology* 8/4 (1993): 259–79.

3. Caddeo, 2:263–65.

4. Ibid., 1:25, 1:311–12.

5. Umberto Carrara, *Columbus*, ed. and trans. Francisca Torres Martinez (Madrid, 2000), Book X.

6. Caddeo, 2:269–72.

7. See José Chabás and Bernard R. Goldstein, *Astronomy in the Iberian Peninsula: Abraham Zacut and the Transition from Manuscript to Print*, *Transactions of the American Philosophical Society* 90/2 (2000): 2, 6–15, 153–54. For the prediction of the eclipse by Zacuto, see *Tabule tabula[rum] celestiu[m] motuu[m] astronomi zacuti* (Lerida, 1496),

NOTES

fol. 168; Hernando's copy is Colombina 12-1-9, and his note on how to calculate the first day of each month is on the rear flyleaf of the same volume.

8. Rusconi, 292–93, 80–81.

9. Caddeo, 2:287–89.

10. *Textos*, 339, 344, 354, 362; Guillén, 111–13. On Ovando making Columbus pay for the costs of the return journey, see La Duquesa de Berwick y Alba, *Autógrafos de Cristóbal Colón y Papeles de America* (Madrid, 1892), 44–46. On Las Casas, see *Historia de Las Indias*, 2:119.

11. The idea that what weighs on Columbus's conscience is Beatriz's infidelity (Guillén, 111–12; refuted by Jos) is confusing and unconvincing. As Guillén points out, Beatriz is also remembered in Diego's wills of 1509 and 1523; Guillén further provides an overview of arguments for why Columbus never married Beatriz.

VI. Shoes & Ships & Sealing Wax

1. "Memorial de las Cosas que hay de Hazer y Dezir en Castilla," in La Duquesa de Berwick y Alba, *Autógrafos*, 77–79. The suggestion that this document was drawn up at Diego's death in 1526 (Rusconi, 8) is plainly wrong, given the ephemerality of most of the items in the list; Rumeu is clearly right in assigning this to 1509 (Rumeu, 6), a date also followed by Guillén (117).

2. *Obras*, 256.

3. Further confidence in this method of reconstructing a list of Hernando's books in 1509 can be taken from the fact that none of these volumes (i.e., ones bearing a location of purchase but no date) was printed after 1509.

4. On the importance of Crastonus's *Lexicon Graeco-Latinum* for Greek language learning, see John Considine, *Dictionaries in Early Modern Europe* (Cambridge, 2008), 27. Burke, *Social History of Knowledge*, 84–85.

5. Hernando bought his volume of Pico della Mirandola's *De rerum praenotione libri novem* (Colombina 12-5-9, *Registrum B* 3782) and Lorenzo Valla's translation of Thucydides (Colombina 2-6-15, *Registrum B* 2816) in Toledo in 1509, likely when the court was there in February. One of the alchemical treatises is a manuscript of *Sedacius totius alchimie*, and the note of gift from Cristóbal de Sotomaior, son of the Countess of Camiña, is recorded as *Registrum B* 3785 (Guillén, 116); Guillén, *Hernando Colón*, 118, claims Sotomaior also gave a printed alchemical work, but his source is unclear. See Troy S. Floyd,

353

The Columbus Dynasty in the Caribbean (Albuquerque, 1973), 123–30,
for the state of gold mining in 1509.

6. Burke, *Social History of Knowledge*, 84–85. Hernando would eventually
own many copies of Angelo Poliziano's treatise on universal knowledge,
the *Panepistemon*, included in the *Annotationes veteres* of Sabellicus
that he bought in 1512 (Colombina 15-6-8), the *Opera omnia* of
Poliziano purchased in 1515 (Colombina 6-5-15), and a lost separate
edition of 1532 (*Abecedarium B*, col. 99; it provides an incorrect
Registrum B number, so further details are unavailable). Hernando's
copy of the 1498 Suda is listed in *Abecedarium B*, col. 1708.

7. See Luis Arranz, *Diego Colón* (Madrid, 1982), 97–102, and appendix
documents XV and XVI, which give the letter of nomination and the
official conferral of the governorship. The transfer of power to the
Duke of Alba's factor Juan de la Peña is given in Muro Orejón, *Pleitos
Colombinos*, 8 vols. (Madrid, 1964–89), 1:191–93. See also Thomas,
Rivers of Gold, 228. On the payments to Hernando, see Navarrete,
Documentos Inéditos, 529, and Guillén, 111.

8. For details of the party that crossed in 1509 see Floyd, *Columbus
Dynasty*, 137. The jewel is described in *Testamento*, xviii.

9. Caddeo, 2:193–95; Thomas, *Rivers of Gold*, 414.

10. For Diego's will see Arranz, *Diego Colón*, 194–95; see also the
"Instrucción del almirante D. Diego Colón para Jerónimo de Agüero,"
in La Duquesa de Berwick y Alba, *Autógrafos*, 61–63, where Hernando
begs the Duke of Alba to come to his brother's aid, and Guillén,
Hernando Colón, 109–10; Guillén also suggests that this document was
from 1511, but as Aguilar was at that point considered missing, it
seems more likely that this was from 1509. Las Casas's later claim that
Hernando returned to continue his studies (Guillén, 116) does not
explain the precipitousness of his departure or the long delay between
his return and the resumption of his formal studies.

11. The "Proyecto de Hernando Colón en nombre y representación del
Almirante, su hermano, para dar la vuelta al mundo" is now preserved
in the New York Public Library as Obadiah Rich Collection, Rich
num. II.i, 6, and is transcribed in Arranz, *Diego Colón*, 338–43.

12. See Navarrete, *Documentos Inéditos*, 16:383, and Rumeu, 27, 48–49;
Guillén, *Hernando Colón*, 87. Hernando describes the *Colón de
Concordia* in the opening of the *Declaración del derecho* . . . (Real
Biblioteca II/652 [3], fol. 1^{r-v}), which is available online and transcribed
in Navarrete, *Documentos Inéditos*, 16:383.

NOTES

13. At this point Hernando may already have been aware of Xenophon's *Oeconomicus*, in which a well-ordered ship is seen as the model for the proper functioning of a household and indeed the state; the contents of the ship, in turn, are known by Xenophon's sailor "just as well as a man who knows how to spell can tell how many letters there are in *Socrates* and in what order they come" (*Oeconomicus*, §8.11–16, trans. E. C. Marchant [Loeb], 463).

14. The copy of the Qur'an is *Registrum B* entry 2997; Hernando purchased François Tissard's *Grammatica Hebraica et Graeca* in Seville in 1511 (Colombina 12–3–23[5]), which is bound together with further guides to Greek by Tissard (12–3–23[1]) and by Manuel Chrysoloras (12–3–23[4]) purchased that year.

15. On Peter Martyr's embassy to Egypt, see *Una Embajada de los Reyes Católicos a Egipto*, ed. and trans. Luis García y García (Simancas, 1947). The *Hieroglyphica* is contained in a Greek miscellany volume (*Habentur in hoc volumine haec . . .* [Venice: Aldus Manutius, 1505]), of which Hernando's copy survives as Colombina 118–6–19 (*Reg. B* 5615); it has no purchase note of any kind, which may mean an early purchase or simply a lost purchase note. A useful introduction to early-modern linguistic thought is provided in Umberto Eco, *The Search for a Perfect Language* (London, 1997).

16. For the quotation, see page 116 (sig. [hvii^v]). Early-modern Egyptologists were unaware of the phonetic values of the hieroglyphs, which awaited the discovery of the Rosetta Stone and Champollion's decryption; the key text on Renaissance hieroglyphs is now available in English: Karl Giehlow, *The Humanist Interpretation of Hieroglyphs in the Allegorical Studies of the Renaissance*, trans. Robin Raybould (Leiden, 2015). On the discoveries on the island of Mona, see Jago Cooper, Alice V. M. Samson, et al., "'The Mona Chronicle': The Archaeology of Early Religious Encounter in the New World," *Antiquity* 90/352 (2016): 1054–71; quotation from page 1062. An example of Jacobo de Testera's work can be seen in the Codex Testeriano Bodmer, *Cod. Bodmer*, 905. On the pillars discovered by Charles Cottar at Sevilla la Nueva, see https://www.academia.edu/978498/The_Frog-legged_Lady_of_New_Seville_European_Motif_or_Evidence_of_Spanish-Indigenous_Syncretism_in_Early_Colonial_Jamaica.

17. *Testamento*, x, 8–9.

18. Hernando was granted an *encomienda* of three hundred Indians as part

355

of the settlement of the *Pleitos* (AGI, Indiferente, 418, L.3, fol. 97v), while a further document of 23 August grants Hernando permission to pass the *encomienda* on to someone, but also suggests that he intends to travel to Hispaniola at the end of five months (AGI, Indiferente, 418, L.3, fol. 154r–154v). The first part of the process started by Isabel de Gamboa, in the diocesan court of Burgos, cannot be followed in detail, as the records of processes in the diocesan court prior to 1813 were destroyed during the Peninsular War. The substance of the case, however, is repeated in the Sacra Rota trial detailed in chapters 6 and 7.

19. Hernando's volume of Flavio Biondo's *De Roma triumphante* (13–4–7) was bought in Seville in 1511; the date comes from the *Registrum B* (3092), as the book itself does not bear a purchase date, further confirming the suggestion that the volumes with a location of purchase but no date are early purchases. It is only sparsely annotated, but it is annotated all the way through, perhaps suggesting that he was using it to prepare for his entry to the Eternal City. He also owned a copy of Biondo's *Ab inclinatione Romanorum Imperii*, similarly purchased in Seville and with no date supplied (either in purchase note or *Reg. B*, suggesting an early purchase date), though it is hardly annotated at all.

VII. The World City

1. Charles L. Stinger, *The Renaissance in Rome* (Bloomington, 1998), 21; Rumeu, 29.

2. Stinger, *Renaissance in Rome*, 32–38. The assumption here that Hernando stayed at San Pietro in Montorio is based on the reading of Hernando's will, following McDonald, 35, and Guillén, 83, where his bequest to the "convento de señor san francisco de observancia" (*Testamento*, 130–31) is taken to indicate that he stayed there when in Rome; San Pietro in Montorio was the major recipient of Spanish patronage at the time, which would make sense of the fact that Hernando highlights its Spanish connections in his will. Hernando's copy of the *Mirabilia urbis Roma* is Colombina 14–1–4(2), which is bound with several other guides to Rome also bought in 1512, including one in German and one in Italian. It is worth noting the printing date of Hernando's copy of the *Mirabilia*—1493—as it gives a sense of how long printed volumes could remain on booksellers' shelves after printing, even when the volume in question was (like this one) ephemeral.

3. On Albertini's guides, see Roberto Weiss, *The Renaissance Discovery of Classical Antiquity* (Oxford, 1969), 84–86. Hernando's copy of Albertini's *Opusculum de mirabilibus nouae et veteris urbis Romae* (Rome, 1510) is Colombina 4–2–5(5); his copy of Giuliano Dati's script for the mystery play, *Incomincia la passione de Christo historiata in rima vulgari* (Rome, 1510), is Colombina 6–3–24(1). Both were bought between Hernando's arrival and the end of 1512.

4. Mitchell Bonner, *Rome in the High Renaissance* (Norman, 1973), 42–43, 51; Jacques Le Saige, *Voyage de Jacques Le Saige, de Douai à Rome* (Douai, 1851), 26.

5. On the Tempietto, see Jack Freiberg, *Bramante's Tempietto, the Roman Renaissance, and the Spanish Crown* (Cambridge, 2014), 144, 151. Giorgio Agamben has recently provided an excellent summary of the concept of universal empire and its links to apocalyptic thought in his *The Kingdom and the Glory* (Redwood City, 2011).

6. The records are contained in ASV, *S. R. Rota, Manualia Actorum*, 83, in about two hundred pages of entries between fols. 150r and 933v. I am immensely grateful to Christine Grafinger of the Vatican Archive and Kirsi Salonen for their help in locating these documents, and to Kirsi and Patrick Zutshi for help in decoding them. Kirsi Salonen's *Papal Justice in the Late Middle Ages: The Sacra Romana Rota* (Oxford, 2016) is the indispensable guide to the workings of the court, and I rely entirely on it here; see page 18 on the court's importance, page 43 on the process of referral to the SRR, pages 56–66 on the day-to-day workings of the court, and page 76 on the location of sessions.

7. Isabel de Gamboa's life can be reconstructed through a series of documents in the Archivo General de Simancas, including Consejo Real de Castilla, 80/2, which details a suit between Isabel de Gamboa and relatives of her first husband, Martín Ruiz de Arteaga of Guernica, over the custody of their children and the goods belonging to them; this document also mentions her second husband, one Captain Salazar, whom Diego's will vaguely identifies as "Petisalazan" (Arranz, *Diego Colón*, 195). Isabel's daughter with Salazar (also called Isabel), who was a lady-in-waiting to Germaine de Foix, is the plaintiff in a further suit (AGS, Consejo Real de Castilla, 666, 23). Hernando's name first appears on ASV *Man Act* 83, fol. 207v.

8. Angela Nuovo, *The Book Trade in the Italian Renaissance*, trans. Lydia G. Cochrane (Leiden, 2013), 389–420; and Brian Richardson, *Printing, Writers and Readers in Renaissance Italy* (Cambridge, 1999), 112–18.

9. The list of those lecturing at the Studium Urbis in 1514 is published as an appendix to Filippo Maria Renazzi, *Storia dell'Università degli Studii di Roma* (Rome, 1803), 235–39. Hernando's reference, in his volume of Silvestro da Prierio Mazzolini's *Clarissimi sacre theologie* (Colombina 12–6–35), to hearing lectures on the text by one "magistro sebastiano" ("prima novembris 1515 incepi hu[n]c libru[m] exponente eu[m] magistro sebastiano Rome i[n]mediate post 24 am. horam octoq[ue] prima folia tantu[m] in octo lectionibus exposuit") is widely agreed to be a reference to Sebastianus Veteranus, who is shown to be lecturing at the Studium Urbis in the 1514 list; see Guillén, *Hernando Colón*, 84, citing Wagner.

10. Nothing is known about the first holder of the chair of natural history at the university (Paul F. Grendler, *Universities of the Italian Renaissance* [Baltimore, 2003], 59). On the relations between mercantile practice and information exchange in general, see Burke, *Social History of Knowledge*, 155. On Luca Pacioli, see Argante Ciocci, *Luca Pacioli e la Matematizzazione del sapere nel Rinscimento* (Bari, 2003).

11. Gabriel Naudé, *Advis pour dresser une bibliothèque* (Paris, 1627), 130–31; see Burke, *Social History of Knowledge*, 105. On the Medici library and the Vatican Library, I have closely followed the chapter by A. Rita, with tables by C. Grafinger, "Per la storia della Vaticana nel Primo Rinascimento," 237–307, in Antonio Manfredi et al., *Storia della Biblioteca Apostolica Vaticana*, vol. 1, *Le Origini della Bibilioteca Vaticana tra Umanesimo e Rinascimento (1447–1534)* (Vatican City, 2010). On Parentucelli's *Canone*, see Maria Grazia Blasio, Cinzia Lelj, and Giuseppina Roselli, "Un Contributo alla lettura del Canone Bibliografico di Tommaso Parentucelli," in *Le Chiavi della Memoria: Miscellenea in Occasione del i Centenario della Scuola Vaticana di Paleografia Diplomatica e Archivistica* (Vatican City, 1984), 125–65. The division of Roman libraries into Greek and Latin rooms is mentioned by Isidore of Seville; see Lionel Casson, *Libraries in the Ancient World* (New Haven, 2002), 97. The notion of canonicity is derived from biblical scholarship, but Parentucelli was pioneering in applying it to a wider selection of learning.

12. Hernando bought the *Respecti d'amore* (Rome, 1506; Colombina 6–3–24[13]) in Rome in 1512, as stated in a note that does not include a month, and the *Storia della Biancha e la Bruna* (6–3–24[19]) also in Rome, with no date at all; this may suggest that the estimate of 1520 for

NOTES

the printing of this text is wrong, as Hernando's undated purchases tend to come from 1512 and before. The other pamphlets bound with these two (such as the *Storia de Fuggir le Puttane* [Colombina 6–3–24(18)], bought in June 1513 for two quatrines), which all treat erotic subjects, were printed in 1513 or before, suggesting these may have been bought at the same time, either already bound or bound soon after.

13. Hernando's copy of the *Hypnerotomachia Poliphili* was the 1500 Venice edition and is listed as *Registrum B* entry 3872; the entry in the *Abecedarium B* might be missed as it is listed with the title reversed (as "Poliphili Hypnerotomachia en toscano," col. 1344). Hernando's list of the "Pasquili carmina" is given on *Abecedarium B*, col. 1268, made up of twenty-two titles covering most years between 1509 and 1526, as well as including other works attributed to Pasquino.

14. The story about the cost of raising the roof of St. Peter's is in Condivi's life of Michelangelo (*Michelangelo Buonarroti: Life, Letters, and Poetry* [Oxford, 2008], 26–33). On the 1507 Jubilee Pardon see Stinger, *The Renaissance in Rome*, 155.

15. Argote de Molina's description of Hernando's ambassadorial mission to Julius is discussed in E. Jos, *Investigaciones*, 609–14.

16. Stinger, *The Renaissance in Rome*, 57–58; Manfredi et al., *Storia della Biblioteca Apostolica Vaticana*, 1:263.

17. Hernando notes in his copy of Dionisio Vázquez, *Oratio habita Rome in apostolica sacri palatii capello i[n] die cinerum nona februarii Anno domini 1513* (Colombina 8–2–38[38]), that he heard the sermon in person ("viva voce") by the author in Rome. Passages from the *Julius Exclusus* are taken from *The Erasmus Reader*, ed. Erika Rummel (Toronto, 1990), 216–38, 218, 228.

VIII. The Architecture of Order

1. Michael Bury and David Landau, "Ferdinand Columbus' Italian Prints: Clarifications and Implications," in McDonald, *Print Collection of Ferdinand Columbus*, 189–90.

2. Piers Baker-Bates, *Sebastiano del Piombo and the World of Spanish Rome* (Oxford, 2016).

3. Bonner, *Rome in the High Renaissance*, 65–76; Stinger, *The Renaissance in Rome*, 97–98. The menu is taken from Paolo Palliolo, *Le Feste de Conferimento del Patrizio Romano* (Bologna, 1885), 76–88.

4. *Suetonius Tranquilus cum Philippi Beroaldi et Marci Antonii Sabellici commentariis* (Colombina 2–5–11) contains the index as well as the

note that Hernando was being lectured to on this by "Mag[ist]ro Castrensi" between 23 July and 5 August 1515. The Lucretius index is in *In Carum Lucretiu[m] poeta[m] Co[m]me[n]tarii a Joa[n]ne Baptista Pio editi* . . . (Colombina 6-4-12). Alison Brown, *The Return of Lucretius to Renaissance Florence* (Cambridge, MA, 2010), 77-78.

5. McDonald, *Print Collection of Ferdinand Columbus* and *Ferdinand Columbus: Renaissance Collector*, ch. 3; *Obras*, 253-318.

6. Stinger, *The Renaissance in Rome*, 76, 121. Hernando's book purchases from late 1515 and early 1516 closely track the movements of the papal court in this period; he purchased the *Compendium rerum decennio in Italia* by Niccolò Machiavelli (1506) in Viterbo during a visit in October 1515 (*Registrum B* 2241).

7. Caddeo, 1:13. On the dispute over Diego's rights in the New World and his recall in 1514, see Floyd, *Columbus Dynasty*, 146-48.

8. AGS, Consejo Real de Castilla, 666, 23, from 26 May 1516, refers to both Captain Salazar and Isabel de Gamboa as "difuntos," giving a latest possible date for her death.

IX. An Empire of Dictionaries

1. The manuscripts of the *Cosmografía* consist of a ms. of 678 folios in the Biblioteca Colombina (Colombina 10-1-10), and a separate two gatherings of 41 folios now held at the Biblioteca Nacional de España (BNE ms. 1351). Crespo points out that while the entry numbers go up to 6,477, only 4,043 entries are found in the surviving manuscripts (*Los Grandes Proyectos* [Madrid, 2013], 42), and he follows Laborda's count of 4,245 entries, with a total of thirteen hundred towns receiving a full treatment (62-64), and a further two thousand only featuring in distance measurements. Though Martínez (*Obras*, 242) points to the entry number 9,967, suggesting that a further third of the project may have been lost, he suggests caution in making this assumption, given that there are no entries between 6,635 and 9,967. Martínez discusses the relationship between the Colombina manuscript and the detached gathering in the BNE in *Obras*, 225-26. Crespo suggests the rather fitting name of the "libreta de campo" in *Los Grandes Proyectos*, 49.

2. For useful discussion of the distinctions between "information" and "knowledge," or "data," "information," and "knowledge," see Burke, *Social History of Knowledge*, 11, and ch. 5, and Ann Blair, *Too Much to Know* (New Haven, 2011), 1-2. For the instructions on mapmaking, see *Descripción*, 1:22-24, and *Obras*, 47-48, 217-18.

3. See *HoC*, 9–10; Anthony Grafton, *Leon Battista Alberti* (London, 2002), 244; and *Worlds Made by Words: Scholarship and Community in the Modern West* (Harvard, 2009), 41; Stinger, *The Renaissance in Rome*, 65–69; Jessica Maier, *Rome Measured and Imagined* (Chicago, 2015), 25–26. Hernando bought the 1493 *Quatripartitus ptolomei* (Venice: Bonetus Locatellus) in Medina del Campo at an unregistered date for 170 maravedís (*Reg. B* 3152; lost); the 1508 *Geographia* (Rome: Bernardinum Venetum de Vitalibus) in July 1512 (*Reg. B* 3527, Colombina 119–8–5) for twenty-eight *carlines*; and the 1513 edition (Argentinae: Ioannis Schotti) in April of 1516 (*Reg. B* 3558, Colombina 15–8–19) for twenty-three *julios*. The 1478 edition supposedly inherited from Columbus is mentioned in Crespo, *Los Grandes Proyectos*, 35, though no source is given; Guillén also mentions it (115) but again provides no evidence that it was inherited from Columbus.

4. Hernando probably encountered the mapmaking ideas of Ptolemy before he went to Italy, perhaps in the form of the *Introduction to Cosmography* published by the leading light of Spanish humanism, Elio Antonio de Nebrija, in 1498. A copy of Nebrija's treatise, which expounded Ptolemy's ideas for a *graticula* (a little grate, or grid) on which maps should be laid out, was among Hernando's undated and probably early purchases. From his early youth Hernando would have known Nebrija at least by reputation and perhaps much more intimately, as Nebrija seems occasionally to have taught at the court of the Infante Juan. Hernando may also have heard Nebrija lecture when the court visited Salamanca, where the eminent scholar presided not only over the intellectual life of the university but also over its printing industry, with the most groundbreaking Spanish editions of classical texts emanating from Nebrija's house on the Calle de los Libreros. Whatever Hernando's relationship with Nebrija was in the 1490s, he would certainly have become close to him in the new century, when Nebrija was (among many other things) involved in the production of Peter Martyr's monumental history of the New World, the *Decades*. Indeed, it may have been Nebrija himself who prompted Hernando to begin the project of the *Description*: the pair were both in Alcalá de Henares in the summer of 1517 when Hernando made his first entry, as recorded in a copy of Nebrija's newly published treatise on chronology, which he gave Hernando as a gift. Nebrija's volume, once again drawing on the observations of Abraham Zacuto, produced tables of the different day lengths in cities throughout Spain—a curious

undertaking, though more understandable when one realizes that these observations could be used to produce the longitudinal measurements required for Hernando's map. Crespo, *Los Grandes Proyectos*, 48–49.

5. See Jerome's commentary on Daniel, and Daniel DiMassa, "The Politics of Translation and the German Reception of Dante," in *Translation and the Book Trade in Early Modern Europe*, eds. José María Pérez Fernández and Edward Wilson-Lee (Cambridge, 2014), 119–20.

6. *Obras*, 48; On the use of the Alphonsine and Nebrija's parallels, see Crespo, *Los Grandes Proyectos*, 48.

7. Jean Michel Massing, "Observations and Beliefs: The World of the Catalan Atlas," in *Circa 1492*, ed. Jay A. Levenson (Yale, 1991).

8. *Descripción*, 1:18, 20, 25, 29, 30, 39–41, 43, 44, 55; 3:35–36. These are the sections attributed to Hernando by Martínez (201–4, 224–26). Michel de Certeau, *The Practice of Everyday Life* (Berkeley, 1984), 120.

9. Crespo, *Los Grandes Proyectos*, 54, points out that dates noted on various entries by the emissaries range between 1517 and 1520. On the Republic of Letters and its collaborative scholarly practices, see Grafton, *Worlds Made by Words*. Though there is no evidence that a formal questionnaire was provided to the gatherers of information for the *Description*, the conventional form of the information amounts to the same thing and provides an antecedent for the questionnaires later used as instruments of state. See Burke, *Social History of Knowledge*, ch. 6.

10. See *HoC*, 10, on the resistance of landlords to later sixteenth-century surveys, and 1081 on Maximilian I. Crespo, *Los Grandes Proyectos*, 52, suggests Hernando would have had to have royal blessing for the project from the start and suggests that Gattinara, Cobos, Granvelle, or Cisneros might have sanctioned the project before Charles's arrival; however, no evidence is available for this.

11. Though we cannot be certain that Hernando wrote this anonymous treatise, it was attributed to him at an early stage and was bound together with other writings undoubtedly by Hernando, and it certainly bears all the hallmarks of Hernando's thought. The "Coloquio sobre las dos graduaciones que las cartas de Indias tienen," Real Biblioteca II/652 (7), is contained in the same manuscript as the "Declaración del Derecho" and the "Memoria" by the Bachiller Juan Pérez. The attribution of the colloquy by Ursula Lamb and others to Pedro Medina seems extremely unlikely, as Medina would have been in his early twenties when it was written (as it says the *Padrón Real* is a

decade old) and would not publish anything on cartography for two decades afterward. See Ursula Lamb, "Science by Litigation: A Cosmographic Feud," *Terrae Incognitae* 1 (1969): 40–57; and "The Sevillian Lodestone: Science and Circumstance," *Terrae Incognitae* 19 (1987): 29–39. Marín Martínez (81) includes the colloquy as potentially by Hernando.

12. Thomas, *Rivers of Gold*, 437–39; "Portuguese Cartography in the Renaissance," *HoC*, 994; on Reinel in Seville in 1519, *HoC*, 987. There is precedent for Hernando's cartographic espionage in the "Cantino planisphere," which Duke Ercole d'Este sent his servant to steal from the Portuguese in 1502. The idea that Hernando's espionage was cartographical is supported by his mention of cartographic espionage in his report from Badajoz: see below at page 253. See A. Texeira de Mota, "Some Notes on the Organization of Hydrographical Services in Portugal," *Imago Mundi* 28 (1976): 51–60, on the 1504 laws forbidding the export of Portuguese maps; also Burke, *Social History of Knowledge*, 144. Crespo, *Los Grandes Proyectos*, 55, cites M. M. Delgado Pérez, *Hernando Colón*, as saying that Hernando was accompanying the court of Leonor of Portugal, though this would not explain his going incognito.

13. *Tragedie Senece cum duobus commentariis* (Venice, 1510; Colombina 1-4-19), flyleaf verso: "Sábado seis de marzo de 1518 comencé a leer este libro y a pasar las notas dél en el índice en Valladolit y distraído por muchas ocupaciones y caminos no lo pude acabar hasta el domingo ocho de julio de 1520 en Bruselas de Flandes en el qual tiempo las annotaciones que ay desde el numero 1559 en adelante aún no están pasadas en el índice porque quedó en España."

14. *Diccionario o Vocabulario Latino* (Colombina 10-1-5), fol. 6r; "A: prime littere nomen est ta[?m] graecis qua[m] ceteris gentibus vel quia omnes littere hebream a qua [?e]manaru[n]t imitantur vel quia est prima infa[n] tiu[m] nescentiu[m] [v]ox vel quia in pronu[n]ciatione prius et interius more qua[m] reliquae sonat." The last part of the entry is rather difficult to transcribe, so the translation provided here is an approximation of the likely sense, though the literal translation is "because in pronouncing it sounds earlier and more deeply by custom than the others." I am grateful to Richard Flower for his advice here. *Obras*, 665–84; Nebrija, *Gramatica castellana* (Salamanca, 1492), aiiʳ ("siempre la lengua fue compañera del ímperio"), expanded upon in the prefatory letter that follows. The definition quoted here uses Isidore's *Etymologiae* (1:iii–iv) as one of its sources—including the

claim (at 1:iv: 17) that *A* is the first letter as it is the first sound made by babies—though it is unclear if directly or indirectly.

15. Ann Moss, *Renaissance Truth and the Latin Language Turn* (Oxford, 2003), 15–17. See also Considine, *Dictionaries in Early Modern Europe*, and Byron Ellsworth Hamann, *The Translations of Nebrija* (Amherst, 2015). Hernando is using Nebrija's monumental Spanish–Latin dictionary of 1495 as well as Niccolò Perotti's encyclopedic commentary on the poet Martial, the *Cornucopiae*, as the foundations for his dictionary; see *Obras*, 681. (Incidentally, this was probably the first European book to use Arabic numerals on both sides of the page; see Blair, *Too Much to Know*, 49.) Hernando's method does seem to aim for authoritative definitions from his historical examples, but also allows for historical variation. Although he owned a copy of the *editio princeps* of the *Suda* (Colombina 1-4-11, *Lexicon Graecum Souida*, Milan 1499, no date of purchase), he does not appear to have used it; likely his Greek was not good enough for this purpose.

16. Erich Peterson has pointed out the link between census taking, of which Hernando's *Description* is a form, and millenarianism, drawing on a tradition in which the fact that the Incarnation occurred during Augustus's census of the Roman Empire is theologically significant; see Agamben, *Kingdom and the Glory*, 10.

17. A good account of the election wrangling is given in Manuel Fernández Alvarez, *Charles V: Elected Emperor and Hereditary Ruler* (London, 1976), 28–32.

18. This volume of pamphlets bound together ("sammelband") is Colombina 4-2-13, mostly acquired in Rome in September and November 1515; Hernando's reading notes show that he read them between 28 September and 15 October 1519 in Seville. He did not strictly read the pamphlets in the current order, which may indicate that he flicked back and forth, or that they were originally bound in a different order.

19. Floyd, *Columbus Dynasty*, 198–99; Rumeu, 83; *Testamento*, 14–15. Las Casas, *Historia de las Indias*, 3:359. This *Capitulación de Coruña* was ratified by the crown on 3 March 1525 (*Testamento*, xv).

X. The Devil in the Details

1. Jeffrey Ashcroft, *Albrecht Dürer: Documentary Biography* (New Haven, 2017), 1:560; Thomas, *Rivers of Gold*, 425, 431.

2. Ashcroft, *Albrecht Dürer*, 1:563–64.

3. *Ioan. Goropii Becani Origines Antwerpianae* (Antwerp: Christophe Plantin, 1569), 178–79.

4. *A. C. Mery Talys* (London, 1526).

5. Considine, *Dictionaries in Early Modern Europe*, 19. Hernando's copy of the *Antibarbarorum* survives as Colombina 12–2–26; on page [2], Hernando has written as follows: "Este libro medio el mesmo autor como parece en la octaua plana." Hernando's copy of Valla's commentary on the Donation of Constantine is *Registrum B* 295, and was purchased in Nuremberg in December 1521. Erasmus, "The Antibarbarians," in *The Erasmus Reader*, ed. Erika Rummel (Toronto, 1990), 62.

6. Hernando's (no longer extant) copy of the *Psalterium David et cantica aliqua in lingua Chaldea* is listed in *Abecedarium B*, col. 1405, as "Psaltarium in lingua chaldica . . . R[ome] 1513," and is given *Registrum* number 5967. On this text and Johannes Potken's mistake about its Chaldaic origin, see Donald F. Lach, *Asia in the Making of Europe* (Chicago, 1977), 2:510–11. Alphabetization was in use from the time of the *pinakes* of works drawn up for the Library at Alexandria; see Blair, *Too Much to Know*, 16. On the invention of the author, see Michel Foucault, "What Is an Author?," in *The Foucault Reader*, ed. Paul Rabinow, 101–120, and Roger Chartier, *The Order of Books* (Redwood City, 1994), ch. 2. See Erasmus's discussion of the letter to the cardinal of Mainz and its leaking in the 1520 letter to Cardinal Campeggio, in *Correspondence of Erasmus, Letters 1122 to 1251, 1520 to 1521*, trans. R. A. B. Mynors (Toronto, 1974), §1167, 108–21.

7. Hernando's copy of Budé's *De Asse et partibus eius* is Colombina 118–7–39 and was purchased in Florence in January 1516. Maximilian I granted Friesland independent sovereignty with the caveat that Austria could redeem it for one hundred thousand guilders (George Edmundson, *History of Holland* [Cambridge, 1922], 14).

8. Gertrude von Schwartzenfeld, *Charles V: Father of Europe* (London, 1957), 53–54; Fernández Alvarez, *Charles V*, 38; Rainer Kahsnitz and William D. Wixom, *Gothic and Renaissance Art in Nuremberg, 1300–1550* (New York, 1986), 305–6.

9. The official bull of excommunication was issued on 3 January 1521; on this, and the successive steps by which Luther felt he was released from the Church, see Richard Rex, *The Making of Martin Luther* (Princeton, 2017), 156–57, 250n. See also discussion of the inflationary logic of indulgences, pages 12–13.

10. On Reformist books in Hernando's collection, see Klaus Wagner, "La

reforma protestante en los fondos bibliográficos de la Biblioteca Colombina," *Revista Española de Teologia* 41 (1981): 393–463. Hernando purchased Melanchthon's *Epistola Philippi Melanchth. ad Joh. Oecolampadium de Lispica disputatione* (*Registrum B* 1525) for two maravedís in Cologne in late November and is said by Wagner to have read it there (396), and Luther's *Acta apud D. Legatum Apostolicum Augustae recognita* in Mainz on 26 November (no. 913 in the *Memorial de los Libros Naufragados/Reg. A*).

11. Rumeu, 83–84; *Testamento*, 28–29. A further document of 4 March 1523 suggests that these two thousand ducats had still not been paid (AGI, Indiferente, 420, L.9, ff. 126v–127).

12. Andrew Pettegree, "Centre and Periphery in the European Book World," *Transactions of the Royal Historical Society*, 6/18 (2008): 101–28; Christopher Hare, *A Great Emperor: Charles V, 1519–1558* (London, 1917), 65; Karl Brandi, *Emperor Charles V*, trans. C. V. Wedgwood (London, 1939), 131. On Hernando's endurance as a rider see the letters of Clenardus (*Correspondance*, 3:181–82). Hernando's first book purchase in Venice is on 9 May; Sanudo records news of Luther's condemnation as a heretic on 11 May (*Diarii*, xxx, 217), and on 12 May Gasparo Contarini was writing from the Imperial Court to the Signory of the kidnap (*CSP Venetian*, §209), which Sanudo records on the eighteenth.

13. Marin Sanudo, *Venice: Città Excelentissima: Selections from the Renaissance Diaries of Marin Sanudo*, ed. Patricia H. Labalme and Laura Sanguineti White, trans. Linda L. Carroll (Baltimore, 2008), 54–58, 208–9. The *relazione* gives Suleiman's age as twenty-three, but he would actually have been twenty-seven at the time.

14. Ibid., 59; a good account is also provided in Peter Martyr's report on his Egyptian embassy, *Una Embajada*, 34–36.

15. Sanudo, *Città Excelentissima*, 21–22.

16. Ibid., 27–30.

17. *Obras*, 738–42.

XI. No Place Like Home

1. Hernando's copy of the 1518 Basel edition of More's *Utopia* (*De optimo reip. statu deque noua insula Utopia libellus* . . . [Basel: Johannes Frobennius, 1518]) survives as Colombina 12-2-39; Hernando notes on page 167 "Hu[n]c libru[m] perlegi Bruselis 26 et 27 diebus mensis martij 1522."

2. The expense of cutting the Utopian type is confirmed by the printer of the English translation by Ralph Robinson, Abraham Veale, who explains the absence of the alphabet from his edition by citing the expense of the type. See Émile Pons, "Les Langues imaginaires dans le voyage utopique," *Revue de Littérature Comparée*, October–December 1930, 589–607 (my translation).

3. On Dürer's design, see Ashcroft, *Albrecht Dürer*, 2:661–70.

4. A detailed description of materials for the pageant is found in SP 1/24 f. 226, "The Emperor's Visit," 5 June 1522, *Letters and Papers, Foreign and Domestic, of the Reign of Henry VIII*, vol. 3, §2305. See D. E. Rhodes, "Don Fernando Colón and his London book purchases, June 1522," *The Papers of the Bibliographical Society of America*, vol. 52 (New York, 1958).

5. Caddeo, 2:196–97, 236–37.

6. Hernando mentions the "forma de navegación p[ar]a su alta y felicisima pasaje de flandes en españa" on fol. 2r of the "Declaración del derecho" of 1524; see Real Biblioteca II/652 (3).

7. *Testamento*, 133–34.

8. Hernando's copy of the *Carta de Relación* is *Registrum B* entry 272, which notes that Hernando purchased it in Valladolid "on 2 December 1521," an evident mistake for 1522 as it notes just previously the publication in Seville on 8 November 1522.

9. *Obras*, 687–765, 715.

10. On the *cedula*, see *Obras*, 163, and Crespo, *Los Grandes Proyectos*, 58. On the relationship of knowledge gathering to empire in the Spanish context, see Burke, *Social History of Knowledge*, ch. 6; Bernard S. Cohn, *Colonialism and Its Forms of Knowledge* (Princeton, 1996); and Barbara E. Mundy, *The Mapping of New Spain* (Chicago, 1996).

11. Considine, *Dictionaries in Early Modern Europe*, 29. Hernando appears not to have known Calepino's dictionary when he began his dictionary in 1518, as Calepino is not among the sources for which he develops a shorthand (Nebrija, Palémon, and Perotti, as well as the *Grammatica ecclesiastici*; see *Obras*, 681); the close similarities between many of his entries and those of Calepino would, then, seem to stem from their synthesizing many of the same sources. The catalogues provide somewhat confusing evidence on the matter: the *Abecedarium B* lists only a 1530 edition of Calepino, though the *Registrum B* entry at 1963 appears to have overwritten a previous entry, showing a purchase of a

copy at Medina del Campo in July 1519. It is possible that the 1519 purchase was lost or that it was simply read to death: it seems that Calepino was (toward the end, at least) a significant presence in the library, as the Bachiller Juan Pérez uses his name to illustrate a point in the *Memoria* (regarding the treatment of pseudonyms; *Obras*, 66).

XII. Cutting Through

1. For the note in the Seneca, see Colombina 1–4–19, *Tragedie Senece cum duobus commentariis* (Venice: Philippo Pincio, 1510), fol. XCII^v^, sig. q.ii^v^. Diego's arrival in Spain on 5 November 1523 is recorded in AGI, Patronato, 10, N.1, R.15.

2. AGI, Patronato, R.48, 12; Guillén, *Hernando Colón*, 123.

3. Hernando's opinion, signed 13 April 1524, is contained in the "Parecer que dio D. Hernando Colón en la Junta de Badajoz sobre la pertinencia de los Malucos," AGI, Patronato, R.48, 16; it is transcribed in Navarrete, *Expeditiones al Malucco*, 333–39. His further opinions submitted to the emperor (on 27 April and after the Badajoz conference) are also contained in Navarrete, 342–55.

4. See the "Declaración del derecho," Navarrete, *Documentos Inéditos*, 16:391–92.

5. AGI, Patronato, R.48, 16, 1^r^–2^v^. See Crespo, 48–49. Hernando is credited as the first to have suggested this solution in Julio Rey Pastor, *La Ciencia y la Técnica en el Descubrimiento de América* (Buenos Aires, 1942), 96–97.

6. This story is recounted in Jerry Brotton, *History of the World in Twelve Maps* (London, 2013), 200; Brotton's account of the conference is on pages 200–217.

7. Hernando is referring to Arcangelo Madrignano's translation, the *Itinerarium Portugallensium e Luistania in Indiam*, "q[ue] fue impreso año de 1508" (Milan: Giovanni Antonio Scinzenzeler, 1508), which he bought in Rome in 1512 (*Reg. B* 2163); the passage "en el cplo [i.e., capitulo] 6[0] se cuenta 3800 leguas desde lisbona a calicut" is at f[v]^v^. The *Abecedarium B* suggests that Hernando's copy of Pedro Margalho's *Margellea logices vtrivsq[ue] scholia* (Colombina 118–5–48[2]) was not acquired until 1536, though this may be replacing an earlier copy; it is one of only two copies of the work noted on the Universal Short Title Catalogue. On the development of numbering and layouts to aid reference and memory, see Blair, *Too Much to Know*, 36–40; and Mary Carruthers, *The Book of Memory* (Cambridge, 2008), ch. 7.

8. On Hernando's arguments for the rights of the Spanish, dated by Rumeu (78) to the end of the Badajoz conference, see the "Declaración del derecho que la rreal corona de Castilla tiene a la conquista de las provincias de Persia, Arabia e Yndia, e de Calicut e Malaca," Real Biblioteca II/652 (3).

9. On the development of textual locators in printed books, see Blair, *Too Much to Know*, 49–51. Though similar arguments for "fixity," first made by Elizabeth Eisenstein in her influential *Printing Press as an Agent of Change*, have been subject to much criticism and revision (see, for instance, *Agent of Change*, eds. Sabrina A. Baron et al. [Amherst, 2007]), it is nevertheless clearly the case that contemporaries *thought* this allowed for secure referencing.

10. The passage in question, on fol.[v]^v of the 1508 *Itinerarium Portugallensium e Luistania in Indiam*, actually occurs in chapter 58; but farther down on the same page, chapter 59 is actually labeled 61, so counting backward from that must have caused Hernando's mistake. On the length of the epitomes, see *Obras*, 344–47. On the theme of the excess of books, see Blair, *Too Much to Know*, esp. 55–61.

11. *Obras*, 53.

12. Juan Pérez's statement that there should be "at most four" books of laws is not further explained, though it may be predicated on the division of law into canon, ecclesiastical, and common laws; see *Obras*, 51. On classical and medieval projects of compilation and condensation, see Blair, *Too Much to Know*, esp. ch. 1.

13. On the codicil, see Rumeu, 83. Hernando's letter to Charles is AGS, Estado, 13, fol. 333. Hernando's defense of his brother's rights is given in the "Papel de Fernando Colón," Navarrete, *Documentos Inéditos*, 16:376–82. On the madness of the infinite library, see Jorge Luis Borges, "The Total Library," in *The Total Library: Non-Fiction, 1922–1986*, ed. Eliot Weinberger (London, 1999), 214–16.

XIII. The Library without Walls

1. *Testamento*, 36–37. On Hernando's failed attempt to buy another property from the Conde de Orgaz earlier in 1526, see Guillén, 125.

2. *Testamento*, 138–40. For the late-sixteenth-century descriptions, see Juan de Mal Lara, *Recibimiento que hizo la muy noble y muy leal ciudad de Sevilla a la C. R. M. del Rey D. Philipe N. S.* (Sevilla, 1570), fol. 50; and Guillén, 126.

3. *Testamento*, 77–79 (for the contract with Alonso de Zamora and his

wife, Maria Rodríguez), and the inventory of Hernando's papers, XCIII, 263, item 29, ". . . dize memoria de plantas e ortelanos"; this is clearly distinct from the various documents related to the acquisition of the Huerta de Goles contained in the same inventory. It should also be remembered that Hernando's Arana relatives were tied to the circle in Córdoba around the apothecaries of the Esbarroya family, in which Columbus is thought to have first encountered the uncle of Hernando's mother, Beatriz; see Guillén, 108.

4. Caddeo, 1:174; 2:30, 193.

5. *Testamento*, 75–77. Brian Ogilvie, "Encyclopaedism in Renaissance Botany," in *Pre-Modern Encyclopaedic Texts*, ed. Peter Binkley, 89–99; and Brian Ogilvie, *The Science of Describing* (Chicago, 2006), 30–34 et passim; Alix Cooper, *Inventing the Indigenous* (Cambridge, 2009); Hubertus Fischer, Volker R. Remmert, and Joachim Wolschke-Bulmahn, eds., *Gardens, Knowledge and the Sciences in the Early Modern Period* (Basel, 2016).

6. Antonio de Villasante may have been the discoverer of *guayacán* from his Taino wife. On Hernando's attempt to recruit the potter-physician to be Clenardus's Arabic instructor, see *Correspondance de Nicolas Clénard*, 1:151–52, 2:93–94.

7. *Obras*, 55, 365–427, esp. 396–402. On the use of indexes to subject matters in medieval *florilegia*, see Blair, *Too Much to Know*, 36.

8. *Obras*, 55.

9. AGI, Indiferente, 421, L.12, fols. 40r–40v; Rumeu, 81n. *HoC*, page 1101, gives this as the first date when such an order was issued. Guillén, *Hernando Colón* (134), suggests that Hernando's appointment as acting *pilót mayor* explains his three-year stay in Seville between 1526 and 1529.

10. *HoC*, 1100. The letter sent from the Consejo de Indias thanking Alonso de Chaves, on behalf of the king, for his work in teaching the pilots to use the astrolabe and quadrant and maps, "según relación de Hernando Colón" (AGI, Indiferente, 421, L.13, fol. 295v), suggests that this is apparently going on in the Casa de Goles; see Guillén, 127. Eustaquio Navarrete, *Noticias para la Vida de D. Hernando Colón*, in *Documentos Inéditos*, 16:357–60, notes a mention by Loaisa regarding a college for mariners that Hernando proposed setting up in the house in the Puerta de Goles in 1526, as mentioned in various histories of Seville (Luis de Peraza, *Origen de la Ciudad de Sevilla*), though this likely refers to a later period. The maps corrected in Hernando's hand are in Ptolemy,

Claudii Ptolomei . . . Geographi[a]e opus (Colombina 15–8–19); the example of the *insula anthropophagorum* is on the second map in the "Tabula Moderna" section.

11. *HoC*, 22.
12. The letter of 1528 instructs Diego Ribeiro to come to the Consejo to fill them in on the "bombas" that are being made in La Coruña (AGI, Indiferente, 421, L.13, fol. 295r–295v). Hernando's note on the ineffectiveness of Spanish artillery is in Colombina 4–2–13(9), sig. [Aii]ʳ.
13. Brandi, *Charles V*, 242.
14. Luigi Guicciardini, *The Sack of Rome*, trans. James H. McGregor (New York, 2008), 114–15; J. Hook, *The Sack of Rome* (London, 2004), 176–78; Stinger, *The Renaissance in Rome*, 320–22; André Chastel, *Le sac de Rome, 1527* (Paris, 1984).
15. Manfredi, *Storia della Biblioteca Apostolica Vaticana*, 311. The Ostrogoth destruction of Roman libraries is recorded in Cassiodorus; see Casson, *Libraries in the Ancient World*, 74–75; and Pedro Mexia, *Silva de Varia Lección* (Seville, 1540). Although more recent studies have suggested that the Library of Alexandria disappeared slowly over centuries, early modern accounts almost always figure a catastrophic destruction: see, for instance, Francesco Patrizi, *A moral methode of ciuile policie contayninge a learned and fruictful discourse of the institution*, trans. Richard Robinson (London, 1576), sig. T[1]ʳ⁻ᵛ.
16. There is some confusion regarding the date of Hernando's departure, as Chapman ("Printed Collections of Polyphonic Music Owned by Ferdinand Columbus," 41) notes Hernando making purchases from the end of August 1529, though Wagner's itinerary still has Hernando in Seville on 30 August. Burke, *Social History of Knowledge*, 86; A. Salmond, "Theoretical Landscapes: On Cross-Cultural Conceptions of Knowledge," in *Semantic Anthropology*, ed. D. Parkin (London, 1982), 65–87.

XIV. Another Europe and the Same

1. For Clenardus's letters, see *Correspondance de Nicolas Clénard*, ed. Alphonse Roersch, 2 vols. (Brussels, 1940), 1:55–6, 200–201, 218–20; 2:33–35, 156–57, 180–83; and Joseph Klucas, "Nicolaus Clenardus: A Pioneer of the New Learning in Renaissance Portugal," *Luso-Brazilian Review* 29/2 (1992): 87–98.
2. Konrad Eisenbichler, "Charles V in Bologna: The Self Fashioning of a Man and a City," *Renaissance Studies* 13/4 (1999): 430–39.

3. AGS, Estado, leg. 21, fol. 22. "Don Hernando Colon Dizeque ha mas de quarenta años q[ue] sirve al Casa Real de V. Mt. y que por no ser molesta nole ha suplicado lehagame[n] por sua s[er]vise y esperando esse determinase/el pleyto de su padre y que agora viendo que aquel es ynmortal hallandose biejo y pobre ha determinado seguir la yglesia porque el papa le ha prometido [???] porella . . ."

4. There is no small tragic irony in that Hernando's mother, Beatriz, seems also to have been put to the exigency of borrowing from the Grimaldis at the end of her life against the promise of what she was owed by Diego and Hernando; see Guillén, 112. On Sanuto's book sale see Sanuto, *Città Excelentissima*, introduction, xxvi, and 39–40.

5. Walter Benjamin, *Illuminations* (Pimlico, 1999), 30.

6. On the Umayyad library of Córdoba, see Padover in James W. Thompson, *The Medieval Library* (New York, 1967), 360–62.

7. The Qur'an that Hernando had acquired in 1510, for instance, is listed as "Elalcora[n] en linda letera arabica" in the *Registrum B* (2997), but in the *Abecedarium B* as "Alcoran en arabigo" (col. 65). The first book in Geez is lost, but is in *Abecedarium B*, col. 1405, as "Psaltarium in lingua chaldica . . . R[ome] 1513" and is given a *Registrum* number of 5967. On the manuscripts brought back from Tunis by Diego Hurtado de Mendoza, see Anthony Hobson, "The *Iter italicum* of Jean Matal," in *Studies in the Book Trade in Honor of Graham Pollard*, Oxford Bibliographical Society Publications, NS 18 (1975), 33–61; Hobson points out that this number is likely an exaggeration, as Mendoza's collection of Arabic manuscripts only numbered 268 when they reached the Escorial in 1571.

8. François Rabelais, *Oeuvres complètes*, ed. Jacques Boulenger and Lucien Scheler (Paris, 1955), 194–202, 207–13. These translations are my own, though I have often relied on the commentary of Screech's translation for guidance.

9. *Correspondance de Nicolas Clénard*, 1:55–56, 200–201, 218–20; 2:33–35, 156–57, 180–83.

10. Ibid., 1:25–28, 2:6–10.

11. The biographical note occupies the margins of five pages starting from Psalm 19 in *Psalterium Hebreum, Grecum, Arabicum, & Chaldeum cum tribus Latinis interpretationibus & glossis* (Genoa, 1516). Hernando's (lost) copy is given the *Registrum B* number 5095; see *Abecedarium B*, col. 1405.

12. The *Life* attributes this rumor to Oviedo as well, though as Caddeo

points out, Oviedo's *Historia general*, while recounting the claim, suggests that it is false (Caddeo, 1:76–80 and n.). See Rumeu, 71–72, on Charles's commissioning Oviedo to develop this line of argument.

XV. The King of Nowhere

1. Caddeo, 1:23; 2:5.
2. Ibid., 1:14–20, 80–91.
3. Ibid., 1:161–62. I am grateful to Professor Fernández-Armesto for pointing out that this scene of Columbus sighting land first is cribbed from a version of the *Alexander Romance*.
4. For related discussions of the genealogy or tree-of-knowledge model, see Gilles Deleuze and Félix Guattari on the "rhizome" in *Mille plateaux* (Paris, 1980) and Burke, *Social History of Knowledge*, 86–87.
5. Hernando's copy of *De scriptoribus ecclesiasticis* (Paris, 1512) is Colombina 3-3-28 and appears as 2156 in the *Registrum B*; it was purchased unbound in January 1516 at Florence for 116 old quatrines and was later bound in Rome for 40 quatrines. On Renaissance chronology, see Anthony Grafton, *Joseph Scaliger* (Oxford, 1993) and *Defenders of the Text* (Cambridge, MA, 1994) and *Worlds Made by Words*, chapter 3, in particular on Trithemius: though Grafton calls Trithemius's library ambitions "encyclopaedic" and "universal," it is clear from the corresponding passage that this was limited to works in ancient languages from within Christendom.
6. Burke, *Social History of Knowledge*, 15. Juan Luis Vives, "De Tradendis Disciplinis," in *De Disciplinis: Savoir et Enseigner*, ed. Tristan Vigliano (2013), 273–86.
7. Caddeo, 1:34–35. The manicules appear in Sabellicus, *Secunda pars enneadum Marci Antonii Sabellici ab inclinatione romani imperii . . .* (Colombina 2-7-11), Decade X, Book 8 (f. CLXVIII, sig. [x.v]^r). Hernando places next to the phrase "(quas Columbus iunior archipirata illustris cruento proelio oppresserat)" a marginal note, "Columbus iunior archi/pirata illustris," together with a large, prominent manicule. Though Rumeu de Armas (99–100) mentions the note that Hernando was reading this in 1534, Rumeu has clearly taken it from the *Registrum B* and has not looked at the original volume and therefore seen this clearly significant note. Hernando places a further manicule against a mention of Columbus's further discoveries, in identical handwriting, on fol. CLXXI, sig.x.viii^r, with the note "Christophorus colu[m]bus pater meus." A good comparison for the

handwriting is Hernando's copy of Pico della Mirandola's *Opera* (Colombina 12–5–10, A[x]ʳ), which contains similar preliminary capital *C*'s.

8. Hernando may well have had a more conscious notion of this than he anywhere formulates, drawing perhaps on Xenophon's *Oeconomicus* (a lost edition of which—*Registrum B* 94—he purchased in 1521), which demonstrates the order that arises out of a calm, methodical way of proceeding, using as its foremost example a well-managed ship. See *Oeconomicus*, 8, 23, and Agamben, *Kingdom and the Glory*, 18.

9. *Testamento*, xxxvi; Rumeu, 17/84; Rumeu, 84, and *Obras*, 86, confirm that this is a life pension. An order of 20 November 1536 requires the royal officers of Santo Domingo to pay Hernando a pension of one thousand ducados for life (AGI, Santo Domingo, 868, L.1, ff. 14r–14v); it is unclear whether this is part of the arbitration arising from the *pleitos colombinos*, though it would seem unlikely that it came unprompted by the generosity of the emperor; it is also unclear whether this includes or is supplemental to his existing pension. See also Guillén, 129.

10. *Correspondance de Nicolas Clénard*, 1:151–52; 2:93–94.

XVI. Last Orders

1. Among the books Hernando noted he was reading or having read to him in these final years are Aymar Falconaeus, *De tuta fidelium nauigatione inter varias peregrinoru[m] dogmatu[m]* (Colombina 15–3–5[1], reading October 1536); the *Expositio noue[m] lectionum que pro defunctis decantari solent* (Colombina 14–3–12[3], November 1537), a meditation on death; and a medical treatise by Gaspar Torella, Obispo de Santa Justa, *Pro regimine seu preservatione sanitatis. De ioculente & poculente dialogus* (Colombina 15–4–26, November 1538). The order to exhume Columbus is found on 2 July 1537 in the *Viajes del Emperador*. Hernando's license to transport household slaves to the New World is AGI, Indiferente, 423, L.19, ff. 4v–5r (31 March 1539), and the provision for burial while abroad in his will is found in *Testamento*, 128; on the epitaph see Guillén, 132–33.

2. The *Memorial al Emperador* is transcribed in *Testamento*, 241–43, which also contains the "testamento" (123–61) and the further notes by Marcos Felipe (226–46) ; the *Memoria* of the Bachiller Juan Pérez is transcribed in *Obras*, 47–76. On Hernando's music collection, see Catherine Weeks Chapman, "Printed Collections of Polyphonic Music

Owned by Ferdinand Columbus," *Journal of the American Musicological Society* 21/8 (1968): 34–84.

3. *Testamento*, 139.

4. It is also clear from Hernando's collecting practices that he did not mean "books" in a narrow sense here, so the library was not necessarily restricting its ambitions to those cultures that produced written codices. An interesting parallel to Hernando's conception can be seen in the *Speculum Maius* of Vincent de Beauvais (composed 1244–55), a popular medieval encyclopedia, though there are enormous differences in the scale of books available and the breadth of acceptable texts; see Blair, *Too Much to Know*, 41–43.

5. The Bachiller Juan Pérez mentions in the *Memoria* a "Sala de Teología," which may indicate that the library was still in multiple rooms at the time of Hernando's death and that the plan to establish a single library room was still in progress; *Obras*, 47. On the belief that the works of the ancients would not have been lost if they had had printing, see Blair, *Too Much to Know*, 47.

6. *Obras*, 53: "The great usefulness of this book of epitomes is clear, because in it one can know in brief the substance of what is treated diffusely, and anyone who does not have many books to read, at the least will have this one that will show them what is treated of in many" (my translation).

7. Blair, *Too Much to Know*, 92.

8. As Guillén (129) and others suggest, this petition to the emperor was likely never sent.

9. *Testamento*, 138–40, 210.

XVII. Epilogue: Ideas on the Shelf

1. *Obras*, 23–25; Guillén, 120 (on the Inquisition marks in the *Antibarbarorum*, Colombina 12-2-26, title page and page 9).

2. The best introduction to these other library projects is Roger Chartier's *Order of Books*; see Burke, *Social History of Knowledge*, 46, on Salomon's House and the Casa de Contratación.

3. This passage from Biondo is beautifully captured and analyzed in Grafton, *Worlds Made by Words*, 137–38.

LIST OF ILLUSTRATIONS

Impressions of many of the images used as illustrations in this book were owned by Hernando himself; references are provided here to the inventory numbers they bear in his *Memoria de los dibujos o pinturas o Registrum C* (Colombina 10–1–16), as well as to their entries in Mark P. McDonald's *Print Collection of Ferdinand Columbus, 1488–1539*, 3 vols. (London, 2004).

Maps
The four maps in the prelims are reproduced courtesy of the British Museum © The Trustees of the British Museum.

In-Text Illustrations
A Drawing of the City of Cadiz, 1509 (España, Ministerio de Educación, Cultura y Deporte, Archivo General de Simancas MPD, 25, 047).

Illustration from *De insulis nuper in mari Indico repertis* (Basel, 1494, ee [1]ᵛ; photo by MPI/Getty Images).

Giovanni Battista Palumba, *Diana Bathing with Her Attendants*, c.1500; (Hernando's inventory number 2150; see McDonald, 2:386; public domain from the Metropolitan Museum of Art).

Native Americans ride on a manatee, 1621 (courtesy of the John Carter Brown Library at Brown University, 04056; JCB Open Access Policy).

A page showing an eclipse from the Mayan *Dresden Codex* (Sächsische Landesbibliothek, Dresden, Mscr.Dresd.R.310, http://digital.slub -dresden.de/werkansicht/dlf/2967/55; CC-BY-SA 4.0).

left dressed as a fool; various drowning figures, cargo, and parts of the boat floating in the sea; illustration to Cicero, *Officia* (Augsburg: Steiner, 1531), woodcut (© The Trustees of the British Museum).

World map by Diego Ribeiro, produced under Hernando's supervision during his time as *pilót mayor*, 1529 (photo by Fine Art Images/Heritage Images/Getty Images).

A perspective of Seville, showing Hernando's house at the Puerta de Goles, from *Civitates orbis terrarum* (Cologne: Petrum à Brachel, 1612–18, vol. 1).

"Horti Publici Academiae Lugduno-Batavae cum areolis et pulvillis vera Delineatio." by Jan Cornelisz van 't Woudt (Willem Isaacsz. van Swanenburg, 1610). From the Rijksmuseum, RP-P-1893-A-18089.

Instruction in an apothecary's shop, from Hieronymus Brunschwig, *Liber de arte distillandi de Compositis* (Strasburg, 1512), Aaa.vv (from *Das Buch der Cirugia* published Strasbourg in 1497; litho, Hieronymus Brunschwig [1450–c.1512]; after/Private Collection/The Stapleton Collection/Bridgeman Images).

Hans Weiditz, *Winebag and wheelbarrow; satire on gluttony with a fat peasant facing right spitting and resting his large belly on a wheelbarrow*, c.1521 (Hernando's inventory number 1743; see McDonald, 2:311; engraving, Hans Weiditz [c.1500–c.1536]/Private Collection/Bridgeman Images).

Psalterium Hebreum, Grecum, Arabicum & Chaldeum (Genoa, 1516), c.vii^v.

Plates

Sebastiano del Piombo, *Portrait of a Man, Said to Be Christopher Columbus* (portrait of Christopher Columbus, 1519. Found in the collection of Metropolitan Museum of Art, New York. Artist: Sebastiano del Piombo, [1485–1547]; photo by Fine Art Images/Heritage Images/Getty Images).

Portrait of Hernando Colón (BCC Sevilla).

Early map of Hispaniola, pasted into Biblioteca Colombina 10-3-3 (BCC Sevilla).

Elio Antonio de Nebrija [1441–1522], Spanish humanist, Nebrija teaching a grammar class in presence of the patron Juan de Zuniga ("Introducciones Latinae," National Library, Madrid, Spain; photo by Prisma/UIG/Getty Images).

Sixtus IV Appointing Platina as Prefect of the Vatican Library, 1477, by Melozzo da Forlì (1438–94), detached fresco transferred to canvas (photo by De Agostini/Getty Images).

INDEX

INDEX

medicine, 148, *266*
  Arabic, 266
  Columbus's voyage with, 47
  drugs from New World plants and, 265–66
  Erasmus and, 308
  Hernando's interest in, 307–08, 310
  Hernando's recipes for, 5, 120
  library categorization and, 123, 172, 238, 257, 317, 320
  medical publishing in France and, 307, 310, 314
  native people of Americas and, 51, 52, 264–65
Medina del Campo, Spain, 33, 43, 55, 112, 126, 233, 293, 314
Melanchthon, Philipp, 214
Memoria de los dibujos o pinturas o Registrum C (Hernando Colón), examples of images in, *38, 118, 212, 290*
Memorial de los Libros Naufragados (*The Catalogue of Shipwrecked Books*, Hernando Colón), 5, 239–40
Méndez, Diego, 103, 105, 110
Michelangelo, 153–55, 157, 318
Milan, 217, 273, 274, 285, 315
millenarian theories, 68–73, 75, 129
Mirabilia urbis Roma (guide to Rome), 139–40
Moctezuma, Emperor, 201–02, 233–34
Moleto, Giuseppe, 337
Molina, Argote de, 138–39, 326–27
Molucca islands, 189–90, 241, 244, 250, 251, 252–53, 269, 272
Monardes, Nicolás, 265–66
Moniz Perestrelo, Dona Filipa, 23, 27, 79
Monserrate, 44
Monte, Vincentio de, 281
Monterrey, Spain, 185
Montesinos, Antonio, 136
Montpellier, France, 307
Moors of Spain, 88
  architecture and, 35, 79
  north African trade routes and, 27
  war against, 18, 21, 22, 26, 72
More, Thomas, 122, 202, 231, 301
  translations by, 206, 300
  Utopia, 224, 225–30, *228*, 261, 292
Müntzer, Thomas, 283
Munzer, Hieronymus, 36, 46–47

Mure, Konrad von, *Magnus elucidarius*, 204
music, 3
  Hernando's collection with, 118–20, *118*, 140, 260, 310, 313
  printed, 3, 310, 313
  street singers and, 151

"narrow Atlantic" hypothesis, 23–24, 182
national libraries, 328–29
nationalism, 329, 331
native people of Americas, *84*
  atrocities of conquistadors and settlers and, 53, 135–36, 310, 326
  at Cariay (Central America), 92–93, 324
  Columbus's interpreters for, 30
  conversion to Christianity and, 30, 50, 52, 59, 69, 70, 72, 129
  currencies and, 88–90, 211
  encomienda system and, 135–36, 137
  European notions of naked innocence and, 17–18, 29, 47–48, 60
  guanín pendants and, 92, 93
  Hernando on the rights of, 136
  La Navidad and, 14, 31, 44–46, 47
  languages of, 18, 29, 30, 134–35, 228
  Mayan people, 87–90, *88*, 234
  Pané's survey of, 50–52, 264
  Paria region and, 60, 62, 92
  Taino people, 111, 121; on Hispaniola, 36, 46, 49–52, 62, 70, 83, 84, 86, 264; on Isla Mona, 134–35; on Jamaica, 103, 104, 105, 106–09, 110, 135
Natural History (Pliny), 51–52, 120
natural philosophers, 86, 166
navigation
  Atlantic shipping routes and, 79–81, 188
  Chaves's cartographical process for, 270–71
  Columbus's circumnavigation proposal and, 82, 128–29
  dead reckoning used in, 80
  Harrison's marine chronometer and, 329
  Hernando's circumnavigation proposal and, 129, 130, 132, 136
  lack of accurate longitude measures and, 80, 90, 91, 107, 108, 245–48, 251–52, 329

395